www.MesorahMatrix.com

MESORAH MATRIX

David Birnbaum / Mesorah Matrix Series

LIGHTS OF CREATION & TRANSCENDENCE

Sanctification

Editors

David Birnbaum & Benjamin Blech

LEAD ESSAY: **Jonathan Sacks**

EXPLORING HIGHER DIMENSIONS

New Paradigm Matrix™

Published by NEW PARADIGM MATRIX

Library of Congress Cataloging-in-Publication Data

Birnbaum, David.

Sanctification / David Birnbaum and Benjamin Blech.

ISBN 978-0-9843619-9-1

1. *Kedushah*.   2. Sanctification.   I. Title.

21st CENTURY PUBLISHING

589 Fifth Avenue   #710   New York, NY 10017

www.MesorahMatrix.com

fax: (212) 398-9438

Distributed by J Levine / MILLENNIUM

Danny Levine, Managing Director

Direct Contact to Publisher

NPM1000@yahoo.com

Sanctification / *Kedushah*

The commandment to be holy is at the very center of the Torah and the quest for personal holiness could easily be said to be the single mission that defines Jewishness at its most profound level. But what does it mean, really, to be holy? How does one attain such an exalted status? Are there many paths towards holiness or only one? How should Jews identify the holy in their midst? And how should they relate to the holy men and women of other faith groups? These and many other questions are posed and answered in this volume by some of today's most creative and thoughtful Jewish authors. Their answers will surprise and delight, but also inform and inspire. This is a book for all who have taken the scriptural injunction to be holy to heart…and wondered how exactly to fulfill it purposefully and successfully…and also with intellectual and spiritual integrity.

Zornberg

Bulka

Blau

Carmy

Blech

Cohen Helfgot

Friedman

Goldberg

Kugel

Berman

Mescheloff

Shatz

Schiffman

Sacks

Riskin

Sanctification

David Birnbaum and Benjamin Blech

Editors

NEW PARADIGM MATRIX

www.NewParadigmMatrix.com

David Birnbaum & Benjamin Blech

Sanctification

Kedushah

with essays by

Saul J. Berman, Yitzchak Blau, Benjamin Blech, Reuven P. Bulka,
Shalom Carmy, Alfred Cohen, Rachel Friedman, Alfred Goldberg,
Nathaniel Helfgot, James Kugel, David Mescheloff, Shlomo Riskin,
Jonathan Sacks, Lawrence H. Schiffman, David Shatz, and Avivah Zornberg

New Paradigm Matrix Publishing
New York
2015

From the Editor-in-Chief

May 10, 2015

It is a privilege to be serving as Editor-in-Chief of this unique 10-theme series. I am honored to be working with world-class editors Benjamin Blech, Martin S. Cohen, Saul J. Berman, and Shalom Carmy.

It is our hope and prayer that the series be a catalyst for intellectual and spiritual expansion – as well as a unifying force both for our people as well as for individuals of good will globally.

Sincerely,

David Birnbaum

Mesorah Matrix series

in-progress

jewish thought & spirituality

10-theme

10-volume

200+ original essays

150 - 180 global thought leaders

a decade-long unified endeavor

genre: *applied scholarship*

www.MesorahMatrix.com

21st CENTURY PUBLISHING

Mesorah Matrix series

> *Sanctification*

Tikkun Olam

Birkat Kohanim

The Kaddish

Modeh Ani

Havdalah

Search for Meaning

U-vacharta Ba-chayim

Eheyeh asher Eheyeh

V'Shamru

AN ICONIC LEGACY SERIES FOR THE 21ST CENTURY

10-VOLUME SERIES......200+ ESSAYS......A GLOBAL EFFORT

150 - 180 ESSAYISTS....SPANNING THE WORLD'S TOP JEWISH THOUGHT LEADERS

A DYNAMIC CONTEMPORARY GLOBE-SPANING ENDEAVOR AND COLLECTION

ESSAYISTS COVER A VERY WIDE SPECTRUM OF JUDAISM:

THE COMPLETE SERIES TO DATE IS AVAILABLE ON-LINE GRATIS
IN FLIP-BOOK FORM......AND DOWNLOAD-ABLE GRATIS
+
AVAILABLE IN SOFTCOVER VIA AMAZON
+
AVAILABLE IN E-BOOK FORM VIA VARIOUS MODALITIES

A UNIQUE STUDY AND REFERENCE TOOL FOR CLERGY, ACADEMICS,
STUDENTS & LAY INTELLIGENSIA

A STELLAR CORE COURSE OF STUDY – WHETHER FOR ONE SEMESTER OR
MULTI-YEAR

AND... AS AN UNINTENDED CONSEQUENCE, THE SERIES HAS
BROKEN DOWN BARRIERS - AND SERVED AS A FORCE-MULTIPLIER –
IN UNIFYING THE JEWISH PEOPLE

IN DEPTH & BREADTH......SCOPE & SPECTRUM
A LANDMARK SERIES
UNIQUE ACROSS THE 3,500+ YEAR SPAN OF JEWISH HISTORY

This New Paradigm Matrix work
is available via multiple modalities:

amazon: www.MesorahAmazon.com

eBooks: www.NPMeBooks.com

online: www.MesorahMatrix.com

contact: NPM1000@yahoo.com

a unique, timeless and potentially multi-semester
Contemporary Jewish Thought course text

a *sui generis* series • original essays • broad spectrum

About the Editors

David Birnbaum is a philosophical writer, historical chronicler and *conceptual theorist*. His first work *God and Evil* (KTAV, 1988) is considered by many to be a breakthrough *modern day classic* in the field of theodicy. See God-And-Evil.com.

Editor-in-Chief Birnbaum is known globally as "the architect of Potentialism Theory" – a unified philosophy/cosmology/metaphysics. The paradigm-challenging theory (see ParadigmChallenge.com) is delineated in Birnbaum's 3-volume *Summa Metaphysica* series (1988, 2005, 2014). See Philosophy1000.com.

A riposte to *Summa Theologica* of (St.) Thomas Aquinas, the Birnbaum treatise challenges both the mainstream Western philosophy of Aristotelianism and the well propped-up British/atheistic cosmology of Randomness. See Potentialism Theory. com.

The focus of 150+ reviews/articles, Summa Metaphysica has been an assigned Course Text at over 15 institutions of higher learning globally. See SummaCoverage.com.

Summa Metaphysica was the focus of an international academic conference on Science & Religion in April 16-19 2012 (see Conference1000.com). The work has been very widely covered globally. See RewindSumma.com.

David Birnbaum is the Editor-in-Chief of the *Mesorah Matrix* series on Jewish thought and spirituality. The *sui generis* series spans 10-volumes and 10 themes. The entire series is comprised of 200+ specially commissioned original pieces from 150-180 global Jewish thought leader essayists. See Mesorah1000.com.

In the history realm, David Birnbaum is the author/chronicler of the 2-volume *The Crucifixion – of the Jews*, and of the 7-volume *Jews, Church & Civilization*. His Crucifixion series, in particular, traces a direct trajectory from the Canonical Gospels in the First Century to Auschwitz in the Twentieth. See History1000.com.

David Birnbaum has served on the faculty of the New School for Social Research in Manhattan. He is a graduate of Yeshiva University High School (Manhattan), CCNY (City College of New York) and Harvard. His commentary blog is www.ManhattanObserver.com.

See also David1000.com

About the Editors

Benjamin Blech is a tenth-generation rabbi. He has been a Professor of Talmud at Yeshiva University since 1966, and was the Rabbi of Young Israel of Oceanside for 37 years.

Rabbi Blech received a B.A. from Yeshiva University, an M.A. in psychology from Columbia University, and rabbinic ordination from the Rabbi Isaac Elchanan Theological Seminary.

He is the author of 15 highly acclaimed books, the last one of which – *The Sistine Secrets: Michelangelo's Forbidden Messages in the Heart of the Vatican* – has now been translated into sixteen languages.

His book *Understanding Judaism: The Basics of Deed and Creed* was chosen by the Union of Orthodox Jewish Congregations as "the single best book on Judaism in our generation". He has also published hundreds of articles in both scholarly and popular publications; he is a noted feature columnist on Aish.com.

In a national survey in The Jewish Week 2001, Rabbi Blech was ranked #16 in a listing of the 50 most influential Jews in America. He is a recipient of the American Educator of the Year Award.

He is a past President of both the National Council of Young Israel Rabbis, as well as the International League for the Repatriation of Russian Jewry, Rabbi Blech has also served as officer for the New York Board of Rabbis as well as the Rabbinical Council of America.

Recent books of Rabbi Blech also include *If God is Good, Why Is the World So Bad?*, *The Book of Passover: A Celebration*, and *Eyewitness to Jewish History*.

In March 2017, Mesorah Books released a new Haggada by Rabbi Blech entitled *Redemption, Then and Now* (see JewishWorld cover story 4/7/17).

DAVID BIRNBAUM MAJOR WORKS

As Author

3-volume *Summa Metaphysica** (www.philosophy1000.com)

2-volume *The Crucifixion* (www.crucifixion1000.com)

7-volume *Jews, Church & Civilization* (www.civilization1000.com)

As Editor-in-Chief

10-volume *Mesorah Matrix* (www.mesorah1000.com)
(target completion: June 2019)

As Conceptualizer

3-volume *Summa Spinoffs* (www.Spinoffs1000.com)

8-volume *Potentialism Theory* via Graphic-Narrative
(www.TheoryGraphics1000.com)

As Commentator

www.ManhattanObserver.com

YouTube channels

Summa Metaphysica

Mesorah Matrix

*

Summa I: Religious Man / God and Evil
Summa II: Spiritual Man / God and Good
Summa III: Secular Man / The Transcendent Dynamic

BENJAMIN BLECH MAJOR WORKS

Understanding Judaism: The Basics of Deed and Creed (1991).

The Secrets of Hebrew Words. (1991).

Your Name Is Your Blessing: Hebrew Names and Their Mystical Meanings (1999).

If God Is Good, Why Is The World So Bad? (2003).

The Book of Passover: A Celebration (2005).

Eyewitness to Jewish History (2007).

With Roy Doliner: *The Sistine Secrets: Michelangelo's Forbidden Messages in the Heart of the Vatican* (2008).

Sanctification / *Kedushah*

Sanctification

from Essay by Chief Rabbi Lord Jonathan Sacks

... And there is the priestly task of *kedushah*, sanctifying life by honoring the sacred ontology, the deep moral structure of the universe, through the life of the 613 commands, a life of discipline and self-restraint, honesty and integrity, respect and love, the code set out in the chapter of the Torah that opens with the momentous words, "Be holy for I, the Lord your God, am holy." Other cultures and faiths drew inspiration from its wisdom and prophetic traditions, but *kedushah* remained a specific Jewish imperative that made us different. Even so, it contains a message for the world, which Jews bear witness to whenever and wherever they remain faithful to it.

Our vocation remains, to be *mamlekhet kohanim v'goi kadosh*, "a kingdom of priests and a holy nation."

– "The Ethic of Holiness" (August, 2012)

Sanctification / *Kedushah*

TABLE OF CONTENTS

Benjamin Blech

Preface

Benjamin Blech

This series is long past due.

In particular, this book is a much needed response to the meaning of the biblical mandate that summarizes the mission of the Jewish people. The Torah commands us "You shall be holy, for I the Lord your God am holy" (Leviticus 19:2). The terse directive begs for clarification. What is it exactly that we are required to do? The wisest of all generations have struggled to define the meaning of the word holy.

In one of the early dialogues of Plato, we find Socrates questioning Euthyphro who is about to prosecute his father on the ground that to do so is an act of piety. Socrates asks Euthyphro how he is so certain that his action is the correct moral choice deserving of being considered holy. Socrates does not want to know what is holy in this particular case only, but instead to know what is holy *in any and all* cases. If he had that standard, if he knew the essence or common-nature of holiness, then he could judge Euthyphro's case as well. What he believes he cannot do is to judge the correctness of Euthyphro's course of action without that standard (and he does not think that Euthyphro can either (15d). And so Socrates says to Euthyphro at the end of their inconclusive dialectic:

And so we must now go back again, and start from the beginning to find what the holy is. As for me, I will never give up until I know. (15c)

Socrates admits that he does not know. But a Jew cannot afford the luxury of uncertainty. To do so would be to lead a life removed from one's divine vocation, lacking purpose and meaning. Holiness is our reason for being. It is our personal obligation as well as our communal responsibility. It is the commitment God placed upon us when he entrusted us with his Torah at Sinai and enjoined us to be "a kingdom of priests and a holy nation" (Exodus 19:6).

And so we need to understand the essence of holiness, the meaning of sanctity, the significance of sacredness. These words cannot remain abstractions. They must point us to ideas relevant to our lives, to concepts guiding us to correct behavior, to aspirations in harmony with heavenly ideals.

The German theologian Rudolf Otto, in his classic study on holiness (*Das Heilige*, 1927 – freely translated into English as *The Idea of the Holy*), states that "holiness is a category of interpretation and valuation peculiar to the sphere of religion." For a Jew that definition is far too constricting. Holiness in the Bible is a life-affirming principle meant to transform every act, no matter how seemingly devoid of spirituality, into an experience of service to God and awareness of our divine image.

Mitzvot, divine imperatives that govern every waking moment of our days, are meant – as the opening words of the blessing prefacing their performance remind us – to "sanctify us." What is the meaning of this sanctification? Sanctity is a word that seeks to encompass an entire philosophy of life. But as William James so correctly pointed out in his deservedly famous *Varieties of Religious Experience*, "Philosophy lives by words, but truth and fact well up in our lives in ways that exceed verbal formulation."

Holiness, sanctity, sacredness are abstractions. We feel their reality but have difficulty defining them. Yet define them we must if we are to fulfill God's will even as we seek to realize our purpose on earth.

All this is by way of explaining the genesis of this book you are about to read.

A short while back, I was approached by David Birnbaum, the iconoclast thought leader. Birnbaum is impacting the reshaping of the face of the Jewish world across-the-board: in philosophy, spirituality, and history. Beneath-the-radar, his Mesorah Matrix series has effected another neo-revolution: a unification of sorts of the Jews via the global group project of the 150+ trans-denominational Jewish thought leaders united in purpose for this landmark endeavor. Shoulder-to-shoulder. *Achduth* at its finest.

David Birnbaum prevailed upon me to take on the task of recruiting the finest Orthodox minds of our generation – theologians, rabbis, professors and internationally renowned scholars – to reflect on the theme of sanctification and contribute essays for a groundbreaking contemporary work on this topic. For me, launching the first volume of this series has been a remarkable endeavor and a true labor of love.

Birnbaum outlined a visionary plan for a *sui generis* landmark ten-volume series addressing ten themes within Judaism. In the ensuing years Editor-in-Chief Birnbaum turned out to be consistent: consistently demanding top quality, consistently insisting on authentic vibrancy, and consistently pressing that we reel-in the world's top talent.

The eager acceptance of the project's mandate by the very distinguished and well-known names of this volume's contributing authors is perhaps the best testimony to the long-unfilled need this seminal work serves. What makes it particularly noteworthy and – with the admitted bias of a very pleased editor – a modern classic of Jewish thought is the wide range of approach to a single subject, made possible by the extraordinary assortment of scholarly backgrounds and intellectual attainments of our contributors.

For some, like the former Chief Rabbi of the United Kingdom, the Lord Rabbi Jonathan Sacks, in his masterful essay on "The Ethic of Holiness," the question that needs most to be addressed is the tension at the heart of Judaism between the universality of ethics and the seemingly particularistic claim of holiness. As Sacks puts it, "What turns tension into paradox is that persistently throughout Tanakh we hear the idea that Jews and Judaism have significance not just for ourselves but for all humanity. How can *kedushah* [holiness], a way of life and mode of being specific to the Jewish people and not demanded by God of all humanity, become an inspiration to all humanity? How can a nation that dwells alone be a role model for nations that do not dwell alone? How can the particular be of relevance to the universal?" Ingeniously resolving this question, we are led to understand the difference between the prophetic and wisdom traditions of other cultures with the Jewish emphasis on the imperative of holiness to which we are meant to give witness.

Shalom Carmy, in his very thoughtful and insightful piece, "Hired For the Day," examines three projects that beckon to modern men and women in quest of sanctification: "the ascetic impulse, the altruistic impulse, and the mystical impulse," and concludes with a striking insight into a well-known midrash that will almost certainly have great meaning for the reader, much as the author confides it has had for him personally.

Aviva Zornberg begins her important essay, "Impressions: Facing the Rock," by pointing out a fascinating truth relating to biblical narrative about the theme of sanctity. Ultimately, she points out, according to Sforno, "You shall be holy" (Leviticus 19:2), represents the ideal of *imitatio dei* – God's wish for the human being to be "in Our form and after Our image" (Genesis 1:26). Indeed, to sanctify oneself is equivalent to sanctifying God: "If you sanctify yourselves, I account it as if you had sanctified Me." In view of this, she notes, it is striking that there seems to be little in the way of biblical narrative that deals with this central concept of sanctification, and this, despite the fact that it is precisely the strength of narrative to flesh out elusive processes and particularly to convey them in temporal and social contexts. The Hebrew *root kadesh*, as adjective or as verb, transitive or intransitive, seems shy of narrative frameworks.

Yet, she correctly points out there is but one exception: The only narrative that focuses its ultimate meanings on this issue is the enigmatic episode of the rock at Merivah. Here, God pronounces the last word on the narrative: it is the failure of Moses and Aaron to "believe in Me *to sanctify Me before the eyes of the Israelites*" that defines their fate: "Therefore you shall not lead this congregation into the Land" (Numbers 20:12).

By exploring the complex layers of this narrative – "its resonances receding back to the beginning of the Exodus and beyond" – Zornberg approaches, in the way that narrative alone can, "an understanding of the intertwined ideals of emuna and kedushah (faith and sanctification)."

From a totally different perspective, James Kugel offers a highly original piece, "The Man Who Mistook His Tefillin for a Hat," in which by way of an imaginary tale of a man who mistakenly wears his *t'fillin* to work, he vividly illustrates an important point: "The everyday is, by definition, not holy: it is ordinary, not special, and normally taken for granted. What is most characteristic of Judaism is that this connection of the everyday things of daily life to God is not articulated internally, through some wished-for, heightened state of awareness, but externally, through some particular act, binding *t'fillin* to one's head and arm, reciting the words of the Shema, or uttering a series of blessings as one moves through the routine act of getting up in the morning."

Nathaniel Helfgot offers us a profound examination of the concept of sacred space in Jewish thought as well as "its meaning for us today as we struggle to experience a sense of the sacred and numinous in our fast-paced and ever-changing world and the secular ethos that finds no room for the holy," incorporating important insights from Abraham Heschel, Joseph B. Soloveitchik, and Yeshayahu Leibowitz, and from the latter's sister, Prof. Nehama Leibowitz as well as others.

Lawrence H. Schiffman, in his most interesting essay "The Dead Sea Scrolls Sect as a Replacement Temple," takes us back to the formative time of the beginning of Christianity as well as the start of Talmudic Judaism to discover the religious ideas of holiness and sanctity that were so crucial to the Dead Sea sect in Qumran.

Shlomo Riskin elaborates on the approach of Rabbi Soloveitchik, in his essay "Sanctity of Time, Sanctity of Place, And Sanctity of The Human Being," to demonstrate how sanctity must be brought into the world through the dimension of time as manifested in our festivals, through the dimension of the space as manifested in the sanctuary, and through human beings responsible for actualizing the existence of divine holiness within every aspect of the universe.

Saul Berman, in "The Holiness of God: Its Meaning, Actualization, and Symbolic Embodiment," focuses on the usage of the term *kadosh*/holy in the text of the Torah in order to elicit the pattern of its use as a way of arriving at a systematic understanding of its accurate meaning, integrating rabbinic teachings to demonstrate applications of these usages within Jewish thought and law.

David Shatz takes up the question of "Separation or Engagement?" as he shares with his readers the intriguing dilemma of which model we are to pursue in our quest to achieve holiness based on the foundations of the various concepts that have given expression to this divine mandate.

I have selected for synopsis but a few of the fascinating articles that await you in order to whet your intellectual appetite, even as I promise that all of the offerings in this collection will fill you with gratitude for the insights of some of the most distinguished thinkers of our time.

In 1931, Ludwig Wittgenstein wrote in his notebook: "Amongst Jews 'genius' is found only in the holy man". Of all the gifts Jews have given to the world, the passion for holiness – the pursuit of the holy in our personal lives and the commitment to sanctity as communal responsibility – is the one aspect of our genius that may well represent our greatest contribution to humankind. It is the genius that has shaped us and accounted for our miraculous and incomprehensible survival. It is the genius that offers the world its only hope for continued existence.

I pray that this work, by enabling us to better understand its biblical parameters, will bring us closer to a time when the idea of holiness will be as much understood and beloved on earth as it is in heaven.

A Note from the Editors

Every effort has been made to retain a good level of consistency between the essays that appear here in terms of the translation and transliteration of Hebrew. Many of our decisions have, needs be, been arbitrary, but we have done our best to create a book that will be as accessible to newcomers to the study of Judaism as it is inspiring to cognoscenti. The four-letter name of God, left unpronounced by pious Jews as a sign of reverence, is mostly rendered in this volume as "the Eternal" or "the Eternal One." Other divine names are either transliterated or translated to create in English something akin to the way the text reads in Hebrew. All translations are their authors' unless otherwise indicated.

Essays

The Ethic of Holiness

Jonathan Sacks

There is a paradox at the heart of Judaism, which remains the defining tension in Jewish life today. On the one hand, the Torah gave the world the first universal vision of humanity. We are all children of the one God, Creator of heaven and earth. That was a radical idea then; it still is. In the ancient world, each nation had its own god or pantheon of gods. The Canaanites had Baal; the Moabites, Chemosh; the Egyptians, Ra, the god of the sun. That was polytheism. In the contemporary world, each culture—indeed, each individual—has his or her own version of the moral life: "whatever works for you." That is relativism: polytheism for a secular age.

There is one God, the God of all, who created every person in the divine image and through Noah made a covenant with all humanity. Not everyone recognizes this fact but, said the prophets, one day they will. We will recognize that we are all children of the one God, and therefore members of the same family. War will cease and the knowledge of God will cover the world, in Isaiah's lovely phrase, "as waters cover the sea" (Isaiah 11:9). Ancient though this idea is, it is the single most pertinent vision for the twenty-first century, the "global age" which sees a diversity of cultures, respecting one another under the overarching sovereignty of God.

That is the universalistic perspective of Judaism. On the other hand, however, the Torah challenges this entire constellation, as the coin of faith has another side as well. The Jewish concept of *k'dushah*, holiness, is not universal. Not all times and places are equally holy;

nor are all people. The word *kadosh*, holy, means "set apart, different, distinctive, dedicated." The Israelites are called in the Torah a *goy kadosh* (Exodus 19:6) or an am *kadosh* (Deuteronomy 7:6; 14:2, 21; 26:19; 28:9), a holy nation and a holy people. This means that they are not like others. Other nations may contain holy individuals, but none aspires to that condition for the nation as a whole. It is this that lies behind Balaam's description of Israel as "a nation dwelling alone, not counting itself among other nations" (Numbers 23:9). God is universal. Holiness is not.

In this context an observation of Rabbeinu Bahya[1] is particularly pertinent. Before performing a *mitzvah*, we recite a blessing: "...who has *made us holy* through the commandments and has commanded us to..." Yet there are many commandments over which we do not make this blessing: giving *tzedakah*, for example, or visiting the sick, or doing some other act of hesed. In general, commands between us and God require a blessing. Those between us and our fellow humans do not. Why so?

Rabbeinu Bahya's answer is that there are two kinds of commandment: rational (*muskalot*) and traditional (*m'kubbalot*). Only the latter bring holiness (*m'kubbalot hein hein ikkar ha-k'dushah*). The rational, interpersonal commands—not stealing, lying, or committing adultery; doing acts of kindness to others—are human universals. Even thieves, says Yehudah Halevi, have a code of honor among themselves.[2] It is the commands that exist only because they were commanded that bring holiness, for these alone are distinctive and non-universal.

Hence is the tension at the heart of Judaism: ethics are universal but holiness is not. What turns the tension into a paradox is that persistently throughout the Tanakh, we hear the idea that Jews and Judaism have significance not just for ourselves but for all humanity. Moses says, "This is your wisdom and understanding in the eyes of the nations, who will hear about all these decrees and say, 'Surely this great nation is a wise and understanding people'" (Deuteronomy 4:6).

Solomon at the dedication of the Temple envisages a time when "the foreigner who does not belong to Your people Israel but has come from a distant land because of Your name" will come to pray at the Temple (1 Kings 8:41). Zechariah says that a time will come when "Ten people from all languages and nations will take firm hold of one Jew by the hem of the robe and say, 'Let us go with you, because we have heard that God is with you'" (Zechariah 8:23).

How can this be? How can *k'dushah*, a way of life and mode of being specific to the Jewish people and not demanded by God of all humanity, become an inspiration to all humanity? How can a nation that dwells alone be a role model for nations that do not dwell alone? How can the particular be of relevance to the universal?

Three Moral Voices

To understand the answer we have to first grasp the complexity of Judaism. By and large, secular moral philosophers from Plato to John Stuart Mill failed because they thought that the moral life was simple. For Plato, knowledge led to goodness. The only cause of evil was ignorance. Plato failed to wrestle with the many destructive passions—hate, envy, fear, aggression, anger—that make people do evil even though, in their sober moments, they know that what they are doing is wrong. John Stuart Mill sought the "one very simple principle" that defined the limits of liberty. But liberty, as we know from the Bible, is not that simple. It is hard to balance individual freedom with collective order. As the Book of Judges says, "At that time there was no king in Israel; everybody did what was right in their own eyes" (Judges 17:6, 21:25). Is that liberty or chaos?

The Torah does not try to simplify the moral life. It recognizes its complexity. There is a prophetic voice that speaks of righteousness, justice, kindness, and compassion. There is a wisdom voice that speaks of prudence, self-control, honesty, and integrity. And there is a priestly voice that speaks of *k'dushah*, holiness. These are all part of a moral vision that recognizes the different aspects of the human condition.

The prophets were interested in personal relationships (including a personal relationship with God). The wisdom books look at what we would now call "sustainability." They ask us to consider long-term outcomes. "Who is wise?" asked the sages, and they answered, "One who sees the consequences of one's actions" (Pirkei Avot 4:1). Hardest to understand is *torat kohanim*, "the law of the priests," which seems (and this is an ancient and quite mischievous claim) to be more interested in ritual than in ethics. It is not so. The priestly vision is moral through and through. But it is a special kind of morality, one that has fallen out of favor in the modern world and now needs to be reclaimed.

The Code of Holiness

The place to begin our inquiry is in the Holiness Code of Leviticus 19 (the *parashah* whose very name, *k'doshim*, embodies the idea of holiness). Here we find the great moral commands: Don't steal. Don't lie. Don't defraud your neighbor. Don't hate. Don't take revenge or bear a grudge. Respect your parents. Be honest in business. Love your neighbor as yourself. Love the stranger. Interwoven with these, however, are commands of a quite different kind: Don't crossbreed your livestock with other species. Don't plant your field with two kinds of seed. Don't wear clothing of mixed wool and linen. Don't lacerate yourselves. At first sight the chapter looks like a jumble of rules with no connecting thread, no overarching logic. That is a measure of how hard it has become to understand the idea of *k'dushah*.

What is unique about the priestly voice is set out in the very first chapter of the Torah. The creation narrative of Genesis 1 is not cosmological. It is not there to tell us what happened in the Big Bang some 13.7 billion years ago and the subsequent slow coalescence of energy into chemical elements, stars, planets, life, and humanity. It is, instead, an ethical creation story. The key word, appearing seven times, is tov ("good"): "And God saw that it was good" (Genesis 1:4, 10, 12, 18, 21, 25, 31). *There is moral order, as well as scientific order, in the universe.* That is the central priestly principle.

The idea that there is order in the universe is not unique to Judaism. On the contrary, most ancient cultures believed this. But what they saw was not *moral*, but *political*, order. The monarch ruled the nation just as the sun rules the sky. Cosmology was used in the ancient world to justify class-bound hierarchical societies, with their divisions into rulers and ruled, free people and slaves. Judaism rejected this absolutely.

Often we fail to understand the significance of the statement that "God created humans in the divine image. In the divine image did God create the human; male and female God created them" (Genesis 1:27). What is radical in this verse is that it is not just that *some* people are created in God's image. (This is what other nations believed— about their rulers.) What is radical in the Torah's conception is that *everyone* is created in God's image—regardless of color, culture, class, or creed. Hence the profoundly egalitarian thrust of the Bible and of Judaism ever since.

The central problem to which Judaism is an answer is not political, the justification of the use of power. Judaism is skeptical about politics because it deeply distrusts the use and abuse of power. The central problem in Judaism is the perennial tension between two aspects of reality: God's creation and humanity's freedom. The greatest act of love and faith on the part of God was to endow each of us with freedom—but the freedom to do good comes indivisibly with the freedom to do bad. *God creates order. Humans create chaos.* The whole of Judaism is generated by that one tension, as the stories of Adam and Eve, Cain and Abel, and the generation of the flood make clear. God could solve the problem at a stroke by taking away our freedom. But that is something God will never do because God desires our freedom. God is a loving parent and we are God's wayward children.

The essential insight of the priests is to recognize and create respect for the moral order of the universe. To do this involves making distinctions. The key verb of *torat kohanim*, priestly consciousness, is the same as it is in Genesis 1 (where it appears five times): *l'havdil*, "to recognize, make, and honor differences"—differences between heaven and earth, day and night, life and death, animal and plant, pure and impure, sacred and profane, permitted and forbidden, good and evil. The chief task of the priest is to maintain the boundaries between domains. Thus, no trace of contact with death is allowed in the sanctuary, which is dedicated to the God of life. Wool, an animal product, should not be mixed with linen, a plant one. Meat, which involves killing an animal, should not be mixed with milk, which involves keeping an animal alive.

An ordered universe is a moral universe in which everything has its integrity and its place in the scheme of things. Sin, for the priest, is disorder. So falsehood undermines human trust. Theft damages people's right to what they own. Bribery threatens the justice on which society depends. Hatred, violence, and revenge create chaos, the opposite of order. Order is best preserved through love. Just as God loves us, so too we should love others—both our neighbors and the strangers among us—for everything is God's creation and everyone is created in God's image. The priestly universe is not a cold, detached, scientific place but one driven and sustained by love. That love was expressed in one of Judaism's most ancient rituals and one still performed today: *birkat kohanim*, the priestly blessing. It is no accident that the *b'rakhah* recited by the priests before blessing the people is the only one that specifies that it must be performed with love (*l'vareikh et ammo yisrael b'ahavah*).

Sacred Ontology

The idea that the moral life is rooted in the order of the universe is one that was lost at some stage in the Enlightenment. That was when rationalist philosophers began to think of human beings as radically distinct from the rest of nature. Immanuel Kant sought to locate morality in the human power of reason. Adam Smith and David Hume found it in human emotion. Jeremy Bentham sought to create a scientific morality by calculating the consequences of different courses of action, and so on. The problem was not that these views were false. It was the opposite: they all embodied some fragment of the truth. But because each claimed to be the whole and only truth, the result was confusion—the confusion that we call moral relativism. Alasdair MacIntyre's great work, *After Virtue*, is an account of the failure of the Enlightenment project.

The thinker who wrote most deeply about these matters—unfortunately, he also wrote obscurely, so he is little read and little known—was a sociologist called Philip Rieff (1922–2006). Rieff, who wrote about Freud and "the triumph of the therapeutic," believed that morality must be based on what he called a *sacred ontology*, by which he meant precisely what I have described as priestly consciousness. There is a moral order in the universe that must be respected, guarded, and sustained. It is this that is the basis of the moral imperative, the "Thou shalt" and the "Thou shalt not." What made the modern world unique and destined to eventual failure was its attempt to rid the world of commands and prohibitions, and the attendant feelings of guilt and responsibility. In the end, that leaves us as lonely, self-obsessed, narcissistic individuals without a shared world of meanings and social order.

Rieff was a pessimist. He thought that we had gone too far and there was no way back. In fact, however, there are serious grounds for hope, for we are beginning to realize again the extraordinary, yet vulnerable, order of life itself. Recent cosmology has shown how precisely tuned the universe was for the emergence of life. The decoding of the genome has revealed the astonishing complexity of "the book of life." We now know that the absence or misplacement of just a few of the 3.1 billion DNA letters that make up the human genome can result in devastating genetic disability. Ecological study tells us how delicately balanced biodiversity is and how easy it is to unwittingly damage the earth's environment, threatening the future of life itself. Chaos theory has famously shown how the beating of a butterfly's wings in one part of the world can cause a tsunami in another. Small acts can have large repercussions, and local disorder can create global disequilibrium.

Let us now go back to the list of commands in Leviticus 19, the Holiness Code. It no longer seems as strange as it did at first. Translated into contemporary terms, we would understand it to be saying something like this: Respect the integrity of the environment. Be cautious before engaging in genetic engineering. Be careful about how you treat animal and plant species. Don't place a stumbling-block before the blind (such as by tempting people into mortgages they can't repay, or by creating financial instruments so complex that no one understands them). Don't undermine the trust on which an economy depends. Don't use the media, either print or electronic, to spread hatred or you will create forms of terror and violence you can't control. And so on.

Each failure to respect boundaries and limits may seem small considered in itself, but the cumulative effect of this tendency will be to destroy the finely tuned balance on which both the natural and human orders depend. Marriages will break down. Children will suffer. Banks will no longer trust one another. The economy will stall. The media will sow cynicism and disrespect. Governments will lack authority. Inequities among people will grow. People will consume natural resources faster than they can be replenished. Resentments will fester. Violence will increase. And a great civilization—in this case, the West—will begin to decline, eventually taking its place with the great superpowers of the past, none of which today survives except as archaeological ruins and relics in museums.

That is what happens when morality loses its grounding in a sacred ontology—when, in Jewish terms, it loses its sense of *k'dushah*.

The Jewish people has never lost its sense of *k'dushah*. That is why, alone among the civilizations of the ancient world, it never died. It lost everything else: its land and its sovereignty, its Temple, its kings, priests, and prophets. But it never lost the disciplines and consciousness of *k'dushah*. It dedicated—and still dedicates—the first moments of the working week to a ceremony celebrating distinctions, order, and boundary-maintenance. The Havdalah ceremony uses the same verb as God did in creating the universe and as the kohanim did in their service in the sanctuary.

It was this survival, against all the laws of history, that earned the awe of those who studied Jewish history—among them Blaise Pascal, Leo Tolstoy, and Winston Churchill, who said, "Some people like the Jews, and some do not. But no thoughtful man can deny the fact that they are beyond question the most formidable and the most remarkable race which has ever appeared in the world." Moses' prophecy came true: "This is your wisdom and understanding in the eyes of the nations, who will hear about all these decrees and say, 'Surely this great nation is a wise and understanding people'" (Deuteronomy 4:6).

The Jewish Tasks

Just as there is not one moral voice in Judaism but three, so there is not one Jewish task in the world but three. There is the *wisdom* task, in this case specified by Jeremiah in his famous letter to the Jewish exiles in Babylon: "Seek the peace and prosperity of the city to which I have carried you into exile. Pray to the Eternal for it, because if it prospers, you too will prosper" (Jeremiah 29:7). The sages called this attitude one of *darkhei shalom*, the ways of peace. It was the world's first-ever formula for becoming a creative minority, contributing to society without losing one's identity. It remains the best way of structuring the diverse, multicultural societies of the West today.

There is the *prophetic* task, beautifully expressed by Isaiah in the passage we read as the *haftarah* on Yom Kippur: "Is not this the kind of fasting I have chosen: to loose the chains of injustice and untie the cords of the yoke, to set the oppressed free and break every yoke? Is it not to share your food with the hungry and to provide the poor wanderer with shelter—when you see the naked, to clothe them, and not to turn away from your own flesh and blood?" (Isaiah 58:5–7). Jews continue to be inspired by the prophetic ethic, which is why they are to be found disproportionately as doctors fighting disease, economists fighting poverty, businesspeople fighting unemployment, lawyers fighting injustice, and teachers fighting ignorance. Wherever there is hopelessness, there you will find Jews giving people hope.

And there is the priestly task of *k'dushah*: sanctifying life by honoring the sacred ontology, the deep moral structure of the universe, through the life of the 613 commands—a life of discipline and self-restraint, honesty and integrity, respect and love. It is found in the code set out in the chapter of the Torah that opens with the momentous words, "Be holy for I, the Eternal your God, am holy" (Leviticus 19:2). Other cultures and faiths drew inspiration from its wisdom and prophetic traditions, but *k'dushah* remained a specific Jewish imperative that has made us different. Even so, it contains a message for the world, to which Jews bear witness whenever and wherever they remain faithful to it.

Our vocation remains: to be *mamlekhet kohanim v'goy kadosh*, "a kingdom of priests and a holy nation" (Exodus 19:6).

NOTES

[1] Commentary to Numbers 15:38.
[2] *Kuzari* II 48.

Hired for the Day

Shalom Carmy

Don't say: I cannot hear all of the Torah and observe all of the commandments written in it, about which it is written, "Longer than earth is its measure" (Job 11:9). It is like a king who had an endlessly deep pit and told a member of his family to hire workers to fill the pit. He then hired workers. The foolish one went and gazed at the pit and said, "When will I fill it?" The shrewd one said, "What do I care, since I am hired for the day? I rejoice that I found work for myself." So God says: "What do you care? You are hired for the day; do your day's work."[1]

There is nothing so physically and spiritually destructive as diverting one's attention from this world. And, by contrast, how courageous is halakhic man who does not flee from this world, who does not seek to escape to some pure, supernal realm.[2]

I

"Sanctification" and "sanctity" are Latin words; "holiness" is a Germanic word. Both translate the Hebrew word *k'dushah*. The editors of this volume, in their letter of invitation, used the two European words interchangeably. Almost all Jewish or non-Jewish discussions of *k'dushah* in English prefer the term "holiness" or "the holy." What conscious or unconscious factors led the editors of this book to settle on "sanctification"?

One possibility is that "holiness" functions as a noun rather than as a verb; the transitive verb "hallow" is uncommon, *pace* the Gettysburg Address. "Sanctification" is a noun derived from the verb "to sanctify." If this book is more about the dynamic of *making* things holy than about being holy, then "sanctification" seems to be a more suitable word. Yet, as Rabbi Soloveitchik often observed, holiness in Judaism is always a characteristic of human beings or a state brought about through human action. Holidays, for example, are holy because they fall out on dates specified by the Jewish calendar, and the calendar is determined by the Sanhedrin (or its successor entity, acting for the Jewish people). That is why the Kiddush that expresses the sanctification of the festivals ends with the words, "Blessed are You, Eternal One, who sanctifies Israel and the [solemn] times"; it is Israel who sanctifies the date. We recite a different formula for the Sabbath, "...who sanctifies the Sabbath," because the Sabbath is determined by the weekly cycle and not through the calendar proclaimed by the rabbinic court. Nonetheless, Rabbi Soloveitchik noted, the Yerushalmi proposes a different text for this blessing: "who sanctifies *Israel and* the Sabbath"—so that even the Sabbath is, in some sense, dependent on human proclamation. Thus holiness and sanctification, even as technical halakhic institutions, are ultimately about what human beings make of themselves. Our reflection on the meaning of sanctification today must be rooted in the human condition.

Sanctification has a particular role in Christian theology. At the risk of oversimplification, the Christian believes himself or herself to be justified, accepted, and forgiven by God, through faith and not through works of righteousness—regardless of human initiative. Of course the Christian desires to live a worthwhile life, and that is manifested through good works. The process of becoming a righteous, saintly human being is called sanctification. In its liberal version, whose secularized form dominates contemporary therapeutic philosophies, this means that we are all okay regardless of our moral record (i.e., that we are justified by our faith); nevertheless, we still want to look upon our existence and pronounce it worthwhile. To talk about sanctification in this context is to pose the question about the meaning and significance of our lives.

"Sanctity," in common parlance, has another connotation. When we speak of the "sanctity of life" we ordinarily refer to something about human existence that makes it inviolable. We speak of an attribute of humanity in which all participate—regardless of our achievements, whether moral, religious, or worldly. We like to think that we, and other human beings, are entitled to a certain respect and dignity by virtue of our humanity, that certain things ought to be done for us and ought not to be done to us. The ideal of the *sanctification* of human life and the conviction of the *sanctity* of human life are different, but the verbal link carries with it some natural association as well. We may feel anxious about the fate of the sanctity of life in our culture because we fear it is in danger of erosion. We may feel anxious, even desperate, about sanctification: not because we are worried about the respect of other human beings, but because we yearn for self-respect and, if we believe in God, because we care about how we appear before the Almighty.

These usages, I think, indicate what "sanctification" connotes for contemporary English speakers. Insofar as our subject is the meaning of sanctification in contemporary Western society, we will not here discuss the intricacies of *k'dushah* as a property of objects: we will not comment on how reciting *Kiddush*, for example, contributes to the sanctity of the Sabbath and festivals; or on the meaning of the word *kiddushin* in the marriage ceremony; or on the laws concerning the consecration of money or objects and the ensuing status of those objects. I will not discuss the details of the laws about the sanctity of the synagogue, even though they apply to our everyday conduct. I will use the Hebrew concept of *k'dushah* only to the extent that it helps clarify the discussion of its putative English equivalent.

Let us, then, examine briefly three projects that beckon to modern men and women in their quest for sanctification.

II

The Ascetic Impulse

K'dushah is related to separation. In Maimonides' great law code, the
Mishneh Torah, the volume concerning *k'dushah* is devoted to laws
concerning sexual and dietary prohibitions. Naḥmanides' commentary
to the verse "You shall be holy" (Leviticus 19:2) is a classic exposition
of the idea of separation. The holy individual goes beyond the
separation mandated by divine law: the Torah prohibits eating pig
or shellfish, and it enjoins ritual purity in certain situations; holiness
mandates abstemiousness even in partaking of permitted foods, and
it also seeks to extend the standards of ritual purity to a broader range
of situations. This ideal of *k'dushah*, it must be emphasized, is one
ingredient in a life determined by thorough-going adherence to the
halakhah, the law, and to the personal relationship with God that the
law defines.

The thought that life attains heroic spiritual significance by voluntarily
overcoming ordinary human restraints and limitations can be
attractive to modern people who do not subscribe to these religious
underpinnings. The noted scholar of modern German literature, J.
P. Stern, wrote a long book, *The Dear Purchase*,[3] on the theme that
excellence, for many German intellectuals, became a function of
such self-transcendence: think of Nietzsche, Mann, Kafka's "Hunger
Artist." Stern maintained that this idea became prominent because
the power of traditional religious life-plans had waned, leaving behind
only the residue of asceticism, and he argued that this idea lies in the
background of German political ideology of the interwar period.

Closer to home, the liberal American icon, Oliver Wendell
Holmes, Jr., articulated his creed while addressing fellow Civil War
veterans:

> I do not know what is true. I do not know the meaning of
> the universe. But in the midst of doubt, in the collapse of

creeds, there is one thing I do not doubt, that no man who lives in the same world with most of us can doubt, and that is that the faith is true and adorable which leads a soldier to throw away his life in obedience to a blindly accepted duty, in a cause which he little understands, in a plan of campaign of which he has no notion, under tactics of which he does not see the use.[4]

In this view, the individual, or the band of comrades, discerns no meaning to life and death beyond the recklessness and solidarity of self-sacrifice. The bluntness and brutality with which Holmes proclaimed his ideal is not unconnected to his having reached manhood with a purely secular outlook on the universe. For those who think like Holmes, this vision offers an alternative of sorts to religious sanctification. It is not, of course, a hospitable outlook for those who care about the sanctity of the human being. In Holmes's words one can hear a premonition of his later tolerance, from the Supreme Court bench, of forced sterilization in the name of eugenics: "three generations of imbeciles are enough."[5]

The Altruistic Impulse

It was precocious of Holmes to learn nihilism from the Civil War. President Lincoln at Gettysburg gestured to the more familiar notion of consecration through death on the battlefield: it is for a cause one understands and deems worthy of the ultimate price (in his case, sustaining the Union and the survival of the American experiment in republican government). I am not sure how many Americans today would be willing to give up 600,000 lives—their own and those of their children—for a political system, or even to emancipate the slaves. It seems safe to say that most people concerned about living a sanctified life today would associate this notion with living in a way that puts the welfare of others ahead of one's own personal benefit. Susan Wolf's influential essay "Moral Saints" defines saintliness entirely in terms of sacrificing one's interests for those of other people; among most of her readers, ethics is synonymous with "what we owe each other," so that the only way to raise ethics to the level of sanctification would be to dedicate oneself to others, beyond the customary reach of duty.[6]

The last phrase is a gross understatement. What Lincoln consecrated was not merely supererogatory behavior, but extreme, life-and-death action. To be sure, the commandment to love God "with all your heart and all your soul and all your possessions" (Deuteronomy 6:5) includes the possibility of dying to sanctify God's name. Some Jews meditate daily on this possible eventuality. All religious individuals think about it regularly—in light of the political realities of our time, how could we not? But at the same time, most of us, barring combat soldiers, will not have the opportunity to engage in such extraordinary actions on behalf of others—and if we do, it is likely to happen not through our contrivance and not as we would have planned. Such sanctification thus cannot ordinarily be a life-project.

Whether Lincoln was ever a conventional Christian believer is doubtful. What is evident is that the kind of religious faith that he took seriously did not rejoice in the easy grace and taken-for-granted justification of liberal therapeutic theology. Quite to the contrary: when Lincoln spoke of God it was to consider the awesome responsibility we assume before the Divine, as when he reminded the nation, in his Second Inaugural Address:

> Yet, if God wills that [the war] continue, until all the wealth piled up by the bondsman's two hundred and fifty years of unrequited toil shall be sunk, and until every drop of blood drawn with the lash shall be paid by another drawn with the sword, as was said three thousand years ago, so still it must be said that "the judgments of the Lord, are true and righteous altogether."[7]

Most current idealization of sanctification through dedication to human welfare lacks the dramatic decisiveness of physical violence, martyrdom, and bloodshed. As a result we are also less likely to grasp the dangers in heroic self-sanctifying self-giving. Human beings are created in the image of God, but they are not God. To treat them as if they are divine is to distort that image. When we seek to make a human being or a group of human beings more than human, we are liable to end up making them less than human. This is the story of nationalism in the modern world. More insidiously, because the decisive dimension of physical compulsion is absent, such distortions readily infiltrate the projects of lovers who seek to assign ultimate value to their personal relationships, or of parents who become overly invested in their children, or of political activists all fired up with their passion for the ideal social order as they perceive it. Our desire to "empower" others often becomes the project of controlling them, enslaving both sides of the relationship in the process. Today we even see an attempt to sanctify existence by manufacturing a neo-pagan cult of nature in place of the personal, commanding God of Scripture.

Human beings deserve better than this. Investing absolute value in helping other people makes them, in effect, objects of our benevolence and pawns in our desire for sanctification. This is the social worker's fallacy: "I am here to help others; what the others are here for, God only knows." Likewise, reducing ethics to everyday altruism is unlikely to provide altruistic people with the sense that their lives are truly worthwhile. In the early nineteenth century, John Stuart Mill was brought up to believe that being ethical was identical with striving for the greatest happiness of the greatest number. He writes in his *Autobiography* that in early adulthood he came to ask himself:

> Suppose that all your objects in life were realized; and that all the changes in institutions that you are looking forward to, could be completely affected at this very instant: would this be a great joy and happiness to you? And an irrepressible

self-consciousness distinctly answered, "No!" At this my heart sank within me: the whole foundation on which my life was constructed fell down.[8]

How Mill repaired the philosophy that his father had taught him, and how he was able to continue as a utilitarian (albeit one with a broader idea of what constitutes happiness), is not our concern here. One inference we can make from Mill's crisis is that the do-gooder's idea of happiness is impoverished. Another is that the entire idea of anchoring the meaning of life exclusively in benefit to others begs the question of what is truly valuable. If a grand life of difficulty and risk for its own sake—like that celebrated by Holmes and pondered by Stern's German modernists—is too much at variance with normal human life to serve as a foundation for a sanctified existence, then Mill's altruism (however effortful its pursuit in the short run) lacks the sense of majesty that we would want to attach to a sanctified human existence.

The Mystical Impulse

The two secular ideologies we have just tried on each contain one ingredient of a sanctified life. On the one hand, the ascetic irrationality of Holmes's "dear purchase" captures the total commitment, the passionate love, required of human excellence. On the other hand, the liberal rationalism of the social worker rightly stresses that such a life must be centered on something other than oneself. A third approach may be found in a popular strand of mysticism, which understands religious practice as a set of actions and "intentions" aimed at affecting God. At first blush, this is nothing but a restatement of fundamental Jewish doctrine: Judaism assigns the human being, the image of God, enormous responsibility; human action is therefore significant and potentially world-altering. The power of religious action is not dependent solely on its visible, measurable worldly impact. If the question of sanctification is about how human beings can, by their own actions, make their lives profoundly worthwhile, this language seems like the answer to a prayer. From this perspective, human beings are indeed agents of their own sanctification. Moreover, within a kabbalistic framework, human actions create external spiritual entities and are even said to affect God and to redeem the fallen world.

Upon reflection, however, it becomes evident that mystical formulations of Judaism go beyond Jewish fundamentals: adding may end up detracting. Judaism, as expressed in the *halakhah*, indeed glorifies the human being's capacity to participate in the creation of the world. This is understood in terms of various models of personal relationship to God: simply, one obeys God. Obedience leads to more intimate modes of relationship: one imitates God and even becomes a partner with the Divine in creation. Just as certain almost invisible or trivial gestures express immense, immeasurable love between friends and lovers, parents and children, so too the precise performance of divine commandments bears significance and spiritual power indiscernible to the indifferent eye.

Now retain the idea of spiritually effective human actions, *mitzvot*, focus more and more on the supposed effects that these spiritual forces exert on high, but take away or downplay the implicit or explicit personal connection to God effected through subordinating ourselves to the commandments and responding to God creatively. What is left is not the experience of God, but instead some occult celestial mechanics, conformity to the rituals of which casts enchantment via a mysterious metaphysical realm, bathing its votaries in warm feelings of spiritual elevation and conferring upon them, at least for a while, an aura of sanctity. No doubt this is not the way things are for serious kabbalists, whose lives emerge from a thorough grounding in *halakhah* and its culture—at least I hope it is not. What I have described here is closer to magic than to the service of God. As such, it has the frisson but not the strenuous adventure of profound nihilism; it generates the self-approval of the social activist without affecting the real world; it exploits the idea of God, and it even engages in *mitzvot* and rituals without the unrelenting commitment to obey—or the fear and trembling that Lincoln, for example, felt in the face of human responsibility in earnest. Adding mystical trumpets and flourishes to traditional religion does not enhance religious reality; rather, such embellishments are liable to make it fanciful.

III

The limitations and pitfalls we have noted in these popular attempts at constructing a sanctified existence lead one to wonder whether the entire exercise is misguided. Perhaps sanctification, in the sense explored earlier, is not the watchword for those whose ladder is pitched in present-day Western culture and who aspire to something better. Judaism surely does not subscribe to the therapeutic doctrine of justification in which God forgives us unconditionally. Is it possible that the doctrine of sanctification, with which that doctrine is allied, is equally unhelpful within a Jewish framework?

Why should this be so? It is natural for people to want to know where they are going. It is inevitable that people will want to assess their progress in terms of some standard. Am I a better person today than I was a year ago, ten years ago, forty years ago? One may break down the analysis and consider particular virtues: relations to family, or to strangers; the development of one's talents; dedication to Torah study; and so forth. One might mark progress in sanctity in fairly circumscribed areas, like those listed by Naḥmanides: greater discipline in indulging one's physical appetites; greater care not to engage in idle or malicious speech; greater aversion to wasting time; greater devotion to, and joy in, doing good to others. To take one seemingly minor issue: imagine what a revolution it would be if more people took seriously the sanctity of the synagogue, not by weaving metaphysical halos about it, but simply by behaving respectfully and refraining from idle chatter and casualness in the house of God! If people were to strive to act this way, one might discern overall a more whole-hearted dedication to goals worthy of all-consuming passion.

However, it would be comic or presumptuous to ask whether one was becoming, or had become, a more holy or a more sanctified person over the past year. It would be even more comic, I think—almost like a Monty Python sketch—to assess one's progress in sanctifying the universe as a whole, or in sanctifying a large number of things in the universe. The ideal of sanctification is simply too general and too fuzzy to serve as a practical guide.

If we are attracted to sanctification as a slogan, it is partly because we want more out of life than simply the accumulation of prescribed actions: we crave an ideal that elevates us and transforms us (preferably without extreme pain or the sacrifice of our worldly values) in a manner that neither everyday secular existence nor the life of routine religious observance can. Perhaps because the secularized doctrine of justification caters to our need to "accept ourselves" unconditionally, we also want a framework of moral striving that can underwrite the move from absolute self-acceptance to unconditional self-approval.

Perhaps we feel insignificant, or are tempted to think of ourselves as insignificant. We may be doing work that is not appreciated and is often of dubious value to ourselves or to others. We suspect, often rightly, that our fellowship is more anonymous and our closer relationships are more fragile and insecure than we can easily tolerate. We lack a vivid connection to God as intimate Commander, Guide, Judge, and Friend; our engagement in organized religion is shrouded in gray conformity. And so, in the absence of achievements in which we can honestly believe or of all-consuming passionate love, we yearn for a doctrine that affirms the cosmic import of our actions in spite of appearances.

During the period that I groped my way toward Orthodoxy, I often thought about the rabbinic statement: "One should always view oneself, and the world, as balanced between merit and guilt. If one performs a single commandment one is fortunate, for one has decided oneself and the whole world to merit..."[9] The Talmud does not say that the individual and the world are really poised between salvation and damnation: it is quite possible that the small action that I will perform in the next moment has no overwhelming cosmic significance. Rather, we are told to think of ourselves—and the world—as *if* our actions have that significance. In the over forty years that have passed since I reached my present theological position, my skepticism about general, vague ideals has increased, as has my faith in the eternal significance of each moment.

In the midrash cited as an epigraph for this essay, the shrewd worker says: "I am hired for the day; I rejoice that I found work for myself." One aspect of the midrash has become clearer to me over time. The king did not hire the workers directly, but rather assigned the task to a member of his household. The foolish worker despairs at the cosmic insignificance of his labors, while the shrewd worker is satisfied to do his work with no illusions about its cosmic importance. Neither worker has encountered the king prior to being hired. The shrewd worker enters into the spirit of the work joyously but anonymously: he has no reason to assume that the king knows him or cares for him. It is only as the story unfolds that the king dispenses with the supervisor and addresses the shrewd worker directly, commending his judgment. The king does not assure the worker that the assignment has some obscure hitherto unsuspected world-changing impact. He doesn't even tell him that the work is outstanding. All he does is remind the worker that he is fortunate to have a day's work for himself, and that the day's work awaits him.

I'm not sure I would have noticed this point forty years ago. Today it means a lot to me.

NOTES

[1] *Yalkut Shimoni* §863 (to Deuteronomy 11).

[2] Rabbi Joseph Soloveitchik, *Halakhic* Man (Philadelphia: Jewish Publication Society, 1983), p. 41.

[3] Cambridge University Press, 1995.

[4] Oliver Wendell Holmes, Jr., "The Soldier's Faith," in Max Lerner, ed., *The Mind and Faith of Justice Holmes: His Speeches, Essays, Letters, and Judicial Opinions* (Piscataway, NJ: Transaction Publishers, 1988), p. 20.

[5] Cited by Lawrence Meir Friedman in *American Law in the Twentieth Century* (New Haven: Yale University Press, 2004), p. 110.

[6] Wolf's essay was published in *The Journal of Philosophy* 79 (August 1982), pp. 419–439.

[7] The biblical quotation is Psalm 19:10.

[8] John Stuart Mill, *Autobiography* (Auckland, New Zealand: The Floating Press, 2009), p. 134.

[9] *Midrash Tanhuma*, ed. Warsaw, *Va-yeileikh*, ch. 2.

The Man Who Mistook His *Tefillin* for a Hat

James Kugel

Tefillin, sometimes called "phylacteries," are two little black boxes, inside of which are parchments inscribed with certain biblical passages. They are worn by Jews during morning prayers: one of the boxes is tied to the upper arm with a leather strap, and the other is connected to a leather headband, so that it sits on the hairline at the top of the forehead. *Tefillin* are worn inside, usually in the synagogue or, if one prays at home, then at home. While it is theoretically permitted to wear *tefillin* outside as well, in practice this is rarely done today, in part because of the various restrictions mentioned in connection with their use.[1]

A hat, by contrast, is made to be worn outside, in the street. In Judaism, it is an altogether ordinary object. True, the Talmud instructs Jews to cover their heads when walking any distance greater than the minimal "four cubits" (six feet) as a sign of modesty and submission to God. But what *kind* of hat is a matter of indifference, indeed, any form of head-covering will do. Thus, these two objects, the "head" part of the *tefillin* and the hat, are each worn on the head, but they are in some sense opposites, the one sacred and the other ordinary, the first belonging to the world of the inside and the second to that of the outside.

For this reason, I will need to explain how it happened that Morris Kleinberg, an otherwise scrupulous observer of Jewish laws and customs, stepped out of his Manhattan apartment building one day wearing the "head" part of his *tefillin* instead of his customary fedora.

It had all started earlier that morning. Kleinberg, having overslept, failed to attend morning prayers at the synagogue, as was his custom. Now he had to pray hurriedly at home instead. Of course, his regular *tefillin* were kept next to his seat in the synagogue, but Kleinberg had been careful to acquire a second pair, which he kept at home in case of just such an emergency. He thus strode purposefully into his living room, opened the drawer in which this home pair of *tefillin* was stored...and then suddenly realized that half of the pair was missing. Some weeks earlier, he had noticed a white spot on the black lacquer of his arm-*tefillin* and had brought it to the synagogue to be retouched, since white spots are forbidden. There it remained; Kleinberg had simply forgotten to pick it up. Now, all he had available was the head part of his *tefillin* and the headband to which it was attached. Is it permitted for one to pray with the head part on one's head but without having the arm part strapped to one's arm? Kleinberg was not sure, but on reflection, he decided that it must be and so proceeded to place the head-*tefillin* on his head as usual, saying the appropriate blessing.

If only he had the other part bound tightly to his arm, he surely would not have failed to remove both it and the head-*tefillin* at the conclusion of his prayers. But somehow, sliding his suit jacket back over his shirtsleeve and encountering no encumbrance of the arm box, he forgot the head-*tefillin* entirely. Stranger still: the slight pressure exercised by the leather headband on his temples somehow convinced him that he was already wearing his everyday hat. Thus it was that he left his apartment that morning with the head part of his *tefillin* on his head instead of his hat.

"Good morning, Hector," he said to the doorman as he stepped outside. Hector, an undiscerning sluggard, grunted his usual vague response and otherwise said, and indeed noticed, nothing. Kleinberg spotted a cab as soon as he reached the curb and hopped in, announcing the address of his company's building in a clear voice: "Broad Street, corner of Pine." He was somewhat puzzled to see the cabdriver peer inquisitively into the rearview mirror once or twice.

He in turn glanced at the name printed on the driver's certificate: Tan Wing-mei. Kleinberg said nothing. Arrived at his destination, he proceeded on his way to the corner coffee shop to pick up his morning espresso. As he walked down the street with the little black box still strapped to his head, its leather straps dangling down next to his tie, Kleinberg felt one or two passers-by staring at him. A woman even raised her index finger as if to say something, but Kleinberg hurried by. What *is* with these people? Pilar, the girl behind the counter at the coffee shop, smiled broadly at him when he came in and hurried to bring him his espresso. She said not a word. Kleinberg also stopped at the corner kiosk, as was also his custom, to pick up that morning's *Wall Street Journal*. Everywhere people now seemed to be looking at him a bit strangely, but this did not particularly trouble him. He had long ago noticed that people sometimes do stare. New Yorkers are so used to everyone being enclosed in an halo of resolute indifference, one that is specifically designed to separate each from the other, that when someone (usually an out-of-towner, or sometimes a resident whose halo has mysteriously come loose)— when someone seems to be walking about without this protective film, all eyes are magically drawn to him. That must be it, thought Kleinberg, who had experienced such staring before; it must be one of those mornings. Thus it was that he entered his office building with the incongruous head box still strapped to his forehead. It was only when he reached the elevator that Jamal, the morning elevator boy, looked up and said, "Hey, Mr. K., what's that on your head?" Kleinberg instinctively lifted his hand to where his hat ought to have been and only then discovered to his horror that the head box that he thought he had returned to its place in the drawer had in fact been in plain sight since he had left his apartment. "Oh!" he exclaimed, and then again, "Oh! Oh!" He quickly removed the head box and stuffed it and its leather straps into the right pocket of his jacket. "What was that?" Jamal persisted. "Nothing, just a. . . nothing," Kleinberg answered. Thus ended a mildly embarrassing incident, whereby that which belongs to the inside was mistaken for that which belongs to the outside.

#

But this is not quite all there is to say on the matter. I believe that, considered from a distance, Kleinberg's error that morning had a kind of symbolic quality to it. In fact, I like to think of him rounding the corner of Broad and Pine Streets with the head part of his *tefillin* firmly planted on his forehead and its straps a-flapping, his own expression mingling determination with a touch of bewilderment, just now passing that woman who raises her finger to question what she is seeing, as a kind of statue, or rather a *tableau vivant*, of Judaism itself. In particular, I believe he is at this moment a near-perfect embodiment of what is perhaps Judaism's most striking characteristic, what might be called its concern for the "sanctification of daily life." Before getting to that subject, however, I wish to start off with a more down-to-earth question, the one that Jamal asked a minute ago: "Hey, Mr. K., what's that on your head?" What is it indeed?

The thing that Kleinberg had on his head was a small leather cube, approximately one inch square, inside of which were four separated compartments. Each compartment contained a different piece of parchment inscribed with biblical verses: Exod. 13:1-10 in the first, Exod. 13:11-16 in the second, Deut. 6:4-9 in the third, and Deut. 11:13-21 in the fourth. Kleinberg, it must be admitted, had only the foggiest notion of his head-*tefillin*'s contents; it was enough to know that the little box, along with the box of the arm-*tefillin*, had to be worn for morning prayers. But the reason why these passages were the ones enclosed in that little black box, and the reason why this fairly odd-looking accoutrement should have found itself on his head in the first place, are not straightforward.

The Torah says, in the four passages just mentioned, that its words are to be bound "as a sign upon your hand, and as frontlets between your eyes." Actually, the "frontlets" part is something of a guess; no one knows for sure what the word *totafot* means in Hebrew.[2] In one of these four passages (Exod 13:9), the word "memorial" (*zikkaron*) appears instead of *totafot*, but this hardly clarifies things. But quite apart from the precise meaning of the words, a real question arises from a reading of these four passages: what exactly are people being told to do?

About this there is a historic debate. Some Jews (notably some Karaites, who flourished in medieval and early modern times; apparently the Samaritans as well, and probably some Jews in more ancient days) maintained that this commandment does not involve actually tying anything to one's arm or head. Rather, exponents of this position argue, its aim is to instruct Jews to hold the Torah's words dear, binding them close, as it were, to one's head and heart. And the exponents do have a point. One of the four verses, Deut 11:18, says more specifically: "You shall put these words of Mine on your heart and on your soul; and you shall tie them for a sign upon your arm, and they shall be as *totafot* between your eyes." The second part of the sentence seems to be a metaphorical reiteration of the first part: "Don't ever let these words of Mine be far from you! Tie them to yourself, keep them forever close!" Such a reading is supported by other verses in the Bible. Proverbs 6:20-21 says, "My son, keep your father's commandment and do not neglect your mother's teachings; *tie them upon your heart forever and bind them around your neck.*" This certainly does not seem to be a reference to *tefillin*; is it not simply the case that the parents' teachings are to be cherished and held close, and for that reason are compared to some sort of ornament worn close to the body? The lovesick maiden of the Song of Songs similarly says to her beloved, "Set me as a signet upon your hand, as a signet on your arm" (8:6), once again in the sense of, "Don't forget me, not for one minute!" Once again, an external ornament is invoked to signify metaphorical closeness. Another passage in Proverbs reads: "My son, do not forget my teaching, and may your heart keep my commandments... bind them around your neck, write them on the writing tablet of your heart" (3:1-3). Just as there does not seem to be any physical writing tablet on a person's heart, so the previous "bind them around your neck" ought likewise to be seen as figurative speech, a metaphor for keeping the parent's words constantly in mind. So, all in all, it might seem that the whole idea of binding the *tefillin* to one's arm and head is a kind of literalization, turning an originally metaphorical commandment into a physical act.[3]

And yet, this commandment was not understood metaphorically—not in rabbinic Judaism and not in at least some Jewish groups in pre-rabbinic times, as may be evidenced in a number of sources.[4] The reasons are no doubt complicated, dependent on both exegetical and other considerations.[5] But what I wish to suggest here is that the decision in favor of actual, physical *tefillin* is altogether consistent with a particularly striking aspect of the "sanctification of daily life" mentioned earlier. Almost wherever possible, biblical commandments that might otherwise seem to be non-specific and/or addressed to one's internal state of mind are concretized into specific, *external* acts, so that, faced with a choice between "Keep these words in mind" and "Physically attach these words to your head and arm," Judaism has—odd as it may seem—generally opted for the latter from ancient times on. Let me mention a few other examples of this same tendency:

Deuteronomy 30:20 urges Israelites to "love the Lord your God, to obey Him and *hold fast to Him*, for by this you will live and long endure upon the land that the Lord has sworn to give to your forefathers..." There is nothing particularly mysterious about the phrase "hold fast to Him." It occurs elsewhere in the Bible in similar contexts: "serve Him and hold fast to Him" (Deut 10:20) "to walk in all His paths and to hold fast to Him" (Deut 11:22), "to keep His commandments and to hold fast to Him" (Josh 22:5). In all these, "holding fast" implies following closely all that God has ordained. But that is not how this phrase was interpreted in rabbinic texts:

> *And hold fast to Him*: But is it indeed possible for a person to ascend on high and hold fast to *fire*—since it is said elsewhere "For the Lord your God is a consuming fire" [Deut 4:24] and "His throne is of tongues of flames" [Dan 7:9]? Rather [it means]: Hold fast to Torah sages and their students and I will account it for you as if you had ascended on high (*Sifrei Debarim* 49).

Here, the impossibility of "holding fast" to God physically has not led to the obvious metaphorical explanation of the phrase. Rather, this metaphorical embrace has been, as it were, brought down to earth and connected to something altogether concrete and close at hand, "Torah sages and their students." This, in turn, was further concretized and specified in later sources:

> *To love the Lord your God and to hold fast to Him*: But is it possible for someone to cling to the *Shekhinah* [God's earthly presence]? Rather, anyone who marries his daughter to a scholar of Torah and conducts business with Torah scholars and causes Torah scholars to benefit from his possessions, Scripture accounts it as if he is clinging to the *Shekhinah* (b. *Ketubot* 111b).

So it is with other *mitzvot* as well. The commandment to "love the Lord your God and to serve Him with your whole heart" (Deut 11:13)—which, considered on its own, might seem to address a person's whole attitude toward the Almighty—was taken as a reference to a specific act, namely prayer (b. *Ta'anit* 2a), and this understanding was then further codified by Maimonides as the requirement that each person pray to God at least once a day.[6] This is another act of specifying and concretizing.

The same might well be said of the requirement to recite the *Shema* every morning and evening. The Torah says: "You shall love the Lord your God with your whole heart and soul and strength. And you shall keep in mind these words that I am commanding you this day. Teach them to your children and speak about them as you sit about your house or walk along on a journey, when you lie down and when you get up" (Deut 6:5-7). Moses speaks these words at the beginning of a long address, his final charge to the Israelites in the book of Deuteronomy. In context, he might seem to be saying to his audience, "Keep the things that I am telling you today in mind and talk about them all the time, wherever you happen to be." The phrases "as you sit about your house or walk along on a journey, when you lie down and when you get up" are an instance of what classical rhetoricians referred to as *merismus*, a figure of speech "in which totality is expressed by contrasting parts."[7]

Understood in this way, the words cited could scarcely be taken as an actual commandment; after all, who can keep in mind the entire contents of Deuteronomy every minute of the day, no matter where or when? But rather than therefore treating this paragraph as some sort of generalized exhortation, Judaism concretized it into the prescription of a specific *act*, to be repeated twice daily. That is, "these words that I am commanding you" were understood to be specifically the words of this very paragraph rather than the whole of Moses' speech, and the *merismus* was explained as an explicit prescription of when those words were to be recited, at the time "when you lie down and when you get up" (m. *Berakhot* 1:1-2). If so, here is another act of turning the apparently general to something specific and concretizing it into a fixed act, in this case one to be repeated twice each day.

Such an understanding of Deut 6:5-7 is attested well before the rise of rabbinic Judaism. It is found in a number of pre-rabbinic sources,[8] including, somewhat obliquely, these words from the Qumran *Community Rule* (10:10, 13-14):

> With the entrance of the day and of night, I shall enter into the covenant of God,[9] and with the going out of evening and of morning I shall speak of His laws...When I begin to stretch out my hands and feet, I will bless His name; when I begin to go out and in, to sit and get up, or upon lying down on my couch, I will extol Him; I will bless him with the offering of my lips....

It is noteworthy that this apparent reference to Deut 6:5-7 seems to represent a halfway position in the process of narrowing and concretization described above. While the *merismus* of "when you lie down and when you get up" has been resolved into two specific times ("the entrance of the day and of night"), the actual words to be spoken remain unspecified ("I shall speak of His laws"), just as in Deut 6:7 ("and speak about them"). The same is true of the *Letter of Aristeas* (late second or first century BCE): "He also commands that on going to bed and rising, men should *meditate on the ordinances* of God" (160).

A similar sort of reading is connected to another famous passage in Deuteronomy:

> For the Lord your God is bringing you into a goodly land, a land of rivers and fountains and torrents gushing forth in hill and vale; a land of wheat and barley, vines, figs, and pomegranates, a land of olives and honey; a land where you may eat food without stinting, since you will lack nothing there; a land whose stones are [rich in] iron and from whose hills you shall mine copper. And you will eat and be satisfied and bless the Lord your God for the goodly land which He has given you. (Deut 8:7-10)

No doubt a first-time reader would see the last sentence of this passage as a continuation of the fulsome praise that precedes it: one who inherits all this abundance, it seems to say, will naturally express gratitude for the gift of this goodly land. But of course that is not how this passage is understood. As early as the book of *Jubilees* (early second century BCE), there is evidence suggesting that the last sentence of the passage was understood as a specific commandment, to say a blessing after eating a meal:

> And he [Abraham] ate and drank. Then he blessed God Most High, who created heaven and earth and who made all the abundance of the earth and gave it to human beings so that they might eat and drink and bless their Creator (Jub 22:6).

It seems likely that in this case, as so often in *Jubilees*, a particular event in the life of one of Israel's forefathers is being presented as a precedent for what was later to become a commandment of the Torah, in this case, that of Deut 8:10. In other words, even at this early date, what might otherwise be seen as a generalized biblical encomium of the land of Israel was already being understood by the author of *Jubilees* as requiring a specific, external act to be performed after eating a festive meal (cf. Jub 2:21).[10] Such a hypothesis is backed up by some of *Jubilees'* contemporaries, for example, Ben Sira's assertion:

> Like a sealing-clasp (חותם) on a purse of gold, so is the praise
> of God after a wine feast (35:5 [ms. B])

(Here, "sealing-clasp" is meant to imply the act of *sealing* or ending the evening with praise.)[11] From only a slightly later period, several texts found among the Dead Sea Scrolls—4QDeut[n], the so-called "All Souls Deuteronomy," 4QDeut[j], and 4Q434a—suggest that the same passage ending in Deut 8:10 was being copied for liturgical use, in all likelihood as part of a fixed practice of reciting a blessing after the meal.[12]

#

Some of the above examples highlight another aspect of this "sanctification of daily life": it is not simply a matter of concretizing and specifying, but of connecting divinely given commandments with the quotidian, the everyday. Putting on *tefillin* each day, supporting the Torah scholars in one's midst, saying a blessing after a meal—all these insist that the realm of the sacred is in the here-and-now; commandments that might otherwise seem vague and location-less are to be anchored in daily life. There are further illustrations of this tendency.

The book of Leviticus contains the commandment, "You shall not take revenge or hold a grudge" (Lev. 19:18). On the face of things, this hardly sounds like a prohibition relevant to most people's daily lives. "Revenge," in biblical Hebrew as well as English, smacks of bloodshed and violence (Gen 4:24, Num 31:2, etc.); perhaps precisely for that reason, it is asserted to be the province of God (Deut 32:35), not men, and the great majority of biblical occurrences of this verb (נק"ם) do in fact refer to divine revenge. Indeed, that would seem to fit well with the prohibition of humans taking revenge in our verse. As for the adjoining prohibition of holding a grudge, is it not mentioned because holding a grudge is simply the starting point of any act of revenge?

Such, however, is not the explanation of these twin prohibitions as found in the tannaitic midrash *Sifra*:

> *You shall not take revenge*: What does taking revenge include? Suppose someone said, "Lend me your scythe," but the other person did not lend it. Sometime later, the second man said to the first: "Lend me your spade." He replied: "I won't lend it to you, just as you would not lend me your scythe." This is what is prohibited by, "You shall not take revenge." *You shall not hold a grudge*: What does holding a grudge include? Suppose someone said, "Lend me your spade," but the other person did not lend it. Sometime later, the second man said to the first: "Lend me your scythe." He replied: "This will show you that I'm not like you. You wouldn't lend me your spade [but I'll still lend you my scythe]." This is what is prohibited by, "You shall not hold a grudge."

Here, the prohibition of taking revenge is removed from the realm of theoretical violence and, as it were, domesticated into the sort of petty act that an ordinary person might encounter in the most everyday of circumstances. "Revenge" is defined so as to include almost any tit-for-tat refusal. As for holding a grudge, the described instance would seem to have almost nothing in it worthy of reproof—and yet, even the mild reminder "I'm not like you" is considered a violation of the prohibition of grudges. Here then, a verse in the Torah is deemed to refer to two rather trivial actions, things that might naturally come up in ordinary, daily life—even though, on the face of things, that might not seem to be what the verse is saying. In the process, what might have seemed a rather vague and generalized prohibition has been concretized to cover two specific (and rather ordinary) *acts*.

One of the commonest forms of connecting everyday occurrences to the divine is the requirement to recite a fixed blessing on various occasions. The Mishnah prescribes a number of such blessings:

> A person who sees a place where miracles were wrought for Israel is to say: "Blessed [are You who have] worked miracles for our ancestors in this place." At a spot from which idolatry has been uprooted, one is to say: "Blessed...who has uprooted idolatry from our land." For shooting stars, earthquakes, lightning, thunder, or storm-winds, one is to say, "Blessed... whose strength and might fill the world." For mountains, hills, seas, rivers, and deserts, one is to say, "Blessed...who created the world." ...For rainfall or the receipt of good news, "Blessed [are You...] the good and the doer or good." On hearing bad tidings one should say, "Blessed is the true judge." (m. *Berakhot* 9:1-2)

The requirement to connect the events of this world to God—not only the unusual or awe-inspiring ("shooting stars, earthquakes, lightning, thunder, or storm-winds") but even more everyday phenomena (seeing "mountains, hills, seas, rivers, and deserts" or even receiving good or bad news)— is clear throughout this chapter of the Mishnah. Indeed, the blessings prescribed in the corresponding chapter of the *Tosefta*[13] are somewhat more extensive, and many of them are still more obviously rooted in the everyday ("One who sees pleasant-looking people or beautiful trees should say the blessing..."). The effect—to connect the everyday to the divine—is reflected as well in the saying attributed to R. Meir at the end of that chapter:

> R. Meir said: There is no one in Israel who is not surrounded by *mitzvot*. He has *tefillin* on his head, *tefillin* on his arm, a

mezuzah at his doorway, and four fringes surrounding him [on his clothing]. It was in reference to these that David said: "With seven [things][14] each day do I praise You" (Ps 119:164)[15]

Perhaps the most striking instance of this tendency is that of *birkhot ha-shahar*, the blessings that are to be said upon getting up in the morning. The things that *all* people do in the morning—wake up, open their eyes, straighten up, put their feet on the floor, start to get dressed, and so forth—all these and more are to be accompanied by a particular blessing (some of them, but not all, fashioned after some biblical description of God). Thus: "Blessed are You, O Lord. . .who enable the blind to see" (Ps 146:8) is said when a person first opens his eyes; "...who straighten those who are bent" (Ps 146:8) when he sits up; "who established the earth upon the waters" (Ps 136:6) when he steps onto the floor; "...who direct a man's steps" (cf. Ps 37:23) when he begins to walk; and so forth (b. *Berakhot* 60b-61a). There could probably be no more evident instance of rabbinic Judaism's conscious effort to connect the most ordinary things of daily life to an awareness of the divine.

Once again, the origins of this overall mentality surely go back earlier than the rabbinic period. It is well known, for example, that the Qumran texts feature regular, statutory prayers to be recited at fixed times. The idea of such prayers is so familiar that it is worth recalling what prayer was in an earlier day: a cry for help or words of praise or thanksgiving *tied to particular, usually one-time events*. True, this association of thanksgiving with, specifically, miraculous divine intervention never disappeared;[16] but it was complemented, and eventually surpassed, by the idea of fixed, statutory blessings and prayers tied to the most ordinary occurrences.[17] At Qumran, for example, there were set prayers to be recited each day, morning and evening.[18] The most detailed prayers of this sort are the "Words of the Luminaries," whose very name[19] suggests their connection to what might be seen as the most ordinary of circumstances, the rising of the sun at dawn. Another, highly fragmentary set of prayers from Qumran likewise highlights the same, everyday event:

And when the sun [goes forth] to illuminate the eart[h], let
them bless....

When the sun goe[s f]orth over the [earth, let them bless
and utter these words: Blessed is the God of Israel,] who has
renewed our joy with the light of day...(4Q503, fragments
33-35, col 1 and 2).

In a famous passage about the Essenes, Josephus offers a
description of practices similar to those suggested by these Qumran
texts and their focus on the morning sun:

Their reverence toward God is somewhat idiosyncratic. Before
the rising of the sun, they speak nothing of everyday matters,
but offer certain prayers handed down from their ancestors
[and addressed] to it [i.e. the sun], as if beseeching it to rise...
(*Jewish War* 2:128-131).[20]

Noteworthy as well is Philo's description of the regular, communal
prayers of a Jewish community called the *Therepeutai*, a group which
he describes as "philosophers" who "spend their time pursuing
solitude in gardens or solitary fields":

Twice each day they pray, at dawn and in the evening. At
sunrise they pray for a fine, bright day, "fine" and "bright"
in the true sense of the heavenly daylight which they pray
may fill their minds. At sunset they ask that the soul may be
wholly relieved from the press of the senses and the objects
of sense and, sitting where she [the soul] is consistory and
council chamber to herself, pursue the quest of truth....

They stand with their faces and whole body turned to the
east and when they see the sun rising they stretch their hands
up to heaven and pray for bright days and knowledge of the
truth and the power of keen-sighted thinking. After the
prayers they depart each to his private sanctuary. (*De Vita
contemplativa* 27, 89)

(The connection of these early prayers with the rabbinic *Yotzer Or* in use today is clear enough.) Here then is further early evidence of an early tendency to focus the worship of God on the everyday things of life, and once again through a series of specific, external acts—*external* in the sense that, even for the philosophical, solitary *Therapeutai*, their inner desires are to be expressed concretely each day in the external act of fixed, communal prayer.

#

I have suggested that the tendency of Judaism that I have been tracing might be described as the "sanctification of daily life," but here a minor lexical clarification is in order: there is a difference between sanctity and sanctification. Sanctity is the state of being holy, or what is called in Hebrew *kedushah*. The *sanctity of life*, as expressed in various biblical commandments and incorporated in Jewish practice, is indeed an important notion, but it is different from *sanctification*. Sanctification, in Hebrew as in English, is the act of making or declaring something sacred that *was not necessarily sacred before*, or raising something to a higher degree of sanctity. In Hebrew this idea is expressed through the *pi'el* form of this verbal root (i.e., with the *dagesh* in the *daleth*): לקדּש primarily means to make or declare someone or something holy and so to *transform it or its status*. God thus sanctifies Aaron and his sons to make them fit to serve before Him (Exod 29:1 etc.); presumably, before this they were like everyone else. Similarly, to sanctify (לקדּש) the Sabbath means to treat it as holy (Exod 20:8, Jer. 17:24), different from the other days of the week. The sanctification of God's name (קידוש השם) means to raise it—or Judaism, the service of God—up to a higher level. Examples could be multiplied. Thus, a more accurate phrase for the phenomenon described herein might be the *sanctification of the everyday*.

The everyday is, by definition, not holy: it is ordinary, not special, and normally taken for granted. What is most characteristic of Judaism is that this connection of the everyday things of daily life to God is not articulated internally, through some wished-for, heightened state of awareness, but externally, through some particular act, binding *tefillin* to one's head and arm, reciting the words of the *Shema*, or uttering a series of blessings as one moves through the routine act of getting up in the morning.[21]

Returning to Morris Kleinberg, his act thus seems to represent both aspects of the sanctification of the everyday that I have been tracing. The very *tefillin* that he has mistaken for a hat are themselves the product of an ancient decision to externalize and concretize a commandment that might otherwise have been understood to refer to an internal act of reflection, and his wearing the head-*tefillin* out from the quiet of his living room into the hurly-burly workaday world represents the intrusion of the sacred into the everyday. This second aspect is certainly as remarkable as the first: that little black box poking its way before him, sticking itself into the secular busyness of lower Manhattan, seems so out of place! And yet it is an appropriate symbol of the insistence that the Torah has everything to do with the everyday.[22]

#

There is something else worthy of mention in connection with this *tableau vivant*, and that is the mass of detailed requirements associated with Kleinberg's *tefillin*. They have not been made just any which-way, or even solely on the basis of what is specified in the four Torah passages that they contain. To begin with, the little black boxes have to be black, completely black. (It will be recalled that a tiny white spot in the lacquer had caused Kleinberg to bring his arm-*tefillin* to be touched up by someone at the synagogue.) No one knows why this is so; having *tefillin* that are entirely black is one of those practices categorized as a "*halakhah* given to Moses at Mount Sinai," that is, a practice about which there is no disagreement, but also no ancient source. The boxes also have to be made of leather, and tied down with leather straps (likewise completely black). The way the arm part of the *tefillin* is tied to the upper arm is rather complicated, with the leather strap going from where the box is placed, at the height of one's heart, downwards into a series of seven loops on the forearm and ending in another series of loops and ties on the hand and fingers. All these have to be observed if the biblical commandment is to be deemed properly fulfilled—although, of course, the actual biblical texts say nothing of these loops and ties. The knot at the back of the headband also has to be tied in a specific way and the four parchments of biblical quotes have to have been inserted in a certain order—itself a matter of dispute—and so on and so forth.

One might well wonder why all these details are necessary. What difference does it make if a person, having already accepted the idea that the apparently metaphorical images of Exod 13:1-10 etc. really refer to attaching actual passages of Scripture to the arm and head—what difference does it make if the person then takes one of those biblical passages or all four or for that matter a whole small-print Bible and binds it onto his arm with straps, snaps, flaps or any other device that could result in attaching those words to his body? And what difference could it make if the straps are black, brown, gray or some other color—what does this have to do with this pious concretization of the Torah's commandment (which specifies no color in particular)? Why keep adding rules and rules and more rules when there does not seem to be any reason to do so? This is indeed part of the "sanctification of the everyday," a kind of sanctifying every last detail.

In the broad perspective, this makes of Judaism a rather unique form of devotion. I happen to know, for example, that Kleinberg's cabdriver, Mr. Tan, is a Buddhist. If he, having ventured to ask about the thing on Kleinberg's head, had gone on to interrogate his passenger about the nature and purpose of *tefillin*, he would certainly have been puzzled by some of the things that Kleinberg would have said—and with good reason. While Buddhism nowadays has split into many quite distinct forms, I think it is fair to say that, in general, it is fundamentally different from Judaism in some obvious respects:

such practices as meditation or various kinds of yoga, the whole notion of liberation and Nirvana, and the doctrines of karma and rebirth are all quite far from mainstream Jewish beliefs and practices. In fact, although quite a few generalizations about Buddhism as a whole would nowadays be open to question, it would not be wrong to suggest that one great underlying theme of classical Buddhism is that of the ultimate disparagement of, and the escape from, the everyday world. One hopes ultimately to escape the cycle of death and rebirth that characterizes this earthly existence; one meditates to empty the mind of everyday concerns, to go *within* in order to enter what is certainly a deeper and truer realm. Judaism, on the contrary, is all about the everyday details: apart from the laws of *tefillin*, Jewish law touches on such topics as the permitted and forbidden uses of electricity on the Sabbath; the minimum quantity of *matzah* that one is required to consume on the first night of Passover; why a neat pile of apples at the side of the road may not be considered abandoned property, but why a similar number of apples scattered over a large enough area can indeed be considered abandoned; and so on and so forth. In all these and myriad other matters, there is simply *the* right way to proceed in one's daily dealings with the everyday world, and this right way goes down to the minutest details. Here, Mr. Tan shakes his head sadly.

One might think that Judaism's two principal "daughter religions," Christianity and Islam, would be closer to Judaism in this respect. Again, generalizations are inevitably only approximately correct, but I think that, despite certain recognizable affinities, neither of these faiths can quite compete with Judaism's total devotion to the little, niggling details of daily life as the focus, and locus, of one's dedication to following the divine will. It is not that these other traditions are not sometimes interested in niggling details, but those details have a somewhat different quality. Early Christians seem to have preferred arguing about shades of meaning in creeds and ideas: the one-letter difference between the doctrines of *homoiousios* versus *homoousios* (that is, the belief that Christianity's founder was of an essence *similar* to that of God as opposed to the belief that his essence *was the same* as that of God)—this really got out the knives in the fourth century of the common era. True, the practical details of sacraments such as baptism and communion were sometimes the subject of clerical debate, but unless I am mistaken, these were far from the everyday concerns of the faithful. Pilar, the young woman in the coffee shop, is a devout Roman Catholic. Try telling her about *tefillin* some time; she is polite, but deep inside it will all sound to her like a lot of nitpicking superstition. Islam may appear to be a bit closer to Judaism in this respect, but I think it would be fair to say that, apart from matters directly connected to fulfilling the five "pillars of religion" (*arkān a-dān*) in Islam, the nitty-gritty particulars of daily life are not the focus of Muslim piety.

Where does this obsession with (indeed, multiplication of) little details come from? It might not be inappropriate here to go back to the very beginning. In the Exodus narrative, when the Israelites reach Mount Sinai, God approaches the people with what is essentially a deal:

> You have seen what I did to the Egyptians, how I bore you on eagles' wings and brought you to Me. Now then, if you will obey Me faithfully and keep My covenant, you will become My treasured possession among all the peoples, since all the land is Mine. And you will be to Me a kingdom of priests and a holy nation. (Exod. 19:4-6)

In plain English, in this deal God proposes to adopt Israel as His own special people on condition that they "obey Me faithfully and keep My covenant," that is, keep the laws that God is about to promulgate. These begin with the Ten Commandments in Exodus 20, and then continue with the all the laws that appears in the next three chapters, Exodus 21-23, indeed, with all the laws of the Torah as a whole, 613 by traditional count.

But what seems most significant for our subject is the very next sentence: "And you will be to Me a kingdom of priests (*kohanim*) and a holy nation." The import of this sentence is likely to elude modern readers not steeped in the basic reality of the priesthood in ancient times. Gods in much of the ancient Near East did not generally have close relations with ordinary citizens—that would have been far too dangerous.[23] For this reason, the gods were housed in specially constructed palaces (i.e., temples), where their every need was attended to by a trained cadre of religious specialists, the priests. The priests were the ones who operated the temple on a day-to-day basis, and who penetrated to its most sacred parts; it was they who presided over what was the most significant area of divine-human interaction, the offering of animal sacrifices. Such an arrangement characterized Israelite worship as well: the temple priests offered sacrifices and thus acted as the *ex officio* go-betweens between the Deity and the rest of the population. Since they were the ones who were permitted to come close to God, they are therefore referred to as "those who come close to Me" (Lev 10:3).

In the light of this, the proposal in the passage cited that Israel become a "kingdom of priests and a holy nation" must stand out as utterly strange. It does not seem likely that Exod 19:6 was suggesting that ordinary laymen offer sacrifices and perform the other functions of priests elsewhere in the ancient Near East. Rather, as the context implies, the entire people are to be like *kohanim* and come close to God by scrupulously carrying out divine laws, the same laws that were about to be promulgated at Mount Sinai. In keeping with this, it is striking that the standard phrase "to serve God/the gods," which in various ancient Near Eastern languages (including biblical Hebrew) refers to the offering of sacrifices, is also used in the Torah to refer to ordinary people *keeping God's laws* (see Deut 6:13, 10:12-13; 13:5). Such a conception of things appears to be quite unparalleled anywhere else in the ancient Near East.

This obligation to serve God through obedience to His laws is expressed in the Torah in regulations governing the most mundane, everyday details imaginable: the fringes that are to be tied at the corners of four-cornered garments; cloven-hoofed mammals, numerous species of birds, and the fins and scales of fish; an axe-head that flies off its handle and accidentally kills someone; skin diseases, seminal emissions, menstruant women, sheaves left behind in the field, a muzzled ox on the threshing floor, and quite a bit more. One might argue that the rabbinic love of pinning down detailed instructions, what might sometimes even be called legal *hyper-specification*, is the product of a long evolution, and in a sense this is so. But it is rooted in the very idea that 'avodat ha-Shem, the service of God, is incumbent on everyone, and the inclusion under that rubric of all the varied laws promulgated in the Torah. Since God was regularly encountered not (or not only) in His earthly sanctuary, but in the everyday keeping of His commandments, distinguishing the right way of keeping them from the wrong way might be deemed as important as following the proper priestly procedure in His temple, sacrificing animals or burning incense in the prescribed fashion.

#

All this brings us back once again to the symbolism of Morris Kleinberg on the way to his office. His wearing his *tefillin* instead of his hat that morning did not merely represent the intrusion of what belongs to the inside into the outside, and not merely the intrusion of the sacred into the everyday world, but as well the extension of the sacred to include the most specific little details. What better image is there of Judaism itself, which seeks to serve God not by staring off for twenty years at the mountaintops visible from an isolated monastery, but in all the ordinary little things of daily life, things already mentioned and so many more, governing relations between parents and children, buyers and sellers, neighbors and neighbors? It is here, Judaism says, that 'avodat ha-Shem, the service of God, is to take place, day after day. People sometimes say that the devil is in the details, but for Judaism the opposite is the case: the divine has everything to do with all those rules governing kosher food, the particular words of blessing that are to be said on encountering a monarch, the proper procedures of sale and purchase, ritual baths, and so on and so forth. That is what Kleinberg's *tefillin* are doing on a New York street, intruding the realm of the sacred into the honking, smelly world of lower Manhattan.

As for the stares of the passers-by, they are also part of this *tableau vivant*. Judaism's characteristic concretizing of the potentially abstract and sanctifying of the everyday make it, in the broad perspective, a rather strange form of devotion, different from the regular acts of piety practiced in other faiths and for that reason often misunderstood. At the same time, Kleinberg's determined look, along with his lack of awareness of the basic fact of his *tefillin*'s incongruous intrusion into this everyday street scene, are equally important. Although his attention has been, since the moment he woke up this morning, largely focused on carrying out the various commandments that a Jew is to perform every day, he has not spent much time reflecting on anything like my theme of Judaism's sanctification of the everyday. Why not? I know him to be a thoughtful fellow: it is certainly not because he is not otherwise given to reflection. But he is utterly the product of Exod 19:5; what he does every day, his Jewish daily routine, does not call for internal reflection, but external performance of the commandments in all their details. The very essence of Judaism is 'avodat ha-Shem and, in a way, this itself might be seen as the greatest act of externalizing and concretizing. Without these, Judaism would not be Judaism; indeed, it is precisely this that Scripture epitomizes in its brief command, "Know Him in all your paths" (Prov 3:6).

NOTES

¹ In earlier times, the stated ideal was to wear *tefillin* throughout the day, both inside and outside, although the evidence for this having been followed in practice is somewhat mixed; see S. Stern, *Jewish Identity in Early Rabbinic Writings* (Leiden: Brill, 1994), 67-71 and the sources mentioned below, n. 4. It is also said that *tefillin* were sometimes worn outside in combination with a turban or hat; see Tur, OH 41. However, a number of restrictions on the wearing of *tefillin* all day are also mentioned in classical sources (see b. *Shabbat* 49a, Tur, OH 37), so that *tefillin* today are generally worn only during morning prayers.

² See Jeffrey Tigay, "On the Meaning of T(W)TFT," *Journal of Biblical Literature* 101 (1982) 330; H. Rand "The Etymology of Totafot," *Judaism* 42 (1993) 160-63. However, as M. Weinfeld observed, "It must be admitted that all the ink that has been spilled in the attempt to understand the etymology and original significance of this word has not led to any definite results"—*The Ten Commandments and the Reading of the Shema—the Permutations of a Declaration of Faith* (Tel Aviv: ha-Kibbutz he-Meuhad, 2001), 139.

³ Long after the current practice had been established, the medieval commentator Samuel b. Meir dared to suggest that it was based on a misunderstanding. Citing the first of the four passages, "Bind it for a sign upon your hand..." he observed: "According to the straightforward meaning of the text, it is to be a memorial for you always, as *if* it were written on your hand... Similarly 'as frontlets between your eyes' means like some sort of ornament or gold chain that people customarily put on their foreheads for decoration."

⁴ These have been studied recently in Yehudah B. Cohn, *Tangled Up in Text: Tefillin and the Ancient World* (Providence: Brown University Press, 1998) 55-87. The earliest material evidence of *tefillin* is found among the Dead Sea Scrolls and was first discussed by H. Haberman, "Phylacteries in Antiquity," *Eretz Yisrael* 3 (1954), 174-77, cf. Y. Yadin, *"Tefillin* (Phylacteries) from Qumran," *Eretz Yisrael* 9 (1969) 60-85. The Qumran *tefillin* arguably go back to the second century. In all, remnants of approximately forty-five separate parchment slips traced to Qumran have been identified as belonging to *tefillin* or *mezuzot*, as well as around twenty-five *tefillin* boxes (battim); see the discussion and sources cited in Cohen, *Tangled Up*, 55-79. The literary evidence for *tefillin* is somewhat ambiguous: see the Septuagint translation of Exodus 13; Letter of Aristeas 157-158; Philo, *SpecLeg* 137-142; Josephus, *Jewish Antiquities* 4:213. Cohn, *Tangled Up*, loc. cit. expresses doubt that these literary sources refer to physical *tefillin*, but the issue remains controversial. Philo's understanding of this commandment as referring to *tefillin* is maintained in Naomi G. Cohen,

Philo Judaeus: His Universe of Discourse (Berlin: Peter Lang, 1995) 144-155. On who actually wore *tefillin*: S. Stern, *Jewish Identity*, loc cit.; Cohen, 106-124.

[5] The further specification in Deut. 6:9 and Deut. 11:20 (but *not* found in Exod. 13:1-10 or Exod. 13:11-16), "and you shall write them on the doorposts of your house and on your gates" might have aided in the concretizing reading (see Weinfeld, op. cit., 141-42). See also Othmar Keel, "Zeichen der Verbundenheit," in P. Casetti et al., *Mélanges Dominique Barthélemy* (Fribourg: Editions Universitaires, 1981), 165-66. So too, the use of amulets within and outside of Jewish society had a role: Cohen, *Tangled Up*, 45-46.

[6] *Hilkhot Tefillah*, 1:1.

[7] On the merismus of Deut. 6:7 see A. M. Honeyman, "Merismus in Biblical Hebrew" *Journal of Biblical Literature* 71 (1952), 11-18.

[8] See J. Kugel, *Traditions of the Bible* (Cambridge: Harvard University Press, 1998) 830-32, 867-70.

[9] On the covenantal aspect of these words, M. Weinfeld, "Prayer and Liturgical Practice in the Qumran Sect," in D. Dimant et al., *The Dead Sea Scrolls: Forty Years of Research* (Leiden: Brill, 1992), 241-58.

[10] See J. Kugel, A Walk through Jubilees: Studies in the Book of Jubilees and the World of its Creation (Leiden: Brill, 2012), 126.

[11] Note that Ben Sira 32:11-13 also refers to blessing God after a banquet, again without specific allusion to Deut 8:10.

[12] See S. A. White, "4QDtn: Biblical Manuscript or Excerpted Text?" in H. W. Attridge et al., *Of Scribes and Scrolls: Studies on the Hebrew Bible, Intertestamental Judaism, and Christian Origins* (Lanham, Md: University Press of America, 1990), 13-20; M. Weinfeld, "Grace After Meals in Qumran," *Journal of Biblical Literature* 111 (1992) 427-40. Not all have found this identification convincing: R. Kimelman, "A Note of Weinfeld's Grace After Meals," *Journal of Biblical Literature* 112 (1993) 695-96; D. Falk, "Prayer in the Qumran Texts," in W. Horbury et al., *Cambridge History of Judaism* (New York: Cambridge University Press, 1999) 3:865.

[13] *Tosefta* 6, Erfurt ms. chapter 7; see also b. *Berakhot* 54a-64a.

[14] The verse is apparently being understood in this fashion, rather than the more usual, "Seven times each day do I praise You."

[15] Cf. b. Menahot 43b.

[16] It is often stated as a general principle, e.g. לכם נסים, תהיו אומרים שירה כשהקב"ה עושה (j. *Pesahim* 10 [37:4]). On the expression "utter praise" (לומר שירה or sometimes לומר הימנון) and some further examples in rabbinic and pre-rabbinic texts: J. Kugel, "Biblical Apocrypha and Pseudepigrapha and the Hebrew of the Second Temple Period" in T. Muraoke and J. F. Elwolde, *Diggers of the Well: Proceedings of the Third International Symposium on the Dead Sea Scrolls and Ben Sira* (Leiden: Brill, 2000) 166-77.

[17] E. Fleischer, "On the Beginning of Obligatory Prayer" *Tarbiz* 59 (1990), 397-441.

[18] See 1Q9:26-10:1-8, which specifies fixed prayers to be said each day, morning and evening, as well as at the *tequfot*, the beginnings of months, festivals, New Year, and so forth. In general see Daniel Falk, *Daily, Sabbath and Festival Prayers in the Dead Sea Scrolls* (Leiden: Brill, 1998); idem, "Prayer in the Qumran Texts," in W. Horbury et al., *The Cambridge History of Judaism* vol. 3 (Cambridge: Cambridge University Press, 1999), 852-76; James Davila, *Liturgical Works*: Eerdmans Commentaries on the Dead Sea Scrolls (Grand Rapids: Eerdmans, 2000), 203-38 E. Chazon (ed.), *Liturgical Perspectives: Prayer and Poetry in Light of the Dead Sea Scrolls* Proceedings of the Fifth International Symposium of the Orion Center (Leiden: Brill, 2003); Eileen Schuller "Prayer, Hymnic and Liturgical Texts from Qumran," in E. Ulrich and J. C., VanderKam, *The Community of the Renewed Covenant: the Notre Dame Symposium on the Dead Sea Scrolls* (Notre Dame, Ind.: Notre Dame University Press, 1994) 153-71; J. Penner et al., *Prayer and Poetry in the Dead Sea Scrolls and Related Literature* (Leiden: Brill, 2012). On *berakhot* at Qumran: Eileen Schuller, "Some Observations of Blessings on God in Texts from Qumran," in Attridge et al., *Of Scribes and Scrolls*, 133-43; B. Nitzan, Qumran Prayer and Poetry (Hebrew), (Jerusalem: Mosad Bialik, 1996) 87-103. M. Weinfeld, has explored connections between prayers at Qumran and in rabbinic Judaism: "Prayer and Liturgical Practice in the Qumran Sect," in D. Dimant op. cit., 241-58.

[19] The title "Words of the Luminaries" appears on the back of the first column of 4Q504 and "probably relates to the work's liturgical function as prayers for the days of the week, with...*hamme'orot*, "luminaries," serving as a term for the day, the unit of time for which these prayers were designated (compare Gen 1:14-18)," E. Chazon, "Scripture and Prayer in the 'Words of the Luminaries'" in J. Kugel, *Prayers that Cite Scripture* (Cambridge: Harvard Center for Jewish Studies, 2006), 25-41. These prayers, as well as those designated "festival prayers" (4Q509+505), follow a complex pattern, which integrated daily praise and petition with reflections on events recounted in Scripture—this last an example of what had already become a conventional feature of late biblical prayers. On this phenomenon: Judith Newman, *Praying by the Book: the Scripturalization of Prayer in Second Temple Judaism* (Atlanta: Scholars Press, 1999). See also E. Chazon, "Is *Divrei ha-Me'orot* a Sectarian Prayer?" In D. Dimant et al., The Dead Sea Scrolls: Forty Years of Research, 3-17; also Davila, op. cit, 239-66.

[20] That the prayers are apparently addressed to the sun (instead of addressed to its Creator) is apparently what Josephus means by describing this prayer as "idiosyncratic" (ἰδίως), but it seems most unlikely that this is an instance of real sun-worship; cf. the prayer of the *Therapeutai* below. Another opinion: Tessel Jonquière, *Prayer in Josephus* (Leiden: Brill, 2007), 54-55.

[21] Some of the issues raised by this concretizing tendency and religious consciousness were discussed in the well known study of my former teacher and colleague, Isadore Twersky z"l, "Religion and Law," in S. Goitein, ed. *Religion*

in a Religious Age (Cambridge: Association for Jewish Studies, 1974), 69-82.

[22] All the more so because, in an earlier day, to wear *tefillin* into the marketplace and elsewhere was the stated ideal; see above, note 1.

[23] The literature on Mesopotamian temple worship is quite considerable: see in connection with cultic "danger" Mary Douglas, *Purity and Danger* (London: Routledge & Kegan Paul, 1966), and more generally A. L. Oppenheim, *Ancient Mesopotamia: Portrait of a Dead Civilization* (Revised edition completed by Erica Reiner) (Chicago: Chicago University Press, 1977), 183-97; J. M. Beard and A. North, "Introduction" to their Pagan Priests: *Religion and Power in the Ancient World* (London: Duckworth, 1990), 1-14; F. Wiggermann, "Theologies, Priests, and Worship in Ancient Mesopotamia," in J. Sasson, *Civilizations of the Ancient Near East* (New York: Scribner, 1995) 1857-70.

Separation or Engagement?
Imitatio Dei and The Nature of Holiness

David Shatz

The Eternal said to Moses: Speak to the entire congregation of Israel and tell them, "You shall be holy, for I, the Eternal your God, am holy." (Leviticus 19:2)[1]

For I, the Eternal, am your God, and you shall sanctify yourselves and you shall be holy, for I am holy....You shall be holy, for I am holy. (Leviticus 11:44–45)

You shall be holy to me, for I the Eternal am holy, and I have set you apart from other people to be mine. (Leviticus 20:26)

***

If asked to define "holiness," a knowledgeable Jew is likely to invoke the idea, advanced by our sages, that *kadosh* means *parush*, "separated."[2] Thus, for example, the Jewish people are called a *goy kadosh* (Exodus 19:6), meaning that they will be or, rather, should be—separate and apart.[3] Likewise, the priests are called *k'doshim* (e. g., at Leviticus 21:6–8); and the Sabbath is holy because it is so distinct from other days. The imperative for Jews to be *k'doshim*, therefore—whether this is taken as a command to individuals or as a command to the people as a whole—may be taken as mandating separation from certain aspects of the world. We might next ask, "What is it that enables the Jewish people (and/or its individual members) to achieve the separation that constitutes *k'dushah*?" The answer, it would seem, is this: adhering to divine laws—especially prohibitions. Jews may even be expected to go beyond these prohibitions, and refrain even from permissible activities. "Sanctify yourself in that which is permitted to you."[4]

K'dushah, then, entails separation. Yet, notwithstanding this widely known association, some thinkers, especially in contemporary times, often speak of Judaism (and *halakhah* in particular) as mandating engagement with the world, active participation in its affairs. We often speak of "sanctifying the mundane." This motto is most naturally taken as identifying engagement with the mundane, rather than separation and withdrawal, as the means for attaining holiness.[5] In short, Jewish explications of holiness or sanctity exhibit an intriguing polarity or dialectic—separation yet engagement.

Which model should we adopt? Are both valid? Should one carry more weight than the other? How shall we understand the relevant notions of separation and engagement? What implications do they carry for Jewish societies in our times? This essay will explore these questions by probing the foundations of each conception of *k'dushah* (separation and engagement) along with their respective weaknesses. My main text will be Leviticus 19:2 (quoted above) and rabbinic materials that interpret it and similar verses.[6]

We live in a time in which, arguably, the theme of separation dominates traditional Jewish life. My thesis is that once we assign weight to the notion of *imitatio Dei* as presented in the verses with which we began ("for I, the Eternal your God, am holy"), the separation view and the engagement view may be understood, as several authorities posit, as reflecting two aspects of God. Both aspects must be imitated, and to focus exclusively on separation is to overlook a key theme of the Torah's presentation of *k'dushah*— namely, *imitatio Dei*. Moreover, I will argue that engagement is in some respects a clearer form of *imitatio Dei* than is separation, although a certain looseness remains in linking *k'dushah* to emulation of God.

A word on method. In approaching Leviticus 19:2, it is from one point of view best to focus on the biblical text in the interest of arriving at its *p'shat*, and to set aside those midrashic interpretations that lack clear textual proof and that may be designed purely for moralistic purposes. Nevertheless, although capturing *p'shat* in the biblical verses is important, if our interest is in examining what Judaism has to say about *k'dushah*, we cannot embrace a sola *Scriptura* approach. We cannot eschew interweaving the biblical text with later aggadic and halakhic interpretations, from the sages of the rabbinic period to Maimonides to Rabbi Joseph B. Soloveitchik and beyond. Judaism is dynamic, not static; and, as Rashbam observed, new interpretations appear every day that become part of our interpretive tradition.[7]

I

In his valuable and bold essay "*imitatio Dei* and the Idea of Holiness," Leon Roth (1896–1963) argues that "wherever in Scripture man is called upon to be holy in the way that God is holy, the substance of such summons is negative, and never positive."[8] Roth cites a slew of biblical verses that connect *k'dushah* specifically to negative prohibitions, the category of lo ta·aseh.[9] A negative prohibition clearly is a call to separation. Arguably, therefore—and as Roth in fact does argue—*k'dushah* primarily entails refraining from certain deeds and thoughts. Roth summarizes: "Holiness is essentially a negative concept."[10]

The case for this "negative" separation approach is far from airtight. After all, the commandments in Leviticus 19 that immediately follow the command *k'doshim tihyu* include the imperatives to fear parents and to observe the Sabbath—both, ostensibly, positive commandments. Roth attempts to analyze these duties as negative commandments, but his analysis is not altogether convincing.[11] In addition, it is precisely before the Ten Commandments were given that God charged the Jewish people with becoming "a kingdom of priests [i.e., a people that serves God] and a *holy nation*" (Exodus 19:6). Accordingly, numerous commentators, following the midrash, state that the imperatives in Leviticus 19 are in essence a reformulation of the Ten Commandments.[12] Taking note of the words in Leviticus 19:2, "Speak to all the congregation of Israel," the sages remark: "This portion was said *b'hak·heil*"—that is, Leviticus 19 was addressed to all of Israel, just as the Torah was revealed to all at Sinai.[13]

What impact does the association of Leviticus 19 with the revelation at Sinai have on Roth's thesis? Well, it is true that the Ten Commandments are mostly negative. But according to Maimonides and others, the first commandment, "I am the Eternal your God," is a positive command to believe in God or rather (to put it accurately) to know God's existence (i.e., to be able to prove it)[14]—although, to be sure, others take it as a prologue rather than as a commandment unto itself. Furthermore, although the fourth commandment as stated in Exodus 20 conveys a negative aspect of Shabbat (cessation of labor) and on a purely literal level merely a positive mental aspect ("remember"), from a broader halakhic perspective, which includes rabbinic legislation, Shabbat obviously includes positive aspects such as honoring and enjoying Shabbat, eating three meals, and reciting Kiddush. (The sages regarded the Shabbat commandment in Exodus and its counterpart in Deuteronomy as complementary positive and negative aspects, "stated in one utterance.") It could be argued that although the positive rabbinic laws obviously apply to the Sabbath, the biblical stress on the negative aspects supports Roth to an extent. But what of the fifth commandment, "honor your father and mother"? That seems to imply a positive duty, alongside any negative ban against disrespect. In short, the attempt to associate *k'dushah* exclusively with negative imperatives is unconvincing. Roth's observation, then, is predominantly but not entirely correct for Leviticus 19, and is even more problematic if we link Leviticus 19 to the Ten Commandments as the sages do.[15]

However, there is another problem as well—one that will occupy us for the rest of this essay.

II

Leviticus 19:2 reads: "Speak to the entire congregation of Israel and tell them, 'You shall be holy, for I, the Eternal your God, am holy.'" In these words, as well as those quoted earlier from Leviticus 11:44 and 20:26, we have the theme of *imitatio Dei*: *k'doshim tihyu* is a command to be like God. This is how Abba Shaul construes Leviticus 19:2: "The retinue of a monarch, what must it do? Imitate the monarch."[16] Thus, the Israelites should be holy because God is holy. So too, in another midrash: "As I am *kadosh*, you shall be *k'doshim*; as I am parush, you shall be *p'rushim*."[17]

But how can that be the case? How can mastery over egocentric drives be an act of emulating God? God has no egocentric drives! And how does a person's refraining from worshipping idols, crossbreeding animals, sowing with two kinds of seed, wearing *shaatnez*, eating fruit before a certain time elapses, consuming blood, removing certain hairs on the head, and allowing a daughter to become a prostitute—all of which (and more) appear in Leviticus 19—how does observing these prohibitions help us to resemble the Divine?[18]

This problem—how does *imitatio Dei* operate in the case of holiness, given that it is unclear how God could observe the commandments in Leviticus 19—hounds explanations given by the commentators. For instance, Rashi and others maintain that *k'doshim tihyu* refers to abstaining from the forbidden sexual relations itemized in Leviticus 18. Yet how could we ascribe that type of separation to God?[19] Or consider the sages' declaration, "Sanctify yourself with that which is permitted to you."[20] With this formula they expand *k'dushah* to include separating oneself even from technically permitted acts. Elaborating on their thesis, Naḥmanides famously explains that, although the Torah has no specific laws against being a glutton or drunkard, or using foul language, or indulging in abundant sex with one's wife, such behavior nonetheless violates the prescription of *k'doshim tihyu*.[21] Yet given this interpretation of holiness, how are we to imitate God? Surely it is odd, if not bizarre, to think of God as observing or not observing such extra restraint. We therefore have a tension between the idea of *k'dushah* as separation, on the one hand, and the idea that achieving *k'dushah* constitutes *imitatio Dei*, on the other hand.

In truth—and rather obviously—the *imitatio Dei* problem is not confined to prohibitions, but extends to positive commandments as well. Consider Maimonides. In the prologue to his *Sefer Ha-mitzvot* (Book of Commandments), where he enumerates the 613 commandments using a rigorous set of principles for inclusion and exclusion, Maimonides refuses to list "Be holy" as a commandment unto itself. Rather, for him, *k'doshim tihyu* encompasses all 613 commandments. Divine instructions to "be holy" are "charges to fulfill the whole Torah, as if God were saying, 'Be holy by doing all that I have commanded you to do, and guard against all things I have enjoined you from doing.'" Indeed, Maimonides states: "There is no difference between [God] saying, 'You shall be holy' and 'Obey My commandments.'"[22] Like Rashi, Maimonides has his own support from the classical sages—in this case, a Sifrei text that states, "'And you shall be holy' [Numbers 15:40]—this refers to the holiness of all the commandments (*k'dushat kol ha-mitzvot*)."[23] For Maimonides, to be holy is simply to perform the commandments. Warren Zev Harvey nicely explains Maimonides' view as follows: when we fulfill the *mitzvot* of the Holy One, we are holy.[24] Maimonides reiterates his understanding of *k'doshim tihyu* in his *Guide for the Perplexed*,[25] asserting that the purpose of all *mitzvot* is to "quell the impulses of matter."[26] In this latter conception of the teleology of *mitzvot*, he does not distinguish between lusting for illicit sex or non-kosher food, on the one hand, and desiring to harm one's comrade for personal gain, on the other. *All* of the *mitzvot* require us, to some degree, to escape corporeality—"the impulses of matter."[27] Holiness involves *all* commandments.[28] This homogenization of the ritual and the ethical fits well with the fact that Leviticus 19 mixes the ritual and the ethical with no distinction, just as in the Torah portion Ki Teitzei (Deuteronomy 21:10-25:19).

But once again our question rears its head. God does not perform the commandments, and certainly not all of them. Where, then, is the imitation? If we interpret "Be holy" as relating to *mitzvot*, whether positive or negative, we ostensibly have no way to analogize between human holiness and divine holiness.

Harvey notes that when we interpret the Bible, and in particular when we interpret anthropomorphic expressions such as "God's face" or "God descended," we employ the principle that "the Torah speaks in the language of human beings," in order to blunt the implication that God has a body. God is designated by terms predicated of human beings that humans can understand. "There is, however," writes Harvey, "one exception to this anthropomorphic pattern…in which God is not designated by the language of man, but man according to the language of God…   '[H]oly' designates God primarily and created things only by extension."[29] If so, the meaning of *k'dushah* for human beings and for God could be different. But ki *kadosh* ani ("for I am holy") cannot then be understood; we would not know what to imitate! This problem with fathoming God's *k'dushah* is intensified by the sages when they say, "My [God's] *k'dushah* is higher than yours."[30]
Let us consider some responses to this problem.

III

The responses to the *imitatio Dei* problem that I consider in this section will assume the "separation" understanding of *k'dushah*. In later sections we will see how the "engagement" view addresses the questions we have posed.

Approach #1

The first strategy for explaining *imitatio Dei* is to assert that the resemblance between human and divine holiness is merely an analogy, and a loose one at that, even verging on metaphor. The resemblance is grounded in God's transcendence. God is *metaphysically* "apart" and transcendent, unique, wholly other, utterly different; we, as individuals and as a people, are "apart" and "transcendent" in a different way. Our acts of separation, of refraining from certain acts, are but rough analogues of God's metaphysical transcendence, but analogues nonetheless.[31]

Now, there is some logic in this idea, since when we remove ourselves from the world and control biological appetites, we in a sense separate ourselves from the material world—we are becoming transcendent. So the idea "Master your drives, because I am metaphysically transcendent" makes *some* sense. But the analogy may simply be too weak and tenuous to ground an imperative for humans to be transcendent on the grounds of *imitatio Dei* alone.[32] This is, in fact, Roth's somewhat despairing response. The *imitatio Dei* principle cannot really be applied to *k'dushah*, he avers, since God does not have the obligations that humans have. Rather, *imitatio Dei* is invoked only *l'tiferet ha-musar*—that is, as "window dressing" (the phrase is that of the translator of Roth's essay), an adornment to Jewish obligations. In sum, one approach to our problem at hand is to capitulate: the resemblance is not strong, after all.

Approach #2

A second strategy is to shift attention away from God's transcendence (where the analogy between God and humans is weak) to God's immanence. God is transcendent and yet also immanent in the world, as brought out in the famous contrast set out in the prophetic verse familiar from the liturgy: "Holy, holy, holy is the Lord of Hosts [i.e., transcendence]; the earth is full of God's glory [i.e., immanence]"

(Isaiah 6:3). Any analogy between human and divine holiness must take immanence into account—and perhaps the appeal to immanence will provide a more cogent understanding of *imitatio Dei*.

This last point has been pursued by several commentators. Rabbi Meir Leibush Malbim argues, in his commentary to Leviticus 19:2, that whenever we conquer our natures (as we do through observing *mitzvot*) we come to resemble the God who exerts control over nature and can interfere with its workings, altering their normal course. This is one point of comparison, and Malbim sees another as well. Malbim understands the notion that humanity was created *b'tzelem elohim* (in the image of God) to mean that we possess free will. Human beings exercise free will over their "small chariot" (namely: the body), in a way that is not subject to and determined by laws of nature. In this way human beings, in Abba Shaul's words, "imitate the Sovereign." Elsewhere, Malbim adds that since God does only good, human beings are like God only when they do good.[33]

Thus for Malbim, the imitation of God's holiness is imitation of divine immanence, to *the exclusion* of divine transcendence.[34] Malbim is also interested in explaining a rabbinic passage that addresses whether God's holiness *depends upon* human holiness.[35] His interpretation of this odd passage is that God will interfere with nature—that is, perform miracles for Israel—only when Israel conquers its material nature and performs *mitzvot*. In this sense, God's holiness (=immanence) depends on ours, even though God's inherent holiness does not.

Malbim's shift from transcendence to immanence as the locus of *k'dushah* resembles the view, prevalent since the nineteenth century, that *k'dushah* demands engagement with the world in the form of activity to better the world.[36] Malbim's view is not quite the same as this one, however, because Malbim stresses two elements that are not salient in the engagement view: humanity's conquest of material nature, and God's working miracles.

A weakness in Malbim's account, perhaps, is that not all *mitzvot* truly conquer material urges. There is no natural "urge" to wear *shaatnez*, for example. But a deeper problem is that once again the analogy is loose, since there is no conquering of urges where God is concerned. Thus, while Malbim's account makes a contribution toward unraveling the imitation theme in Leviticus 19:2 by shifting the analogy from transcendence to immanence, even so we are left with an analogy that is essentially metaphorical: God can use divine free will to interfere with nature, and we use our human free will to "interfere" in our own, personal natures.[37]

Approach #3

A third response is that *k'dushah* is a property that a being can possess *intrinsically*—in the way it can possess, say, a specific height and weight. God possesses the property of holiness as part of the divine essence; human beings can acquire it by performing (or by refraining from performing) certain actions. We do not know what the property of *k'dushah* is like in the case of God—or even in our own case. The midrash says, "My [God's] *k'dushah* is higher than yours."[38] What we do know is only that through *mitzvot* we can attain a state that is sufficiently like God's *k'dushah* that it can be called *k'dushah*;[39] but exactly how our *k'dushah* compares and contrasts with God's, and indeed what God's (or our own!) *k'dushah* is, is beyond our ken. To be sure, some verses suggest that no comparison is possible between human and divine holiness, which might suggest there is no common property called *k'dushah*. This perspective about the incomparability of God is found, for example, in the following verses: "To whom can you liken Me, to whom can I be compared—says the Holy One" (Isaiah 40:25); "Who is like You, majestic in holiness" (Exodus 15:11); "None is holy like the Eternal" (1 Samuel 2:2). However, these verses can all be taken to express differences in degree—that is, differences in the levels of *k'dushah* attained by God and by human beings respectively.

The approach to holiness just described—that holiness is a quality intrinsic to a subject, one that we cannot perceive with our senses—has been called an "essentialist" or "ontological" approach.[40] Attacks on "essentialist" or "ontological" views of the Sabbath, sanctuary, Jewishness, the land of Israel, Jerusalem, Torah, *t'fillin*, and *m'zuzah* are common today,[41] and some important sources, including statements by Maimonides as well as earlier rabbinic texts, support the rather different view that holiness refers to a certain set of relations.[42] Rabbi Joseph B. Soloveitchik writes:

> Judaism has always maintained that holiness is not something objective inherent in an object, prevailing independently of the way this particular sacred object is treated. We denied the idea that there is sanctity per se, a metaphysical endowment which persists irrespective of man's relationship to the object. Such an approach to the idea of the sacred would border on fetishism and primitive taboos. Sanctity is born out of man's actions and experiences and is determined by the latter.[43]

Although he is speaking of sacred objects as opposed to humans attaining *k'dushah*, the Rav's discomfort with viewing holiness in terms of metaphysical qualities suggests that he would not view human beings attaining *k'dushah* in terms of "something inherent in the object." Why is there opposition to the notion that *k'dushah* is an intrinsic property? Some of the critics are concerned about ethical and political repercussions of, say, viewing Jews as intrinsically different from non-Jews with regard to holiness (e.g., "Gentiles have lower-level souls than Jews"), and about the prospect that assigning intrinsic holiness to the land of Israel will produce extremism.[44] There is also a danger of creating cults centered on an "intrinsically holy" individual. For these reasons, perhaps it is best to say, with Menachem Kellner, that "holiness characterizes 'God-liked behavior'"—and that's all.[45]

Because of the difficulties in treating holiness as an intrinsic property,[46] I submit that the best solution to the *imitatio Dei* problem as it affects a negative separation approach is to move in two stages.

First, we should concede that we have only a vague, near-metaphorical analogy between a transcendent God and human beings, who separate from the world and transcend it by observing commandments; and only a vague, near-metaphorical analogy between an immanent God who freely interferes with nature and human beings, who exercise free will to conquer their own natures. Second, we may underscore the analogy between God and humans with respect to engagement, as opposed to separation. With that in mind, let us turn now to the view that *k'dushah* requires engagement with the world, especially ethical engagement.

IV

Initially, it is tempting to associate the view that *k'dushah* requires engagement with the world with a "centrist" or "Modern Orthodox" orientation, while assigning the separation view to the Orthodox right. But in truth, a large step toward an engagement view is taken by Rabbi Moses Sofer (the Ḥatam Sofer), the very sage who famously declared, against the modern outlook, that "the new is biblically prohibited,"[47] and it is found as well in writings of his son, Rabbi Avraham (the Ketav Sofer) and other commentators.[48] A key element in the engagement approach (reminiscent of our earlier discussion) is that God is both transcendent and immanent. The Ḥatam Sofer, while not ignoring *p'rishah* in the sense of separation, infers from the rabbinic assertion that "this section was stated *b'hak·heil*" that *k'dushah* perforce must take place within the context of a society. Unlike those Gentiles who, he says, separate themselves from the world because they hate the world, Jews, he asserts, are p'rushim who are nonetheless involved with people—loving them and bringing them closer to Torah and the service of God.[49] The Ketav Sofer, in a similar spirit, maintains that to emulate the elohim ḥayyim, the living God, we must be engaged with life.

In fact, in a wide-ranging study of holiness, Eliezer Berkovits concludes: "Rather than indicating transcendence, it [holiness] seems to be inseparable from the idea of immanence. Far from meaning inaccessibility, it reveals closeness and association. It is not the *mysterium tremendum* [the description applied by Rudolf Otto]. If anything, it is its very opposite."[50] This identification of holiness with immanence connects with the views of both Malbim and the Ḥatam Sofer, though Berkovits has something else in mind about what holiness means (namely, closeness to God) and hence about how holiness and immanence are related. One need not go so far as Berkovits (and I think one should not), and deny altogether that *k'dushah* implicates transcendence. But immanence as an aspect of *k'dushah* cannot be denied. Accordingly, a person who is *kadosh* must be both removed from the world and, like God, involved in society with the aim of benefitting others. Whereas Malbim emphasized our conquest of our natures as the analogue to immanence, the views now under discussion tether the analogy with divine immanence to *mitzvot bein adam la-ḥaveiro*, laws governing interpersonal relations.

What about Roth's point that the laws in Leviticus 19 are negative prohibitions, which suggests only separation from the world? One reply, reflected in the already-cited Ketav Sofer, is that in addition to the positive aspects of the commandments noted earlier, the negative prohibitions of Leviticus 19 are themselves predicated on Jews living a material life: participating in a family (verse 2); harvesting (verses 9–10); leaving fallen fruit of a vineyard for the poor and the stranger (verse 10); paying workers promptly (verse 13); conducting court proceedings (verse 15); interacting with others (verses 17–18, which include the famous command to "love your neighbor as yourself"); plowing, sowing, and making clothes (verse 19); owning slaves (verse 20); conducting business affairs (verses 35–36); along with other activities that I have omitted. Judaism, then, allows for earthly activities (even if we can't conclude from the examples *per se* that the Torah encourages them)—but it places restraints on how these activities should be conducted.

The two most famous exponents of the "engagement" view of holiness are Rabbi Samson Raphael Hirsch and Rabbi Joseph B.

Soloveitchik. In his commentary to Leviticus 19:2, Rabbi Hirsch refers to *k'dushah* as "self-mastery," control over one's appetites.[51] But throughout his works he also champions engagement in ways too numerous to list. Let me adduce one telling passage from his commentary on the *haftarah* of *parashat Emor*, the Torah reading that sets out regulations governing the priests. In that *haftarah*, taken from Ezekiel 44, the prophet describes the activities of the Zadokite priests and the regulations that govern them. At one point we are told that, after leaving the special precincts of the Temple pursuant to performing the sacrificial service, when the priests move to the outer courtyard in which the populace is assembled they must remove their special clothing and change to other garments (Ezekiel 44:19). Why must they change clothes?[52] Because, says Rabbi Hirsch, the true test of *k'dushah* is not what the priest does in the Temple, but what he does when he brings Judaism to the street, to the larger world.[53] This is not to assert that Rabbi Hirsch advocated "social action" and *tikkun olam* as they are conceived today. Rather, he seems to be saying that when Jews conduct themselves as they should, they present a model for the world. But his stress on social morality cannot be marginalized.

Perhaps the most robust articulation of the engagement view of holiness is found in the writings of Rabbi Joseph B. Soloveitchik. In *Halakhic Man* and other writings, Rabbi Soloveitchik stresses that, in Judaism, holiness is not to be attained in a transcendent realm, but rather in this world: "An individual...[becomes holy] through actualizing the *halakhah* in the empirical world."[54] The Rav offers this gloss on Leviticus 19:2: "Holiness consists of a life ordered and fixed in accordance with *halakhah* and finds its fulfillment in the observance of the laws regulating biological existence." He is referring, no doubt, to both positive and negative commandments. Creativity is also, for Rabbi Soloveitchik, an aspect of *imitatio Dei* and holiness. The realization of *halakhah* makes the human being a creator of worlds (an activity that obviously constitutes *imitatio Dei*), and this is (part of) the meaning of *k'dushah*.[55] Moreover, he writes: "The intellect, the will, the feeling, the whole process of self-creation, all proceed in an ethical direction."[56] In his essay "Majesty and Humility," Rabbi

Soloveitchik states that "God purposely left one aspect of creation unfinished in order to involve man in a creative gesture and to give him the support to become co-creator and king."[57]

What I have presented thus far, however, is only one aspect of holiness in Rabbi Soloveitchik's thought. At least in other works, he does not ignore separation. On the contrary, we find strong connections between *k'dushah* and "self-denial, self-despair, and self-sacrifice."[58] In fact, he writes: "Sacrifice and holiness are synonymous concepts in Judaism."[59] He subsumes self-denial and self-sacrifice (such in the laws of *niddah*) under *imitatio Dei* by invoking God's act of *tzimtzum* (contraction) in kabbalistic thought.[60] This represents another way of dealing with our problem of understanding the analogy between human and divine holiness.[61]

Returning now, however, to the theme of engagement, one aspect of the imperative to engage with the larger world emerges in the following passage by the Rav:

> Since we live among gentiles, we share in the universal historical experience. The universal problems faced by humanity are also faced by the Jew. Famine, disease, war, oppression, materialism, atheism, permissiveness, pollution of the environment—all these are problems which history has imposed not only on the general community but also on the covenantal community. We have no right to tell mankind that these problems are exclusively theirs....The Jew is a member of humanity.[62]

These sentiments echo the Rav's classic article "Confrontation." In that essay he regards interfaith cooperation on social issues as imperative for Jews, even though, at the same time, he forcefully rejects calls for interfaith dialogue on theological issues. He writes: "Yes, we are determined to participate in every civic, scientific, and social enterprise. We feel obligated to enrich society with our creative talents and to be constructive and useful citizens."[63] And he writes: "We stand with civilized society shoulder to shoulder over against an order that defies us all."[64] The Jews are both strangers and residents in their host societies—in Abraham's phrase, *geir v'toshav anokhi immakhem*, "I am a stranger and a resident among you." Every Jew has a dual identity: both a Jewish identity and a human identity.[66] We are strangers in our host societies; but we are obliged to participate in their affairs. The reason Jews did not historically follow this mandate, says the Rav, is that their host societies treated them in ways that made such cooperation impossible.[67] It is interesting that Rabbi Soloveitchik seldom invokes the notion that Jews are "a light unto the nations" (Isaiah 42:6, 49:6). Perhaps he wants to stress the equality of Jews with others in facing social problems, and not the Jews' superiority. In any event, it is clear that he relates holiness to engagement in the world. Famously, he achieves this by viewing halakhic activity in this world as an act of "bringing down" transcendence. This is a far cry from requiring separation. More to our present purpose, though, he views creative action directed toward completing creation as expressive of *imitatio Dei*. Rabbi Menachem Genack, a close student of the Rav, frames the point this way:

> [The Rabbis] insisted that we achieve holiness within the context of society, involved and engaged with the community....Human holiness must be achieved not through negation, but through affirmation; not through isolation, but through engagement; not by abjuring the world and adopting a monastic life, but by the riskier approach of confronting the world and its imperfections. This approach chances failure, but it brings us to the path of redemption.[68]

To repeat, however: for Rabbi Soloveitchik, separation (or more precisely, withdrawal) imitates God as well—by paralleling *tzimtzum*.[69]

V

In sum, prominent modern rabbinic thinkers relate *k'dushah* to engagement with the world and to ethical conduct. Their approach creates a clear analogy between divine immanence and the human conduct prescribed by God. Just as God acts to benefit the world, so do we; just as God creates, we create, and we channel our creativity toward ethical goals. (Rabbi Soloveitchik would add that we channel creativity toward *talmud torah* as well.) It must be acknowledged, to be sure, that locating *k'dushah* specifically in the areas of creativity and interpersonal relations limits the analogy between human k'dushah and divine k'dushah, for it excludes seeing the observance of ritual laws as *imitatio Dei*. To subsume such observance under *imitatio Dei* requires either falling back on the loose analogy we explored in section III above, or invoking *tzimtzum*. So we have one clear form of *imitatio Dei*, and one looser one. Note that we can make our desired analogy (with respect to immanence) specific by referring to the larger biblical canvas—God's caring about the poor, widows, and orphans, and providing sustenance to all creatures—and, all the more so, by including actions listed in the Talmud such as visiting the sick, burying the dead, and clothing the naked.[70]

But we confront an important question: can we truly connect the ethical imperatives just mentioned with the concept of holiness as it functions in biblical and midrashic texts?[71] Or is the connection between k'dushah and ethics a modern invention ignored in earlier times?[72] There are, I maintain, several premodern precedents that support the ethical dimension of holiness.

1. Earlier we mentioned the statement of Abba Shaul that *k'doshim tihyu* imposes upon us the obligation of *m'hakkeh la-melekh*, "imitating the king." To be sure, his statement does not expressly mention ethical traits or action as the proper mode of imitation. However, the same Abba Shaul elsewhere refers to imitation of ethical traits in particular. Specifically, on the words, *zeh eili v'anveihu* (Exodus 15:2), usually translated as "this is my God, and

I will glorify Him," Abba Shaul comments: "[It means that] I will resemble God. Just as God is compassionate and gracious (*raḥum v'ḥannun*), so too you should be compassionate and gracious."[73] Thus, Abba Shaul's statement about *m'ḥakkeh la-melekh* probably refers to the ethical traits of compassion and graciousness.[74]

2. In the Mishneh Torah,[75] when prescribing the "middle path" as the correct path of conduct, Maimonides quotes the Sifrei on the verse "You shall walk in God's ways" (Deuteronomy 28:9), which interprets those words as implying *imitatio Dei*. Maimonides' citation of the Sifrei reads: "Just as God is called gracious, you should be gracious; just as God is called merciful, you should be merciful; just as God is called holy, you should be holy."[76] The texts we have of the Sifrei do not mention holiness; it is Maimonides who adds "holy" to the traits "compassionate" and "gracious." Maimonides thus connects ethical characteristics (graciousness and mercifulness) with holiness. It is a bit mysterious how he arrived at the version of the Sifrei that he presents, but the bottom line is that he connects *k'dushah* with ethical traits.[77]

3. In his *Guide for the Perplexed*, Maimonides explains that Moses wished to emulate God's attributes—that is, to govern the people by imitating the attributes by which God governs the cosmos. Maimonides states:

    > For the utmost virtue of man is to become like unto Him, may He be exalted, as far as he is able; which means that we should make our actions like unto His, as the sages made clear when interpreting the verse "Ye shall be holy." They said: "He is gracious, so be you also gracious; He is merciful, so be you also merciful."[78]

The rabbinic statement that Maimonides cites is actually not a statement that the midrash makes with regard to Leviticus 19:2; rather, the statement is attached to Deuteronomy 28:9, "walking in God's ways." The effect of the mis-citation is to once again connect the idea of holiness to emulation of God's ethical attributes.[79]

4. Thus far I have cited rabbinic material. How firm is the biblical basis for connecting *k'dushah* and righteousness? To answer this question, let us return to the essay by Leon Roth cited earlier. Roth argues that when the Bible attributes holiness to God, it is in the context of affirming divine justice or righteousness (expressed at times by the words *tzedek* or *tz'dakah*). The most familiar of these associations is Isaiah 5:16, which is incorporated into the High Holy Day liturgy: "And the Lord of Hosts is exalted by *mishpat*, and the Holy God evinced as holy by *tz'dakah*." Roth cites a midrashic gloss on Leviticus 19:2 that begins: "Scripture elsewhere states…" and then quotes the familiar Isaiah 5:16 as the verse connected to *k'doshim tihyu*.[80] On this basis, Roth asserts a connection between divine holiness and divine *tz'dakah*.[81] The translation of Roth's Hebrew article renders *tz'dakah* as "righteousness"; the JPS translation of Isaiah, however, renders *tz'dakah* as "retribution" (which carries an import similar to *mishpat*, the parallel word in the first part of the verse). That latter translation makes more sense in both the biblical context of the verse and also in the midrashic passage referring to God's acts toward the wicked. This connotation of *tz'dakah* may seem to pose an obstacle to Roth's linkage of *k'dushah* and righteousness. At the same time, Roth believes that God's imposing punishment on the wicked is an aspect of divine righteousness—thereby preserving the nexus between *k'dushah* and righteousness. Interestingly, the High Holy Day *mahzor* mutes the retribution theme when it places its citation of Isaiah 5:16 not immediately after the lines that describe the devastation of the wicked (in the section *u-v'khein tzaddikim*, "and the righteous will see and rejoice"), but instead in between an affirmation of God's eventual sovereignty and an affirmation of God's choice of and love for Israel and their sanctification through *mitzvot* (*v'kiddashtanu b'mitzvotekha*). The *mahzor's* placement of the Isaiah verse at a distance from the theme of retribution may reflect a certain sensibility, one that does not restrict *tz'dakah* to retribution in connecting God's *k'dushah* and *tz'dakah*.

Roth invokes other verses to substantiate the connection between divine holiness and divine righteousness. Ezekiel 28:22 speaks of God executing judgment upon Tzidon, and then concludes "and I shall be sanctified in her" (*v'nikdashti vah*); Ezekiel 38:22–23 expresses a similar sentiment. Isaiah suggests a connection between divine kindness and divine holiness: "The poorest among people shall rejoice in the Holy One of Israel" (Isaiah 29:19).[82] The designation "the Holy One of Israel" also appears when speaking of redemption.[83] Most significant for us is Isaiah 57:15–16: "the One who forever dwells and whose name is holy, [and declares:] I dwell on high in holiness, reviving the spirit of the lowly and contrite and withdrawing divine anger." Further, "God in the *holy* habitation" is the champion of orphans and widows (Psalm 68:6).

Independently of Roth, Rabbi David Shapiro marshals evidence for the nexus between holiness, whether human or divine, and ethical behavior.[84] Indeed, his central thesis is that "*The attainment by reality in all its phases of the highest reaches of its moral faculties constitutes holiness.*"[85] Shapiro quotes Rudolf Otto's 1917 classic, *The Idea of the Holy*, which speaks of a process in religion whereby "the numinous is throughout rationalized and moralized, i.e., charged with ethical import, until it becomes the 'holy' in the full sense of the word."[86] Judaism reflects this ethical character of holiness. On the holy Sabbath, the Jew's servants rest, so that "all sovereignty of man over man is abolished"; equality is affirmed and no life may be taken, even for judicial punishment.[87] The holy festivals "are celebrated by opening our doors to the needy and the stranger so that they may rejoice with us."[88] The holy land of Israel does not tolerate evildoers; the holy Temple is in part a medium for ethical instruction; the jubilee year expresses equality and freedom from slavery.[89] God's name is sanctified when Jews act ethically and it is desecrated when God is associated with injustice.[90]

Rabbi Shapiro's association of ethics with the Sabbath and festivals initially has the odd effect of making it seem that Judaism does not endorse values like equality and freedom on weekdays. But in a private correspondence, Rabbi Yitzchak Blau has responded to this objection that differentiation in society and economic disparity may be inescapable: Shabbat reminds us, once a week, of another potential order. We value equality on weekdays but it is unattainable then—either for pragmatic reasons or because of a clash between equality and other values.

A critique of the identification of holiness with ethics is proffered by Isaac Heinemann in his discussion, already cited, of Rabbi Samson Raphael Hirsch's account of *mitzvot*. Heinemann states that "Hirsch confines the ideal of *k'dushah* within the four ells of ethics (*musar*)." (Heinemann notes affinities with Hermann Cohen's view that holiness is the ethical.) It strikes me that although Hirsch does speak that way at times, he is not really talking about ethics but rather about spiritual development, and there are many places where he portrays *k'dushah* as separation in the service of that goal.[92]

Nonetheless, it can be objected that Leviticus 19 and parashat *Ki Teitzei* make no distinction between the ritual and the ethical, but rather blend all laws together—and not all ritual laws carry ethical import. So, if we want to link ethics and holiness, a bit more should be said about integrating these laws.

In this regard, let me make two suggestions. First, one way of linking ethics to the separation view of *k'dushah* (in the form of restraint from drives) is to argue that our conquest of drives ultimately leads us to ethical righteousness. Given that the "ritual" requirements of *k'dushah* in Leviticus 19 necessitate restraint of urges and desires and the curbing of egoism, such restraint and such mastery over egoistic drives can lead to strength of will in the case of *mitzvot bein adam la-haveiro*. Such a theory was advanced by Rabbi Eliezer Berkovits, and I have assessed it elsewhere.[93] Utilizing this approach, we may say that adhering to ritual is part of *k'dushah* because it promotes ethical conduct, but only the ethical aspect constitutes an imitation of God.

Second, might it be the case that Maimonides came to link holiness to *imitatio Dei* precisely for the reason we have been giving—namely, that *imitatio Dei* as regards k'dushah cannot be linked to all the *mitzvot*, but only to ethical ones? Perhaps for this reason Maimonides confines the theme of *imitatio Dei* to the moral realm: it cannot be applied to observance of all the commandments. Admittedly, this contradicts Maimonides' statements that k'dushah refers to doing all the *mitzvot*. Nonetheless, perhaps in his view the only *mitzvot* whose performance involves *imitatio Dei* are those that command the practice of graciousness, lovingkindness, etc. The others perhaps reflect *k'dushah*, but not *imitatio Dei*. I do not know whether this interpretation is correct, but it is I believe an interesting possibility.

Conclusion

In this paper I have pointed to two contrasting obligations that enable individuals and the Jewish nation to attain *k'dushah*. One is the obligation of *p'rishah* (separation), which the sages explicitly identify as *k'dushah*. Our initial problem was linking *k'dushah* thus defined to *imitatio Dei*, in accord with Leviticus 19:2 and other verses. If *k'dushah* amounts to performing the commandments—whether particular commandments or the entire corpus—how could God perform or not perform the commandments? I replied that in a loose way (and I have stressed just how loose it is), *p'rishah* mirrors and imitates God's transcendence. Malbim, however, sought to parallel *p'rishah* to immanence: control over one's natural urges parallels God's control over nature.

The other obligation implicated in *k'dushah* is engagement, which imitates God's immanence, insofar as God acts to better the world. The imperative "Be holy because I, the Eternal your God, am holy" is far easier to articulate when we focus on *imitatio Dei* as the imitation of immanence (divine action) than when we view it as the imitation of transcendence. The analogy between God's involvement in improving the world and our efforts at achieving that goal are clear. It is much more difficult to find parallels between God's transcendence and humanity's transcendence—although some analogy, however loose, must be drawn in order to retain the *p'rishah* element. The upshot is that ethical conduct (and, for Rabbi Soloveitchik, creativity—which itself is ethically directed) is a primary element in achieving *k'dushah*, and perhaps even the main element. To further explicate the connection between *k'dushah* and holiness, I suggested as well that (1) ritual observance, on one theory, leads to ethical observance; and (2) although Maimonides held that *k'doshim tihyu* is shorthand for "do all of the *mitzvot*," perhaps he confined the imitation of God that is linked to holiness to imitation of the "ethical" attributes of compassion and lovingkindness.

Ultimately, the dual movements of engagement and separation closely resemble the dialectic of Adam the first and Adam the second in Rabbi Soloveitchik's *The Lonely Man of Faith*,[94] and also in his essay "Majesty and Humility."[95] Admittedly, one difference between Rabbi Soloveitchik's view and what I have suggested here is that the dual movement we are considering does not necessitate an oscillation between poles.

Contemporary Judaism contains, at one pole, groups and individuals who isolate themselves from the problems of the larger society, and at times even from moral challenges in Jewish society. At the other pole are those Jews for whom social action and *tikkun olam* are the be-all and end-all, Judaism's exclusive goal. Withdrawal is less an imitation of God's transcendence than social involvement is an imitation of God's immanence. If we think of *k'dushah* as requiring both imitation of transcendence and imitation of immanence, and do not neglect immanence but rather highlight it, then a theological framework for social duties becomes clear—and our further duty is to integrate both of these aspects of God, transcendence and immanence, in our quest for both wholeness and holiness.[96]

NOTES

[1] In translating the Tetragrammaton as "the Eternal" rather than "the Lord," I am deferring to the editor's decision to use this translation throughout as explained by Rabbi Blech in his preface to this book.

[2] Sifra, *K'doshim*, on Leviticus 19:2; Vayikra Rabbah 24:5. See also Rashi to Leviticus 20:25–26, where he takes the *k'dushah*, holiness, of the Jewish people to connote their being *muvdalim*, separated.

[3] Mekhilta D'Rabbi Yishmael, *Ba-ḥodesh*, Yitro 2.

[4] B. Yevamot 20a.

[5] Nothing in this essay hinges on whether "sanctify the mundane" truly has this positive implication, but it is, as I said, a natural inference to draw from the expression.

[6] I will not here enter into the question of how the concepts of *tumah* and *tohorah* (purity and impurity) relate to *k'dushah*. But see Maimonides, *Guide of the Perplexed* III 47, and the articles by Rabbi Moshe Lichtenstein in *Daf Kesher*, found at http://etzion.org.il/dk/idx/archive.htm.

[7] See Rashbam to Genesis 37:2.

[8] See Leon Roth, *Is There a Jewish Philosophy? Rethinking Fundamentals* (London: Littman Library, 1999), pp. 15–28 (translated from Hebrew by Raphael Loewe), at p. 17. See also Aḥad Haam, *Al Parashat D'rakhim* (Berlin, 1921), vol. 4, pp. 48–49. Roth was the first professor of philosophy at The Hebrew University in Jerusalem.

[9] To wit: Leviticus 11:41–44, 20:25–26, 21:7–8; Deuteronomy 7:3–6, 14:1–2, 21; 23:15; Exodus 29:34; 30:32; 30:37.

[10] Roth, p. 19.

[11] See Roth, pp. 17–20.

[12] See Vayikra Rabbah 24:5, and Sifra, *K'doshim* on Leviticus 19:2. For example, Leviticus 19:3 echoes the fourth and fifth commandments (about keeping Shabbat and honoring parents), and Leviticus 19:16 is linked to the sixth commandment (prohibiting murder). Leviticus 19 uses a plural, however, rather than the singular mode of address found in the Decalogue; see also Menachem Genack, "Kedoshim: You Shall Be Holy," in Daniel Z. Feldman and Stuart Halpern, eds., *Mi-tokh Ha-ohel* (Jerusalem: Maggid Books, 2010), pp. 293–295, quoting Rabbi Joseph B. Soloveitchik.

[13] See Vayikra Rabbah 24: *she-rov gufei torah t'luyin bah*—most of the essentials of the Torah depend on (or are found in) these laws.

[14] These two formulations (believing vs. knowing) reflect two approaches to translating, from the Arabic, the first commandment in Maimonides' *Sefer Ha-mitzvot*.

[15] Construing holiness as bound up exclusively with negative prohibitions is even more implausible when we look at the positive practices associated with

the Sabbatical and Jubilee years and the land of Israel. Admittedly we should be careful to distinguish holy objects, acts that sanctify objects or times, and being a holy people. For a discussion of a variety of complexities surrounding *k'dushah*, see the interview conducted with Rabbi Aharon Lichtenstein by Rabbi Chaim Sabato in *Mevakshei Panekha: Conversations with Rabbi Aharon Lichtenstein* (Tel-Aviv: Yediot Aḥronot and Ḥemed, 2011), pp. 109–124.

[16] Sifra, *K'doshim* on Leviticus 19:2. Some texts spell the word *m'ḥakkeh* (assumed in the translation above to be spelled with a *kof*, meaning "imitate") with a *kaf*, meaning "await [the monarch]." But, problematically for this alterative reading, Abba Shaul invokes the theme of *imitatio Dei* elsewhere as well—as we will see later.

[17] Sifra, *Sh'mini* 12:3 (on Leviticus 11:43) and 12:4 (on Leviticus 11:44); see also Sifra, *K'doshim* 10:21 (to Leviticus 20:26).

[18] Roth recognizes the problem of interpreting the *imitatio Dei* motif and, as we shall see below, he adopts a drastic solution. Eliezer Berkovits argues against several interpretations of *k'dushah* and points to the *imitatio Dei* problem. See Berkovits' essay, "The Concept of Holiness," in his *Essential Essays in Judaism*, ed. David Hazony (Jerusalem: The Shalem Center, 2002), pp. 247–314; the *imitatio Dei* problem is mentioned on p. 314. The essay is reprinted from *Man and God: Studies in Biblical Theology* (Detroit: Wayne State University Press, 1969), pp. 141–223.

[19] Rashi's association of holiness with sexual restraint has rabbinic roots, however. See Vayikra Rabbah 24:6, B. Yevamot 20a, and Y. Yevamot 2:4 (but cf. Rashi to Deuteronomy 22:9). Warren Zev Harvey cites refraining from idolatry as the critical separation. See his article, "Holiness: A Command to *imitatio Dei*," *Tradition* 16:3 (Spring 1977), pp. 16–17.

[20] B. Yevamot 20a, in the name of the talmudic sage Rava; cf. Rashi to B. Sanhedrin 53b, s.v. r. *y'hudah maḥalif.*

[21] See Naḥmanides' commentary to Leviticus 19:2. When and how to do more than is required is explored by Rabbi Yitzchak Blau in his essay elsewhere in this volume.

[22] See principle 4 of Maimonides' prologue. See also Maimonides, *Guide for the Perplexed* III 33. See also Rabbi Joseph B. Soloveitchik, *And From There You Shall Seek* [*U-vikkashtem Mi-sham*] (New York: Toras HoRav Foundation, 2008), p. 124: "There is one commandment that includes all 613, namely 'You shall be holy'…" Maimonides also quotes the Mekhilta, *Mishpatim*, which states that whenever God creates a mitzvah, Israel's holiness is augmented.

[23] Sifra, *K'doshim* 10 on Leviticus 20:7; Sifrei Bemidbar 115, on Numbers 15:41.

[24] Harvey's formulation is in his essay cited above, pp. 18–19. Harvey points out that the liturgical formulations *kid'shanu b'mitzvotav* and *v'kiddashtanu b'mitzvotekha*, both meaning that God has "sanctified us with

the commandments," fit well into the assertion that *k'dushah* encompasses all *mitzvot*.

[25] See Guide III 47; in Shlomo Pines' translation (Chicago: University of Chicago Press, 1963), the relevant passages are on pp. 595 and p. 433. For more on Maimonides' view of holiness, see Menachem Kellner, *Maimonides' Confrontation with Mysticism* (Oxford: Littman Library, 2007), chapter 3, and the next section of this essay. I have used Kellner's translation of the *Sefer Ha-mitzvot* passage, p. 94 (which in turn adapts that of Charles B. Chavel).

[26] *Guide* III 8.

[27] In M.T. Hilkhot Yesodei Hatorah 7:1; however, when Maimonides speaks of the prophet sanctifying himself, he makes reference to his separating himself from the common run of people, rising above them in achievement and perhaps even potential. This is *k'dushah*, separation, in a different sense.

[28] By contrast, the section of Maimonides' Mishneh Torah that he calls *Sefer Ha-k'dushah* deals with laws of sexual relations, laws of *kashrut*, and laws of ritual slaughter. He says: "In these two respects [he seems here to include *kashrut* and ritual slaughter as one], the Omnipresent sanctified us by separating us from the nations." See Kellner, *Maimonides' Confrontation with Mysticism*, pp. 94–95, nn. 27, 29.

[29] Harvey, pp. 8–9.

[30] Vayikra Rabbah 24:9.

[31] God's otherness is accompanied by human consciousness of that otherness. See Sol Roth, *The Jewish Idea of Community* (New York: Yeshiva University Press, 1977), ch. VI, especially pp. 95-98.

[32] Roth, pp. 22–23. Roth draws an analogy to a passage in B. Sukkah 30a on another topic.

[33] See Malbim to Genesis 1:26 and 28. He states there that, of all created things (including angels), only human beings have free will, and this grants human beings dominion over "a small world."

[34] See also Berkovits, "The Concept of Holiness."

[35] Vayikra Rabbah 24:9.

[36] This view will be discussed further below.

[37] As we shall see below, Berkovits—independently of Malbim—maintains that *k'dushah* refers to God's immanence. But in putting forth this thesis, he does not emphasize its utility in solving the *imitatio Dei* problem.

[38] Vayikra Rabbah 24:9.

[39] Again, God would possess the attribute by the essence of divine nature; we would attain it through our efforts.

[40] See Kellner, *Maimonides' Confrontation with Mysticism*, ch. 3. See also Sol Roth, *The Jewish Idea of Community*, pp. 103-107.

[41] The concepts just cited are the ones that Kellner discusses.

[42] For more on this idea, see Nathaniel Helfgot's essay elsewhere in this volume. Cf. also the interview with Rabbi Lichtenstein in *Mevakshei Panekha* (note 15 above).

[43] Rabbi Joseph B. Soloveitchik, *Family Redeemed: Essays on Family Relationships*, eds. David Shatz, Joel B. Wolowelsky, and Reuven Ziegler (New York: Toras HoRav Foundation, 2000), p. 64. See also his *The Emergence of Ethical Man*, ed. Michael S. Berger (New York: Toras HoRav Foundation, 2000), p. 150: "Objective *k'dushah* smacks of fetishism." At times Rabbi Soloveitchik refers to *k'dushah* as a "transcendental quality" (e.g., *Family Redeemed*, p. 74) but I will not venture here to explain such locutions.

[44] Rabbi Soloveitchik criticizes the view of Yehudah Halevi and Moses Naḥmanides that the land of Israel possesses "an objective metaphysical quality" called holiness (p. 150); instead, he maintains that human actions create the land's holiness. See also the texts of Maimonides discussed by Kellner (*Maimonides' Confrontation with Mysticism*, pp. 107–115), which accord with Rabbi Soloveitchik's view.

[45] The *Daat Mikra* commentary on Leviticus 19:2 (Jerusalem: Mosad Harav Kook, 1991) struggles to explain what it means for God to be *kadosh*, apparently taking *kadosh* as a property, and possibly troubled by how *imitatio Dei* can be achieved vis-à-vis holiness. *Daat Mikra* argues that there are no equivalents in human language to the notion of "divine holiness" that exhaust its meaning, and that "the holiness that flesh and blood individuals are made to reach is but a feeble imitation of God's *k'dushah*, which cannot be fathomed" (p. 56).

[46] Sometimes people explicate transcendence in terms of our inability to know what God is like. But it is not clear that transcendence, so construed, could really be a property of *God*. Does it not refer to a property of *us*—namely, our inability to conceive of what God really is?

[47] A pun on the law of *ḥadash*. The Ḥatam Sofer's position is considerably more complex than the stereotype of him; see Aaron Schreiber, "The Ḥatam Sofer's Nuanced Attitude Towards Secular Learning, *Maskilim*, and Reformers," *Torah u-Madda Journal* 11 (2002–2003), pp. 123–175.

[48] I am indebted here to the references and explications in Yehudah Nahshoni, *Hagut B'farashiyyot Ha-torah* (Bnei Brak: Yehudah Nahshoni, 1981), vol. 2, pp. 488–492.

[49] Ḥatam Sofer presents this amidst other possibilities, one of which he expresses with reluctance. The Hebrew word *p'rushim* (singular, *parush*) literally means "those who are apart" and was the Hebrew name of the sect generally referred to in English as the Pharisees.

[50] Berkovits, "The Concept of Holiness," p. 314.

[51] *The Hirsch Chumash*, trans. Daniel Haberman (Jerusalem and New York: Feldheim and Judaica Press, 2009).

52 We can see the force of this question when we realize that, in contrast to the kohen, the Pope never appears in public in anything but papal garments.

53 This motif is found also in Rabbi Soloveitchik's writings, especially *Halakhic Man*, trans. Lawrence Kaplan (Philadelphia: Jewish Publication Society, 1983), pp. 94–95.

54 Ibid., pp. 46–47. Objects, likewise, are sanctified by human actions: "Holiness is created by man, flesh and blood."

55 See ibid., pp. 99–137, esp. pp. 100–101. On *imitation Dei* in Rabbi Soloveitchik's thought, see the two essays by Walter Wurzburger in his *Covenantal Imperatives*, eds. Eliezer L. Jacobs and Shalom Carmy (Jerusalem, 2008), pp. 161-190.

56 Ibid., p. 137.

57 "Majesty and Humility," *Tradition* 17:2 (Spring 1978), p. 34.

58 *Family Redeemed*, p. 75.

59 Ibid., p. 63.

60 Ibid., p. 35. One must be careful here, because not all thinkers will embrace kabbalistic concepts, and because even in Rabbi Soloveitchik's own thought it is not clear how literally he uses kabbalistic concepts. Lawrence J. Kaplan argues that he uses them for literary effect; see Kaplan's "*Motivim Kabbaliyyim B'haguto shel Ha-Rav Soloveitchik: Mashma·utiyyim o Itturiyyim?*" in *Emunah Bi-z'manim Mishtanim* (Jerusalem: Mercaz Yaakov Herzog, 1996), pp. 75–95.

61 Rabbi Soloveitchik asserts, too, that *k'dushah* requires "the ability to answer the violent, orgiastic, hypnotic call of nature in the negative" (*Family Redeemed*, p. 110). In that last context he is speaking of consecrating objects.

62 Joseph B. Soloveitchik, *Abraham's Journey: Reflections on the Life of the Founding Patriarch* (New York: Toras HoRav Foundation, 2008), p. 203.

63 "Confrontation," *Tradition* 6:2 (Spring/Summer 1964), pp. 27–28.

64 Ibid., p. 20.

65 Genesis 23:4, in speaking to the Hittites to negotiate a gravesite for Sarah. See "A Stranger and A Resident," in *Reflections of the Rav* lectures of the Rav adapted by Rabbi Abraham R. Besdin (Jerusalem: The Jewish Agency/Alpha Press, 1979), pp. 169–177. This lecture strongly resembles "Confrontation."

66 Ibid., p. 170.

67 "Confrontation," p. 20. Regarding the apparent novelty of the contemporary Orthodox emphasis on *tikkun olam*, see Jacob J. Schacter, "*Tikkun Olam*: Defining the Jewish Obligation," in Raphael Madoff, ed., *Rav Chesed: Essays in Honor of Rabbi Dr. Haskel Lookstein* (Jersey City, NJ: KTAV, 2009), vol. 2, pp. 183–204.

68 Genack, "Kedoshim: You Shall Be Holy," p. 295. I am taking Rabbi Genack's eloquent words somewhat out of context. In context, he is drawing a distinction between God's holiness and human holiness while retaining the *imitatio Dei* motif: "God, however, is entirely independent of the universe. His holiness is manifest in His separation, loneliness, and isolation. God is holy in that He is totally 'Other,' beyond the universe, hidden by clouds of transcendence,

shrouded in infinity. The Rabbis in the Midrash feared that man might try to emulate God and attempt to achieve holiness in the same fashion—by being insulated and aloof, cloistered from the world's temptations, potential cruelty, and vulgarity. [And that is why they said that God's holiness and the human being's holiness are different.]" In my presentation, I stress that God is not insulated.

[69] See again the cautionary note in n. 60.

[70] See B. Sotah 14a.

[71] Certainly *imitatio Dei* is expressed in ethical acts—clothing the naked, visiting the sick, comforting mourners, burying the dead (B. Sotah 14a)—but I am looking for links between *holiness* and ethical imperatives.

[72] See Isaac Heinemann's classic *Ta·amei Ha-mitzvot B'sifrut Yisrael* (Jerusalem: World Zionist Organization, 1956), vol. 2, pp. 150–151. Heinemann doesn't really say that the view is unprecedented, but rather that prior to Hirsch, it was not held by philosophers.

[73] Mekhilta D'Rabbi Shimon bar Yohai, *Shirata*, 3.

[74] Because this connection is likely, the reading of *m'hakkeh* with a kof is probably the correct one.

[75] Hilkhot Dei·ot 1:5–6.

[76] On the textual problems with *Maimonides' quotations, see Kellner, Maimonides' Confrontation with Mysticism*, pp. 99–102, and his citations from Michael Schwartz's Hebrew translation of the Guide (Tel Aviv: Tel Aviv University Press, 2002).

[77] Kellner tentatively suggests that by including holiness with graciousness and mercifulness, Maimonides was emphasizing the "non-ontological character of holiness" (p. 101). I have raised the additional but not exclusionary possibility that he wanted to connect holiness with ethics. I wonder whether Maimonides' mis-citation is an instance of a tendency on Maimonides' part to occasional faulty memory when he cited texts. See Marc Shapiro, *Studies in Maimonides and His Interpreters* (Scranton, PA and London: University of Scranton Press, 2008), pp. 11–55.

[78] *Guide* I 54, Pines translation, p. 128.

[79] My discussion assumes that Maimonides is speaking of the emulation of these attributes in ordinary ethical life. Some interpreters believe he is referring to the attributes that are exercised by political leaders. Discussion of that interpretive possibility is beyond the scope of this essay.

[80] Vayikra Rabbah, *K'doshim* 24:1. Roth notes (p. 25) that Plato expresses the same thought about *imitatio Dei* in his dialogue *Theaetetus*. We must escape to the realm of the gods "with all possible speed, and such escape constitutes being like God as best we may: to become like [Him] means to become righteous and holy" (Roth's translation).

[81] Cf. Sol Roth, *The Jewish Idea of Community*, ch. VI, which cautions against reducing the holy to the ethical.

[82] Other quotations in Roth, some more effective than others, include Isaiah 30:12–18 and Amos 4:1–2.

[83] See references on Roth, p. 24.

[84] David Shapiro, "The Meaning of Holiness in Judaism," *Tradition* 7:1 (Winter 1964–1965), pp. 46–80.

[85] Ibid., p. 51 (italics in the original).

[86] Otto, *The Idea of The Holy*, trans. John W. Harvey (New York: Oxford University Press, 1958), p. 75. Berkovits, "The Concept of Holiness," pp. 312–314, rejects Otto's concept that holiness represents the *mysterium tremendum*.

[87] Shapiro, p. 63. I omit from my footnotes the biblical and rabbinic texts that Shapiro cites in defense of his assertions.

[88] Shapiro, p. 76.

[89] Ibid., p. 66.

[90] Ibid., pp. 68, 69.

[91] Heinemann, vol. 2, pp. 148–154. Harvey notes that God is hallowed through both righteousness (Isaiah 5:15) and sacrifices (Leviticus 22:32).

[92] For further discussion of Hirsch on sanctification, see Yitzchak Blau, "R. Hirsch on Sinfulness, Physicality, and the Sacrificial Order," at http://vbm-torah.org/archive/modern/07modern.htm.

[93] See my essay, "Berkovits and the Priority of the Ethical," *Shofar* 31:4 (Summer 2013), pp. 85-102, and also "The Seeming Disconnect Between Ritual Observance and Moral Behavior," in *Rav Shalom Banayikh: Essays Presented to Rabbi Shalom Carmy*, eds. Hayyim Angel and Yitzchak Blau (Jersey City, NJ: KTAV, 2012), pp. 283–299. Harvey writes, however: "While the imperative of 'walk in His ways' is moral, the *imitatio Dei* of the command to be holy is *religious*."

[94] This work originally appeared in *Tradition* (Summer 1965), and has been republished many time (most recently, by Koren Publishers, 2011).

[95] See n. 56 above.

[96] I thank Rabbi Yitzchak Blau for his comments on an earlier version of this essay, and Aaron Segal for helpful communication on the topic.

Impressions: Facing the Rock

Avivah Zornberg

Failure to Sanctify?

The process of sanctification represents a biblical and rabbinic ideal of human development. The Torah commands, "You shall make yourselves holy" (Leviticus 11:44), "You shall be to Me a kingdom of priests and a holy nation" (Exodus 19:6), and "You shall be holy for I, the Eternal your God, am holy" (Leviticus 19:2). This indicates a process in time—a "morality of aspiration,"in Lon Fuller's terms[1]— that is subtly but clearly different from Koraḥ's claim that "the whole community—all of them are holy" (Numbers 16:3).

In biblical law, this process is often mapped out in terms of specific ritual laws: removing pollutions of various kinds, preparing the people for entry into sacred space, and preparing the accoutrements of sacred space for the indwelling of God. However concrete the practices of sanctification may be, the overarching ideal of holiness both transcends and motivates its practices. And that ideal in some sense resists being reduced to its ritual elements.

In that sense, the practices of holiness have often been associated with restraint, rather than action—a fastidiousness, for instance, about sexual purity. In the verse "You shall be holy for I, the Eternal your God, am holy" (Leviticus 19:2), the command to be holy, *k'doshim*, is understood by the sages as an injunction to be *p'rushim*, to be *separate*[2]—that is, one should keep away from whatever endangers holiness. A sense of dedicated difference comes to inform one's way of living ordinary, everyday life.[3] One implication is that holiness and sanctification are felt to be indefinable in positive terms. As a kind of *via negativa*—the notion that God is diminished by any positive description, which must necessarily be limited—human holiness likewise can only be intimated by what it is not. Ineffable, it can only be protected both by its legal safeguards and by the sensibility of those who care about it.

Ultimately, according to Sforno, "You shall be holy" represents the ideal of *imitatio Dei*, God's wish for the human being to be created "in our form and after our image" (Genesis 1:26).[4] Indeed, to sanctify oneself is equivalent, say the sages, to sanctifying God: "If you sanctify yourselves, I account it as if you had sanctified Me."[5] In biblical law, the collective is the implicit bearer of this ideal; for the rabbis, the focus shifts to the individual and the capacity of the individual to "sanctify God." In sanctifying oneself one effectively bears witness to God's holiness, as one's state of being in itself declares God's holiness in the world. Human holiness evokes for others the reality of God's holiness.

In view of this, it is striking that there seems to be little in the way of biblical narrative that deals with this central concept of sanctification, despite the fact that it is precisely the strength of narrative to flesh out elusive processes and to convey them in temporal and social contexts. The root *kof-dalet-shin*, either as an adjective or as a verb, used transitively or intransitively, seems shy of narrative frameworks.

In fact, I believe that the only narrative that focuses its ultimate meaning on this issue is the enigmatic episode of the rock at Merivah. Here, God pronounces the last word on the narrative: it is the failure of Moses and Aaron to "have faith in Me, to *sanctify Me* before the eyes of the Israelites" that defines their fate: "...therefore you shall not lead this congregation into the land" (Numbers 20:12). I suggest that by exploring the complex layers of this narrative—its resonances both with the beginning of the Exodus story and beyond—we may approach, in the way that narrative alone can, an understanding of the intertwined ideals of *emunah* and *k'dushah*, faith and sanctification. In this narrative, uniquely, a space is created in which a crucial process, in failing to happen, leaves its deep imprint.

Here is the story in its entirety, found in Numbers 20:

> [1]The Israelites arrived, the whole community, at the wilderness of Zin on the first new moon, and the people stayed at Kadesh. Miriam died and was buried there. [2]The community was without water, and joined against Moses and Aaron. [3]The people quarreled with Moses, saying, "If only we had perished when our brothers perished in the presence of the Eternal. [4]Why have you brought the congregation of the Eternal into this wilderness, for us and our beasts to die there? [5]Why did you bring us up out of Egypt to bring us to this evil place, a place with no grain or figs or vines or pomegranates? And there is no water to drink!"
>
> [6]Moses and Aaron came away from the congregation to the entrance of the Tent of Meeting, and fell on their faces. The Presence of the Eternal appeared to them, [7]and the Eternal spoke to Moses, saying, [8]"Take the rod, you and your brother Aaron, and gather the community, and before their very eyes speak to the rock so that it gives forth of its water. So you shall produce water for them from the rock and you shall provide drink for the congregation and their beasts."
>
> [9]And Moses took the rod from before the presence of the Eternal, as he had been commanded. [10]Moses and Aaron assembled the congregation in front of the rock; and he said to them, "Listen, you rebels, shall we produce water for you from this rock?"[11]And Moses raised his hand and struck the rock twice with his rod. And copious water emerged, and the community and their beasts drank.
>
> [12]And the Eternal said to Moses and Aaron, "Because you did not trust Me enough to affirm My sanctity before the eyes of the Israelite people, therefore you shall not lead this congregation into the land that I have given them." [13]These are the waters of Merivah—meaning that the Israelites quarreled with the Eternal, through which God affirmed the sanctity of the Divine.

The story begins with the death of Miriam, her burial, and the lack of water. The people attack Moses and Aaron who seem to flee from them[6]—from the presence of the community to the presence of God. God's glory then appears to them. On every other occasion where this happens in the book of Numbers, it is followed by stern words of judgment.[7] Here, however, God speaks tenderly about providing water to nurture the people: Moses is instructed to personally and intentionally produce the water *for them* and to bring it to their lips. When Moses strikes the rock twice, the water simply "emerges" (he does not directly produce it), and he does not personally tend to the people's needs (rather, "the community drank").

It is at this point, when the narrative seems to have come to a happy conclusion, that God declares the inscrutable decree, couched in language that rings with uncanny lucidity: "*Because* you did not trust Me enough to affirm My sanctity before the eyes of the Israelite people, *therefore* you shall not lead this congregation into the land…" (verse 12).[8] In this logical form the death sentence is even more shocking, for the explanation itself needs explaining. Moses and Aaron did not trust in God? They failed to sanctify God? But the self-evident tone of the decree is carried over to the last sentence, where the waters are named for the people's "quarrel" with God, who *is* "sanctified by them." We are left with the apparent coherence of a closure that purportedly justifies the original name of the place— Kadesh (verse 1)—without, in fact, clarifying anything. How is God sanctified in this place where Moses and Aaron have failed to sanctify the Divine?

This enigmatic narrative has been the subject of multiple interpretations. *Or Ha-ḥayyim*[9] in fact counts ten such theories, only to conclude that none is satisfactory; in spite of this—or perhaps because of this—he declares that the reader is still obliged to make sense of this most resistant narrative.[10] This pattern of criticizing previous theories and suggesting a new one has its absurd side. *Or Ha-ḥayyim* quotes Luzzatto: Moses committed one sin and various commentaries have attributed to him more than thirteen different sins! Critical ingenuity ends up riddling Moses' character with endless flaws—surely a perverse exercise!

But the history of exegesis of this narrative demonstrates at least one thing quite clearly: that the Torah has not provided a clear answer to the question of Moses' culpability. Too many different understandings of Moses' failure hover over a gap in narrative meaning.

Scenarios of Sanctification

The classic explanation of Moses' sin is found in Rashi's comment to verse 12: Moses was commanded to speak to the rock, not to strike it. Rashi writes: "If you had spoken to the rock and it had produced water, I would have been sanctified before the eyes of the community. They would have said, 'If this rock, which does not speak or hear and has no need for sustenance, fulfills God's word, how much the more so should we do likewise!'"

Rashi emphasizes the public nature of the scene, noting that it is enacted before the eyes of the mass of Israelites—the same mass from whom Moses and Aaron have just fled. God finds Moses and Aaron fallen on their faces and urges them to return to face the people. Publicly acting before their faces and their eyes, Moses and Aaron are to speak to the rock. But how would this have generated faith, or trust, or sanctification? What, after all, is the difference between striking a rock and speaking to it? One might say that striking the rock is precisely what is meant by "speaking" to it.[11] How else does one communicate with a thing, an inanimate object that is impervious to words? A blow with a stick is just the language that a rock understands!

But Rashi's scenario of sanctification is intriguing. The rock's obedience to God's words would have produced a thoughtful response in the people, who would have seen themselves in the place of the rock. By an imaginative act of introjection,[12] they would have come to recognize the power of God's word in their own vulnerable and dependent lives. Their own human situation would have been highlighted by the miracle of the rock. The purpose of the whole exercise was the impact it would have on the people's eyes. Failing to speak and instead hitting the rock, Moses misses the point; the imaginative process is short-circuited, as the double blow of the rod induces in the people no self-reflection.

Many commentaries are unsatisfied by Rashi's reading. In the narrative, after all, God tells Moses to "take the rod" (verse 8): for what purpose is he to take it, if not to strike with it? And striking the rock does produce the water that God had promised. There is no indication in the narrative that God is displeased with this act—until the shocking coda that immediately follows.

Rambam takes a different tack.[13] Moses' sin lays in his address to the people and not in his striking the rock. An inappropriate anger informs his words: "Listen, you rebels…" Moses is punished, however, not for the anger itself, but rather because God at this moment is not personally angry with the people: Moses is thus misrepresenting God, who has just spoken solicitously of them. It is the public context of Moses' angry outburst that leads to God's judgment. Moses has failed to create in the people the trust that a sense of God's love would have generated; he has not sanctified God by conveying a sense of divine nurturing concern for the people. The gravity of such a moment of misrepresentation, Rambam implies, justifies God's decree.

The Turning Point

Instead of criticizing the people for their complaints, God turns to the leaders. God's glory appears, on this occasion, not to the whole people but to Moses and Aaron alone. A portentous moment looms for the leaders, rather than for the people.[14] For the first time, the focus of God's scrutiny shifts, and it is Moses who is held accountable for God's sanctity in the people's eyes. As a result of this judgment, Aaron will die in the near future (Numbers 20:23–29). Moses will lead the people through the battles of Transjordan and the final months of the fortieth year. Miriam has already died, just before our narrative (Numbers 20:1), and midrashic tradition connects her death with our narrative, suggesting that the miraculous well that had accompanied the people on their journeys vanished when she died. The people thirst for water when this vital resource—Miriam's presence and her well—disappears.

This pivotal narrative, then, crystallizes an important motif in the history of the wilderness. This is the turning point: both an ending and a beginning. The three leaders fade from the scene, and the people reach a moment of transition.

The historical context of this moment is signalled in the first verse: "The Israelites arrived, the whole community, at the wilderness of Zin." Rashi, citing *Midrash Tanḥuma*, comments on the unusual harmonics of the expression: "'The Israelites…the whole community'—for those who were to die in the wilderness had already died, and these were set apart for life." Suddenly, a dramatic turning point comes to light: this is the moment when all the dying is done. The death of a generation has been completed, and God's original decree after the sin of the spies has been fulfilled. Those who survive are now set on a different journey, to life and not to death. Perhaps that is why the law of the red heifer, offering purification from death-pollution, had just now been promulgated (Numbers 19).

The poignant moment between death and life, however, carries its own mystery. We suddenly become aware that thirty-eight years have passed without our noticing. Behind the scenes, a generation has vanished into the sands. There is something uncanny about this hidden passage of time, with its harvest of so many deaths. A new generation is suddenly identified in the midrash, but in the Torah the intervening thirty-eight years go unrecorded. Suddenly the people arrive at Kadesh, at the border of Edom, at the threshold of the promised land. In the blink of an eye, we find ourselves looking back at the unrecorded wilderness trauma. Like a traveller whose sense of continuous time and space is disrupted by a sudden sight of the Grand Canyon, the reader moves from the story of Koraḥ,[15] for whom the earth opened and closed, to our narrative of the rock. What had seemed continuous is now revealed as an abyss.

The "complete community," which has achieved the form in which it will enter the land, now loses its original leaders, one after another. There is, I suggest, a similarly uncanny character to these individual death narratives. Miriam dies—just the stark fact is reported—and suddenly there is no water. Abruptly, Moses and Aaron are sentenced to death; we are thus compelled to re-read the preceding narrative which, on a first reading, gave no hint of a sin that might merit such punishment. Aaron dies at the top of Mount Hor, where Moses divests him of his priestly robes and dresses his son in those very garments. Moses too dies at the top of a mountain, but he dies alone, overlooking the land. He dies "by the mouth of God" (Deuteronomy 34:5)—by a kiss?[16] He is buried (va-yikbor oto, Deuteronomy 34:6)—but who buried him? God? Or does he bury himself?[17] "And no man knows his burial-place until this very day" (Deuteronomy 34:6)—Moses, the quintessential man, did not know where he was buried?[18] These narratives cry out for interpretation. They are haunted by untold histories; couched in silences, they represent the fraught nature of moments of transition.

These narratives of transition are preceded by the mysterious law of the red heifer. This law becomes the epitome of the unfathomable in midrashic thinking:[19] a hair of the quasi-mythical red heifer both purifies those polluted by contact with death and also, in a different context, pollutes the pure. Yalkut Shimoni quotes Kohelet 7:23, "All this I tested with wisdom; I thought I could fathom it, but it eludes me," and comments: "Solomon said, 'I understood the whole Torah; but when I arrived at the passage of the red heifer I would search it, investigate it, interrogate it.'"[20] About this law of the red heifer, fraught with existential issues—life and death, purity and impurity—

even Solomon the wise is baffled. Similarly, as generations of commentators have testified, no key has yet been found to unlock the mystery of the rock episode at Merivah.

The rock and the rod: these are the objects that mark this transitional moment between the wilderness and the land. As we remember their history, these objects begin to vibrate before our eyes; they are *things* that are charged with narratives, with laws— ultimately, with *words*. They gleam secretly with hope and fear, with past and future, with the intense experience of those who live with them.

Two Rock Stories

God tells Moses to "take the rod." This rod was last seen in Moses' hand in that original water-from-the-rock episode at Rephidim. We read there: "The Eternal said to Moses, 'And the rod with which you struck the river—take it in your hand…and strike the rock; and water will issue from it and the people will drink.' And Moses did so before the eyes of the Israelite elders" (Exodus 17:5–6). There, Moses did exactly what was expected of him, striking the rock before the eyes of the Israelite elders. The rod did its work. And it was Moses who named the place in such a way as to register his criticism of the people: strangely, it too is called Merivah (Exodus 17:7).

What follows that early rock-water episode is the battle with Amalek: "Moses then told Joshua, 'Go forth to fight the Amalekites; tomorrow I shall stand on the hilltop *with the rod of God in my hand*'" (Exodus 17:9). The battle is waged, with the Israelites in the field and Moses on the hilltop, the position of his hands somehow governing the vicissitudes of the battle: "And it was that whenever Moses would raise up his hand, Israel would prevail; and whenever he would rest his hand, Amalek would prevail. But Moses' hands grew heavy, so they took a stone and placed it under him and he sat upon it. And Aaron and Hur supported his hands from either side, so that his hands were stable (*emunah*) until the sun set" (Exodus 17:11–12).

Here again, the rod seems to be in use—at least in the sense that Moses plans to hold it in his hand. Surprisingly, though, there is no further reference to the rod. Moses' hands alone are the focus of the narrative, determining the fortunes of the battle. They rise and fall; they are heavy and must be supported. But no mention is made of the rod in those hands. Trying to visualize the battle, the reader's imagination falters: is there a rod in his hands, as they rise and fall, or not? At any rate, we have seen this rod for the last time until the moment of our narrative forty years later, when Moses is again commanded, "Take the rod…"

In comparing the two events, we are struck by the fact that both rock-water sites are named Merivah ("dispute"), although they are clearly located in different places[21] and the incidents took place at different times. Aside from God's instruction in the first narrative to strike the rock, we also notice the impersonal, factual tone of God's words there. In the second narrative, God address Moses and Aaron by name, emphasizing their relationship; they are to address the rock "before the eyes of the people," and with an awareness of their perspective; the rock is personified ("it will give forth its waters"), while Moses will be animated by the intention of providing water *for them*; he will personally give them (and their cattle) to drink. Subtly, God's language animates the inanimate, the rock and the water, drawing a contrast with both Moses and the people.

As for the rod, it is once again in Moses' hand, in this different place and time. Where has it been in the interim? The text notes that "Moses took it from before the presence of the Eternal, *mi-lifnei Adonai*" (Numbers 20:9), presumably referring to the Ark located in the Holy of Holies.[22] In effect, this suggests that in the intervening thirty-eight years since the first rock-water episode, the rod had been lodged "in the presence of the Eternal." Like the jar of manna, which was stored "in the presence of the Eternal, as a memento for your generations" (Exodus 16:33), the rod is also described as stored "as a memento in the presence of the Eternal" (Numbers 17:25)—removed from active use, as a significant memento of the people's history.

Meshekh Hokhmah[23] suggests that "as a memento" (*l'mishmeret*) implies that the object is suspended from its normal usage within time and space, in order to sacralize its miraculous status. As soon as the tabernacle was erected in the second year in the wilderness, both the jar of manna and the rod were laid in storage "before the presence of the Eternal" (although the manna would continue to sustain the people until the end of the wilderness period). The act of preserving a specimen for future generations demonstrates the miraculous status even of the manna, which would continue to be in daily use, so that familiarity would not breed contempt.[24]

The manna is thus represented as occupying a paradoxical space in the lives of the people. It is to be a part of life in nature and in time—collected and consumed daily—and yet, by being preserved for the future, the manna "in the presence of the Eternal" also becomes a symbol of the starkly miraculous. Poised between nature and miracle, it is already absent: a keepsake for the generations, even as it continues to fall daily upon the camp.

Like the manna, the rod is laid away as a symbol of the miracles of the Exodus.[25] The rod comes to represent an early period of powerful and miraculous divine interventions into the natural order. Until God tells Moses to "take" it in the second rock-water narrative, it has been retired from active service; it has become a museum piece. What were its original characteristics? In what situations had it been used? And how do the associations of these historical moments impact on one another in memory?

The Posture of Trust

In the first rock-water story, God instructs Moses: "Pass in front of the people" (Exodus 17:5).

Rashi's comment to that verse subtly deflects our first reading of God's words:

"Pass in front of the people"—and see whether they stone you! Why have you spoken slander against My children? "And your rod, with which you struck the river"—What is the force of the words, "with which you struck the river"? They are apparently superfluous. But they were added because the Israelites had said of the rod that it was intended only for punishment. By the rod, Pharaoh and the Egyptians had been stricken with many plagues in Egypt and at the Sea of Reeds. Therefore, it is said here: "Take the rod, with which you struck the river"—they shall see now that it is effective also for good.

As Rashi tells the story, a tense drama of fear and suspicion is being enacted between Moses and the people. Moses has, in fact, just expressed his fear of being stoned by them. To this God replies, "Pass before them! You are slandering them by speaking of them as a lynch mob!" What will happen if Moses passes unprotected in front of them? They will witness a benevolent use of that rod that heretofore had been used only to "strike"—that is, to plague the Egyptians. This rod, in other words, is fraught with punitive, destructive meaning, bringing death and suffering to the Egyptians. As soon as the Israelites see that the rod can be an instrument of benevolent (and not only destructive) power, their aggression will abate.

In this midrashic reading, God reproaches Moses for "slandering the people." At first, he is paralyzed in a posture of fearful antagonism, facing a people for whom the rod has only one set of associations. These obvious punitive associations are now to be inverted; the rod will act beneficently, giving life-sustaining water rather than turning water into deathly blood. The familiar rod of the plagues suddenly becomes uncanny. Imbued with memories of the past, the rod is now destabilized. Apparently, a rod is not always a rod. Implicitly, Moses' relation to the people is affected by this old-new usage of the rod. In effect, God is teaching Moses how to shift the people's traumatic associations, and how to evoke in them a measure of trust.

When Moses then goes up to the hilltop to oversee the battle against Amalek, he announces that the rod of God will be in his hand. And yet, as we have noticed, the rod seems to disappear from the narrative. Like the conductor of an orchestra, Moses seems to conduct the progress of the battle...but where is the conductor's baton? Does he conducts with bare hands? Moses' hands are heavy, so he is seated on a stone and Aaron and Hur support his hands: "And his hands were *emunah* until the sun set" (Exodus 17:12).

The description is dense with physical detail, haunted by hands, so that we feel the strain involved in holding the position that will bring his people victory. "His hands were *emunah*"—simply translated, this means that his hands held steady, so that the people prevailed. But Rashi shifts the drama from the physical to the spiritual plane: "Moses held up his hands outspread toward the heavens in faithful and constant prayer." The steadiness of his hands becomes an expression of a difficult posture of the soul, the posture called *emunah*—faith, trust, stability—which is the characteristic of true prayer.

A tableau is enacted in which Moses prays with his hands outstretched toward the heavens. But if we are to visualize the scene in this way, where is the rod? Ramban treats the question in all seriousness, asserting that Moses went up the mountain so that he could see the people in battle and "look upon them in benevolence." They will then see him absorbed in seeing them, spreading his hands heavenward and praying; as a result, they will trust him and will be filled with courage. But in this case, at the moment of prayer with hands outstretched, Moses cannot be holding anything in his hands.

The very nature of prayer and of *emunah* precludes the use of the rod. Ramban suggests that the rod was raised to bring down destruction upon the Amalekites, in the same way that it had been raised to bring plagues upon the Egyptians. In spite of its recent conversion to beneficent purpose in the Merivah story, the rod is clearly an instrument of violence, and violence is no stranger in battle. But the essential role of Moses in this narrative is to discard the rod and spread his hands in prayer. It is the vulnerable open hand, held high, that brings victory to the people.

What is the connection between Moses' hands and the people's triumph? Do his hands hold magical power to determine the fortunes of war? The question is raised in a well-known mishnaic passage:

> Did Moses' hands really make the fortunes of war or break the fortunes of war? Rather, this comes to teach that as long as Israel was looking upward and submitting their hearts to their heavenly Progenitor, they would prevail; but if not, they would fail.[26]

If Moses' hands do not have magic power, what role do they play? According to this midrash, victory in battle depends on the spiritual attitude of the people, on their hearts' connection with God. Another midrashic passage, however, shifts the emphasis: "As long as Moses held his hands high, Israel would gaze at him and trust (ma·aminim) in the One who commanded Moses to do this. And because of this, God performed miracles and prodigies for them."[27] Here, the people's hearts are affected by the position of Moses' hands. By gazing at him as he prays, they are led to their own place of emunah. Moses' hands are thus the visual link between the people and God.

Who, then, is Moses for the people? In the moment of emunah, seeing him evokes for them their own spiritual possibilities. What this moment costs is implied in the human heaviness of his hands, in his need for support, and in the discarding of the rod, with its well-practiced gestures of authority and confidence. But when they look at him, the people instinctively replicate his posture: "When he kneels, so do they; when he prostrates himself, so do they; when he stretches his hands to heaven, so do they. Just as the prayer leader prays, so too does the whole people pray after him."[28]

This is a radical description of the mimetic relation of Moses and his people. Moses is to pray from a position where he can be seen; the spiritual life of his people is attuned, in some sense, to his. "Before their eyes," he goes through the gestures of humility and trust in the presence of God. An intimate and personal prayer experience thus becomes a visual and spiritual focus for others. In the context of the battle, Moses and the people are engaged in two incompatible processes: the people's hands and eyes are involved in waging war, while at the same time they are fixed in mutual absorption on Moses and imitating his prayer gestures. Moses holds the rod of power and violence, while at the same time his hands are outstretched in the posture of one who grasps at nothing.[29] It is the open-handed posture of the caress: tender and tentative, yet attentive.

Such a tableau, the midrash concludes with astonishing aplomb, is the model for every prayer community. The work of souls who attach themselves to a leader and, like children, repeat prayers after him, is done in the very midst of the cut and thrust, the ambitions and drives, of life. It is as if, in prayer, all of one's competence is disarmed, and one allows oneself the dangerous vulnerability of trust.

In this narrative, Moses' hands, either with or without the rod, come to represent a dynamic epiphany of connection with God; hands high or low, Moses' figure becomes an object of intense suggestiveness for those who see him. Their position brings power (*g'vurah*) to his people, or to their enemies. The final stable position of his hands becomes an icon of faith, which will conserve for the future an early moment of private and collective experience.

Therefore, some forty years later when God tells Moses to "take the rod," the earlier moment of *emunah*, encompassing the first rock-water episode, flickers into potent life. This time, however, the staff fails to ignite *emunah*. Moses fails to find the posture that will make sense of this later moment. The space between himself and his people and the rock remains unsanctified. And God responds: "Because you did not trust in Me, to sanctify Me before the eyes of the Israelites, therefore you shall not lead this congregation into the land" (Numbers 20:12).

The remembered moment when Moses looked in love at the people looking at him (as Ramban puts it) is later suffused with a kind of "aura." Robert Alter describes Walter Benjamin's use of this term: "an object imagined is felt to have numinous value, an effect of the sacred, because it is steeped in memory."[30] A form of personal revelation, the moment holds a "potency of the truth" that has to be recuperated in the later time. For Benjamin, the aura is associated with involuntary memory, originating in the unconscious and capable of endless epiphanies: "For an experienced event is finite," Benjamin writes in his essay on Proust, "at any rate, confined to one sphere of experience; a remembered event is infinite, because it is *only a key to everything that happened before it and after it*."[31]

The Plagues: Blows on the Heart

Suffused with associations, the early rock-water episode is remembered by Moses when rod and rock again come together. We are not, I suggest, thinking only about two texts, two narratives separated by time and space, and marked by similarities and differences. We are thinking about the way the earlier narrative becomes fraught with memory in the later moment. The Torah itself gently reminds us of this linkage between moments by introducing a flashback into a yet earlier narrative: God's earlier reference to the rod describes it as "with which you struck the river" (Exodus 17:5). In a regressive series, each appearance of the rod evokes the associations of an already extinct past.

The plagues (*makkot*), for instance, begin with a literal *makkah*, a "blow" of the rod that turns the Egyptian river into blood. This most concrete act of violence resonates with unconscious meanings. Fish die and stink in the river. Here, by means of the rod, water becomes blood; later, rock will become water. Here, blood seeps uncannily through the trees and the stones in all the land of Egypt; later, the water will spill straight into the thirsty mouths of the people. Death and life, liquid and solid, soft and hard, desire and disgust, voluntary and involuntary—sensory images of the first plague are mirrored and transformed in the miracle at Rephidim.

On another level, unconscious meanings cluster around the issues of power and authority: Moses strikes and "kills" the sacred river, which is Pharaoh—who is his father, and who holds the power of life and death. Such aggression is bound up with terror. When God later refers to the rod at Rephidim, a process of transformation is initiated—generating life.

The primal horror of the bloody river in the end achieves nothing: "And Pharaoh's heart was hardened, and he did not listen to them.... He paid no heed even to this [literally: 'did not take it to heart']" (Exodus 7:22–23). Pharaoh's heart remains unaffected by the blow of Moses' rod. Ultimately, all the plagues (*makkot*)—all the blows (*makkot*) of Moses' hand and rod, whether physical or gestural— are aimed at Pharaoh's resistant heart. The adjectives *kaveid*, *ḥazak*, and *kasheh* repeatedly convey a sense of the stiffness, hardness, and density of this heart. Impenetrable and unimpressible, this heart is to be battered into submission. One might say that this heart, imagined as a tactile organ, looms over the text—as though contemplating this powerful, perverse organ can provide the Israelites with ways of thinking about other things, such as their own hearts.

Time and again, Pharaoh's heart tightens and closes against the impact of God's hand, often represented by Moses' hand. Before the seventh plague, hail, God has Moses tell Pharaoh: "This time, I am sending all of My plagues against your heart" (Exodus 9:14). In Rashi's reading, God is here referring to the final plague, the ultimate blow: the death of the firstborn, in which will be contained the cumulative terror of "all My *makkot* (plagues/blows)." Will the Egyptians acknowledge the terrifying impact of God's words upon their hearts? Will they "take to heart" Moses' warning and protect their servants and livestock from the hail by bringing them indoors (Exodus 9:21)?

What is clear, however, is that all these blows—up to, and possibly even including,[32] the final concentrated blow—do not penetrate Pharaoh's heart. Ramban suggests that the bombardment of plagues has a perverse effect: Pharaoh is afraid and clenches his heart ever more tightly.[33] In other words, these *makkot*, these blows of hand and rod, are not simply a series of events. They act dynamically within Pharaoh's memory, altering the field at every stage. Pharaoh's history is one of increasing intransigence; such histories too lie within the human range.

Seeing and Believing

At the same time, Moses too lives with the clusters of memories aroused by his rod. His attack on the river takes its license from a still earlier narrative, his first encounter with God at the burning bush. There, God had announced the divine scenario of redemption, which included the condensed narrative of the plagues: "I will stretch out My hand and smite Egypt with all My wonders that I will work in their midst; after that, he [Pharaoh] will let you go" (Exodus 3:20). In this projected future, Moses is to play an essential role. As God's emissary, Moses will effectively[34] liberate the people from Egypt: "Go, I will send you to Pharaoh and you shall free My people, the Israelites, from Egypt" (Exodus 3:10).

In a real sense, he is to be the redeemer. Moses protests: Who am I? Who shall I say sent me? God answers, and Moses listens in silence to God's scenario of redemption—consisting of nine verses in the Torah text. At the end of God's speech, Moses protests with considerable force: "Then Moses spoke up and said, 'But they will not believe me; they will not listen to my voice. They will say: God did not appear to you'" (Exodus 4:1). God then responds with two signs: Moses' rod is transformed into a snake and then reverts to its original form, and his hand becomes leprous and also reverts to its previous status:

> The Eternal said to him, "What is that in your hand?" And he replied, "A rod." God said, "Cast it on the ground." He cast it on the ground and it became a snake, and Moses fled from it. Then the Eternal said to Moses, "Put out your hand and grasp it by the tail"—whereupon he put out his hand and seized it, and it became a rod in his hand—"that they may believe that the Eternal, the God of their ancestors— the God of Abraham, the God of Isaac, and the God of Jacob—did appear to you." (Exodus 4:2–5)

The rod is introduced as the first of the "signs" that God offers in response to Moses' protest. At this crucial point, Moses' doubts surge from the depths of his being. This time, they cannot be resolved by God's words alone. Moses' body has to deliver a sign that will affect the people's belief in him and in his narrative. Or, in a larger sense, the sign will affect his own belief in the people's belief in him and in his narrative. The reflexive nature of Moses' protest implicates him in his skeptical description of the people: "They will not believe me!" The nexus between him and the people will fail: they will not trust him, and he will be incapable of arousing trust. In the face of God's assurance ("They will listen to your voice," Exodus 3:18), he cries out, "They will not listen to my voice!" Moses' complaint implies that he will be incapable of conveying, by voice or words, a credible narrative of revelation.

Indeed, a passage in the Talmud diagnoses the leprosy that afflicts his hand in the second sign as a punishment for suspecting the innocent. God praises the Israelites as "believers, children of believers."[35] Ostensibly it is *their* faith (or trust) that is at issue here, but it is *Moses* who requires signs, indications that will allow him to trust them! As the Talmud puts it, the people's faith is amply proven, since the Torah vouches for them: "He performed the signs before the eyes of the people, and the people believed" (Exodus 4:31). God gives the people credit for *emunah*. Moses, on the other hand, must undergo experiences in which his body becomes an instrument of *emunah*, capable of eliciting *emunah* in the people.

At the burning bush, God asks Moses, "What is that in your hand?" (Exodus 4:2)—and the reader is thus led to see the rod in Moses' hand. Perhaps, as Rashi suggests, God is drawing Moses' attention to the *thing* in his hand: do you acknowledge that it is a rod? Moses names it, only to have it transformed into a snake. In other words, Moses is being made aware that his own understanding of things is limited: his names turn out to be inadequate or provisional. Forms will change and new names will have to be found. The rod—the extension of the power of his own hand, more potent, more effective—is transformed into a sinuous, uncanny creature that turns against him: "And Moses fled from it" (Exodus 4:3). After the snake reverts to a rod in his hand, God's attention turns to that very hand: "Put your hand into your bosom" (Exodus 4:6). When he removes it, his hand is "encrusted with snowy scales" (Exodus 4:6).[36] In and out again, and it reverts *ki-v'saro*, into the vulnerable, soft flesh that signifies life.

After each of the signs, God speaks of *emunah*, the effect of the sign on the people's belief. They will believe the first sign, God says. If they don't believe the first sign, they will believe the second. And if they believe neither, if they don't listen to Moses' voice, then he should pour water from the river, and it will turn to blood. Strangely, God's stance in relation to the people's belief seems to shift: the first sign will produce belief; but if it fails, the second will succeed; but if they both fail, Moses should perform the water-blood transformation (which is not called a "sign"), but God does not promise that it will affect the people's belief. Assurances turn into contingency plans, which turn into acknowledgment of possible failure.

Perhaps this indicates that the underlying issue is Moses' faith in the people's faith. The first two signs offer an opportunity of moving Moses to that faith. In both cases, his bodily integrity and his confidence in his own knowledge of things are shaken. Transformations rapidly affect him: life and death switch places, and then switch back again. There is fear, and recoiling from his own alienated body. In the end, there is just his own flesh: vulnerable, impressible, volatile; a reminder of the existence of others and of the mutuality of flesh. The messages that are the "voice of the sign" (*kol ha-ot*, Exodus 4:8) are not magical effects, but rather human meanings transmitted by a messenger who is himself the instrument of *emunah*.

Suckling Moses

If it is indeed Moses who is, at least in part, the target of the signs, then the experience of transformation resonates with a sense of isolation that is part of his narrative from its earliest days. His life begins in a world that wants him dead. Set adrift by his mother in the Egyptian river, he is taken into the bosom of the Egyptian princess, who is persuaded by his sister to hire a wet-nurse from among the Hebrews—his own mother, in fact—to nurse the baby "for her." The fact that Moses is nursed by his own mother appears to be a deceptively "normal" situation. But it is fraught with history, its meanings complicated by power relationships: his mother has been hired by the princess to nurse the baby "for her."[37]

The Torah pays great attention to the arrangements for Moses' nursing, as though to convey the deep structure of Moses' formation, the ways in which the earliest experience of nurturing may be registered and enriched in memory by unconscious imagination. To suckle a child is to be an *omenet*, one who offers a first encounter with a loving, trustworthy world. *Omenet* comes from the same Hebrew root as *emunah*; the notions of trust, faith, and solidity are embodied in the primal human connection of the infant with its nursing mother. However, that word is never used in this narrative. If *emunah* is a recurring theme in the early narratives we have looked at, it is significantly absent in this explicit description of the nursing relationship. Here, the physical facts may be secondary to the emotional grounding that is signified by them. Moses is born into a world of genocide and then nurtured in an equivocal setting, situated between two worlds. The confirmation of being, so simply achieved by others, does not quite happen for him.

In this vein, when the infant Moses cries in his box in the river, one midrash hears in his sobs a kind of unconscious solidarity with his suffering people: "She opened [it] and saw there was a child— behold! a boy (*naʿar*) crying" (Exodus 2:6). Since *naʿar* is an unusual term to apply to an infant (as it usually designates a "youth"), *Tzʾror Ha-mor* relates the word to another verse: "Israel is a *naʿar* and I love him" (Hosea 11:1).[38] Uncannily, the baby's voice is thickened by the pain of his people.

A better-known midrash speaks of Moses' nursing history. It was only after many Egyptian wet-nurses had tried—and failed—to nurse the infant Moses that his own mother was hired. However, this baby refused to nurse (*lo yanak*), detaching himself from those breasts—because his mouth was destined to speak with God.[39] Such a precocious awareness of destiny complicates intimate connections. In this history, weaning precedes nursing. Communication with the world will never be straightforward; there will be impediments to Moses' relation with all that is not God.

The Field of Violence

Such layerings of self-experience, extending back in time, create clusters of meaning around voice and mouth, hand and rod. "This rod," God tells Moses at the burning bush, after he has tried in every way to resist his mission, "you shall take in your hand and perform the signs" (Exodus 4:17). Even as it is flesh, this hand is empowered: "And Moses took the rod of God in his hand…'See,' says God, 'all the wonders I have placed in your hand…'" (Exodus 4:20, 21). Moses will return to Egypt, and the people will believe him when he performs the signs "before their eyes" (Exodus 4:30).

But rod and hand are now already saturated with meaning. Rashi's comment to Exodus 4:8, concerning Moses' leprous hand, suggests just how unexpected these meanings may be:

> "They will believe the voice of the latter sign"—As soon as you say to them, "On your account I have been smitten with leprosy, because I uttered slander about you," they will believe you, for they are already familiar with this (i.e., that those who collaborate to harm them are smitten by plagues, like Pharaoh and Avimelekh, who were punished on Sarah's account).

By performing this sign with his hand, Moses will paradoxically be confirming the people's sense of being loved by God, by offering his own painful experience as evidence that those who slander Israel are made to suffer. Rashi converts a simple magical manifestation of power into a message, at Moses' own cost, of validation to his people. For this elaborate message to work, however, it is Moses who will have to find words to frame it. These words—of slander, punishment, affliction—are born in the darkness of Egypt. In order to create trust in his people, Moses will have to speak about his own body with the language of violence and revenge.

In the first memorable event of his life, Moses "goes out" to his brothers: "And he saw their suffering; and he saw an Egyptian man striking a Hebrew, one of his brothers" (Exodus 2:11). In one swift, complex vision of his world, Moses witnesses suffering and violence, the blow (*makkah*) inflicted by one person upon another. Immediately, there is a circumspect glance in all directions, followed by the blow that kills the Egyptian in retaliation. The text relates: "And he turned this way and that, and he saw that there was no man; and he struck down (*va-yakh*) the Egyptian and buried him in the sand" (Exodus 2:12).

Moses' response is described with the same word used of the Egyptian's violence, *va-yakh* (from the same Hebrew root as *makkah*). Like the Egyptian, he strikes to kill—in effect, to save his "brother." In Rashi's reading, his circumspect glance takes in the systemic persecution that lies behind this moment, and also the fact that the persecutor has no redeeming potential.[40] The time-gap between Moses' initial glance and his subsequent act represents a judicious inquiry into the justice of his own act of violence. Perhaps Rashi, in the wake of the midrashic traditions he cites, is sensitive to the irreducible fact that Moses' first recorded act is a *makkah*, an act of violence—which mirrors the violent world into which he has emerged.

The second act follows on the following day. This time he protests against the violence among his own kinsmen: "Why do you strike your fellow?" (Exodus 2:13). From the Hebrew slave's response, he realizes that his own killing of the Egyptian is now public knowledge. He fears for his life and flees. The two episodes are clearly linked, as both address the issue of *makkah*, an infliction of fatal bodily harm. The aggressive Hebrew slave sarcastically questions Moses' role as a self-appointed "chief and ruler over us" (Exodus 2:14), terms that imply the power to inflict punishment. Moses did kill the Egyptian in the name of justice; and yet the fact that he uses the same word, *makkah*, when he protests against the Hebrew slave's violence suggests a more troubling awareness.

In a remarkable talmudic comment, Resh Lakish learns from this narrative:

> One who raises his hand against one's friend, even without hitting that person, is called wicked, as it is said, "And he said to the offender [*rasha*; literally, "the wicked one"], 'Why do you strike (*takkeh*) your fellow?'" It does not say, "Why did you strike," but rather "Why *will* you strike?" Even though he had not yet actually struck him, he is called wicked.[41]

The Torah describes as wicked one who is merely about to strike another. This becomes a legal principle: the menacing act of raising one's hand disqualifies one from giving testimony in a court of law.[42] Such a remark reflects a critical awareness of the nature of human destructiveness. On one level, Moses is justified in killing the Egyptian to prevent the latter from killing the Hebrew; however, the very same impulse of violence (makkah) is, at least in Moses' mind, at work in the fight between the two Hebrew slaves. And this is an impulse that is tainted at its source.

Beyond the world of law, with its nuanced and contextualized licenses to kill, there remains the sense that *makkah* characterizes the field of violence that is Egypt. It implicates all who are born into it, including the Hebrews and even Moses himself, from the moment he ventures out into it. The language of redemption is shot through with destructiveness. In order to liberate Israel and bring them out of Egypt, God inflicts ten "blows" (*makkot*, plagues) on the oppressors. He engages Moses as the divine emissary: in addition to speaking in God's name, Moses is also to raise his hand repeatedly, throughout the unfolding of the plagues as well as at the Sea of Reeds. At the Sea, two different verbs are used (*natah* as well as *ramah*), but the power of the hand that cleaves the water remains palpable. The upraised hand has become a weapon. Much later, Moses records the marches of the Exodus as follows: "The Israelites started out defiantly [literally, "with raised hand," *b'yad ramah*] before the eyes of all the Egyptians" (Numbers 33:3). The meanings of the gesture of a raised hand—swearing an oath, defiance, aggressiveness, destructiveness, even blasphemy[43]—vary according to context, but Resh Lakish's suggestive remark lingers in the mind.

When this characteristic gesture of the Exodus story appears again at Rephidim, in the scene of the battle against Amalek, it undergoes a transformation. Here, Moses wages war by other means; his upraised hand is outstretched in prayer, transformed into *emunah* ("And his hands were *emunah*," Exodus 17:12). The rod is nowhere to be seen. If defiance has become prayer by an extension of the fingers, does this imply a kind of sublimation of primal impulses? By such small adjustments, the body moves into new worlds.

But if the *makkah* is Moses' first significant gesture, it is also to be his last. In the second rock-water episode at Merivah, he both raises his hand and he strikes: "And Moses raised (*va-yarem*) his hand and he struck (*va-yakh*) the rock twice" (Numbers 20:11). The concentrated violence of the moment differentiates it from the first episode at Rephidim. There it had been God who, in the context of a continuous future-tense narrative, commanded Moses to strike. Moses' own act there is presented as a simple act of obedience: "and Moses did so" (Exodus 17:6). At Merivah, in contrast, Moses obeys only until the moment that he takes the rod, "as [God] had commanded him" (Numbers 20:9). After that, even in assembling the people, he speaks and acts with an independence and aggressiveness that is not "as God had commanded." Moses raises his hand and strikes with all the pent-up power that had once split the Sea and rained down death-blows on the killers of his people. Now, the violent power of this hand surges one last time. His life from Egypt onward has come to a dark fruition.

By the Hand of Moses

The history of Moses' hand is complex and layered. Shaped as an instrument of divine anger, it gathers memories of past selves, conserving the experience of particular moments of being. Each memory is itself saturated by previous moments. Revelations from the past cluster around these memories, which flash back like lightning to the beginning, which holds infinite truth. We recall Walter Benjamin on Proust: "For an experienced event is finite…a remembered event is infinite, because it is only a key to everything that happened before it and after it."[44]

The body that holds these memories becomes an instrument of both anger and *emunah*. The Torah was given by the hand of Moses. This metaphor refuses to die; Moses' real hand gives it heft.[45] In a particularly telling moment, when Moses resists all of God's blandishments to become the divine messenger, he ultimately cries out, "Please, Adonai, send by the hand of the one You will send" (Exodus 4:13)—that is, Moses asks that God make someone else the divine agent. And Rashi's comment to that verse makes his demurral even clearer: "Send by the hand of another whom You will choose as Your messenger! I am not destined to bring them into the land and to be their future redeemer. You have many messengers."

From his first encounter with God, Moses apparently senses that he will not, in any case, complete the mission. God wants him, his hand, his agency—but only for the first part of the journey. This knowledge will be officially revealed to him at the end of the story, after the rock-water narrative at Merivah. But the issues of anger and trust have already crystallized; Moses' hand will not be the hand that will move the people out of the wilderness. Moses knows this, as surely as he already knows the power and powerlessness of his own hand—as though God's decree will have been long in place. What will be enacted forty years later at Merivah will flash back to an original moment of revelation at the burning bush.

With Their Own Eyes

By the time Moses has travelled from the bush to the rock, his rod has been long out of use—lodged "in the presence of God," as a memento for future generations. Fraught with associations that gather up the inner history of Moses and his people, the rod has been retired from active service. Now, many years later, God tells Moses, "Take the rod...and speak to the rock" (Numbers 20:8). Does taking the rod mean striking with it? Or does the rod now gleam with its clustering associations, with the aura that plays around it, a thing become words? Moses is told to take it, to hold it, and to speak before the eyes of the Israelites. This is to be a strictly visual endeavor: Moses and Aaron will speak, and the people will watch them speak. What they say will not enter the people's ears but rather their eyes. An almost theatrical scene is to be played out, in which rod and words affect the people like a new epiphany.

For the people's eyes, too, carry memories going back to the beginning of the story. Precisely this expression, "before the eyes of the people," accompanied Moses' original performance of the signs: "[he] repeated all the words...and performed the sign before the eyes of the people, and the people believed" (Exodus 4:30–31). Very simply, miraculous signs create belief in those who witness them. But the suggestion is always present in such scenes that a theatrical performance may involve illusion. Public testimony to miracles may generate faith; seeing is indeed believing. But as conjurers and faith healers know, the eye sees what it wishes to see.

When, for instance, Joseph imprisons Simeon "before the eyes" of his brothers (Genesis 42:24), this may mean that an illusion is being practiced upon them: behind the scenes, Joseph releases Simeon.[46] God too appears and acts before the eyes of the people: "And God shall come down on Mount Sinai before the eyes of the whole people" (Exodus 19:11). Again, the truth of this revelation is attested by its eyewitnesses. But, at the same time, "before the eyes of the people" also suggests limited perspectives, subjective meanings triggered by visual impressions. Much later, Moses cautions the people about the tenuous nature of things once seen: "Take utmost care...so that you do not forget the things that you saw with your own eyes, and so that they do not fade from your mind as long as you live" (Deuteronomy 4:9). Here, Moses is addressing the new generation who, in fact, did not themselves see the revelation at Sinai; all those whose eyes had literally seen it had by then vanished into the sands. How can this new generation be urged to remember things seen only by others? Perhaps it is precisely in the absence of that visual experience that a deepened inner vision, clusters of memories that reach through the generations, can be evoked. "One who internalizes his learning— soveir, working it into one's mind—will not quickly forget."[47] The movement away from concrete vision into the world of thought and memory offers alternative ways of conserving the potency of the past.

Strange Masterpiece

From this point of view, the last words of the Torah open up radical interpretive possibilities:

> Never again did there arise in Israel a prophet like Moses—whom the Eternal singled out, face to face, for the various signs and wonders that the Eternal sent him to perform in the land of Egypt, against Pharaoh and all his courtiers and his whole country, and for all the great might [*yad*, literally, "hand"] and awesome power that Moses performed before the eyes of all Israel. (Deuteronomy 34:10–12)

The Torah summarizes Moses' career of manifest prodigies and miracles, which were awesome and visible to all. Rashi quotes the Talmud and other sources:

> "For all the great might [hand]"—that he received the Torah in the form of tablets in his hands. "Before the eyes of all Israel"—that he was inspired [literally, "his heart lifted him up"] to break the tablets before their eyes, as it is said, "I smashed them before your eyes" (Deuteronomy 9:17).

Breaking down the categories of power manifested by Moses, Rashi focuses on Moses' hands, which received the stone tablets. These are also the hands that performed miracles in "that great and fearsome wilderness" (Deuteronomy 8:15). But finally these hands manifested their supreme strength "before the eyes of all Israel," when they smashed the stone tablets that they themselves had received.

The power of that act is represented by the power—the shock—inflicted by this midashic narrative. It closes with God acknowledging Moses' act: *Yishar koḥakha she-shibbarta*, "Congratulations that you smashed them!"[48] God affirms and blesses Moses' act of iconoclastic power. This is the true climax of Moses' prodigious life, as he himself records it: "I smashed them before your eyes" (Deuteronomy 9:17). And God, in this provocative midrash, validates and privileges this act.

This, Rashi suggests, is the crowning moment of Moses' life, as well as the last word of the Torah. Rashi seems to point to the extraordinary courage that Moses displayed in such a public way: "his heart lifted him up." He has no official imprimatur for this heroic act; he shatters his own conscious expectations of himself and of God. Moses braves the gaze of all those eyes to shatter the concrete, "permanent" representation of God's word. Some extraordinary inspiration raises him above normal considerations to commit this most violent act, and God celebrates the iconoclastic moment.

Moses' heart and hands have here achieved a strange masterpiece. Another midrashic version of the story, however, shifts our impression of the scene. On Moses' narrative in Deuteronomy 9:17, "I seized the two tablets and I cast them out of my two hands, and I smashed them before your eyes," the Jerusalem Talmud reads: "The tablets sought to fly off and Moses seized hold of them."[49] Moses tries with the force of his hands to restrain the tablets as they fly out of his hands, but then apparently yields to their impulse and lets them fly out of his control.

Here, Moses' hands surrender their power in the moment of shattering. Counterintuitively, we are to imagine the force that his hands exerted, seizing hold of the tablets. In smashing the tablets, he paradoxically surrenders control, allowing the tablets to fly! Some unconscious force subverts the mastery of Moses' hands. The tablets wish to fly: what unrecognized longing does the midrash intimate here? The imagery sets heaviness, hardness, and the will to preserve God's words engraved forever on a thing of stone, against lightness, movement, and the thrust of life—that is, the fluidities of oral memory.

The Hand That Writes

By smashing the tablets, Moses undoes the act of engraving, inscribing, and preserving. Moses' hand is, among its other functions, a hand that writes. At the end of his life, he writes the Torah; earlier, he had written—engraved—the second set of stone tablets. Writing down God's dictation, his hand acts as pen. Accepting the divinely inscribed tablets into his hands, he embraces the act of writing.[50]

Michael Fried has written about the work of writers, painters, and surgeons, all of whom represent and remake the world—dissecting, describing, sometimes disfiguring and causing suffering, even in the interest of recovery. He focuses his discussion on the contrast between the "spaces" of reality and of literary representation, which requires "that a human character, ordinarily upright and so to speak forward-looking, be rendered horizontal and upward-facing so as to match the horizontality and upward-facingness of the blank page on which the action of inscription was taking place."[51]

The power relations of the writer's hand, eye, and subject do, in a real sense, *subject*—throw the subject down, as well as subject the reader—onto the blank page. When Moses raises his hand in Egypt and at the Sea, there is physical pain and terror in the world; bodies are cast down on the ground, laid low. (According to Edmund Burke, the ability to hurt is the hallmark of the sublime.) But Moses' hands are also implicated in the production of the Torah itself. We read these narratives as writing on the page: words that have passed through Moses' hands, representing God's voice. And these hands hold conflicted experience: they are flesh; they have been lifted in prayer, palms spread to heaven. This too has happened before the eyes of the people, moving their bodies and hearts to imitation.

Inscribing, describing, dominating, praying—are Moses' hands open or closed? What has happened to the rod? Is it exchanged for the pen or the chisel? What is it that the people see that affects their hearts? Perhaps Moses' hands surrender one kind of power, as the people allow Moses' hands to lead them upward to the source of their gesture…as the narrative surrenders its claim to reduce the moment to the *writable*, and to set it down.

Letters Fly Off

The tension inherent in such moments comes to a climax, I suggest, when Moses undoes God's writing on the stone tablets. Moses' hands open and let the tablets fly. This is done before the eyes of all Israel: it responds to and challenges their human desire to confirm the evidence of their senses—to be redeemed from the terrors of time by an object hard as stone, eternally present, inscribed by God personally.

"If the tablets had not been smashed," says the Talmud, "the Torah would never have been forgotten from Israel."[52] Two different readings of this passage are possible: (1) if only the tablets had not been smashed, then the Torah would never have been forgotten; or (2) smashing the tablets made forgetting possible—which has generated the dynamic world of the Oral Law.

Rav Yitzhak Hutner reads the talmudic text in this second way, elaborating on the virtues of forgetting.[53] The life of the Oral Torah begins here. When conscious memory ends, the mind begins to reconstruct. Because of forgetting, a world of interpretation and vital argument springs up. What the people have once seen is immediately forgotten upon the death of Moses: three hundred laws vanish from the national memory until the judge many generations hence, Otniel ben Kenaz, retrieves them through his pilpul, his brilliantly creative interpretations.[54] In the words of the rabbis, "Sometimes, the unmaking (*bittul*) of Torah is its fulfillment."[55]

Memory holds on to what one knows; forgetting or smashing the icons of the past makes it possible to know differently, to access by a different route that which was once simply present. Here is both loss and gain: stability, continuity, things hard as stone are fragmented, fly off into the air, and draw the human eye upward after them. The sense of the body responding will, in time, turn the eyes and heart upward, participating in the movement of the object, anticipating its trajectory. The eye moves through possible viewpoints, establishing a relationship with what is seen and what is no longer seen.

"Meet it is I set it down," says Hamlet as he seizes his tablets, "that one may smile and smile and be a villain."[56] To "set it down" is to control on the horizontal, on the blank page, the overwhelming impact of human treachery. It is also to remember it forever in this reduced form. To forget it might be to release it to unconscious transformation, elaborating it in a world of diffuse impressions. To set it down, to master it in writing, is to preserve it and to become the curator of experience; to smash it is to restore it to its elements, to pure potential—it is to practice a different kind of learning, internalized and free. Unmaking things, as Susan Stewart argues, perhaps gives value to our making.[57]

So if the survival of the Torah has depended on the organic forgetting of history, Rav Hutner suggests that this has given the Oral Torah its particular dynamism. If Moses' greatest moment was when he smashed the tablets before the eyes of all the people, then an eyewitness report is being invoked to complex ends. The visible, graspable Torah, written by the finger of God, becomes, in an instant, invisible; its letters fly off. The people see the thing unmade, liberated into its elements.

In the Presence of the Rock

At the second rock-water incident, God tells Moses and Aaron to "speak to the rock before their [the people's] eyes" (Numbers 20:8). Once before they had seen sounds: at Mount Sinai, they had "seen the voices" (Exodus 20:15).[58] Something of the power of God's word had affected them with the primal, traumatic impact of vision. Perhaps, suggests the *Meshekh Hokhmah*, now—at the end of the wilderness time, as the Israelites are about to re-enact the Sinai covenant—God wishes them to re-experience the visionary impact of the word.[59] At Sinai, they had been confronted with its demand. Now, each one will envisage Moses delivering it to unimpressible rock. They will bring themselves to bear on the scene; their eyes will be sanctified by seeing holy words.

However, Moses, because of his anger with the people, calls only on their sense of *hearing*: "Listen, you rebels, shall we produce water for you from this rock?" (Numbers 20:10). Seeing God's message would have generated in the people faith, trust, and intimate connection. But Moses fails to engage their depth-perception of the moment. To see God's words is to bring one's personal presence—both conscious and unconscious—to the scene; it is to be affected to the roots of one's very being by something staged before one's eyes.

But for this to happen, one must have eyes that can see. Such an intensity of vision is evoked in the midrash: "Each person saw himself or herself standing in the presence of the rock."[60] This is a scene of presences: the people are gathered *el p'nei ha-sela*, face to face with the rock. Each person sees his or her own presence in the presence of the rock. Looking at the thing, one endows it with a face; a space is created between two faces. One enhances the rock with one's own life.

The Impressionist Moment

The English psychoanalyst Donald Winnicott calls the space between mother and baby "potential space"; it is electric with fantasy and dream. In this space, mother and baby create each other. Facing the rock, each person experiences him or herself facing the rock.

A similar experience is described by John Berger, who writes of the way that the subject of a painting may, breathtakingly, convince the viewer that it has been seen. The light-energy that is transmitted through the painted object "is the true subject of the painting."[61] Aglow with what lies behind the apparent, paintings interrogate appearances:

> Every artist discovers that drawing—when it is an urgent activity—is a two-way process. To draw is not only to measure and put down; it is also to receive. When the intensity of looking reaches a certain degree, one becomes aware of an equally intense energy coming towards one, through the appearance of whatever it is one is scrutinizing....The encounter...is a ferocious and inarticulated dialogue. To sustain it requires faith....Every event which has been really painted—so that the pictorial language opens—joins the community of everything else that has been painted.[62]

To sustain this meeting of two symmetrical energies, running between the eye and the work, requires faith, Berger says. In our scene of potential revelation at the rock, the people are to be invited to see, to look hard, with eyes open wide. This, claims *Meshekh Ḥokhmah*, is precisely what Moses fails to do when he urges the people to simply "listen." He is not merely neglecting their eyes; he is, in a sense, obscuring a way of seeing that both requires and generates *emunah*—hence God's pronouncement, "Because you did not trust Me...' (Numbers 20:12).

Strikingly, Berger meditates on this faith-dimension of a painting:

> Paintings are prophecies received from the past, prophecies about *what the spectator is seeing in front of the painting at that moment*.... [A] visual image...is always a comment on an *absence*....Visual images, based on appearances, always speak of disappearance.[63]

In another essay, still more eloquent about the themes that concern us here, Berger amplifies his thinking about the paradox of the visible and the invisible in a work of art. "The Eyes of Claude

Monet" focuses on the sadness in Monet's eyes, which is not merely
personal but concerned also with the melancholy that pervades his
new Impressionist school of painting. It acknowledges that "visibility
itself should be considered flux."[64] The history of painting will never
be the same again.

"Impressionism" was the term used to describe an early painting
by Monet, "Impression Soleil Levant." In the new painting method,

> ...The optical truthfulness and the *objective* vagueness...
> render the scene makeshift, threadbare, decrepit. It is an image
> of homelessness....An impression is more or less fleeting;
> it is what is *left behind* because the scene has disappeared
> or changed....An impression later becomes, like a memory,
> impossible to verify....The new relation between scene and
> seer was such that now the scene was more fugitive, more
> chimerical than the seer.[65]

"A new relation between what you are seeing and what you have seen"
uncovers the meaning of other lilacs, other water-lilies of one's own
experience. "What I want to represent is what exists between the
motif and me," Monet affirms.[67]

The impressionist painting no longer invites one into an alcove of
changeless time and space. What it shows "is painted in such a way
that you are *compelled to recognize that it is no longer there.*" The viewer's
memories are "often pleasurable...yet they are also anguished, because
each viewer remains alone....*Memory* is the unacknowledged axis of
all Monet's work. His famous love of the sea...of rivers, of water, was
perhaps a symbolic way of speaking of tides, sources, recurrence."[67]

At the end of his essay, Berger singles out a late painting of a cliff
near Dieppe. Here, Berger claims, Monet himself misunderstood the
nature of his own achievement: he believed that he was interpreting
the effect of sunlight as it dissolved every detail of grass and shrub
into a cloth of honey hung by the sea. But he wasn't, and the painting

has really very little to do with sunlight. What he was dissolving into the honey-cloth were all of his previous memories of that cliff, so that it could absorb and contain them all.

In his paintings of the water-lilies during the last period of his life, Monet's aim was "to preserve everything essential about the garden....The painted lily pond was to be a pond that remembered all."[68] "More alone than ever before, more ridden by the anxiety that their own experience was ephemeral and meaningless,"[69] painters wish "to save *all*."[70]

Let us now return to the eyes of the Israelites, and to the "impressionist" moment staged by God in front of the rock. This is a scene about to disappear. Like Monet's cliff, the rock is the stone-hard repository of all previous memories of rocks, mountains, and revelations—as well as of hands, eyes, rods, water, blood, and snakes. What is to be done with this resistant but ephemeral object so that it will yield water? What the impressionist painter does, says Berger, is to infuse the seen into a new relationship with what has been seen. This acknowledges that the impression is what has been *left behind*: fugitive, impossible to verify. In this sense, it is "a comment on an absence"; such visual images speak of disappearance.[71]

Of Words and Rocks

"Take the rod," God says, "and speak to the rock before their eyes" (Numbers 20:8). The address is to be before their eyes; the moment of faith will be known in that way of looking that acknowledges the fleetingness of the moment. What they will see is the rock, the rod — the visible objects; but also the act of speaking to the rock. This is to make a visual impression on them. It will absorb and contain all the memories of words, prophecies, commandments, and decrees.

At a later time, the prophet will say: "Behold, My word is like fire—declares God—and like a hammer that shatters rock!"[72] And, at a still later time, the sages will meditate on this image of a rock, together with their own interpretive activity: "Just as this hammer splits the rock into many fragments, so too does each word that issues from the mouth of God split into seventy languages."[73]

Much later still, Kafka will relate the parable of Prometheus and his rock. He will offer four versions of the myth. The first is the traditional myth: Prometheus is clamped to a rock for betraying the secrets of the gods to men, and the gods send eagles to feed on his liver, which is perpetually renewed. In the second, Prometheus presses himself in agony into the rock until he merges with it. In the third and fourth versions, all the details are forgotten over the course of millennia; everyone grows weary of the story—even the gods, even the angels, even the wound that closes wearily.

What remains after this? What is left behind? "The inexplicable mass of rock. The legend tried to explain the inexplicable. As it came out of a substratum of truth, it had in turn to end in the inexplicable."[74] The substratum of truth underlies all the weariness of time; this is the timeless quality of the inexplicable that will, in Robert Alter's words, "eternally compel urgent questions."[75]

For Berger, Monet's rock is part of the future succession of images that are to be seen with the intense energy of the painter's desire to "save all." The substance of the rock is reduced to a frontier, with light coming from behind it toward one who looks with this visual desire.

We recall Walter Benjamin: "For an experienced event is finite...a remembered event is infinite, because it is only a key to everything that happened before it and after it."[76] Such a remembered event is the scene at Merivah: inexplicable, emerging from a substratum of truth. For the remembering mind, it is a key to everything that came before it and that will follow after it. From Mount Sinai to the rock at Merivah to Kafka's rock, an aura suffuses the vestiges of the sacred. For Walter Benjamin, this aura is the object steeped in memory. For those who stood in the presence of the rock at Merivah, a space was created in which each individual might see him or herself standing in that fraught presence. Like painters, the Israelites are to learn a way of seeing that involves receiving the revelations of the sacred. To be capable of this receptivity, involuntary memory must be allowed its sway.

"To see is to forget the name of the thing one sees," writes Paul Valéry. Seeing in this way dissolves the rock and the rod into a stream of "impressions." The prophet Ezekiel speaks of change, flux, forgetting, as the marks of redemption: "And I will give you a new heart and put a new spirit into you; I will remove the heart of stone from your flesh and give you a heart of flesh" (Ezekiel 36:26). In this vision, the stony heart is an alien presence in human flesh. God's promise of a redeemed reality is to reconstitute the human being as *all flesh*—all impressible, receptive to impressions, responsive to the light-energy coming from behind the visible.[77]

Heart of Stone, Heart of Flesh

In the presence of the rock at Merivah, a critical developmental moment has arrived:

> When a child is small, the teacher hits him and educates him. But when he grows up, he is corrected with words. So, too, God said to Moses: "When this rock was young, you struck it, as it is said, 'And you shall strike the rock' (Exodus 17:6). But now, 'You shall speak to the rock'—recite over it a chapter of Torah and that will produce water from the rock!"[78]

God introduces Moses to a new way of understanding his—and the people's—experience. Instead of regarding his earlier experience with the rock at Rephidim as a precedent for future behavior, he is to regard it as an early stage of the people's development, to be transcended as the child/rock matures. What had once been an effective teaching tool (namely, striking) is now to be replaced by the use of language. The early memory is not cut in stone; it grows by opening to less concrete impressions. So too: now, in memory—involuntary memory—the rock flashes back to the scene of an earlier self. It has become a holding space, preserving both the integrity of self-experience and the acute sense of transformation. The self has evolved. And the rock registers in imagination as capable of maturing; like the stony heart, it is seen in reverie as softening into flesh. If Moses speaks—a chapter, a law—the rock will, like Monet's cliff, essentially dissolve.

Beyond Miracles

This developmental moment—reciting a chapter of Torah in the presence of the rock—becomes, in the reading of *Ha·ameik Davar*,[79] the central image of the narrative. In this view, the moment of Merivah is to prepare the people for the post-miraculous new epoch, which they are now entering. This fortieth year in the wilderness sees a fading-out of miracles and direct interventions by God in human life. In tune with this process, Miriam's death also means the disappearance of her well, which had provided water for the people throughout their travels. Strikingly, *Ha·ameik Davar* claims that this well was not miraculous: it had become a "natural" resource for the people. When it vanished, this crisis needed to be dealt with in the same way as, in the future, in the Holy Land, the people would deal with crises of drought: by gathering and engaging in the dual activities of learning Torah and praying.

The moment at Merivah is therefore a transitional moment; it is precisely *not* a miracle that is called for here, but rather a natural, organic human response to such situations of drought. Now they are to learn how to reactivate natural water-sources: by engaging in words of study and prayer.

So God tells Moses to speak to the rock. Obviously, the rock cannot hear; Moses is to speak not *with* it but *in its presence*. He and Aaron are to speak in such a way as to move the people to inner growth and to prayer. In this way, the rock will—naturally, spontaneously—give forth its own, familiar waters. In addition, as a kind of afterthought, God adds: "You shall bring forth for them water from the rock" (Numbers 20:8). In case the "natural" strategy of Torah and prayer does not work to produce water, then Moses will act alone—in the old miraculous manner, using his rod to produce water. But the miraculous is to be only a fallback position; what God really wants is to educate the people about their new post-wilderness lives in the land, and about the practices that will enable them to live organically in a new place and time.

In this reading, the water that emerges from the rock after Moses has struck it twice is, in fact, inferior to the natural resources that he failed to produce. The miracle of the rod is, at this point in time, anachronistic. Moses loses the opportunity to teach the people the natural resources of generative language. His failure, in this view, is not that he did not speak. It is that he spoke—in the rock's presence—words of anger against the people. Instead of apprenticing them to Torah and prayer, he attacked them for their sins: they alone are responsible for the drought. His tone rings with angry scorn: "Listen, you rebels, shall we produce water for you from this rock?" (Numbers 20:10).

The result is that instead of guiding the people toward their own spiritual resources, instead of acting with Aaron, the man of peace, Moses acts alone: he speaks alone as old chagrins overwhelm him. He then performs the old, banal miracle that he remembers so well from the past. The rod, which had long been withdrawn from circulation, is now used not only on the rock but first—symbolically—against the people. In his exasperation, he strikes the people with his words.

In this startling reversal of conventional readings, *Ha·ameik Davar* redefines Moses' failure. It is not that he fell short of a fully splendid miracle, but rather that he overshot the new "natural" mode of a life shaped by words. As *Ha·ameik Davar* puts it, when it came to the moment, he "forgot" the law that he was about to teach the people:

the words of Torah that would inspire them to pray. Forgetting the law is, in classic midrashic sources, associated with anger. Moses finds himself assailed by anger more than once in his life; at such moments, the midrash remarks, he forgets the law. Here, anger drives him off course, effacing the words that might have allowed the people to glimpse a new way of being.[81]

Generating Holiness

If the miracle of the rod has suddenly come to seem hackneyed, the alternative state of dynamic self-awareness—of being drawn by words toward a place of faith and holiness—could have been evoked only by words of a certain kind. *Ha·ameik Davar* describes the desired use of words as "soft," in contrast to the angry, rejecting words with which Moses in fact addressed the people.

In the Merivah moment, then, Moses does speak to the people, but his language "misfires." His speaking was to have a performative power: words of Torah would have given birth to prayer and, in turn, to water from the rock. Language here was to be an act, not describing but transforming reality. Instead, Moses speaks so as to wither possibilities in the bud. As Rambam reads the scene,[82] Moses' scornful speech misrepresents God's words. He "forgets" to address the inner lives of the people, neglecting the dynamic power of Torah and prayer to create a sense of holiness among them.

The Talmud offers guidance on how holiness may be generated: "'And I shall be sanctified in the midst of the Israelites' (Leviticus 22:32)—How is God sanctified in the midst of the people? By speaking words of holiness in public."[83] So God turns immediately to Moses and Aaron: "Because you did not trust Me enough to affirm My sanctity before the eyes of the Israelite people..." (Numbers 20:12). They did not speak words of holiness so as to create faith in the power of those words. Instead, words were wielded as blunt weapons. The people remain unprepared for the gentler, more organic movements of self-awareness. The miracle that is not God's will drives a wedge between them and the future.

Two-Way Process

The power of language is articulated with great precision by Emerson: "All language is vehicular and transitive, and is good, as ferries and horses are, for conveyance, not as farms and houses are, for homestead."[84] Language as vehicular and transitive: it is designed to move one, not to settle one; like ferries and horses, it "can lead me thither where I would be."[85] The poet takes things as occasions for words, as signs for words. In the presence of the inexplicable rock, words of Torah and prayer might have carried the people into their future lives, already knowing something of their own capacity for transformation. In his reading of the rock narrative, *Ha·ameik Davar* carries us inward, to the impressionable heart of flesh that responds to language.

What, then, is the *emunah*, the faith that has sadly not happened here? The Maharal offers us a key: the experience of *emunah* is the experience of being drawn after God, willingly, by the divine word alone.[86] This experience generates joy. And joy, in turn, demonstrates the existence of *emunah*. Moses is to speak to the rock so that it will transcend its stony nature and be moved in attraction after God. To be attracted to an object is, paradoxically, to be at one's most free, at one's most autonomous.

We remember Berger's artist who discovers the two-way process in which, in one's intense gaze, "one becomes aware of an equally intense energy coming towards one."[87] "To sustain it [this dialogue] requires faith....It is like a burrowing in the dark, a burrowing under the apparent. The great images occur when the two tunnels meet and join perfectly....it is like something thrown and caught." This is the moment of most full and most free being: both receiving and giving in one motion. This is achieved, says Maharal, by language (*dibbur*) alone, not by main force. With a rock responding freely to words alone, the image will leave its trace on the people's imagination, creating a model for their own inner possibility.

Even rocks can discover their own power of response. Rav Yitzḥak Hutner puts it like this: the miracle of the rock that produces water includes the miracle of its effect on the human soul.[89] In other words, the most miraculous thing is the movement of the soul, in being drawn after God. Other images might have served equally well to express the gift of water, such as heavy rains or deep underground springs.[90] But the image of water from a rock has an intimate resonance for those before whose eyes it is enacted. It speaks to the possibility of a new, more responsive nature opening within them. As in a dream or a reverie, the stony heart gives way to the heart of flesh; an immature child grows to discover the power of language for conveyance. Through language, even a rock may be moved from here to there, from jagged dryness to vital flow. This is the joy of which Maharal writes. He calls it *emunah*: faith, trust, two-way processes that draw and are drawn.

The Inexplicable Rock?

The narrative of the rock at Merivah yields its teaching by negation. After the drama has apparently reached resolution—namely, the thirsty people have drunk their fill—God speaks with words that destabilize everything: "Because you did not trust Me enough to affirm My sanctity before the eyes of the Israelite people, therefore you shall not lead this congregation into the land" (Numbers 20:12).

Ironically, there is perhaps no narrative biblical description of the process of faith and sanctification that conveys as much as this description of its absence. What has *not* happened here is an inward (if collective) process that is evoked most powerfully in its failure. Here, we may say, the inexplicable rock comes to life in the text of the Torah.

The disjunction between the apparently happy narrative and God's dire sentence has mystified and provoked generations of readers. Like Kafka's rock, the story comes out of a substratum of truth in turn to end in the inexplicable. The desire to understand, to make the thing a sign of words, generates interpretations of the meaning of both belief (*emunah*) and sanctification (*k'dushah*). The words, inexplicable in this context, become a thing that entitles us to other words. But in the end the mystery remains, focused precisely on that disjunction between the happy miracle narrative of a first reading and God's words that challenge future readings.

Precisely here in this disjunction, we can trace a kind of closure to the story. The last verse reads: "These are the waters of Merivah, where the Israelites quarreled with the Eternal; through which God was *sanctified by them*" (Numbers 20:13). Much ink has been spilled over these words. The place, it seems, has two names: Kadesh, as it is named at the beginning of the story, and Merivah, the name given at the end of the story: "holiness" and "quarrel." The name Merivah is explained in the last verse of the narrative, but the very last words of the verse revert back to the original, unexplained name of the place: "And God was sanctified (*va-yikkadeish*) by them." By a surprising turn, this place of failures and absences does, after all, achieve a different sanctification. In the urgency of generations of readers to find meaning, there is oblique testimony to a passion for the holy. The place will have retroactively earned its name.

This disjunction, strikingly, is the place where Abravanel[91] finds his key to the meaning of the narrative. In his reading, the central reason for God's decree is not given in this narrative at all. There are repressed narratives that account for the decree: namely, the earlier major failures of Moses and Aaron. (Aaron made the golden calf; he did not resist the people's rebellion and die a martyr's death, in sanctification of God's name. And Moses shares responsibility for the disaster of the spies, insofar as his questions to the spies undermined their faith.) But Abravanel's essential provocative point is that the narrative of the rock is intended to obscure the true etiology of sin and punishment. If the reader finds the rock narrative of insufficient gravity to account for God's judgment, then this impression is correct: the rock story screens other, graver narratives.

Abravanel is well aware that his idea of repressed meanings is radical. Why would the Torah hide its meanings, split the narrative of sin and punishment, and merge two separate sins—Moses' and Aaron's—into one? Indeed, he offers another example of this dynamic: the death of Aaron's two sons is indeed "explained" in the text: "they offered strange fire, that God had not commanded, before the Eternal" (Leviticus 10:1). But this does not prevent the commentaries from searching far and wide for "other sins" to attribute to Aaron's sons. The existence of these other interpretations indicates that the Torah may have obscured the true cause of the priests' deaths.

Abravanel does not offer a theoretical justification for his idea. However, such displacements, in which a simple, concrete explanation is regarded as a screen for other things, are familiar to us in modern literary and psychoanalytical texts. In the narrated life of Moses or Aaron or Aaron's sons, some preoccupation is being worked through; there emerges an arc that can only be suggested by the immediate objects of the narrative. In such a vision, the reader's search for unequivocal explanations may be misleading. Moses is in the end unfound, unknown. He is both revealed and hidden. In each event of his life, there are "impressions"—that is, things left behind. For the reader, too, there are impressions—such as those left by remembered events, which are "a key to everything that happened before it and after it."[92]

Kenneth Burke writes eloquently of the world of nature that "gleams secretly with a most fantastic shimmer of words and social relationships."[93] The midrashic literature deals with this "impressionist" world of nature and the supernatural.[94] Secretly, the Torah reveals and conceals. Implicitly, its enigmatic stories entitle the reader to read, and to speak.

Ben Azzai is given to us in a luminous midrash as such a reader and speaker:

> Once, as Ben Azzai sat and expounded Torah, fire flared around him. They went and told Rabbi Akiva, "Rabbi, as Ben Azzai sits and expounds Torah, fire flares around him." He went to him and said, "I hear that as you were expounding Torah, fire flared around you." He replied, "That is so." He said, "Were you perhaps engaged in the secrets of the divine chariot?" He replied, "No. I was just threading words of Torah with one another, and then with the words of the prophets, and the prophets with Scriptures, and the words were as joyful as when they were given at Sinai, and they were as sweet as at their original utterance. And were they not originally given at Sinai in fire, as it says, 'And the mountain burned in fire?'" (Exodus 19:18).[95]

Encircled by fire, Ben Azzai teaches in the manner called *doreish* (i.e., in the genre of midrash): interpreting, searching, soliciting the text for its hidden meanings. Word spreads like fire: "Ben Azzai is sitting and interpreting, with the fire flaring around him." Three times the words are repeated, like an incantation. The fire flickers and flares, making all space unstable. To Rabbi Akiva's accusation ("Have you been engaged in forbidden mystical practices?"), Ben Azzai serenely, almost domestically, replies that he is merely threading beads, bringing texts into electric contact with each other. What he is doing is (merely!) remembering, re-enacting the experience of Sinai. His activity generates joy and sweetness: this is the aura that flickers around him, as sweet and joyful as the original fire of revelation.

What Ben Azzai is doing is no mystery, he says. As in the Maharal's account of *emunah*, he is being drawn into the otherness of God's words and, at the same time, he is drawing together the separate beads—out of context—into fiery new chains of meaning. This, he says, is sweetness and joy: the two-way process of human and divine energies meeting, so that something emerges from behind the appearances, becomes visible, and rejoices.

NOTES

[1] See Lon L. Fuller, *The Morality of Law* (New Haven: Yale University Press, 1969).

[2] Sifra, *Sh'mini* 12:3.

[3] See Ramban to Leviticus 19:2. Ramban focuses on the higher sensibility of holiness that transcends minimal legal requirements. For a more detailed treatment of Ramban's commentary on this verse, see the essay by Yitzchak Blau elsewhere in this volume.

[4] Ovadiah ben Jacob Sforno (c. 1475, Cesena [Italy]–1550, Bologna) was one of the greatest medieval commentators on Scripture.

[5] Sifra, *K'doshim* 1:1.

[6] See ibn Ezra to Numbers 20:6.

[7] See Numbers 14:10ff., 16:19ff., and 17:7ff.

[8] At the close of Deuteronomy, the failure to sanctify God is spelled out again, just before Moses' death: "…because you did not sanctify Me in the midst of the Israelites" (Deuteronomy 32:51).

[9] Hayyim ibn Attar (1696–1743) lived in Morocco and the land of Israel.

[10] *Or Ha-ḥayyim* to Numbers 20:8.

[11] See Ramban to Numbers 20:7.

[12] In psychoanalytic parlance, this process is similar to identification: "I am [not] a rock."

[13] Maimonides, *Hakdamot Ha-Rambam La-Mishnah*, ed. Yitzhak Shilat (Jerusalem: Yeshivat Birkat Mosheh, 1992), ch. 4, p. 240.

[14] See Elchanan Samet, *Iyyunim B'farshiyyot Ha-shavua: Vayikra-B'midbar-D'varim*, Second Series (Yeshivat Birkat Moshe: Maaleh Adumim, 2005), pp. 254–255.

[15] Ramban reads Korah's rebellion as an immediate offshoot of the narrative of the spies, and therefore as happening in the second year in the wilderness.

[16] Rashi to Deuteronomy 34:5.

[17] Rashi to Deuteronomy 34:6.

[18] See B. Sotah 14a.

[19] The law of the red heifer is called a *ḥok* (or *ḥukkah*): the quintessential pure decree, resisting normal rational inquiry.

[20] *Yalkut Shimoni* §759.

[21] The first narrative takes place near *Ḥorev*, at Rephidim; the second near Edom, on the plains of Moab.

[22] Cf. Numbers 17:25. If this rod is identical with Aaron's rod which flowered in the Korah narrative, its history becomes more complicated. I intend here to focus on the history of Moses' rod (called "the rod of God") as it appears in the miracle stories in Exodus and in Numbers 20.

[23] Meir Simhah Hakohen of Dvinsk (Eastern Europe, 1843–1926); see comment to Exodus 16:33–34.

[24] The *Meshekh Ḥokhmah* cites Mekhilta, *Va-yissa* 6:3; and Rambam, *Guide for the Perplexed*, II 29.

[25] See B. Horayot 12a.

[26] M. Rosh Hashanah 3:8.

[27] Mekhilta, *B'shallaḥ* 1 (to Exodus 17:11).

[28] Pirkei D'Rabbi Eliezer (ed. Warsaw, 1852), p. 44.

[29] See Ramban to Exodus 17:9: "While he was praying with his palms outstretched to heaven, he grasped nothing in his hands."

[30] Robert Alter, *Necessary Angels: Tradition and Modernity in Kafka, Benjamin, and Scholem* (Cambridge: Harvard University Press, 1991), p. 104.

[31] Walter Benjamin, *Illuminations: Essays and Reflections* (New York: Schocken, 1969), p. 204; emphasis added.

[32] Even including the plagues at the Sea of Reeds. See *Or Ha-ḥayyim* to Exodus 11:9 for a psychological reading of Pharaoh's intransigence.

[33] See Ramban to Exodus 7:16.

[34] See Rashi's comment to the verse: "Your words will be effective in liberating them."

[35] B. Shabbat 97a.

[36] This is the NJPS translation.

[37] See Exodus 2:7 with its repetition of the word *lakh*, "for you."

[38] Abraham Saba (1140–1508), who lived in Spain, Portugal, and Morocco; here, he cites a midrash that is found in *Torah Sh'leimah* §51.

[39] B. Sotah 12b.

[40] Rashi to Exodus 2:12: "He saw what he had done to him at home and in the field….He saw that no future proselyte would be born of him."

[41] B. Sanhedrin 58b.

[42] See the comment of Rema on Shulhan Arukh, Ḥoshen Mishpat 34:4; and also Torah *T'mimah* to Exodus 2:13.

[43] See Numbers 15:30.

[44] Benjamin, *Illuminations*, p. 204.

[45] See, e.g., Rashi to Numbers 17:5: "'As God spoke by the hand of Moses'— in the same way as Moses was afflicted with leprosy." The dead metaphor is transformed into a specific moment of memory and judgment.

[46] See Rashi to Genesis 42:24.

[47] Y. Berakhot 5:1.

[48] See B. Shabbat 87.

[49] Y. Taanit 4:5.

[50] Moses is classically identified as the *m'hokeik*, "engraver" or "law-maker"; see Rashi to Deuteronomy 33:21, as well as B. Bava Batra 15a.

51 Michael Fried, *Realism, Writing, Disfiguration* (Chicago and London: University of Chicago Press, 1987), pp. 99–100. See also Gillian Beer, *Open Fields: Science in Cultural Encounter* (New York: Oxford University Press, 1996), pp. 14–15.

52 B. Eiruvin 54a.

53 *Sefer Pahad Yitzhak—Hanukkah* (Brooklyn, NY: Mosad Gur Aryeh, 1984), p. 36.

54 B. Temurah 16a.

55 B. Menahot 99b.

56 *Hamlet*, act I, scene v, line 108.

57 See Susan Stewart, *The Poet's Freedom: A Notebook on Making* (Chicago and London: University of Chicago Press, 2011), pp. 1–2.

58 See Rashi to Exodus 20:15, s.v. ro·im et ha-kolot.

59 Meir Simhah Cohen of Dvinsk, *Sefer Meshekh Hokhmah* (ed. Riga, 1927), p. 297.

60 B'midbar Rabbah 19:5.

61 John Berger, *Keeping a Rendezvous* (New York: Pantheon, 1991), p. 129.

62 Ibid., pp. 129–130.

63 John Berger, *Sense of Sight* (New York: Vintage, 1975), pp. 206–207.

64 Ibid., p. 189.

65 Ibid., p. 191.

66 Ibid., p. 193.

67 Ibid., p. 195.

68 Ibid., p. 196.

69 Ibid., p. 196.

70 Ibid., p. 195.

71 Ibid., p. 207.

72 Jeremiah 23:29.

73 B. Shabbat 88a.

74 Franz Kafka, *Parables and Paradoxes* (New York: Schocken, 1961), p. 83.

75 Alter, *Necessary Angels*, p. 92.

76 Benjamin, *Illuminations*, p. 204.

77 Samson Raphael Hirsch, commenting on Genesis 2:21, connects *basar*, "flesh," with the verb *l'vasser*, "to announce, proclaim," suggesting that "the human body is the herald of the spirit to the world"; it brings consciousness of the world and is the medium of impact on the world. See Hirsch, *The Pentateuch*, trans. Isaac Levy (London: Isaac Levy, 1959), vol. 1, p. 68.

78 *Yalkut Shimoni* §763.

79 Naftali Zvi Yehudah Berlin (1816–1893; also called the Netziv); *Ha·ameik Davar: Torat Elohim* (Jerusalem: Chemed, 1975), vol. 4, pp. 174–175.

80 Miriam's well is listed among the ten things created at twilight on the Shabbat eve of creation (Pirkei Avot 5:8). These last-moment creations occupy

a transitional space between the natural and the miraculous.

81 Sifra, *Sh'mini* 60:2 (to Leviticus 10:20).

82 *Hakdamot Ha-Rambam La-Mishnah*, p. 240.

83 B. Megillah 23b.

84 Emerson, "The Poet," in *Selected Essays* (New York: Penguin Books, 1982), p. 279.

85 Ibid.

86 Judah Loew ben Bezalel (1535–1609), *G'vurot Hashem* (Bnai Brak [Israel]: Yahadut, 1982), p. 44.

87 Berger, *Rendezvous*, p. 130.

88 Berger, *Sense of Sight*, p. 131.

89 Yitzhak Hutner, *Sefer Pahad Yitzhak—Pesah* (Brooklyn, NY: Mosad Gur Aryeh, 1984), p. 40.

90 See the comment to Numbers 20:8 by Yaakov Tzvi Mecklenburg in his *Ha-k'tav V'ha-kabbalah* (ed. Frankfurt, 1880), p. 31a.

91 Don Isaac Abravanel (1437–1508) to Numbers 20 (ed. Warsaw, 1863), p. 20b.

92 Benjamin, *Illuminations*, p. 204.

93 Kenneth Burke, "What Are the Signs of What? A Theory of Entitlement," in *Language as Symbolic Action: Essays on Life, Literature, and Method* (Berkeley: University of California Press, 1966), p. 379. See also Richard Poirier, "Frost, Winnicott, Burke," in Peter L. Rudnytsky, ed., *Transitional Objects and Potential Spaces: Literary Uses of D.W. Winnicott* (New York: Columbia University Press, 1993), pp. 216–228.

94 The kabbalistic idea of the *r'shimu* (literally: the impression, the trace) is a major theme in its world of meanings.

95 Shir Hashirim Rabbah 1:10.

·

Sanctity as Defined by the Silent Prayer

Benjamin Blech

Sanctity isn't meant to be an esoteric subject reserved solely for rabbis, theologians, and scholars. It is a theme that has been accorded a blessing that is to be recited by every Jew three times a day as part of the Amidah, the Silent Prayer composed by the Men of the Great Assembly, in order to give voice to our collective desire to communicate with the Almighty.

The Amidah is the paradigm of prayer. It is what the Talmud and rabbinic commentators refer to as "[the] *t'fillah*." It is the one prayer at whose beginning and ending we take three steps backward followed by three steps forward, indicating our awareness of entering and then subsequently leaving the presence of the supreme Sovereign. The wording and structure of this prayer are profoundly significant. Its text carries the spiritual weight of authorship by saintly scholars imbued with prophetic inspiration.

All this is by way of introducing the reader to the importance (as well as the practical relevance) of the insights of the Amidah regarding the theme of holiness. It is within the context of the words chosen for our daily conversations with God that we will discover how the concept of sanctity helps us resolve two of the most pressing problems of life: How can we be certain that God exists? And if indeed there is a God, what does that mean for our mission here on earth?

Can We Ever Prove God's Existence?

Philosophers throughout the ages have debated this issue without coming to a universally agreed-upon resolution. Theists continue to believe and atheists to deny. Each side has its prominent spokespeople, yet in the final analysis neither can present irrefutable proof to declare its position victorious.

For atheists, this inability to fully prove God's existence with the exactitude of scientific methodology or the logic of human reason is sufficient to reject the possibility of a divine Being. What we cannot verify, they claim, must assuredly be discarded.

Yet, many of our most fundamental assumptions can never be verified or proven; they are simply grasped as truths beyond question. There is no proof, for example, of the existence of other human beings besides ourselves, yet we are convinced that they do exist. In the words of Alfred Tennyson:

> Thou canst not prove the Nameless, O my son,
> Nor canst thou prove the world thou movest in,
> Thou canst not prove that thou art body alone,
> Nor canst thou prove that thou art spirit alone,
> Nor canst thou prove that thou art both in one;
> Thou canst not prove that thou art immortal—nay, my son,
> Nor yet that thou art mortal—nay, my son,
> Thou canst not prove that I, who speak with thee,
> Am not thyself in converse with thyself,
> For nothing worthy proving can be proven,
> Nor yet disproven, wherefore thou be wise,
> Cleave ever to the sunnier side of doubt,
> And cling to Faith beyond the forms of Faith![1]

Theists are hardly surprised that the evidence of our senses cannot demonstrate the existence of that which is beyond our senses, nor that our reasoning cannot logically confirm that which transcends the power of our intellect. Only the Almighty can truly grasp the Almighty. As Solomon ibn Gabirol put it, "If I could understand God, I would be God." It is precisely God's greatness that precludes our ability to fully describe God or prove the existence of the Divine.

Where decisive proof cannot play a role, both theists and atheists can share no more than a *belief* in the truth of their position. Both are guided by faith—faith in the truth of their conviction. And that is why both must be judged by the same standard: not which view can be proven, but rather which one is more convincing.

It is in this light that we need to understand the three opening blessings of the Amidah.

The Three-Part Section of Praise

The Amidah is divided into three sections. The first, consisting of three blessings, is called *shevah*, praise. The second section, consisting of thirteen blessings (expanded from an original twelve), comprises *bakashah*, requests. The final section, consisting of three blessings, is known as *hoda·ah*, giving thanks. The Talmud tells us that the opening blessings of praise have a biblical origin:

> Our rabbis taught: From where in Scripture do we learn that we are to say [the blessing of] the ancestors? Because it says, "Ascribe to the Eternal, O sons of might [understood as referring to the patriarchs]" (Psalm 29:1). And from where do we learn that we say [the blessing of] strength? Because it says, "Ascribe to the Eternal glory and strength" (Psalm 29:1). And from where do we learn that we say [the blessing of] holiness? Because it says, "Ascribe to the Eternal the glory of God's name, worship the Eternal in the beauty of holiness" (Psalm 29:2).[2]

These three blessings are called, respectively, *Avot*, ancestors; *G'vurot*, strength; and *K'dushah*, holiness.

It is instructive to ask how precisely these three themes summarize praise of God, which is the ostensible purpose of the opening section of the Amidah. But perhaps a more pertinent question needs to be raised first: of what use is human praise to the Almighty? Why does an all-powerful God need the plaudits of God's creations?

It is abundantly clear that it is not God who requires our admiration; rather, it is we who desperately need to recognize God and to put into perspective the nature of our relationship. To praise God is to acknowledge that we have found the Almighty. We begin the Amidah by verbalizing the three ways that confirm our faith and make us certain we have someone to speak to who hears our prayers.

In short, the first three blessings are the closest we can come to resolving the universal quest for proofs of God's existence. They resonate with the reasons that bolster our conviction that there's someone above us with whom we can share our concerns and in whom we can place our trust.

Avot/Ancestors: Proof from the Patriarchs

This blessing draws on the powerful proof of history to articulate the first reason that convinces us we are right to praise God:

> Blessed are you, Eternal, our God and God of our ancestors, God of Abraham, God of Isaac, and God of Jacob; the great, mighty, and awesome God, God most high.....O Sovereign, Helper, Savior, and Shield. Blessed are You, Eternal One, Shield of Abraham.

In his classic work *The Kuzari*, the medieval philosopher Yehudah Halevi has the king of the Khazars ask the rabbi a profound question: Why is God described, in the first commandment of the Decalogue, as "the Eternal your God, who took you out of the land of Egypt, the house of bondage"? Would it not have been far more persuasive for the Almighty to declare, "I am the Eternal your God, who created the heavens and the earth"? Halevi uses this as a convenient introduction to explain how Judaism diverges from the methodology of Aristotelian philosophy. Very much aware of the profound abyss separating the personal God of the Bible from the God of the philosophers (the latter being self-contained, unmoved, and non-personal—in short, God the Creator), Yehudah Halevi posits that it is *history*, more than anything else, that is decisive for our relationship with the Divine. The God who is revealed in the record of Israel and in the miracles performed on their behalf could not have been reached by philosophical speculation, but only by revelation.

At the beginning of the story of our people's covenant with God, Abraham, Isaac, and Jacob each sought the Divine in his own way—and God personally came in response to each one. The patriarchs knew God not as a concept but as a close friend; for them God was not a belief but a Being whose presence was constantly reaffirmed through direct contact and communication.

This reality of God's nearness is the theme of all of Jewish history. Collectively it was first made manifest by way of the miracles connected to God's deliverance of the Jews from the slavery of Egypt. That is the reason for the emphasis on the Exodus in the Decalogue commanding our commitment to God. And that is how we begin our praise of God: "Sovereign, Helper, Savior, and Shield. Blessed are You, Eternal, Shield of Abraham." There is no room to doubt God's existence when the Almighty has clearly played such a significant role in our story, beginning with our first patriarch and continuing through to our present day.

G'vurot/Strength: Proof from Nature

Maimonides, in his masterwork the Mishneh Torah, first posits
the law that we are commanded to love and to fear God. He then
proceeds to ask how one goes about fulfilling this requirement. His
answer is the response of the philosophers who find confirmation of
the Creator by concentrating on the beauty, profundity, and design
of creation:

> When one contemplates God's wondrous and great deeds and
> creations, and appreciates the infinite wisdom that surpasses
> all comparison, one will immediately love, praise, and glorify
> [God], yearning with tremendous desire to know [God's]
> great name, as David stated: "My soul thirsts for the Eternal,
> for the living God" (Psalm 42:3).
> Upon [continuing] to reflect on these same matters, one will
> immediately recoil in awe and fear, appreciating how one is
> a tiny, lowly, and dark creature, standing with one's flimsy,
> limited wisdom before the One who is of perfect knowledge,
> as David stated: "When I see Your heavens, the work of Your
> fingers...[I wonder] what is humanity, that You should recall
> us" (Psalm 8:4–5).[3]

Maimonides aligns himself with the ancient proof of God from
teleology. The complex design of the world clearly demonstrates the
existence of a Designer. As Philo put it:

> Who can look upon statues or paintings without thinking
> at once of a sculptor or painter? Who can see clothes or
> ships or houses without getting the idea of a weaver and
> a shipwright and a house builder? And when one enters a
> well-ordered city in which the arrangements for civil life
> are very admirably managed, what else will you suppose but
> that this city is directed by good rulers? So then, one who
> comes to the truly great city, this world, and beholds hills and

plains teeming with animals and plants, the rivers, spring fed or winter torrents, streaming along, the seas with their expanses, the air with its happily tempered phases, the yearly seasons passing into each other, and then the sun and moon ruling the day and night, and the other heavenly bodies fixed or planetary and the whole firmament revolving in rhythmic order, must one not naturally or rather necessarily gain the conception of the Maker and Father and Ruler also?[4]

For the midrash, this was in fact the very way Abraham first came to a belief in God: he saw a mansion all lit up and thought at first that the mansion had no owner or architect, for he did not see anyone. Upon further consideration, he realized that was impossible. The mansion, with its magnificent design, must have been built by someone. Extrapolating this to the world, Abraham concluded that there must obviously be a supreme Architect who created and owns it.[5]

The second blessing of praise in the Silent Prayer references God's might in ruling the world. Here we allude to God "making the wind blow and making the rain descend." God continues to play a direct role in seeing to it that nature functions in accord with highly complex laws that demonstrate a universal Lawgiver.

The most remarkable expression of the Almighty's power is God's ability to resuscitate the dead. We see evidence of this in nature when the trees seem to die as they shed their leaves in the fall, only to return to life again in the spring. We acknowledge it in our own lives when we go to sleep, a condition the Talmud refers to as one-sixtieth of death,[6] only to miraculously awaken once more in the morning. The blessing states: "You are eternally mighty, Adonai; the resuscitator of the dead are You, abundantly able to save...Blessed are You, Eternal One, who resuscitates the dead." This is the second reason why we believe in and praise God.

K'dushah/Holiness: Proof from Our Souls

It is the third blessing that has special meaning for us as we seek to understand the true significance of the concept of sanctity in Judaism: "You are holy and Your name is holy, and holy ones praise You every day forever. Blessed are You, Eternal One, the holy God." *Avot*, speaking of God's direct role in the history of our people, and *G'vurot*, addressing the way in which God speaks to us via the extraordinary complexity and design of nature, both convince us of the presence of the Divine. But what do we mean when we say "You are holy"? And what is it that lends credence to this assertion?

Paradoxically, this may seem to be the weakest and yet at the same time the most powerful proof of all—the strongest reason why we can feel confident of God's existence. It has its echoes in the mystical approach to religion popularized by the Baal Shem Tov, founder of the hasidic movement. One of his favorite quotes to his disciples was, "Taste and you will see that the Eternal is good" (Psalm 34:9). Religious experience is compared to tasting food: the taste cannot be described; it simply must be personally felt. The God within us is far more real than what we are capable of proving or of describing.

When a hasidic leader once asked his followers whether they believed in God, they were horrified by the question. "Of course we believe in God," they replied. "How could you possibly doubt our faith?" The rabbi, to their amazement, told them, "Well, I do not. I do not *believe* in God. Do you *believe* that we are sitting at a table? You *know* that we are sitting at a table. So too, to say merely that we *believe* in God is to acknowledge that we lack the certainty of our awareness. We *know* God. God is holy and that spirit of holiness resonates in our souls with the same certainty we have of our own being."

The existentialist movement has popularized the idea that the attempt to prove the existence of God is in and of itself impertinence. God must be encountered rather than discussed. If we are to experience religious truth we must take what Kierkegaard calls "the leap of faith." This idea resonates in the works of Martin Buber, Franz Rosenzweig, and their disciples. That leap of faith is a response to an inner call, a spiritual demand to be heard that can best be defined as the holy within us. It is "the still small voice" that spoke to Elijah with greater force than the strong wind, the earthquake, or the fire—the voice of God that announces its presence from the depths of our souls.

Sanctity is not something we believe in; it is something we *know*, something we taste and feel in a way that transcends the need for any kind of intellectual proof.

Immanuel Kant, in an oft-quoted passage from his *Critique of Pure Reason*, claimed that his certainty of God's existence came from the stirrings of his conscience: "Two things fill the mind with ever increasing wonder and awe, the more often and more intensely the mind of thought is drawn to them: the starry heavens above me and the moral law within me."[7] God is not something outside of us. God is as close as our conscience, as near as our soul. In the words of the Amidah blessing, "Holy ones praise You every day forever"—and we join them in our daily prayers. We dare to claim holiness for ourselves because we have been created in God's image and because part of us is divine.

This is at once both a very mystical as well as a very real awareness. This feeling of sanctity that infuses us with the certainty of God's presence is at the heart of our religious experience. Remarkably, Albert Einstein, despite his massive intellect, himself surrendered to this unfathomable and mystical dimension of God. He wrote the following in 1932:

> The most beautiful and deepest experience a man can have is the sense of the mysterious. It is the underlying principle of religion as well as of all serious endeavors in art and science. He who [has] never had this experience seems to me, if

not dead, then at least blind. To sense that behind anything that can be experienced there is a something that our minds cannot grasp, whose beauty and sublimity reaches us only indirectly: this is religiousness. In this sense I am religious. To me it suffices to wonder at these secrets and to attempt humbly to grasp with my mind a mere image of the lofty structure of all there is.[8]

The third blessing of the Amidah moves us from proofs to perception. As we personally speak to God, it assures us that the stirrings of sanctity within us are far more meaningful than any philosophical speculation. Holiness is the language of the soul, begging us to hear the voice of our Creator.

The first two blessings of praise try to respond to the question of God's existence. The third blessing, alerting us to the concept of sanctity, *negates the need for an answer*. For those of us who do not simply believe—but who encounter—God in every moment of our lives, who grasp holiness as the defining principle that governs our being, inquiring about God's reality is as pointless as questioning our own existence.

Sir Arthur Eddington put it well:

Theological or anti-theological argument to prove or disprove the existence of a deity seems to me to occupy itself largely with skating among the difficulties caused by our making a fetish of this word. It is also irrelevant to the assurance for which we hunger. In the case of our human friends we take their existence for granted, not caring whether it is proven or not. Our relationship is such that we could read philosophical arguments designed to prove the nonexistence of each other, and perhaps even to be convinced by them— and then laugh together over so odd a conclusion. I think that it is something of the same sort of security we should seek in our relationship with God. The most flawless proof for the existence of God is no substitute for it; and if we have that relationship, the most convincing disproof is turned harmlessly aside. If I may say it with reverence, the soul and God laugh together over so odd a conclusion.[9]

The Historic Basis of the First Three Blessings

The third blessing, stressing the concept of sanctity, affirms that our awareness of holiness confirms our belief in the existence of the Holy One. But on a more profound level, the historic basis of this blessing, as pointed out by the midrash, adds a far more powerful dimension. When we recognize who first uttered this blessing and in what context, we will discover what the striving for holiness demands of us.

The first three blessings of the Amidah, we are taught, have their sources in three significant moments in the lives of the patriarchs. The first blessing, praising God as the Shield of Abraham, was uttered by the angels in the aftermath of the story in Genesis about the five kings who rebelled against four kings but were defeated by them.[10] The four kings had kidnapped Lot, Abraham's nephew, in order to force Abraham to come to Lot's rescue, which would then allow them to slay Abraham and put an end to his monotheistic theology. God shielded Abraham from falling victim to their nefarious plan, so that he could survive to promulgate his newfound belief in the one God. When the angels saw how God miraculously intervened to save Abraham's life, they were moved to exclaim, "Blessed are You, Eternal One, Shield of Abraham."[11]

The second blessing, praising God as the One who resuscitates the dead, is related to an event in the life of Isaac, the second patriarch. The seminal event in his life took place when God commanded his father, Abraham, to sacrifice his son. Abraham obeyed, bound Isaac on an altar, and was a moment away from slaughtering him when God sent an angel to stop the offering and explain that it was but a test: God did not, in fact, desire human sacrifice.[12] According to the midrash, when Abraham lifted up the knife, Isaac's fear of being killed caused his soul to leave him. Isaac had, in fact, actually died before the angel could stop Abraham from carrying out God's command. Miraculously, God intervened and restored Isaac's soul to him. That made Isaac the first person who ever experienced coming back to life after dying. As witnesses to this miracle, the angels proclaimed, "Blessed are You, Eternal One, who resuscitates the dead."[13]

It is the historic source of the third blessing, rooted in an incident in the life of Jacob, which is most relevant to us as we seek greater understanding of the meaning of sanctification. The words "Blessed are You, Eternal, the holy God" also echo an exclamation of the angels. They were recited in the aftermath of Jacob's first prophetic vision. He had come to the place on which the Temple would later be built, Mount Moriah. On that very spot Jacob dreamed a dream. He saw "a ladder set upon the earth, and the top of it reached to heaven, and behold the angels of God ascending and descending on it" (Genesis 28:12). This vision inspired Jacob to sanctify God's name: "And Jacob awoke out of his sleep, and he said, 'Surely the Eternal is in this place, and I knew it not'; and he was afraid, and said, 'How full of awe is this place! This is none other than the house of God, and this is the gate of heaven'" (Genesis 28:16–17). And when the angels heard this, they responded by reciting the words that have become the conclusion of our final blessing of praise: "Blessed are You, Eternal One, the holy God."

Note carefully the order in which sanctification took place: first Jacob sanctified God, and only then did the angels declare their sanctification as well. Acknowledging God's holiness is the task of both Jews and angels. Both are required to fulfill this mandate. But remarkably enough, the midrash says that angels are not allowed to praise God until the Jewish people does so first![14] What is behind this strange sequence? It is nothing less than the recognition that angels can only justify their existence by way of their influence on humanity. Their reason for being is to serve as messengers of divine communication, proclaiming the truth of God's holiness to the world. Their mantra is "Holy, holy, holy is the Eternal One of hosts—the whole world is filled with God's glory."[15] When human beings acknowledge God's presence in "the whole world," on earth as well as in heaven, angels are then permitted to sing because they have then fulfilled their purpose.

In Jacob's vision of the ladder, he saw angels ascending and descending. One would have expected the reverse: since the home of angels is in heaven, we would have assumed that the first part of their trip would have been to come *down* from above. Instead, Jacob saw them leaving the lower region of earth to *ascend* to heaven. It was only after they completed their task here that the angels were welcomed above. And it was only after they were able to make Jacob realize that God's holiness was as near as the spot on which he slept that the angels were permitted to join the celestial choir in singing paeans of praise to God.

The Jewish Meaning of Holiness

"The whole world is filled with God's glory." Those are the words of the angels after they offer their threefold exclamation of "holy, holy, holy." With this phrase the angels capture the uniquely Jewish explanation of holiness. It is an idea that for some biblical commentators is implied in the numerical value (*gematria*) of the Hebrew word *sullam*, "ladder," which serves as the focal point of Jacob's vision.[16] *Sullam* ("ladder"), *mamon* ("money"), and "Sinai" all share the same numerical value of their letters, 130. What a remarkable trilogy! What could these three words/ideas possibly have in common?

The answer holds the key to the symbolic content of Jacob's dream. On the very spot that would one day become the site of the holy Temple, Jacob was taught that the essence of Judaism is *the linking of earth and heaven*. Humanity's role is not, as in Christian thought, to forsake this world; it is, rather, to sanctify it. "My kingdom is not of this world" is the teaching of Jesus. In contrast, the message of Moses is "to perfect the world through the Almighty's sovereignty."

Saint Simeon Stylites was the first and probably the most famous of a long succession of stylites, or "pillar-hermits," who, over the course of more than six centuries, acquired a great reputation for holiness throughout Christendom. In an attempt to get closer to heaven and nearer to God, Saint Simeon and his followers decided to remove themselves as far as possible from earth and live secluded with God on top of a self-constructed pillar. At first Saint Simeon's pillar was little more than nine feet high, but it was subsequently replaced by others, and the last in the series apparently towered more than fifty feet over the ground. For these "pillar-hermits," casting off all connection with humanity expressed the true meaning of holiness. In their eyes the top of Mount Sinai was a final destination, a place from which the pious ought to never descend.

Christians built a monastery on top of what they believe to be the location of the original Mount Sinai. For them, that spot is holy. For Jews, holiness is incompatible with estrangement from earth and from humanity. "Do not separate yourself from the community" is the accepted ruling of Hillel,[17] embodying this perspective. Jews understand Sinai as a fulfillment of Jacob's vision of the ladder. Angels served as our models, by ascending and descending, because the journey to heaven requires a return trip back down to earth. Moses climbed to the top of Mount Sinai to get the Torah and then brought it back to the people Israel. His goal was not to bring Jews to heaven; he wanted to bring heaven down to the Jews.

Torah is compared by the sages to water. Just as water is a source of life for the world,[18] so too is the Torah a source of life for the world. Just as water flows down from the mountaintop to bless the land below with its life-giving power and make it fruitful, so too is the purpose of Torah to enhance and nourish everything here on earth.

Those who seek only the sacred are content to stand on pillars, far removed from the world and its challenges. Those who perceive their mission as perfecting the world and transforming the profane into the holy identify their spiritual mission with ladders, rising to the sky but rooted in the ground, linking heaven and earth.

Sinai and sullam—the mountain on which the Torah was given and the ladder of Jacob's dream—also share a message of meaning with the word *mamon*, money. At first glance, the connection seems highly problematic. Money and spirituality seem to be antithetical. The love of money, says the New Testament, is the root of all evil.[19] The Christian Bible declares: "It is easier for a camel to go through the eye of a needle than for a rich man to enter into the kingdom of God."[20]

But Judaism disagrees. Humans do not become saints if we take a vow of poverty. Wealth is not a curse; it is merely a challenge. Holiness is defined by our ability to use wealth to enhance and sanctify the presence of God on earth.

Is money holy or profane? The midrash gives us the answer in the explication of the verse concerning God's commandment to Moses: "This they shall give, everyone that passes among them that are numbered: half a *shekel*, after the shekel of the sanctuary" (Exodus 30:13). God stressed that they shall give "this," illustrating with the actual coin.[21]

Why did God need to do this? Because the midrash tells us Moses was baffled by this command, not knowing what to do. Yet what was so difficult? It seems quite simple. God had specified "half a *shekel*." Why did God have to follow up the command with a visual demonstration? And moreover: why does the midrash add that the coin God showed him was "a coin of fire"?

Our sages explain that what Moses could not grasp was how God could command something as seemingly mundane as half a *shekel* for the holy task of counting Jews. How could currency possibly be used as a way to identify holy people?

"God then showed him a *shekel*, a coin of fire." What does the midrash mean? How can a coin of fire resolve the problem? And did Moses have to be shown the image of a coin in order to know what God was talking about? The explanation is profound: If you, Moses, cannot believe in the relevance of the coin, then let Me illustrate by way of a coin of fire. Fire is the symbol of money because fire destroys, but it also creates. Fire may burn, but it can also cook, warm, and serve beneficial purposes. The same is true of wealth. Precisely because it has this quality, it becomes doubly holy. When we choose to use a potentially destructive object in a positive and productive manner, we have learned the secret of true holiness.

This is a concept we find similarly expressed by a symbol used on the High Holy Days: the *shofar*. Why is the *shofar* the vehicle for bringing us to repentance? What is there about the horn of an animal that may be linked to spiritual rebirth? The horn is one of the four major causes of damage produced by animals.[22] We, too, may at times allow ourselves to be possessed by our animalistic nature, but the *shofar* tells us to take the potentially destructive horn and transform it, thereby becoming holy.

Hasidim have suggested that the Hebrew word for coin, *matbei·a*, may also be read as *mi-teva*, which means "from nature," from the world around us. God told Moses to "take a coin of fire," and we are thus taught that we may find opportunities for great holiness in the world about us. Like fire, a coin may be either creative or destructive. The potential for both exists; the choice is in our hands.

Symbolically, Jacob's dream of the ladder was also about the purpose of Torah at Sinai and the proper use of material blessings. Immediately after Jacob awoke we are told, "And Jacob vowed a vow saying, 'If God will be with me and will keep me in this way that I go and will give me bread to eat and clothing to put on, so that I come back to my father's house in peace, then shall the Eternal be my God; and the stone that I have set up for a pillar shall be God's house, and of all that You will give me I will surely give one-tenth to You'" (Genesis 28:20–22).

The concept of tithing comes from Jacob and this passage. It appears right after he had the vision of the ladder. Why would he speak of something as materialistic as money, immediately after experiencing the most sacred vision of his life? Because that very vision enabled him to comprehend that one *can*—and *must*—serve God even with that which is seemingly secular and profane. Money should not be renounced; it should be used correctly. Wealth is not to be rejected, but rather utilized for its capacity to enhance and expand God's blessings on earth.

And so, too, the potential for holiness exists within everything that God has created. Indeed, that is why God pronounced all that was made, every day of creation, as tov, "good"; and, upon final completion, "God saw everything that had been made and behold it was *tov me'od*, very good" (Genesis 1:31). Not "good" because the world is perfect, but because the world is perfectible—with the help of humans, to whom God entrusted this task. Not "good" because the world is already holy, but because the world has the potential for holiness—if human beings fulfill their mission to become "partners with God in the act of creation."[23] Not "good" because the world is sanctified by God, but because the people with whom God entered into a covenantal relationship have the power to sanctify it.

Perhaps the best summary of this concept is to be found in God's command to "Make Me a sanctuary (*mikdash*), that I may dwell among them" (Exodus 25:8). The Israelites were told to erect a house for the Almighty. And yet we know that God is everywhere and neither needs nor can be contained in a single edifice, no matter how magnificent. The difficulty is resolved by the second half of the verse itself. It does not say, "that I may dwell in *it* [i.e., the sanctuary]." Rather, it says, "that I may dwell among *them*"—that is, among the people. Since "the whole world is filled with God's glory," the purpose of the sanctuary (and this applies to all aids to holiness) is to awaken holy feelings, which then cause God to "dwell among them"—that is, in their hearts.

God is the source of holiness. Humans must discover it and proclaim it. That is our partnership. That is our mission, ever since we entered the covenant at Sinai. God has sanctified us with the commandments and it is we who must sanctify the world and make it worthy of the Almighty's presence.

NOTES

[1] In *Tiresius and Other Poems: The Ancient Sage*, by Alfred Lord Tennyson (1885).

[2] B. Rosh Hashanah 32a.

[3] Mishneh Torah, Hilkhot Yesodei Hatorah 2:1–2.

[4] *De Specialibus Legibus* I:6 (Loeb Classical Library; London and Cambridge, MA: William Heinemann Ltd. and Harvard University Press, 1950), vol. 7, p. 119.

[5] Bereishit Rabbah 39:1.

[6] B. Berakhot 57b.

[7] Immanuel Kant, *Critique of Pure Reason* (1788).

[8] The quotation is taken from a speech by Albert Einstein to the German League of Human Rights in Berlin, in the autumn of 1932. It can be found in the appendix of Michael White and John Gribbin, *Einstein: A Life in Science* (New York: Penguin Books, 1994).

[9] *Science And The Unseen World* (1929; rpt. Whitefish, MT: Kessinger Publications, 2007), pp. 49ff.

[10] Genesis 14:8–10.

[11] *Pirkei D'Rabbi Eliezer*, ch. 27.

[12] Genesis 22:13.

[13] *Pirkei D'Rabbi Eliezer*, ch. 31.

[14] *Tanna D'vei Eliyahu Zuta* 25.

[15] Isaiah 6:3.

[16] See, for example, *Ba·al Ha-turim* to Genesis 28:12.

[17] Pirkei Avot 2:5.

[18] Cf. Song of Songs 4:15, "A fountain of gardens, a well of living waters."

[19] First Epistle of Timothy 6:10.

[20] Matthew 19:24.

[21] *Tanhuma, Ki Tissa*, §7; see also Rashi to Exodus 30:13.

[22] M. Bava Kamma 1:1.

[23] B. Shabbat 10a.

Who Has Sanctified Us
Through His Commandments

David Mescheloff

David Mescheloff

לע״נ א״א מו״ר הרב משה משלוף ז״ל ולע״נ אמי מורתי הרבנית מרים משלוף ז״ל

Introduction

Sanctity—holiness[2]—is the principal, overarching aim of the Torah way of life, both for individuals and for the Jewish people as a whole.[3] It is the ultimate purpose of a life lived in accordance with the covenant between God and the people of Israel, of a life of fulfillment of God's law as expressed in God's commandments.[4]

This essay has three major sections. First we will look at some of the evidence supporting our opening paragraph. We will bring evidence from the Torah—both in general, comprehensive statements, and in verses concerning specific, concrete areas of life. We will also bring evidence from formulations of prayers and blessings by our sages of ancient times. Second, we will discuss what sanctity means as the ultimate purpose of Jewish life, and how *mitzvot* can help[5] to achieve it.[6] Finally, we will present an educational tool that illustrates and clarifies this overall perspective of Jewish life and how its system of divine commandments can lead to a life of holiness. This tool has been used in teaching both children and adults. It has proven of value both for Jews born into religious families and for newcomers to the Torah way of life, both converts and people who were born Jewish.

Part I: Evidence That the Aim of the *Mitzvot* Is Holiness

The evidence that sanctity is the goal of the commandments and the primary aim of Jewish life is rooted in the Torah, as well as in the teachings of the talmudic sages.

A. Evidence in the Torah

As God was preparing the Israelites to receive the Torah, God told Moses to tell them, "'And you shall be a kingdom of priests and a holy nation [dedicated] to Me!' These are the things you shall tell the Israelites" (Exodus 19:6). God's kingdom of priests and "holy nation": this is what the Israelites are charged to become through Torah, *mitzvot*, and the covenant of Sinai. We will now present seven specific commandments (or groups of commandments) whose aim is stated explicitly in the Torah to be sanctification. At first, this may appear to be belaboring the point. However, in Part II it will become clear why it is so significant that each of these areas be specified, and in Part III it will become clear how this elaboration underlies the educational tool we will present. The last selection we will present in this section will address both all of the *mitzvot* as a whole, and two important specific areas of life.

1. *Sanctity in Time* The fourth of the Ten Commandments that were pronounced at Sinai, after the comprehensive introduction we saw above, called upon the Israelites to acknowledge one day of the week as sacred: "Be continuously aware of (*zakhor*, literally, "remember") the Sabbath day, to make it holy (*l'kad'sho*)!" (Exodus 20:7). This calls for making the Sabbath day holy by molding the experience of the sacred day proactively to be pleasant, thought-inspiring, consciousness-raising, and memorable throughout the week. According to rabbinic tradition, this message was stated simultaneously with the command to make the Sabbath day holy by "guarding" it, refraining from any of the activities included in the term *m'lakhah*:[7] "Guard (*shamor*) the Sabbath day continuously, to make it holy (*l'kad'sho*), as the Eternal your God has commanded you" (Deuteronomy 5:11).[8]

Indeed, the source of the sanctity of the Sabbath day is described in the Torah as being an act of God, as is recorded at the conclusion of the major events of the six days of creation: "And God blessed the seventh day and sanctified it (*va-y'kaddeish oto*), for on it God ceased all the *m'lakhah* that God had created [for human beings] to complete" (Genesis 2:3). Thus, too, we read: "Six days *m'lakhah* may be done, but on the seventh day [there shall be] a Sabbath of cessation, sacred to God" (Exodus 31:15). This theme is repeated in the Torah several times.

This was not the Israelites' first encounter with the notion of sacred time. As Moses prepared them for the exodus, God commanded them to recall this unique historical event throughout the generations with a seven-day celebration, a mixture of prescribed actions and prohibitions,[9] creating a holy time: "And you shall have on the first day a [day of] sacred assembly, and on the seventh day a [day of] sacred assembly; no *m'lakhah* shall be done on them, except that which every person eats, that only may be prepared by you" (Exodus 12:16). Ultimately, all of the biblical festivals were characterized as holy times, introduced as follows: "Speak to the Israelites and say to them, 'The appointed times of the Eternal, which you shall proclaim as [days of] sacred assembly (*mikra·ei kodesh*)—these are My appointed times" (Leviticus 23:2).

2. Sanctity in Space   At the heart of the Israelite camp in the desert, they were to create a sacred space: "And they shall make a sanctuary (*mikdash*) [dedicated] to Me, and I shall dwell in their midst" (Exodus 25:8). Indeed, as the Israelites sang praises to God shortly after being freed from slavery in Egypt and being brought miraculously across the Reed Sea, it was already their vision for the future to settle in the land of Israel and construct a sacred place dedicated to God from which they could bring the message of God as Ruler of the universe to all peoples: "May You bring them in and may You plant them on Your mountain inheritance; O Eternal, You have created a firmly-founded place for You to reside; Your hands, O God, have firmly established a sanctuary (*mikdash*)…The Eternal will reign forever and ever" (Exodus 15:17–18).[10] Yet these were not the Israelite's first encounters with the notion of sacred space. Earlier in the book of Exodus, we read: "And [God] said [to Moses]: 'Do not come near to here, remove your shoes from your feet, for the place on which you are standing is sacred ground (*admat kodesh*)" (Exodus 3:5).[11]

3. *Sanctity in Eating* The sanctity of Israel was to be expressed not only in time and place, but also through the very act of eating. Thus, we read: "And you shall be holy people (*anshei kodesh*) for Me, and [so] you shall not eat flesh torn in the field; throw it to the dogs" (Exodus 22:30). The fruit of the tree, during the fourth year after planting, was to be sacred: "And in the fourth year all its fruit shall be sacred to the Eternal, for praising [God]" (Leviticus 19:24). The Torah repeatedly calls upon the Israelites to restrict what they eat, so that they will be holy: "For I am the Eternal your God; consecrate yourselves and be holy, for I am holy, and do not make your souls impure by [eating] any of the creatures that creep on the ground" (Leviticus 11:44).

4. *Sanctity of People* The Torah also teaches about sanctifying certain human beings. This includes the priests (*kohanim*), of whom the Torah states: "And you shall sanctify him (*v'kiddashto*), for he offers up your God's [i.e., the altar's] food; he shall be holy to you, for I, the Eternal, who makes you holy, am holy" (Leviticus 21:8). Similarly, a woman's firstborn male child is sacred and is to be declared sacred, as it is written: "Sanctify (*kaddeish*) every firstborn to Me— every one that opens the birth canal among the Israelites—among the people and among the animals is [dedicated] to Me" (Exodus 13:2). This sanctity was partially transferred to the Levites, as the Torah states: "For every firstborn among the Israelites—among the people and among the animals—is [dedicated] to Me, for on the day that I struck all of the firstborn in the land of Egypt I sanctified them to Me" (Numbers 8:17). And the Torah states that God sanctified the tribe of Levi in place of the firstborn: "For they [the Levites] are surely given to Me from among the Israelites; I took them as Mine

in place of all of the firstborn among the Israelites who opened the birth canal" (Numbers 8:16).

5. *Sanctity in Social Justice and Ethical Relations*   A long list of familial, social justice, ethical, and ritual commandments begins with the following heading: "Speak to the entire congregation of the Israelites and tell them: 'You shall be holy, for I, the Eternal your God, am holy" (Leviticus 19:2). Among the many commandments that follow this introduction are: show deference to one's parents; observe Shabbat; leave portions of the field and the vineyard for the poor and for the Levite; do not steal; do not lie; do not delay paying a worker's daily wages; do not mislead an unsuspecting and unknowing person; do not stand by idly while your fellow is in distress; do not hate in your heart; do not take revenge and do not bear a grudge; do not gossip; love your neighbor as yourself; do not plant forbidden mixtures of seeds; do not make tattoos; love the convert; and many more.

6. *Sanctity in Family Life* Over and above sanctity expressed in time, place, and the act of eating, family relations are a matter of sanctity as well. An extensive list of forbidden sexual relations begins with the following statement: "Consecrate yourselves and you shall be holy, for I am the Eternal your God" (Leviticus 20:7). There follow prohibitions against cursing one's parents, adultery, incest, homosexual relations, bestiality, relations with a menstruant, and eating forbidden animals, fowl, or crawling creatures. The section concludes with the instruction: "And you shall be holy to me, for I— the Eternal—am holy, and I have separated you from the nations, to be [dedicated] to Me" (Leviticus 20:26).

7. *Sanctity in Thought and Belief* The above is a mere sampling of the notion of the sacred as it appears in the Torah, for our sole intent here is to point to the connection between God's commandments in all areas of human life and the striving for sanctity. We conclude this section with one more explicit link between *mitzvot* and sanctity. This source refers generally to all of the *mitzvot*, as well as to two

specific aspects of Jewish life. The third paragraph of the Shema, recited twice daily, reads as follows:

> And the Eternal said to Moses, "Speak to the Israelites and tell them that throughout the generations [to come] they are to make fringes on the corners of their garments, with a blue string on each fringe. It shall be your fringe and you shall look at it, and you shall be aware of [i.e., remember] all the Eternal's commandments, and you shall fulfill them, and you shall not wander after your hearts and after your eyes, after which you go astray. [This is] so that you will be aware of [i.e., remember] and will fulfill all of My commandments, and will be sanctified to your God. I am the Eternal your God, who brought you out of the land of Egypt to be your God; I am the Eternal your God" (Numbers 15:37–41).

"So that you will be aware of and will fulfill all of My commandments, and will be sanctified to your God" is as explicit a statement as is possible: we should think about and fulfill God's commandments so that we may become holy.

This last selection also brings the notion of sanctity specifically to the sphere of one's heart and one's mind—that is, it calls on Israel to adopt holy thoughts and beliefs. There are many beliefs abroad in this world, and many belief systems, and different world outlooks, all of which may be reasonable in one sense or another; however, the ones God commands us to adopt are the ones that lead to holiness.

B. Evidence from Rabbinic Institutions

1. *Blessings before Fulfilling Commandments* Our sages of ancient times instituted a large array of blessings to be recited daily, so that Jews would be accustomed to thinking and speaking of God, and thus thanking, revering, and praising God regularly. The standard opening formula of blessings is *barukh atah Adonai, eloheinu melekh ha-olam*, "Blessed are You, Eternal our God, Ruler of the universe."

Many of these blessings are part of the daily prayer services. Others are expressions of praise, gratitude, and acknowledgment of our dependence on God, such as the blessings recited before and after eating. Another major category of blessings consists of those that are recited as one begins to fulfill a wide range of commandments, some of Torah origin and others of rabbinic origin. Here is a small sampling of commandments over which a blessing is recited: studying Torah, lighting Shabbat and holiday candles, lighting Hanukkah candles, hearing the sound of the *shofar* on Rosh Hashanah, dwelling in the *sukkah* on Sukkot, holding the four species on Sukkot, eating *matzah* and *maror* at the *seder*, counting the *omer*, circumcision, redeeming the firstborn, ritual hand-washing upon rising in the morning and before breaking bread for a meal, donning *tallit* and *t'fillin*, and many more. Each blessing recited before the performance of a *mitzvah* begins with the six words above, and continues *asher kid'shanu b'mitzvotav v'tzivvanu*, "who has sanctified us through His commandments and commanded us," and concludes with reference to the specific *mitzvah* about to be performed (for example, *lishmo·a kol shofar*, "to hear the sound of the shofar"). Thus the sages clearly instituted a regular reminder that God has sanctified us through the commandments, and that this is their purpose.

2. The Silent Standing Prayer (Amidah) Our sages also instituted fixed prayer services to be recited on Shabbat and holidays, morning, afternoon, and night. Those prayers include the following line: "Our God and God of our ancestors…sanctify us through Your commandments (*kad'sheinu b'mitzvotekha*)." Every holiday and high holiday prayer that the sages instituted includes the following praise and gratitude to God, acknowledging the special relationship with the Israel: "You chose us from among all of the nations, You loved us and You wanted us, and You elevated us above all the languages (i.e., cultures), and You sanctified us through Your commandments (*kiddashtanu b'mitzvotekha*)." There can be no doubt that the sages of classical antiquity understood that a life lived fulfilling God's commandments has as its purpose the creation of holy people—both as individuals and as a nation.

C. Implications for Understanding the Commandments

Thus all arguments of the following type are clearly based on a false premise: "The purpose of the ancient Torah and rabbinic commandments was sociological, or psychological, or economic, or political, or to promote private and public health and hygiene, or to promulgate justice and universal ethical values, etc.; and since such purpose is no longer relevant—since it has been met, or since it can be met better in other ways—therefore, such commandments are no longer applicable." As the premise of that argument is false, so is its conclusion. The ultimate goal of the commandments is to promulgate holiness (as we shall describe below). Thus they are eternally binding on the Jewish people, as components of the eternal covenant between God and Israel.

The following question, then, naturally arises. If it is so clear that sanctification is the aim of the commandments, then why have so many Jewish thinkers over the generations suggested sociological, psychological, economic, political, hygienic, ethical, or other reasons for the *mitzvot*? I will suggest a different answer to this question in Part II; here, let me simply raise two other points. First: in a brutal, harsh, evil, unstable world of exile, most Jewish efforts had to be directed toward physical and cultural survival. In such circumstances, the possibility of sanctification (as I will describe it below) may have seemed distant and unimaginable. In a world in which Jewish values, beliefs, and practices came under steady, withering, hostile attack from all sides, support for their legitimacy had to be provided from the areas of life that were most easily, immediately, and closely observable and most widely accepted as legitimate: sociology, psychology, economics, hygiene, education, etc. Indeed, different aspects of the *mitzvot* speak to different aspects of human life; thus, different people may find meaning in *mitzvot* in different ways, and a single individual may find different meanings in the same *mitzvah* at different times in his or her life. Second: one must remember that even those great Jewish minds that found numerous visible, sensible values in the *mitzvot* did not claim that their proposals were the sole reasons for the *mitzvot*.

They would certainly not subscribe to the false reasoning above, concluding that one should abrogate the commandments. A well-known example of this is Maimonides' suggested general purpose for animal sacrifices: that the Torah intended to wean the Israelites gradually from idolatrous practices.[12] The natural, logical conclusion that one would expect in light of such an explanation would be that animal sacrifices would never return to Jewish practice. Nevertheless, Maimonides states clearly that they will be restored.[13]

It seems that the principal way to understand Jewish thinkers' seeking reasons other than sanctity as the aims of the *mitzvot* is as Rabbi Avraham Yitzhak Kook wrote:

> One must not consider at all innovating details [of Jewish law] based on the [commandments'] reasons. This applies even to those reasons stated by our sages, of blessed memory, the authors of the Talmud, and, similarly, the reasons of Maimonides, and a *fortiori* the reasons given by later thinkers. The only value this entire matter [suggesting reasons for the commandments] has is [to serve] as words of encouragement and inspiration toward ethics and proper beliefs, and not to make them a basis for innovations or scholarly analyses.[14]

The purpose of attributing various reasons to *mitzvot* was to encourage their observance, not to replace the true understanding of their purpose—which, as we have seen, was intended to further the pursuit of holiness. Those Jewish thinkers surely did not intend their ideas to be used as the basis for rejecting God's commandments.

Part II: The Meaning of Holiness and How *Mitzvot* Can Help Achieve Holiness

A. The Meaning of Sanctity

Since we are called upon to be holy, "for I, the Eternal your God, am holy," it seems appropriate to examine briefly what we mean when we say that God is holy.

1. *God's Holiness: Transcendental Yet Immanent*   God's holiness has two apparently contradictory aspects. On the one hand, God is ultimately and absolutely transcendental. There is no aspect of this universe to which God can be likened: God is unique. God is not "in" space-time, nor composed of material, nor any of the kinds of "energy" we associate with matter. These statements are subsumed under the first set of fundamental Jewish beliefs about God enumerated by Maimonides. Yet space-time-matter-energy is all that our senses know in this universe. This transcendental nature of God—as absolutely Other, as completely apart, separate, and different—is the thought usually associated with God's holiness. Yet, on the other hand, without God's immanent presence, there could be no universe. God provides the non-space-time-matter-energy infrastructure on which our universe of space-time-matter-energy rests. From the vastest extent of our immense universe, into whose distant recesses we peer back in time through our telescopes (the light "particles/waves" that reach us from the most distant objects began their trajectories through space on their way to our instruments and our eyes billions of years ago, such that we see the spatially distant objects from which that light emanated only as they were very long ago in time), down to the infinitesimally small spaces (Planck lengths, that have never been observed); from the several different types of energy we have come to recognize to what appear to be the densely, tightly packed bundles of energy we call atomic and subatomic particles—all of this exists because of God's free choice to create the universe. The Kabbalists speak metaphorically of a divine spiritual "light" emanating from God, which "supports" all of space-time-matter-energy "from within." By way of contrast, there is a fundamental asymmetry in the relationship between God-the-Creator and the universe that God created: God's existence is absolute, independent, and not contingent on the existence of the universe.

This apparent contradiction is a major theme in our daily public prayers. The theme of the third blessing of every Amidah is God's *k'dushah*, holiness. When the prayer leader repeats this blessing aloud in public prayer, we quote Isaiah 6:3: "Holy, holy, holy is the Eternal

One of Hosts; the fullness of the entire earth is God's glory." The classic Aramaic paraphrase of this verse, quoted elsewhere in our daily prayers, suggests that the threefold repetition of *kadosh*, "holy," indicates God's absolute transcendence beyond time, beyond matter, and even beyond all that we humans experience as abstract "energy." Yet Isaiah's prophetic vision continues, speaking of God in relation to the multitudinous hosts of the world, and concludes with God's immanence, "the fullness of the entire earth is God glory!"[15]

This verse is also recited in the first of the two blessings preceding the morning recitation of the Shema, which focuses on God's creation of the world and concludes with the words, "Blessed are You, Eternal, Creator of lights."[16] Similarly, the expanded paragraph of this first blessing, as it is formulated in the Shabbat morning service, is based on a verse from Hannah's prayer: "None is sacred like the Eternal, for there is nothing without You; and there is no Rock (alternatively: Creator) like our God" (1 Samuel 2:2).[17] All other sacred things may be set apart from everything else, but God's sacredness is unique, for nothing could exist if God were to separate from the world completely; God's unique sacredness includes being simultaneously both transcendent and immanent.[18]

Continuing our attempt to understand God's holiness, let us examine an aspect of God's immanence that is even deeper and more significant than God's role as creator and maintainer of the material universe in which we live—namely, God's manifestation in this universe in relation to human beings in a specifically non-space-time-matter-energy way. This is the intuitive, spiritual experience we have of a relationship with God, as a free "personality." The Talmud reports the following five-fold link between God and the human soul:[19]

To what do the five times David said "O my soul, bless the Eternal"[20] correspond? To the blessed Holy One and to the soul. Just as God fills the world, so too does the soul fill the body. Just as the blessed Holy One sees but is invisible, so too does the soul see but is not seen. Just as the blessed Holy One nourishes the entire world, so too does soul nourish the entire body. Just as the blessed Holy One is pure, so too the soul is pure. Just as the blessed Holy One dwells within the innermost recesses, so too does the soul dwell within the innermost recesses. May the soul, which has these five properties, praise God, to whom one can attribute these five properties![21]

We human beings have a God-like soul, which enables us to sense something beyond this universe of space-time-matter-energy. That intuitive sense opens the way for our spiritual link to God.

We have struggled for millennia against numerous forms of idolatry—some crude and primitive, and others more sophisticated—which perceived of God as material or, in some way, belonging to this natural world or being identical with it. In the course of our struggle, we have sometimes fallen victim to a greater danger: obscuring God's personality.[22] Two fundamental cornerstones of Jewish faith are belief in the freedom of God and the freedom of human beings.[23]

We can learn a great deal about the nature of our personal relationship with God from the nature of our personal relationships with other free human beings. One similarity results from our being "others" to each other: just as we cannot know what is going on in someone else's mind unless the other lets us know, so we cannot know what God has in mind, unless God lets us know. Another similarity results from our freedom: each individual's freedom places restraints on the freedom of every other individual. Free agents may influence the external actions and internal states of others in many ways, from mild to highly aggressive and even coercive. Yet one free agent cannot dictate to another what the other desires; to do so would contradict the notion of freedom.[24] On the other hand, once a free agent has expressed his or her own preferences, another free agent can relate to such expressions of preferences in any way he or she chooses—from joyful acceptance to grudging submission, or even to outright stubborn rejection and resistance. In the context of our authentically free relationship with God, this means that only God can express what God wants,[25] while we have been created with the freedom to relate to God's preferences as we choose.

2. *Human Holiness and the Commandments* Since we are called upon to be holy, "for I, the Eternal your God, am holy," it appears that we are called upon to emulate both paradoxical aspects of God's holiness, as best we can. That is, while remaining fully engaged with this world of space-time-matter-energy, we are to live in a way that demonstrates transcendence—the presence in our lives of a spiritual dimension that is free, that is not subject to the limitations and restrictions of space-time-matter-energy, the material "laws of nature." We are called on to do this both individually and as a nation.

Indeed, the ninth explicit, concrete positive commandment in Maimonides' *Sefer Ha-mitzvot* will help understand our subject. In this work, Maimonides first lists the commandments to affirm God's existence as the First Cause and God's unique oneness, and the commandments to love, to revere, and to worship God through prayer and Torah study (which are the fundamental commandments that bridge the gap between God's transcendence and immanence). The next three commandments Maimonides lists are: to associate with the wise in every possible way so as to learn from their knowledge, their character traits, and their behavior; to take oaths only in God's name, since all truths must be attributed to the Divine; and to strive to be as God-like as possible (e.g., compassionate, righteous, etc.). Maimonides then writes:

> [The ninth commandment is] the commandment that we were commanded concerning sanctifying the name [of God], which was expressed by God saying, "And I shall be sanctified in the midst of the Israelites" (Leviticus 22:32). What this commandment is about is that we are commanded to disseminate this true religion (as described in the preceding commandments) to the multitudes...

A life of *mitzvot* is the means by which we become holy, infusing a fully engaged natural human life, immersed in space-time-matter-energy, with an awareness of the immanent presence of God in the world, and thus disseminating the truth of our Jewish convictions and commitments.[26] We do this by exercising our own free wills in an encounter with God's freely expressed will—that is, the commandments.

3. *Rabbi Kook: Mitzvot Are the Means, Holiness Is the End* Rabbi Avraham Yitzhak Kook wrote about the relationship between *mitzvot* and holiness in the context of the talmudic discussion concerning the Hanukkah lights[27] (among other places). In that discussion, the Talmud presents the blessing instituted by our ancient sages to be recited before lighting the candle: "Blessed are You, Eternal our God, Ruler of the universe, who has sanctified us through His commandments, and commanded us to light the Hanukkah candle." In that discussion the Talmud also distinguishes between *mitzvah*, commandment, and *k'dushah*, holiness. Lighting Hanukkah candles is a *mitzvah*, but the candles have no *k'dushah*. Rabbi Kook expands on this as the distinction between the means—namely, the *mitzvot*—and the end—in this case, *k'dushah*.

Holiness, wrote Rabbi Kook,[28] is the ultimate goal of life, a self-validating and self-justifying way of living. Holiness must not be thought of as a means for achieving any end other than itself.[29] Holiness is an uninterrupted God-consciousness: the awareness of the exalted glory of God engraved deeply in one's heart, the internalization of the truth that the glory of a human being and the splendor of one's soul are directly proportional to the degree to which God's glory is grasped—even if only approximately—within one's soul. This is why no personal benefit or private pleasure of any kind may be derived from something that is holy: to make it clear that no personal pleasure, no advantage of any kind, can be thought of as the purpose of holiness. Holiness is the impression created in the soul by the glory of God; it is the ultimate purpose of creation, greater than any other good that one can imagine or any pleasure that one can call to mind. By way of contrast, *mitzvot* are the means God provided for preparing all of humanity and every individual for the supreme, ultimate goal: sanctity. *Mitzvot* prepare one's soul—both its capabilities for action and its personal qualities—for that ultimate good which humanity and individuals will achieve at some future time, when they reach their final state of perfection. Thus, Rabbi Kook wrote, one should not attribute to *mitzvot* the same value as to holiness. If one were to equate the value of *mitzvot* with that of sanctity, seeing *mitzvot* as an end unto themselves, then the performance of *mitzvot* would not stimulate a person to wonder about the ultimate aim and purpose of *mitzvot*. The *mitzvot* lead us to the path of goodness and life, to what Rabbi Kook referenced as the supreme light that God hid within the living Torah. Thus *mitzvot* are "sacred" only because of the ultimate goal, sanctity, that *mitzvot* help achieve.

Since *mitzvot* are a means to an end, Rabbi Kook continued, one does not have to avoid the thought that *mitzvot* may also serve as means to other beneficial ends, besides their ultimate goal (unlike the case with *k'dushah*, as we have described above). The problem with this, however, is that one might think that the *mitzvot* have "lower aims." For example, one might think that their purpose is only to bring humankind to material perfection, or merely to elevate humankind out of its primitive, wild state. If one looks at *mitzvot* this way, they could appear as inferior and contemptible to those generations that had already risen to a higher level of human civilization, beyond the abominations of idolatry and its associated activities. One must realize that divine *mitzvot*—which are wonderful, wise counsel from omniscient God, designed to lead humankind to eternal success—have sublime, lofty missions. These are so elevated that even when humankind achieves perfection of character and true intellectual perception and awareness, there will still be in the *mitzvot* eternal glory and beauty.

In light of this introduction, Rabbi Kook explained the halakhic limitations placed on two different *mitzvot*, which the Talmud explained on the basis of the principle "so that the *mitzvot* will not be contemptible in one's eyes." We will gain further insight into holiness as the goal of observing God's commandments by considering the following two examples.

The first example is as follows: "It is forbidden to count out coins by the light of the Hanukkah candle."[30] The Hanukkah lights serves to remind us of the miracle of the continued national existence of the Jewish people. Using them to count out coins would be equivalent to seeing the value of the national existence of the Jewish people in the private pleasures that it affords each individual. Attributing this inferior purpose to the *mitzvah* degrades it. Only an uncouth person would think that the highest mission of the candle is to provide light for counting coins. Since money is the principal vehicle for satisfying private, individual desires, this thought-process would reduce the bond of Jewish peoplehood to a group arrangement whose purpose is simply to enable each individual to achieve his or her private material goals. One must realize, instead, that the existence of the Jewish people is for higher, loftier purposes: sanctifying the name of God and living the covenant with God that is Israel's Torah—thus effectuating God's promise to Israel of an eternal national existence that is more powerful, sublime, and exalted than that of any other nation and culture. Degrading the higher purpose of even one *mitzvah*, like the continued existence of the Jewish people, could easily spread to other *mitzvot*.[31]

The second instance discussed in the Talmud there, of a *halakhah* based on the principle of not degrading *mitzvot*, concerns the *mitzvah* of covering the blood of a kosher bird or non-domestic animal that has been ritually slaughtered. The Talmud states that one may not cover the blood by pushing the covering material over the blood with one's feet, "so that *mitzvot* will not become contemptible in one's eyes."[32] Rather, one must use one's hands to scatter the cover over the blood. Rabbi Kook explains this as follows: at first blush, the purpose of this commandment appears to simply be preventing people from eating blood, and from eating *over* blood[33]—idolatrous practices that remained from humanity's primitive, wild days. Indeed, it was surely one of the Torah's aims to elevate humankind from those depths. However, that cannot be the ultimate goal of this commandment; humankind has yet to rise much higher, to a future of even greater grandeur and holiness. Rabbi Kook wrote that while it was impossible to describe in detail the light of human morality that will shine at the future messianic time, he could speculate that one day human beings will rise to so high a moral sensibility that killing animals for food will be totally unacceptable, as it had been from the time of Adam until the Flood. For the present and the foreseeable future, human beings are not ready for such a prohibition; humanity still has a long way to go before being ready for such a step.[34] However, only the Torah's guidance can lead people toward holiness. The practice of covering the spilled blood will—gradually, over the course of many generations—slowly impress on human beings that spilling animals' blood for human benefit is a cause for shame, permitted only as a concession to the current low level of human morality. This *mitzvah* applies only to the blood of birds and non-domestic animals, who procure their own food and do not depend on humans for their very lives. The lesson about not killing animals will thus be more readily absorbed in human consciousness with respect to these creatures. Moreover, the blood must be covered using the same part of the body—the hand—that spilled the blood, to underscore the connection in one's heart between spilling the blood and subsequently covering of the blood in shame. One must not cover the blood using one's foot, as that would wrongly imply that the *mitzvah* had only a primitive, inferior purpose, making the *mitzvah* contemptible—thus impeding the fulfillment of its ultimate purpose, of raising human beings to holiness.

One often hears the suggestion that the purpose of many *mitzvot* is to keep the Jewish people separate from other nations, and that "separateness" is the "holiness" that those *mitzvot* engender. That is undoubtedly an important goal of many *mitzvot*. After all, Jews are one of the smallest nations on earth; without consciously separating ourselves from other nations, assimilation would surely have already brought about our complete disappearance. Undoubtedly, the numbers of Jews lost to assimilation, over the millennia, far exceeds the numbers lost to any other cause. Nevertheless, I believe that Rabbi Kook would see that purpose—mere survival—as one of the inferior purposes that has been attributed to *mitzvot*. Surely our survival is for the sake of a much higher form of sanctity—that is, living at once in this world and in the divine presence.[35] I will now present two ways in which *mitzvot* serve the purpose of leading to holiness.

B. How *Mitzvot* Can Help Achieve Holiness

I will now present two ways in which *mitzvot* serve the purpose of leading to holiness.

1. *Mitzvot—Natural and Beyond* All of God's commandments concern natural human behavior in this world. Indeed, there is nothing unnatural about any of the *mitzvot*. On the other hand, there is no *mitzvah* that is only natural: either the *mitzvah* as a whole or the way it is formulated, or some crucial detail of its observance, imposes limitations or requires that we make choices from among several "natural" options. A person might ask, "Why am I doing (or not doing) this? It isn't natural! Other people don't do (or refrain from doing) this!" or "Why am I doing this in this way (or: at this time)? It's not natural! Other people don't do it this way (or at this time)!"

Stimulating these questions is critically important in order for *mitzvot* to accomplish their ultimate purpose.[36] And whether the answers that are proposed are of a lower nature or of a higher nature, as Rabbi Kook described, the main point will be this: we are immersed in the natural world and engaged in it fully, yet there are things we do that go beyond mere nature. That is because the *mitzvot* are the means by which we imbue our immanent, natural world with an awareness of what is beyond, what is transcendent. This is how we bring holiness—an awareness of our immanent/transcendent God— into our lives in this world. Let us mention briefly a few examples of this.[37]

It is natural to eat. As long as one has food, it is neither natural nor unnatural to refrain from eating certain specific foods. So a Jew may, for example, ask, "Why do I not eat pork? Other people do!" The very question makes one aware that while eating is a natural act, what and how one eats goes beyond what is natural. It brings into the act of eating a dimension beyond the natural. It makes all eating a religious, spiritual act of doing something that is beyond space-time-matter-energy. This is the first step by which *mitzvot* bring holiness into this fundamental, concrete aspect of human life in this world.

It is natural to prepare food with heat before eating it. A Jew who observes the prohibitions of Shabbat may, for example, ask: "Why am I not cooking some rice today? Other people do! I cooked rice myself yesterday; what has changed between then and now?" This question makes a person aware of the fact that, while the progression of time is perfectly natural, there are aspects of how we relate to time that have no basis in nature. It elevates one's sense of time, by introducing an awareness of a spiritual dimension beyond the merely natural: not all periods of time are the same. Indeed, it makes of the very act of cooking (for example) a spiritual act that goes beyond space-time-matter-energy, for one who cooks is always conscious of the fact that there are times when the activity is permissible and times when it is not. Not only does the Sabbath thus becomes holy, but even the act of cooking on a weekday takes on an other-worldly aspect, for one has to ask before cooking, "Is today Shabbat?" This is the first step by which we bring holiness—an awareness of our immanent/transcendent God—into the time dimension of our lives in this world.

It is natural for married men and women to have intimate relations. It is neither natural nor unnatural to refrain from relations from time to time. Yet refraining from relations specifically before a woman has immersed in a *mikveh* is not natural *per se*. So Jews who observe the laws of family purity (*tohorat ha-mishpahah*) must ask themselves, both when relations are permitted and when they are prohibited, "Why may we do this now, when we didn't do this yesterday? This is such a natural thing to do, and others do it naturally whenever they want to!" This heightens one's awareness that doing *mitzvot* is a natural thing, but that it is not limited to the realm of what is natural. Thus at any time during a couple's marriage, both when such relations are prohibited and when they are permissible, the *mitzvah* makes them conscious of the presence within their natural lives in this space-time-matter-energy universe of spiritual considerations that must come from elsewhere. This awareness may not be in the forefront of their consciousnesses during intimacy, but it is surely there in the background.

2. *Mitzvot—Flowing with God's Expressed Will* The fact that *mitzvot* have a dimension beyond the natural is not sufficient in and of itself to create *k'dushah*, holiness. All human beings bear the imprint of the image of God, and the fact that we have free choice means that any human behavior must have a non-deterministic, spiritual dimension. Indeed, certain aspects of contemporary physics suggest that even space-time-matter-energy may not behave in a strictly deterministic fashion. Furthermore, the diversity of human cultures shows that there are many ways to structure personal, interpersonal, family, and social institutions, including matters such as spiritual beliefs, eating, work, and sexual relations, *inter alia*. One must therefore ask: why should the Jewish way of living be thought of as anything other than just another of many human cultures? Why should it lead Jews and the Jewish people to *k'dushah* more than any other culture?[38]

- The answers to this question touch on fundamental aspects of Jewish faith and commitment, and lie beyond the scope of this paper. For our purposes here, let the following observations suffice. There are several general indications ("proofs") of the existence of God, including: God as the Creator (an idea that has been reinforced by the current cosmological notion of "the Big Bang"), God as the First Cause (a variation on the notion of Creator—namely, God as the ultimate answer to the question, "Why is the universe as it is?"), God as the Grand Designer (the teleological argument), God as the source of human morality, and God as the Being than which nothing greater can be conceived (the ontological argument). Each of these relates to a different aspect of God's relationship to the universe, and has had both proponents and opponents for many centuries.

We Jews, while occasionally getting into the fray about the arguments above and others, have our own unique ways of knowing about God. Among them is our national experience of God's revelation at Sinai, which has been passed down authentically and reliably over the generations in an unbroken tradition.[39] Others point to our experience with true prophets, and, in particular, with Moses—part of whose prophecy we experienced with him, and whom we then accepted as the closest any human being will ever come to God. Clearly, in these ways we have knowledge of God, of the divine covenant with us, and of the commandments—because God communicated them to us directly in the most reliable way possible, and our sages and our families have passed them forward in an unbroken tradition over the millennia.

The history of our people, as well—unique among the nations of the world—is proof of the covenant between God and us. Part of that covenant was God's undertaking to guarantee the continued existence of our people, after suffering unspeakable horrors in exile. We have, indeed, suffered in exile more than any other nation; and we are, indeed, still here. Current events, such as the establishment of the State of Israel and the ongoing ingathering of our exiles, constitute the initial fulfillment of promises God made to us in the Torah over 3,300 years ago, reinforcing further our conviction that the Torah, the covenant, and the commandments are, indeed, uniquely from God.

Finally, the Torah and the *mitzvot* themselves testify to their divine origin. The values of human freedom and dignity, of justice, of equality before the law, and others enshrined in the Torah, have gained near-universal recognition over the course of the centuries, and continue to grow, albeit ever so slowly, in their genuine application around the globe. The system of *mitzvot* as expressed in Jewish law and molded by the Oral Torah traditions of millennia are as vital, alive, creative, meaningful, and vibrant today as ever. Countless men, women, and children study the Torah, the Talmud, and other texts of Jewish law intensely every day all around the globe. Their lives are fully engaged with this world, while being immersed in *mitzvot* throughout the course of the day. Every new development at the cutting edge of medicine and technology is immediately examined by brilliant scholars who strive to understand how the innovations blend with traditional Jewish law, which they accept as the word of God.[40]

This is especially true in the State of Israel, where the Jewish people is now again independent and sovereign in its own land. We may no longer relinquish responsibility for politics and government, the economy, international relations, national defense, social policy, national infrastructures, and more, to the host countries of our exile.[41] The Jews of Israel are now responsible for every aspect of our national lives, and the creativity of the Torah world in dealing with all these new challenges is noteworthy. The flowering of Torah literature in recent decades is unparalleled in Jewish history, particularly as it deals with the flood of new technology and the challenges faced by the realities of the new Jewish state. Furthermore, the rich diversity of lifestyles that comes under the heading of "Torah living" and "*mitzvah* observance" is such that these terms cannot really be considered as monolithic, dictating fundamental life choices in a stifling manner. Quite to the contrary, the range of choices can be dizzying! Observing and taking part in this continued and renewed vitality of Torah life, and experiencing the sustained excitement of the revival of our ancient way of living, one can only stand in awe of what can only be a gift from God.

Thus, one who lives the *mitzvot* may be constantly aware, in every possible concrete way, that his or her life in this world stands in an inseparable relationship with God. That is evident in the history of the Jewish people from the time of the exodus and the revelation at Sinai to this very day—in the growing world-wide recognition of Jewish values and of Jewish beliefs about human beings and the world, and in the ongoing, continuous experience of national and individual vitality, creativity, and contribution to making the world a better place that go hand-in-hand with living a personal life of Torah and *mitzvot*.

God has expressed what we are asked to do in order to attain holiness, through the Torah and commandments, and we now freely decide whether and how to live our lives in accordance with God's will. Since God is transcendent, the only way God and we can "be close" is through our free wills, which are not material and are not predetermined in a fixed way by the laws of nature. The degree to which we freely choose to live lives of Torah and *mitzvot* is the degree to which we connect with God's will—and, hence, with God. Since God is free, only God can express the divine commandments to us. Our freedom to blend our wills with the divine will by studying the Torah and by fulfilling the commandments does not extend to the point of our being able to abrogate the commandments—as if we (and not God) were the source of their authority. Thus God's commandments stand unchanged forever. God is the One who knows how God wants us to achieve holiness and closeness to God.

Thus, observance of the *mitzvot* connects us simultaneously both to this world and to a non-natural world, instilling in us an awareness that the non-natural world to which we are linking is our holy, transcendent, and immanent God. This is how *mitzvot* can lead to holiness, as nothing else can.

Part III: "The Tree of Jewish Life"—An Educational Tool for Teaching about *Mitzvot*, Life, and Holiness

This educational tool consists of a series of drawings of a large tree that has seven major branches. In each drawing in the series, the verse "and you shall be [dedicated] to Me [as] a kingdom of priests and a holy nation" (Exodus 19:6) is written at the foot of the tree.[42] In the first drawing in the series the tree is bare, with unmarked branches. In the last, the culmination of an extended period of study, all of the branches are labeled, as are the sub-branches, and the tree is full of leaves, each marking a different theme or specific *mitzvah* or group of *mitzvot*. The drawings are printed on large pages[43] to allow for many details to be added during the course of study, so that a total picture of Torah living can be displayed on one large page.

The series of drawings displays the principal *mitzvot* in every one of seven principal areas in which human life takes place. The principal *mitzvot* are revealed to the learner on one branch at a time, without ever losing sight of the total picture. The learners will study the details of each *mitzvah* on each branch and sub-branch, gradually increasing in detail, in a way that is appropriate for the students, the teacher, and the learning context.

Each student is to receive each picture, in order, as the learning progresses.[44] Sometimes the student will be asked to write on the picture, and at other times he or she will be free to do so as he or she desires. When the learning is complete, each student will have a complete set of eleven drawings.

The series of drawings is designed to give the teacher maximal freedom in deciding what area of life and what *mitzvah* to introduce, at what time, in what order, and in what degree of detail. Furthermore, the teacher can use the series of drawings as a vehicle for expressing his or her own personal understanding of each and every *mitzvah*, and his or her own halakhic and worldview orientation regarding each *mitzvah*. The only two themes that will run of necessity through the entire series of drawings are that *mitzvot* have been given to us in every area of life, and that their ultimate aim is holiness for each individual and for the entire Jewish people.

I will look here at five of the drawings in the series, and describe the others. A comprehensive curriculum of Jewish study can be based on the series, but I will present here only a few brief samples of what can be done with it.

The first drawing in the series is of the bare tree, with seven unmarked branches and numerous sub-branches on each branch, and the verse at its base. After introducing the basic idea, the teacher may guide the students through a discussion of seven different areas that comprise all of life, as they mark each branch themselves. The areas I have chosen are the dimensions of the universe within which we live: time and space (the first two branches on the lower left), the three principal experiential modes of an individual's personal life: thought, emotions, and the body (the first three branches on the lower right), and the two group frameworks within which each human being experiences the world: the closest group of origin, the family, and the larger groups: community, nation, and all of humanity.

The second drawing to give the students, then, is of the tree, with only the seven main branches marked: time, space, thought/belief, emotion/service, the body, the family, and the community/nation/ human race. (See Illustration 1.)

The teacher may then guide the students through marking the secondary branches on each main branch. He or she may do so at this point, moving from branch to branch until all sub-branches are marked. This will be the third drawing to give the students. (See Illustration 2.)

At this stage, the teacher can describe in broad terms both various aspects of Jewish life and a variety of ways of thinking about the *mitzvot*. Thus, for example, I have included both Torah study and prayer as sub-branches on the same branch, "Sanctity of the Heart." A formal basis for doing this is the statement found in the Sifrei and quoted by Maimonides as proof that the commandment "to serve God" is not merely a general instruction, which Maimonides would not normally count in the list of commandments, but rather it has specific operative content: "[The verse that says] 'And to serve

God'—that is prayer; and they also said: 'And to serve God'—that is Talmud [i.e., Torah study]."[45] Maimonides also quotes a *baraita* of Rabbi Eliezer, son of Rabbi Yose the Galilean: "From what source [do we know] that the basic requirement to pray is one of the *mitzvot*? From here: 'You shall revere the Eternal, your God, and you shall serve God' (Deuteronomy 6:13), and they [the sages] said: 'Serve God through the Torah, serve God in the divine sanctuary.'" Thus both prayer and Torah study are forms of serving God with one's heart.[46] This observation leads to the significant conclusion that Torah study is not to be an abstract intellectual experience alone, but is to involve all of the human personality—the heart—in serving God.[47]

At the next stage, the teacher will begin to fill in more specific commandments and areas of Jewish law on the sub-branches. Seven different drawings are useful for this purpose, one for filling in details on each branch while leaving the other branches marked only with their sub-branches. This educational tool is not a substitute for detailed study, but it allows the learner to maintain a broad perspective on life, Jewish living, and holiness as he or she learns the details from other sources, with the help of the teacher. Two of these pages appear here as Illustrations 3 and 4.

Thus, for example, let us consider the drawing in which we begin to fill in the details of the sanctity of time (Illustration 3). The six sub-branches are "Shabbat," "The Three Biblical Pilgrimage Festivals," "The Days of Awe," "The Four Fast Days," "The Two Holidays of Rabbinic Origin," and "The Dawn of Our Redemption." The detailed study of the laws of Shabbat can take a long time, requiring considerable effort. But the tree helps keep things in broad perspective. The leaves show the place of the details that will be studied closely. Thus the *mitzvot* of Shabbat may be broken down in one way into two major parts. One is a study of *zakhor*, the positive actions that give Shabbat its pleasant and holy atmosphere—including Kiddush and Havdalah, preparing for Shabbat throughout the week, honoring Shabbat with special dress, family meals, Torah study, table songs, and more. The other major part is the negative commandments referred to by *shamor*—that is, refraining from *m'lakhah*, from forbidden labor, as a declaration that God is Creator and Master of the universe, not we.

The idea of Shabbat also has three other aspects, which are related to the three Shabbat meals and the three Shabbat public prayer services. These refer to the creation of the material world, the giving of the Torah with its spiritual aims, and the peaceful harmony we anticipate for the world at some future date. All of these can be studied while addressing how they contribute to sanctity, and not losing perspective of the place of all this in the total picture of Jewish life.

As another example, consider the drawing in which we begin to fill in the details of the sanctity of the body (Illustration 4). The two major sub-branches are "Foods of Vegetable Origin" and "Foods of Animal Origin," with another sub-branch with only one leaf, forbidden mixtures. This allows one to maintain a perspective of how this fits into the totality of Jewish life, as one begins to delve into the many details of *kashrut* observance. As all the details are studied, it is expected that the teacher will remind the students from time to time of the various ways in which each "leaf" on each sub-branch constitutes a means for achieving closeness to God and sanctity, by living according to God's commandments. So one may learn, for example, about the forbidden sinew, *gid ha-nasheh*, whose prohibition reminds us not to abandon a person, leaving him or her alone and unaccompanied in a dangerous place.[48] Similarly, one may learn about the various views of how the prohibitions of cooking milk and meat together, and of eating or gaining benefit from such products, can contribute to the heightening of one's moral sensitivity.

After the student has studied the details of the *mitzvot* at "the level of the leaves" and beyond, in an appropriate measure, the course of study can conclude with a review of all of life, and the *mitzvot* that fill and mold all of Jewish life, and how they lead to that ultimate Jewish aim, *k'dushah*, with the help of Illustration 5. It shows "The Tree of Jewish Life" with all branches, sub-branches, and leaves marked, showing a comprehensive view of the path to holiness through *mitzvot*.[49]

Summary

We have seen that the Torah and rabbinic sources down to our own day have established that the aim of a life lived in accordance with God's commandments is sanctification of all of life. We have examined the notion of God's holiness, and the human holiness that is to be modeled on God's, and the way in which fulfilling the *mitzvot* can lead to holiness. Finally, we have examined an educational tool that can be used to teach, in a variety of contexts, all of the components of Jewish life, in detail, without losing sight of the all-encompassing nature of Torah living and its ultimate aim, sanctification.

ILLUSTRATION 1
The Tree of Sacred Jewish Life,
Showing the Seven Major Branches

ILLUSTRATION 2
The Tree of Sacred Jewish Life,
Showing all the Secondary Branches

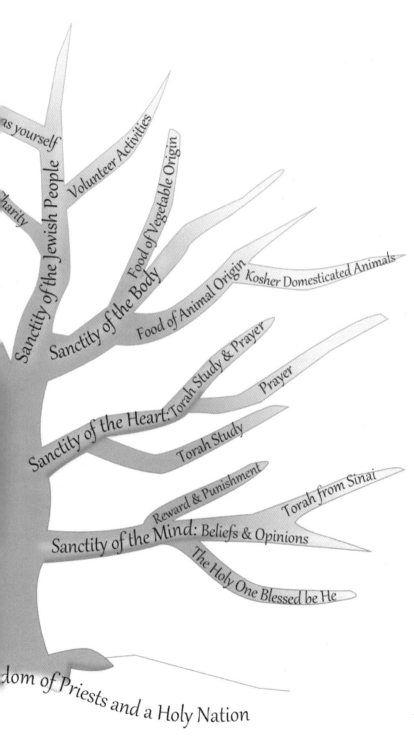

as yourself

Volunteer Activities

Food of Vegetable Origin

Charity

Sanctity of the Jewish People

Food of the Body

Sanctity of the Body

Food of Animal Origin

Kosher Domesticated Animals

Torah Study & Prayer

Prayer

Sanctity of the Heart:

Torah Study

Reward & Punishment

Torah from Sinai

Sanctity of the Mind: Beliefs & Opinions

The Holy One Blessed be He

dom of Priests and a Holy Nation

שופרים

ILLUSTRATION 3
The Tree of Sacred Jewish Life,
Showing Details of Sanctity of Time

ibor as yourself

Charity

Volunteer Activities

Sanctity of the Jewish People

Food of Vegetable Origin

Sanctity of the Body

Food of Animal Origin

Kosher Domesticated Animals

ife

Sanctity of the Heart: Torah Study & Prayer

Prayer

Torah Study

m

Reward & Punishment

Torah from Sinai

Sanctity of the Mind: Beliefs & Opinions

The Holy One Blessed be He

ngdom of Priests and a Holy Nation

שובבי״ם

ILLUSTRATION 4
The Tree of Sacred Jewish Life,
Showing Details of Sanctity of the Body

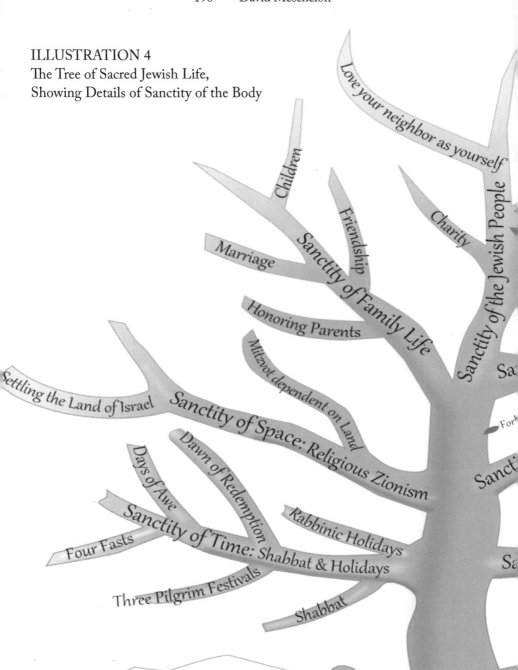

Chametz on Pessah

Produce of Sabbatical Year

Gifts from crops to the poor

Forbidden Admixtures

Volunteer Activities

Chadash

Challah

Kilayim

Orlah & Reva'i

Trumot & Ma'asrot

Food of Vegetable Origin

Kosher wine

Milk & Milk Products

of the Jewish People

Sanctity of the Body

Food of Animal Origin

Kosher Domesticated Animals

Treifa

Meat & Dairy

Blood & Forbidden Fats

Priestly Portions

Gid HaNasheh

Kosher Slaughtering

Kosher Fish

Kosher Birds

Forbidden Insects & Larvae

Non-domestic Animals

Sanctity of the Heart: Torah Study & Prayer

Prayer

Torah Study

Reward & Punishment

Torah from Sinai

Sanctity of the Mind: Beliefs & Opinions

The Holy One Blessed be He

of Priests and a Holy Nation

שורש

ILLUSTRATION 5
The Tree of Sacred Jewish Life,
In Full Detail

o a Bride

orting Mourners

ove the Convert

Hospitality

bor as yourself

Zionist Institutions

Charity

tutions

an Societies

al Institutions

agement

Aid to the Needy

Hevra Kaddisha

Politics

Synagogue

Volunteer Activities

Chadash

Challah

Kilayim

Orlah & Revai

Trumot & Ma'asrot

Jewish Education

Chametz on Pessah

Produce of Sabbatical Year

Gifts from crops to the poor

Kosher wine

Food of Vegetable Origin

Forbidden Admixtures

Treifa

Milk & Milk Products

Meat & Dairy

Blood & Forbidden Fats

Forbidden Fats

Priestly Portions

Gid HaNasheh

Kosher Domesticated Animals

Kosher Slaughtering

Sanctity of the Jewish People

Sanctity of the Body

Food of Animal Origin

Kosher Fish

Kosher Birds

Forbidden Insects & Larvae

Non-domestic Animals

Tallit & T'fillin

Blessings before Mitzvot

Grace after Meals

Praise & Thanks

Morning Service

Afternoon Service

Evening Service

High Holiday Prayers

Torah Study & Prayer

Prayer

Sh'ma Yisrael

New Moon & Holidays

Sanctity of the Heart:

Jewish Thought

Torah Study

Participation in Torah Study

Tanakh

Mishna

Talmud

Ethics

Jewish Law

Reward & Punishment

Resurrection of the Dead

Messiah

G-d Knows What We Do

World to Come

Torah is Eternal

Revelation / Torah

Moses the Greatest Prophet

Torah from Sinai

Prophecy

Sanctity of the Mind: Beliefs & Opinions

The Holy One Blessed be He

Free Will / T'shuvah

One G-d

Serve G-d

Knowledge of G-d's Universe

Virtues / Common Decency

Transcends Space

Transcends Time

fe

n

gdom of Priests and a Holy Nation

עובדיה

NOTES

[1] This essay is dedicated to the memory of my father, Rabbi Dr. Moshe Mescheloff, and my mother, Rebbetzin Magda Mescheloff.

[2] We will use the terms sacred, sanctified, and holy and their cognates interchangeably in this essay, as well as the Hebrew terms *kadosh* (holy) and *k'dushah* (holiness).

[3] This is only one of several ways of articulating the purpose of God's covenant with Israel. Other ways include "perfecting the world," "being a light unto the nations" (that is, teaching humankind a commitment to monotheism, and a proper balance of justice, righteousness, and mercy), "bringing all people to recognize God's rule," "advancing the cause of God in the world," "bringing us closer to the messianic era," and "earning a place in the world to come." We will show later in this essay that Rabbi Avraham Yitzhak Kook, too, identified *k'dushah*—sanctity or holiness—as the ultimate goal.

[4] We will use the terms commandment and *mitzvah* (plural: *mitzvot*) interchangeably in this essay.

[5] *Mitzvot* have the potential to create holiness, but, like any tool, they can be misused and distorted, and may fail to fulfill their potential. Indeed, that has happened repeatedly throughout Jewish history, earning us God's rebuke through the prophets, and bringing upon us exile after exile, including the current long exile, which has not yet ended. To this day, one who so desires can point to the shortcomings of the Jewish people and of individual Jews, even Torah-observant individuals and groups. Creation of holiness through observance of *mitzvot* is a long, challenging process. Therefore, it is unrealistic and unjust to expect full results over the short term, as much as one would like to see more than just the partial results that are evident. The slowness of the process is one reason that *t'shuvah* (repentance) is such an important component of Jewish life, on both the national and individual levels. At first blush, I should have added the word "sadly" after "but" in the first sentence in this note. However, the possibility of misusing *mitzvot*, of their not having the effect of creating sanctity with mechanical certainty, the necessity of *t'shuvah*, and the achievement of *k'dushah* as a process, are all consequences of human beings having free will. The exercise of free will in action, in thought, in belief, and in emotion is the only way that the human spirit, and a relationship with God, can grow authentically and have genuine meaning. Thus it is actually spiritually necessary that *mitzvot* not achieve the goal of sanctity with certainty, automatically or immediately. See notes 24 and 26.

[6] Although I will speak here of *mitzvot* as a means to achieving sanctity, this is not to say that they have no intrinsic value. To the contrary, I will show in

Part II that the *mitzvot*, as a means to achieving sanctity, share in a measure of that sanctity, so that they do have a degree of intrinsic value. This is one way of understanding the statement of Ben Azzai, "The reward of a *mitzvah* is a *mitzvah*"—that is, the *mitzvah* is its own reward (Pirkei Avot 4:2). Similarly, Maimonides wrote: "One should have no aim in studying wisdom other than knowing it. Similarly, the purpose of the truth is only to know that it is true, and the Torah is true, and the purpose of knowing it is to live it [literally, to do it]" (see the introduction to the tenth chapter of Sanhedrin in his Mishnah commentary). Maimonides expanded on this theme there, and wrote: "The sages warned against this as well—that is, that one should not set anything at all as the purpose of serving God and of performing *mitzvot*." The *mitzvot* are not to be related to as instruments toward achieving any goal other than their own intrinsic value, Maimonides wrote. They should not even be thought of as instrumental for the purpose of "earning a place in olam ha-ba (the world to come)," where the soul survives after the physical death of the body—even though, in fact, *olam ha-ba* will be the natural consequence of *mitzvah* observance. The Torah and the sages spoke of rewards for observing the *mitzvot* only for the educational purpose of encouraging such observance, which is often inconvenient, difficult, and not completely "natural" (see Part II, below). The various "reasons" for various *mitzvot* given by Jewish thinkers over the generations were also intended only to encourage observance (see Part II, below). Thus in this essay we will not adopt a commonly held view, that one studies the Torah and observes *mitzvot* in order to earn *olam ha-ba* (this view is commonly attributed to *M'sillat Y'sharim*). To the contrary, our approach will be completely oriented to our lives in this material world. And, even though we will speak of *mitzvot* as being instrumental (in the sense that they are the means by which to attain holiness), it should become clear in our presentation below of Rabbi Kook's view that this is not an instrumental approach in the sense that Maimonides opposed; rather, it is a description of the inherent value of *mitzvot* as part of a very long individual and national process.

[7] The list of thirty-nine characteristic activities included in this term, often mistranslated as "work" (for lack of a better term), has been characterized by Samson R. Hirsch as those activities in which people use their intelligence and practical skills to effect a material change in the world for their own benefit.

[8] Note the emphasis on "as the Eternal your God has commanded you." This emphasizes that observing the Sabbath as God's commandment is what will make it holy; Shabbat is not just a secular day of rest. This verse points toward the Oral Law, where the practical details of the concept of *m'lakhah* are spelled out. In addition, it alludes back to the first report of the giving of the Ten Commandments in Exodus, thus combining the later commandment to "guard"

Shabbat (*shamor*) with the earlier commandment to be continuously aware of Shabbat (zakhor).

[9] Including, among other things, eating *matzah*, and destroying and not eating *ḥametz*.

[10] For more on this idea of sacred space within the land of Israel as articulated in the Song at the Sea, see the article by Rachel Friedman elsewhere in this volume.

[11] Shoes protect a person's feet from being harmed by numerous dangers to be found on the ground. There is no need to be protected from sacred ground; to the contrary, one should come in direct contact with the holiness that is there, absorb it, and should be protected from harm by the holiness alone. Furthermore, shoes become dirty from all that is on the ground as they protect the feet; it would desecrate holy ground to bring such filth to it.

[12] *Guide for the Perplexed* III 32.

[13] M.T. Hilkhot Melakhim 11:1. Indeed, in complete consonance with our thesis here, in the course of stating that animal sacrifices were commanded to be brought before God as part of a weaning of the Israelites from idolatry (*Guide*, ibid.), Maimonides wrote explicitly that the aim of this process was to enable the ultimate fulfillment of God's charge to the Israelites to become "a nation of priests and a holy people."

[14] *T'ḥumin* (Alon Shevut: Tzomet Institute, 1980), vol. 1, p. 9.

[15] The second and third verses recited in the public Kedushah prayer carry the same complex message. A full study of this blessing and these verses is beyond the scope of this article.

[16] It appears that our sages wanted us to do a quick, symbolic review of the Torah before reciting the Shema, for the first of the two blessings relates to the beginning of the first book of the Torah, Genesis, while the second blessing focuses on themes from the last book of the Torah, Deuteronomy.

[17] After the usual opening, praising God "who is the Creator of everything," this blessing continues on Shabbat: "Everything thanks You, everything praises You, and everything says 'None is sacred like God'"—which is a quote of the beginning of this verse from Hannah's prayer. And the section concludes with the words: "None is comparable to You and there is none other than You; there is nothing without You"—the second part of the verse from Hannah's prayer. Thus this paragraph of prayer is framed by the verse from Hannah's prayer, suggesting that the author intended to expand thereby on the theme of the verse. The same theme is reiterated in different ways throughout this blessing: God is simultaneously transcendent and immanent, uniquely sacred.

[18] By way of wordplay, one may suggest the following mnemonic device. Most scholars agree that the Hebrew language is based on three-letter roots as the basic units of meaning, while others suggest that the basic units of meaning are two-letter roots. It seems to me most likely that both are right—that is, some

basic semantic units are two-lettered and some are three-lettered. In any event, it has also been suggested that the basic meanings of at least some of the three-letter roots may be combined from the meanings of two two-letter roots joined together. In this case, the root for "holy," *kof-dalet-shin*, may be thought of as a combination of *kof-dalet*, meaning "bow" or "worship," and *dalet-shin*, meaning either "break the outer cover to release what is inside" or "routine, mundane."

[19] B. Berakhot 10a.

[20] In Psalms 103 and 104.

[21] It is worthy of note that God is called, in this passage, *ha-kadosh barukh hu*, "the blessed Holy One"—for this passage deals with the notion of God's holiness and God's connection with human holiness.

[22] See Samson Raphael Hirsch's comment to Genesis 6:6 in his Torah commentary (trans. Isaac Levy; London: I. Levy, 1963), vol. 1, p. 132. While I believe that every non-Jewish aspect of Christian theology is easily disproven and rejected, the one area where many Christians seem to cling to their faith and to which we have only weak responses is just this: the ability to relate to God "personally," as a person. We have abstracted and de-anthropomorphized God to the point where having a personal relationship with God can be extremely difficult; indeed, it seems to be frequently discouraged. Yet, as Hirsch points out, de-personalizing God is not a necessary Jewish belief. To the contrary, God's presence in the universe stands in an authentic, highly personal relationship to humanity. I believe it would be to our advantage, in our desire to advance the awareness of God's presence in the world, to revive our experience of this.

[23] Hirsch, ibid.

[24] The following aphorism is attributed to Kabbalists: "There can be no coercion in spiritual matters."

[25] Perhaps this perspective provides an insight into the statement of Rabbi Avdimi bar Ḥama bar Ḥasa (B. Shabbat 88a) to the effect that God forced the Torah on the Israelites at Sinai. Before the giving of the Torah, they were free to choose how to worship God; but after God gave the Torah and expressed a preference for Israelite behavior and service of God—i.e., the positive and negative commandments—this became a reality that they could not change through their choice. Only God can choose what God wants; people may not dictate God's commandments to God. However, they are free to choose how to relate to the commandments.

[26] Nahmanides, like Maimonides, interpreted God's call in Leviticus 19:2, "You shall be holy, for I—the Eternal your God—am holy," as a general call concerning the manner in which all *mitzvot* are to be observed, and not as an individual commandment unto itself. (See Naḥmanides' glosses to the introduction to Maimonides' *Sefer Ha-mitzvot*, the fourth principle). Naḥmanides describes this general call to be sacred as a call for a life of self-restraint, going beyond

the letter of the law, refraining from satisfying one's lusts on the grounds that
it is technically permissible to do so. Thus, for example, there is holiness in
avoiding gluttony while eating permissible foods, avoiding drunkenness while
drinking permissible drinks, avoiding excessive sexual activity even within the
bounds of marriage, and avoiding foul language and cursing. Similarly, there is
holiness in developing admirable character traits (see Naḥmanides' commentary
to Leviticus 19:2). It is quite possible that Naḥmanides' dispute with Rashi
concerning the interpretation of this verse was not a matter of principle, but
rather a technical matter. Rashi seems to have applied it specifically to observing
the commandments of prohibited sexual relations, whereas Naḥmanides did not,
seeing it with much broader import—i.e., applying to all of the *mitzvot*. In any
event, I believe that Naḥmanides would agree that all of the commandments
are aimed at creating a holy person and a holy people, as I have argued above.
I believe, too, that Naḥmanides would concur with my presentation here of the
relationship between all *mitzvot* and sanctity. His interpretation of the verse
"You shall be holy" as an additional, general directive concerning how one is
to go about living a Torah way of life only emphasizes that the *mitzvot* have
the *potential* for creating a holy person and a holy people, but they may fail
to achieve their potential if the way of life in which the *mitzvot* are observed
is not appropriate. Indeed, the association of *mitzvot* with repugnant behavior
may create a desecration of God's name. For a more detailed treatment of
Naḥmanides' understanding of holiness, see the essay by Yitchak Blau elsewhere
in this volume.

[27] *Ein Ayah* (ed. Jerusalem, 1986), Shabbat 2:15, and cf. also 2:22–24.

[28] Here and in what follows I will paraphrase what Rabbi Kook wrote, although
his rich Hebrew poetic style makes a straightforward translation into English a
nigh impossible task.

[29] It appears that the notion of a human choice that has no purpose other than
itself, advanced also by Maimonides (see note 6), is genuinely foreign to human
beings. Thus it seems appropriate to acknowledge the difficulty of this concept,
and to be tolerant of the attempts that people make to identify the purpose even
of such choices. In the very selection we are discussing, in which Rabbi Kook
emphasizes that sanctity has no purpose other than itself and must not be said
to have a purpose, Rabbi Kook's opening sentence discusses this very notion:
"The difference between *mitzvah* and *k'dushah* is dependent on this, that the
purpose of sanctity (*mat'rat ha-k'dushah*) is to plant firmly in a human being the
exalted nature and the glory that is appropriate to conjecture in one's heart about
everything that concerns the glory of God…"

[30] B. Shabbat 22a.

[31] Rabbi Kook wrote elsewhere about the degradation of pure spiritual ideas
and their ultimate revival. See, for example, *Orot Ha-t'shuvah* (Jerusalem,

1924), 12:12. In a long paragraph probably intended as a description of the degradation of the Zionist idea and the inevitable ultimate restoration of its original heavenly greatness, much (but not all) of the description can be applied equally well to the process of attributing to *mitzvot* various purposes other than holiness.

[32] B. Shabbat 22a and B. Ḥullin 87a.

[33] Leviticus 19:26.

[34] Rabbi Kook expanded on this idea elsewhere (*inter alia, see his Ḥazon Hatzimḥonut V'ha-shalom Mi-b'ḥinah Toranit* (Jerusalem, 1961). He explains that human violence against other humans would be even worse than it is currently, if humans were unable to take out some of their aggressive, violent urges on animals. Thus, taking the lives of animals is a necessary concession at the present time until human beings will rise to a higher level in relation to their fellow humans. Moreover, human beings need to be reminded that they are not animals: unlike animals, humans are not to live merely in accordance with natural drives, instincts, and urges. This distinction between animals and humans is underscored by the fact that it is permissible to take the lives of animals for food, while the murder of humans remains strictly forbidden.

[35] In any event, the importance of Jewish separateness is referred to by the sages as *havdalah*, and its central significance is reiterated in the weekly blessing recited at the end of Shabbat and holidays (blessing God for separating us from the other nations, *ha-mavdil...bein yisrael la-ammim*). On the other hand, a midrash such as the following (B'reishit Rabbah 32:77) may refer to Jewish separateness, although I suspect its principal significance is in reference to the sanctity that is our ultimate aim, which we seek to share with God: "Rabbi Berekhiah said in the name of Rabbi Shimon: 'There is none like God' (Deuteronomy 33:26), yet 'Who is like the God of Yeshurun'? [It is our] grandfather, Israel [who is like God, even though none is like God]: Just as it is written about the blessed Holy One, 'And God alone will be exalted' (Isaiah 2:11), so too [is it written about] Jacob, 'And Jacob remained alone' (Genesis 32:25)."

[36] Note that the four types of sons enumerated in the Passover Haggadah are characterized according to the questions they ask. They seem to be ranked in descending order, in terms of the sophistication of their questions. The last level (and presumably the lowest) is that of the son who does not know how to ask at all. The Haggadah suggests that such a child be stimulated to ask questions, even by "spoon-feeding" the questions to him. For example, a parent might say, "You might have thought that I should have begun telling you about this at the beginning of the month..." or "You might have thought that I should have begun during the day..." No Jewish spiritual growth is possible without asking questions.

[37] The three examples I will give here illustrate a certain type of negative commandment. Many negative commandments prohibit evil behavior, such

as idolatry, murder, incest, theft, or giving false testimony. However, the aim of other negative commandments is to mold desirable behavior in such a way as to make it holy. Examples of such commandments include the dietary laws (which insist that we refrain from eating certain foods), the laws of Shabbat (which insist that we refrain from performing *m'lakhah* on the seventh day), and the laws of family purity (which insist that we refrain from sexual intimacy at certain times).

[38] It is surely not my intention here to denigrate all the non-Jewish human cultures of the world. Each people makes its unique contribution to humanity, every individual is created in the image of God, and the righteous of all nations have a share in the world to come. Here we are attempting to express the unique contribution to humanity that can be made by the Jewish people, who are, indeed, recognized by significant portions of humanity as the people with a special, ancient covenant with God. I argue here that the unique contribution of Israel lies in fulfilling God's charge to be "a kingdom of priests and a holy nation." Indeed, the system of *mitzvot* is binding only on the Jewish people, not on all peoples of the earth. It should be noted that the thesis presented here is independent of the view of Yehudah Halevi that the Jewish people have an innate proclivity toward the holy and the divine; that is, this thesis holds whether or not one agrees with that view.

[39] This view is generally ascribed to Yehudah Halevi, in his *Kuzari*.

[40] The announcement of the demise of Torah study and *mitzvah* observance, and the declaration that they are out-of-date, primitive, and stuck in a past that will never return, have been repeated and disproven so often that one can only conclude that those who repeat them are stuck in the past themselves, refusing to see the thriving, genuine, faithful Jewish living and learning taking place right before their eyes.

[41] As much as we have contributed and continue to contribute in all of these areas, as loyal citizens, in all of our host countries around the world, nowhere is all of the responsibility and the authority ours as they are in the State of Israel.

[42] A full set of drawings in Hebrew was prepared originally by my sister, Renah Bell, a talented graphic artist, calligrapher, and art instructor. I have used them in teaching in Israel. The drawings in English were redesigned in a new, original formal especially for this book by my multi-talented friend, Ovadyah.

[43] I recommend using at least twice "letter size" (international standard size A3).

[44] The drawings should not be given out all at once.

[45] Maimonides: *Sefer Ha-mitzvot*, positive commandment #5, basing himself on the comment to Deuteronomy 11:13 found at Sifrei Deuteronomy, *Eikev 5*.

[46] In light of this equivalence between prayer and Torah study, one must clarify the sages' distinction between prayer as *hayyei sha·ah*, focusing on life of the moment, in contrast to Torah study, which is *hayyei olam*, focusing on eternal life. See Rabbi Kook in *Ein Ayah*, Berakhot 7:35.

[47] I believe this parallel between Torah study and prayer is well known. Less well known is the following parallel. While most *mitzvot* apply to individuals, there are at least several that are the responsibility of the entire Jewish people as a whole national unit, although the actual fulfillment of the *mitzvah* devolves on individuals. Thus, for example, the commandment to circumcise all males on the eighth day of life seems to be the responsibility of the entire Jewish people (see Maimonides' Introduction to Hilkhot Milah). The first individual responsible for that is the father, but if he does not fulfill his responsibility, then it reverts to the bet din, as representatives of all of Israel. If they do not fulfill the responsibility, then the man must see to it himself when he reaches maturity; he alone will suffer the sanction for violating this *mitzvah* if it remains unfulfilled. Another example is the *mitzvah* of settling the land of Israel (for those who count this as a *mitzvah*), which requires the people of Israel to acquire and maintain sovereignty in the land of Israel, but which individuals fulfill by living in Israel in such a way as to strengthen Jewish sovereignty there. (There has been much speculation as to why Maimonides did not count this as a *mitzvah*; perhaps its application to individuals' behavior did not appear to Maimonides as sufficiently well defined to justify counting it.) Perhaps both Torah study and prayer are commandments that are at least partially of this type. Thus all the requests in our formal prayers are formulated in the plural, and, more fundamentally, the formulation of standardized prayer texts may be seen as a means for the entire Jewish people to fulfill their national responsibility to serve God in this way together, as one people—even as individuals pray both for their own needs and the nation's needs. Torah, as well, was given to the Israelites at Sinai in unison, as a whole "corporate" entity, and not only to a large group of individuals. Thus, too, we can understand why, when a father is better at Torah study than his son, then the father should devote himself fully to that study while the son supports the family (see B. Kiddushin 29b)—for in this way the total sum of the Jewish people's Torah study will be maximized, Torah study being a way for the entire nation to serve God.

[48] On Jacob's way back to the land of Canaan with his family, the night before his reunion with his brother Esau he was left alone overnight, at which time he was injured in a struggle with an unidentified man/angel. Jacob's descendants undertook not to eat the corresponding sinew in a kosher domestic animal, the gid ha-nasheh (generally identified as the sciatic nerve; see Genesis 32:33). The commentator Ḥizkuni suggested that this was to be an eternal reminder never to do what the children of Jacob had done: leaving their father alone and exposed to danger. Of course, this is not the only meaning of the *mitzvah* of gid ha-nasheh.

[49] The *mitzvot* on this "Tree of Jewish Life" were selected in the spirit of Maimonides' selection, in his *Sefer Ha-mitzvot*, of sixty commandments (out of

a total of 613 *mitzvot* in the Torah) that shaped the life of a regular householder living in his day. That was fewer than 10% of all of the *mitzvot*! Similarly, we have selected for our tree the principal areas of Jewish life (including laws of rabbinic origin and customs) that are generally considered relevant today. This reflects the continuing tragedy of our people, for our Temple still lies in ruin, the majority of our people are in exile, intermarriage and assimilation are creating a tragic loss to us of millions of our people, and the revival of our national life in the State of Israel is based on a combination of Turkish Mandatory law, British Commonwealth law, American law, and Israeli secular law, with only a minute amount of Jewish law. As we rejoice in the blessings God has showered on our people in the past two generations, and thank God for them, we know that this is only the beginning, and that we have an unknown distance yet to go before our Torah way of life is fully restored. Thus the picture presented by "The Tree of Jewish Life" may be accurate in terms of Jewish life today, but it is woefully lacking as a presentation of Jewish life of *mitzvot* as we pray it will be in our future.

Searching for Holiness:
The Song of the Sea in the Bible and in the Liturgy

Rachel Friedman[1]

Great is the power of prayer. For to worship is to expand the presence of God in the world. God is transcendent, but our worship makes Him immanent.[2]

Prayer is the search for holiness. That is, when we pray, we seek to bring God's divine presence into our daily experience. Many people are familiar with this idea as expressed in the rules and philosophy of prayer, but many fewer understand how it is expressed in the actual liturgical texts of prayer. This essay examines one example of this theme, in the prayer Az Yashir, also known as Shirat Ha-yam, the Song of the Sea.[3] It is hoped that a literary-theological analysis of the Song of the Sea in its biblical and liturgical settings will inspire a personal connection between this ancient poem and its modern daily readers, and thus enhance the experience of sanctity for those who recite this prayer.

The "Verses of Praise" and the Daily Prayer Service

The Song of the Sea is part of the section of the liturgy known as Pesukei D'zimra, or "Verses of Praise." The Talmud teaches that "a person should first recount the praise of God, and then pray" (B. Berakhot 32b). The rabbis instituted Pesukei D'zimra to prepare the individual for the recitation of the central elements of the daily prayer service—the Shema and the Amidah—by focusing one's thoughts on the Divine and the contemplation of God's glory. Before we can ask God to grant our needs and requests, we must enter the proper state of mind by thinking about, and praising, God.

The broad theme of these selections is praise of God for creation of the splendid and orderly natural universe. Pesukei D'zimra begins with the introductory blessing popularly called Barukh She-amar, which includes ten praises of God, each beginning with the word *barukh* ("blessed").[4] The prayer itself explains its goal, as follows: we intend to praise God through the songs of David (*u-v'shirei David avdekha, n'hallel'kha Adonai eloheinu*). Indeed, the core passages that follow are the six final chapters of the book of Psalms—Psalm 145, commonly known as the Ashrei ("praiseworthy are those..."),[5] and Psalms 146–150, the *halleluyah*-psalms.[6] The remainder of Pesukei D'zimra is mostly composed of passages from the Bible that are also traditionally attributed to David, from the book of Psalms and elsewhere. Pesukei D'zimra then concludes with the blessing of Yishtabaḥ ("May [Your name] be praised"), which enumerates fifteen words of praise and fifteen expressions of glorification of God.

The Song of the Sea stands out from most other selections in Pesukei D'zimra because it is not attributed to David.[7] It is a song found in the biblical book of Exodus, a song recited by the Israelites after they crossed the Sea of Reeds and their Egyptian pursuers were defeated. Why is this song, which begins with the words "Then Moses and Israel sang," included in the category of the songs of David? What was the motivation for including this passage, and the verses that precede and follow it, in the Pesukei D'zimra section of the service?

In order to answer these questions we must consider the significance of the Song of the Sea in its biblical context.

The Biblical Significance of Shirat Ha-yam

The structure and themes of the book of Exodus, based on a plain-sense reading of the biblical account, is as follows:

Book of Exodus: Part 1

1–14	Oppression and Exodus
15:1–21	**Song of the Sea**

Book of Exodus: Part 2

15:22–17:16	Journey begins
18–24	Revelation at Sinai
25–31	Commandment to build the tabernacle
32–34	Sin of the golden calf
35–40	Construction of the tabernacle

On the simplest level, Shirat Ha-yam marks a turning point, the end of the period of the Exodus. The time of oppression and miraculous salvation are over (chapters 1–15:21), and the journey through the wilderness toward the land of Canaan has begun (chapters 15:22ff.). Thus, Shirat Ha-yam is the demarcation line between Part 1 and Part 2 of the book of Exodus. In this sense, it is similar to Song of Deborah (Judges 5), which marks the completion of the conquest of Canaan.

On a deeper, level, however, Shirat Ha-yam is the key to understanding the entire structure of the book of Exodus. Analysis of the passage helps clarify the very nature of the book.

A disagreement regarding the overall theme and purpose of the book of Exodus dates back to the rabbinic period. Is Exodus a book that tells the story of a nation of slaves who are liberated, enter a covenant with God, and, in a culminating crescendo, build a sanctuary in which to serve God? Or is it the story of a nation liberated by God and blessed with divine revelation that then falters by succumbing to idol worship, so that God must command the construction of a sanctuary to fulfill their need for physical worship?

This divergence in opinion reflects two different views as to the actual chronology of events in the narrative. According to the sequence described in the book, and assumed by the thirteenth-century Spanish exegete Rabbi Moses Naḥmanides (among others), God commanded Moses to construct the tabernacle (*mishkan*) immediately following the revelation at Sinai. According to this understanding, it had always been God's intention to have a tabernacle at Sinai and to dwell among the people.[8] The people then sinned with the golden calf, and the Torah therefore reiterates that the command to build the tabernacle was nonetheless fulfilled.

The midrash, however, as well as many of the classical commentators (such as the sixteenth-century Italian exegete Obadiah Sforno),[9] assumes that this is one example of the principle *ein mukdam u-me'uḥar ba-torah*, that the Torah is not necessarily written in chronological order. In fact, the sages argued, the command to build the tabernacle followed the sin of the golden calf; it was only in response to the sin that the concept of the tabernacle was introduced at all.[10]

There is an indication in the text that the book of Exodus records events in their actual sequence—and we can appreciate this through careful study of Shirat Ha-yam. Immediately after the liberation from Egypt, after witnessing their salvation from the Egyptians at the Sea of Reeds, Moses and the people pause to reflect on the new era of history unfolding before them. At this juncture, the Israelites express their heartfelt desire to embrace God in sacred space, proclaiming: *zeh Eili v'anveihu*, usually translated as "This is my God, whom I shall glorify" (Exodus 15:2). Targum Onkelos, however, explains the word *v'anveihu* as deriving from the word *naveh*, habitation: "This is my God, for whom I shall build a sanctuary." The twelfth-century Spanish exegete Abraham ibn Ezra elaborates: "This is my God, and I wish to make a habitation wherein God can dwell with me forever."[11]

At the conclusion of the song, the nation lodges the same request: "You will bring them and plant them in the mountain of Your inheritance, the place You made to dwell in, O Eternal, the sanctuary, my Sovereign, that Your hands established" (15:17). When the Israelites are finally planted in the land of Israel, they will build a permanent structure in God's honor. Shirat Ha-yam begins and ends with the same theme: the Israelites desire a physical location at which they can experience God's presence on earth. Scholars have noted that this theme is prominent in ancient Near Eastern texts as well, where songs often express a desire to build temples to the gods. For example, the Babylonian creation epic Enuma Elish culminates with the building of a temple for Marduk, and the Ugaritic Baal-Yam texts describe the construction of a palace for Baal following his victory over Yam. Thus Shirat Ha-yam, which proclaims the sovereignty of the God of Israel, asks that a temple be built to God's name.

This desire to build a shrine for God is implicit elsewhere in the song as well. Whereas the first eleven verses of the song celebrate God's salvation of Israel at the Sea of Reeds, verse 12 introduces the theme of God's holiness, in addition to the theme of divine power: "Who is like You among the heavenly powers, Eternal One! Who is like You, mighty in holiness (*nedar ba-kodesh*)." Similarly, in verse 13, God is not only the victorious warrior but also the redeemer who guides Israel to the divine destination of holiness: "You have led with might to Your holy abode (*n'veih kodshekha*)." Ibn Ezra asserts that the "holy abode" referred to here is Mount Sinai: the Israelites praise God for leading them to the site of revelation. This explanation is in fact quite logical, given the location of this praise in the song: it occurs after the description of the events at the Sea and before the description of the Canaanite nations' fear of conquest. If the nation's desire for *v'anveihu* (verse 2) is their wish to enshrine God on earth, we might argue that the hope expressed in the song is similarly to build the *mishkan*, the tabernacle, at Mount Sinai.

Israel desired a sanctuary, a sacred place, and God responded by commanding the building of the tabernacle—not as a concession to human frailty, but as a response to the Jewish people's desire for nearness to God, as expressed in Shirat Ha-yam. This indicates that the final 16 chapters of Exodus, the complex and detailed enterprise of building the tabernacle, had always been part of the divine plan, to have the people create an abode for God's presence in the wilderness. Perhaps the tabernacle was a response to the desire for a physical mode of worship, but that desire is not negative. On the contrary: it is the lofty desire to continue to glorify God in a sacred space long after we have concluded singing the song glorifying God's miracles.

The Liturgical Context of the Song of the Sea

With this background in mind, we can understand the function of Shirat Ha-yam as part of Pesukei D'zimra, which consists predominantly of the songs of David. Shirat Ha-yam, the Torah's paradigm for the praise of God as savior, culminates with a request that God invest the divine glory on earth, creating a sacred space for humans to worship God. This is, in fact, the subtext of all of Pesukei D'zimra.

In the Ashkenazic liturgy,[14] Barukh She-amar (the beginning of Pesukei D'zimra) is preceded by Psalm 30 (Mizmor Shir Hanukkat Ha-bayit L'David); according to a prominent rabbinic tradition, this psalm was intended by David to be sung at the dedication of the Temple.[15] In fact, although it was David's son Solomon who would actually build the Temple, one of our primary associations with David is his own desire to build it. It was David who pleaded with God for the opportunity to build a house for divine worship, and when his request was denied, he prepared the plans and materials for its eventual construction.[16]

Pesukei D'zimra continues to praise God, particularly in connection with the divine sanctuary on earth. Hodu, the first passage that follows Barukh She-amar, is a song of thanksgiving composed by David when the portable ark was brought to Jerusalem, in preparation for the ultimate construction of a permanent sanctuary.[17] Psalm 100 (Mizmor L'todah) was recited when one brought a thanksgiving offering in the Temple upon salvation from a hazardous situation.[18] Psalm 145 (T'hillah L'David), the most important passage in Pesukei D'zimra, is introduced with the words *ashrei yosh'vei veitekha*, "Happy are those who dwell in Your house"—words that are not actually a part of that psalm.[18] The final Halleluyah, the magnificent culminating song of Psalm 150, was recited by pilgrims bringing their first fruits to Jerusalem. It begins, "Praise God in God's holy place (*b'kodsho*)."

Following this psalm, we recite three successive verses from the book of Psalms that each begins with the word *barukh* ("blessed"),[21] which would seem to bring closure to the praise begun in Barukh She-amar, where that word is the central theme. We would expect Pesukei D'zimra to end here, but instead, we move on to the passages of *Va-y'varekh* David ("David blessed the Eternal"),[22] *Attah Hu Adonai L'vadekha* ("You alone are the Eternal"),[23] and Shirat Ha-yam. What are these sections doing here? I suggest that they continue the theme that we have begun through the excerpts from the "songs of David": they mark the historical moments when Israel asked God for sacred space on earth.

At the end of his life, David made Jerusalem the capital of his kingdom and he brought the ark there. Denied the chance to build the Temple himself, he assembled the people and charged them with the task of doing so. The *Va-y'varekh* David passage is David's prayer of thanksgiving, which he recited after concluding his preparations for the Temple that would be built by his son Solomon.

The next section, *Attah Hu Adonai L'vadekha* ("You alone are the Eternal"), is an excerpt from a prayer recited by Ezra, Nehemiah, d their community after the return to Zion. Ezra and Nehemiah summon the people to reaffirm their covenant with God and ask God to help them as they rebuild Jerusalem, with the intent of rebuilding the Temple. Indeed, this gathering culminates with the people's affirming their commitment to the Temple service: "We will not leave the house of our God" (Nehemiah 10:40).

Pesukei D'zimra then continues with Shirat Ha-yam (introduced by Exodus 14:30–31, *Va-yosha Adonai*), which describes, as we have said, the very first request for a sanctuary. The song glorifies God as Israel's savior and asks God to invest the divine presence in a sacred space on earth—a *mishkan* (tabernacle) or *mikdash* (temple).

The opening words of Shirat Ha-yam indicate that this composition was recited in immediate response to the miracles that Israel witnessed at the sea: *Az yashir*, "Then they sang." The rabbis of the midrash claim that the verb in this verse is actually in future tense and, strictly speaking, should be translated literally as "then they *will* sing."[24] According to this midrash, this is the song that Moses and the Israelites *will* sing in future, messianic times. Similarly, Rashi writes in his comment to Exodus 15:1: "This is a hint in the Torah to the resurrection."

Thus, to the rabbis, the significance of the Song of the Sea is not limited exclusively to the episode of the splitting of the sea. Similarly, to the compilers of Pesukei D'zimra, the recitation of Shirat Ha-yam does not simply recall a song of praise that had been sung once upon a time, or a request for God's presence that had been lodged ages ago. Rather, Shirat Ha-yam anticipates messianic times and the future Third Temple; it thus constitutes our own praise of God and our own request for *mikdash Adonai kon'nu yadekha*, "the sanctuary, O Lord, that Your hands established" (Exodus 15:17).

Because of these messianic implications, we conclude our recitation of Shirat Ha-yam with other verses that refer to the ultimate redemption and God's universal sovereignty: "For sovereignty is the Eternal's, and God rules over the nations" (Psalm 22:29); "Saviors shall go up to Mount Zion to judge Mount Esau, and sovereignty shall be the Eternal's" (Obadiah 1:21); "Then the Eternal shall be sovereign over the whole earth; on that day, the Eternal shall be one and God's name shall be one" (Zechariah 14:9).

According to our understanding of the thrust of Shirat Ha-yam, it serves as an appropriate capstone to Pesukei D'zimra: it declares the glory of God, crowns God as our sovereign, and asks God to create sacred space for us on earth.

Searching for Holiness: The Song of the Sea in the Bible and in Prayer

In our prayer service, then, the Song of the Sea plays two key roles. First, it provides the final "verses of praise" for Pesukei D'zimra, concluding our introduction to the formal prayer service (which begins immediately thereafter with the Shema and the Amidah). Second, it provides a model for praising God (on which this entire introductory section of the morning prayer service is based). To understand the Song of the Sea, then, is to understand how the compilers of Pesukei D'zimra conceived of the very act of prayer.[25]

Our reading has shown that Shirat Ha-yam (and thus the very enterprise of prayer itself) is about how to create holiness: how to create an encounter with God on this earth and in our daily lives. This biblical song concludes Pesukei D'zimra because it is not only about creating holiness in an abstract sense, but is about doing so in the most concrete way possible: by building a physical space set aside for encountering God.

The Song of the Sea connects us to a historical moment in which the nation of Israel beseeched God, seeking to create sacred space on earth. Since being granted that privilege, our people has been forced by history to transition from one conception of sacred space to another, and then yet another: from tabernacle to Temple to synagogue. But, through all its various expressions, our quest for holiness endures. We continue through our prayers to encounter God wherever and whenever we are.

NOTES

[1] I am grateful to Meira Mintz and Dr. David Shatz for their contributions to earlier drafts of this essay. I am also grateful to Elie Friedman for his valuable suggestions and to Allen Friedman for his continued inspiration.

[2] Abraham Joshua Heschel, *Quest for God: Studies in Prayer and Symbolism* (1954; rpt. New York: Scribner's, 1983), p. 62.

[3] The history of the liturgical recitation of Shirat Ha-yam is itself a fascinating topic but one that is outside the scope of this essay. Shirat Ha-yam was part of the liturgy in the Temple; it was sung by the Levites on Shabbat afternoons in conjunction with the daily offering, the *korban tamid*. After the destruction of the Second Temple, two different customs developed with respect to the inclusion of Shirat Ha-yam in the prayer service. In Babylonia it was not included in the daily service, and even in geonic times it was sung only on Shabbat and holidays; only much later did it become a fixed part of the daily prayer service. In the land of Israel, however, many customs of the Temple were incorporated into the daily service after its destruction, and Shirat Ha-yam was thus included in Pesukei D'zimra from earliest times. See, e.g., Eliezer Levi, *Torat Ha-t'fillah* (Tel Aviv: Abraham Zioni Publishing House, 1967), pp. 123–125.

[4] In the first line of the prayer Barukh She-amar, the words *barukh hu* are a response to the previous phrase and are therefore not counted as a separate line of praise.

[5] In the prayer service, Psalm 145 is introduced with two verses, Psalms 84:5 and 144:15, both of which begin with the word *ashrei*. Therefore, this prayer is commonly referred to as "the Ashrei."

[6] These six psalms correspond to the six days of creation. See, e.g., the comment of Rabbi Jonathan Sacks in *The Koren Siddur with Introduction, Translation, and Commentary by Rabbi Sir Jonathan Sacks* (Jerusalem: Koren Publishers, 2009), pp. 62, 65. The concept of God as Creator is fused with that of God as Sustainer; God created humanity and continues to care for it. Thus, these passages describe not only the wonders of nature, but also the graciousness of God's nurture. Psalm 147, for example, describes God as the One who not only "counts the stars" and rules the cosmos, but also as the One who "heals the broken-hearted and binds their wounds."

[7] The passages from Nehemiah 9:6–11, which immediately precede Shirat Ha-yam in Pesukei D'zimra, and the passages from Obadiah 1:21 and Zechariah 14:9, which immediately follow it, are also not attributed to David. We will discuss these passages later in this essay.

[8] See especially Naḥmanides' introduction to the book of Exodus.

[9] See especially Sforno's introduction to the Torah, where he discusses the content and purpose of the book of Exodus.

[10] *Midrash Tanhuma*, for example, explains that the golden vessels of the mishkan

serve as an atonement (*kapparah*) for the gold used to construct the golden calf. See *Tanhuma T'rumah* §8. This is also the approach adopted by Rashi, who suggests that the bull brought by Aaron as a sin offering at the dedication of the *mishkan* was intended to atone for the sin of the golden calf. See Rashi on Exodus 29:1, s.v. *par ehad*.

[11] See similarly the comment of Sforno on Exodus 15:2: "I will make a habitation so that God may dwell within us." Compare also the NJPS translation of the verse, "I will enshrine Him." Rashi cites Onkelos' translation and also offers an alternative translation: "From the word noi, 'beauty.' I will tell of God's beauty and praise to all people." See also The *Koren Siddur*, p. 80, which translates the phrase as "I will beautify."

[12] Note that this verse uses plant imagery—*titta·eimo* (from the verbal root meaning "to plant")—evoking the concept of rootedness in the land.

[13] Nahum Sarna agrees that this is the most likely interpretation. See *The JPS Torah Commentary: Exodus* (Philadelphia: Jewish Publication Society, 1991), p. 80. This explanation is substantiated by the description of the journey from Egypt found in Psalm 78:54: "[God] brought them to the border of holiness; this mountain that God's right hand acquired." It is also implicit in the language of God's promise at the burning bush: "When you take the nation out of Egypt, you will worship God on this *mountain*" (Exodus 3:12).

[14] The discussion in this section assumes the sequence of Pesukei D'zimra in Nusah Ashkenaz.

[15] See, e.g., Rashi on Psalm 30:1. See also the comment of the thirteenth-century exegete Rabbi David Kimhi (Radak) on this verse.

[16] See 2 Samuel 7 and 1 Chronicles 17, 22:5–19.

[17] 1 Chronicles 16:8–34.

[18] See e.g. Rashi on Psalm 100:1.

[19] The words are from Psalm 84:5; cf. note 5 above.

[20] See e.g. Maimonides, Mishneh Torah, Hilkhot Bikkurim 4:17.

[21] These three verses are the concluding verses of three of the books of Psalms.

[22] 1 Chronicles 29:10–13.

[23] Nehemiah 9:6–11.

[24] See, e.g., Mekhilta D'Rabbi Yishmael, *Shirata* 1 on Exodus 15:1. According to the simple meaning of the biblical text, the word *yashir* is used here as a reference to the past. In biblical Hebrew, the imperfect *yashir* can refer to the past or the future, depending on context. Rashi (on Exodus 15:1) offers a third possibility when he explains, "Then—after witnessing the miracles—it occurred to Moses that he should sing."

[25] It has been suggested that the ten words of praise in Barukh She-amar are meant by its composers to evoke the ten times that God "spoke" (*va-yomer*) in the course of creation (Pirkei Avot 5:1); in this regard, see the comment of Rabbi Jonathan Sacks in *The Koren Siddur*, p. 65. It has also been suggested

that the fifteen words of praise in Yishtabaḥ correspond to the fifteen steps leading to the entrance of the Temple, on which the Levites stood as they sang their hymns (the "songs of ascent," Psalms 120–134). See Sefer *Abudraham Hashaleim* (Jerusalem: Even Israel Publishing, 1995), p. 74. See also the discussion in Bernhard Salomon Jacobson, *The Weekday Siddur* (Tel Aviv: Sinai Publishing, 1978), p. 119. Pesukei D'zimra can thus be understood as beginning with the praise of God as Creator, and concluding with the praise of God as the One who answers our request for God to dwell on earth.

K'dushat Makom: On Sacred Space[1]

Nathaniel Helfgot

Introduction

One of the most iconic pictures in recent Jewish memory shows three Israeli paratroopers immediately after the liberation of the Western Wall on the third day of the Six Day War in 1967. They are shown expressing awe and wonder as they stand before the last remnant of our holy Temple and the touchstone of our history in the land of Israel. In those moments, and in many subsequent months and years, both religious and avowedly non-religious soldiers—and, indeed, multitudes of religious and non-religious Jews in Israel and throughout the world—have felt something special, something unique, something historic, something…spiritual. Indeed, in many published comments in subsequent months, non-religious Israelis expressed feelings of deep emotion and sanctity as they came into direct contact with a historic remnant of the holy Temple in Jerusalem. And this continues until today in the comments one reads on Facebook, in blogs, and in newspaper articles of young Jewish adults who have been given the gift of a Birthright trip by leading Jewish philanthropists and the State of Israel, upon their visit to the Kotel. As one young woman recently put it:

"One thing that really hit me hard was the Kotel," she says. McCombs expected to have "the normal tourist reaction, like, 'Oh, there's the Wall, that is so cool.'" Instead, she found herself in tears. To share the experience "with other people

I'd never known before, seeing how hard hit they were too" added to this uniquely spiritual moment, says McCombs.[2]

This essay is a short examination of the concept of sacred space in Jewish thought and its meaning for us today as we struggle to experience a sense of the sacred and numinous in our fast-paced and ever-changing world and the secular ethos that finds no room for the holy.

In the Beginning: Heschel on the Priority of Time

In his highly influential monograph *The Sabbath*, the noted theologian Abraham Joshua Heschel lays out a fundamental dichotomy between holiness of place and holiness of time in Jewish thought. In Heschel's words:

> Judaism is a *religion of time* aiming at the sanctification of time....The Sabbaths are our great cathedrals, and our Holy of Holies is a shrine that neither the Romans nor the Germans were able to burn....Now what was the first holy object in the history of the world? Was it a mountain? Was it an altar? It is, indeed, a unique occasion at which the distinguished word *kadosh* is used for the first time...it is applied to time: "And God blessed the seventh day and made it holy." There is no reference in the record of creation to any object in space that would be endowed with the quality of holiness...When history began, there was only one holiness in the world, holiness of time. When at Sinai, the word of God was about to be voiced, a call for holiness in man was proclaimed: "You shall be unto me a holy people." It was only after the people had succumbed to the temptation of worshipping a thing, a golden calf, that the erection of the Tabernacle, of holiness in space, was commanded. The sanctity of time came first, the sanctity of man second, and the sanctity of space last.[3]

In Heschel's reading, this is not only a historical reality but one that bespeaks an ongoing statement of our hierarchy of values, such that sanctity of time always supersedes sanctity of space.[4] And even when we speak of holiness of space in Judaism, Heschel writes that

> no place on earth, is holy by itself....The temple became a sacred place...yet the paradox of a sanctity in space was yet sensed by the prophets. The pious people of Israel would sing, "Let us go into His dwelling place; let us worship at His footstool" (Psalm 132:7); but the prophet proclaimed: "Thus saith the Lord: The Heaven is My throne and the earth is My footstool; where is the house that you may build unto Me?" (Isaiah 66:1). If God is everywhere, He cannot be just somewhere."[5]

Heschel continues in this vein for many paragraphs, painting a picture of a Judaism in which the concept of the sanctity of space is downplayed and relegated to a secondary role in the larger drama of humanity's interaction with the Divine.

Critique of Heschel

This sharp antinomy between holiness of time and holiness of space is one of the enduring legacies of Heschel's thought. It has been cited in writing hundreds of times in the half-century since he introduced it to the English-speaking world in 1951. And these ideas have penetrated not only the inner circles of Heschel's natural constituencies in the more liberal movements in American Judaism; they have also had an impact on Orthodox circles and thinking. To take just two examples: First, the great educator and Bible scholar Nechama Leibowitz approvingly cites a number of passages from Heschel's writing cited above, in her discussion of the relationship between the building of the tabernacle and the laws of Shabbat at the beginning of the Torah portion Va-yak·heil.[6] Second, my good friend and teacher, Dr. David Shatz, has noted to me that he vividly recalls a teacher at Yeshiva University High School in the early 1960s assigning his class to read *The Sabbath*, so as to explore the underlying concepts of Shabbat.

As with many of Heschel's antinomies, the reader must grapple with a nagging question. Heschel's extreme formulation of the dichotomy is, like all his writing, elegant, poetic, and edifying. But is it correct?

While it is true that the first element that God describes as "holy" is indeed time (Genesis 2:3), the biblical narrative proceeds to spend many verses describing the special place on earth, the Garden of Eden, where God places Adam and Eve to live their idyllic life.[7] And, most tellingly for our purposes, this place is described as the spatial domain in which God is intensely present, the place through which God literally "walks" during the course of the day; it is also called the place "which is before the Eternal."[8] This term is later used by the Bible to describe the land of Israel as a whole[10] and more specifically the precincts of the Temple —or, in Maimonides' reading, the entire environs of Jerusalem.[11]

Moreover, the entire corpus of the Bible is saturated with the notion of the holiness of space—whether in narratives such as Jacob's awakening in Beth-El (Genesis 28), Moses' encounter with God at the burning bush where God directly tells him that he is standing on *admat kodesh*, terra sancta (Exodus 3:5), or in the detailed laws of the tabernacle contained in so many parts of the five books of the Torah (especially Exodus 25–40). The Temple, the *mikdash*, is of course a central institution in the biblical worldview— and its name is connected to the same Hebrew root as *kodesh*, holy.[12]

As we noted above, Heschel claims that the *mishkan*, the tabernacle, was only introduced to the Jewish people as a concession, reflecting God's lowered expectations of them in the aftermath of the sin of the golden calf. This reading does find support in some *midrashim* and is understood by many to be the view of medieval commentaries such as Rashi,[13] and it is explicit in the writings of Rav Ovadiah Sforno;[14] however, the plain sense of the text and many other voices in the tradition (such as Naḥmanides) see the tabernacle as a fully desirable phenomenon, as part of the divine plan all along and in no way a concession. Furthermore, leaving this debate, the Torah clearly envisions a central role for the holy sanctuary in the land of Israel long before there is any hint of backsliding or sin around a human creation. In the Song of the Sea, at the beautiful closing section of the poem, Moses prophetically declares: *mikdash Adonai kon'nu yadekha*, "the holy place that You, Eternal, have established" (Exodus 15:17). Two *parshiyot* later, at the conclusion of the Book of the Covenant in Mishpatim, the Torah introduces the concept of the three pilgrimage holidays and concludes with the following phrase: "The first fruits of your land should be brought to the House of the Eternal, your God (*beit Adonai Elohekha*)" (Exodus 23:19). And into this reality, the Bible continually drives home the notion that humanity, and specifically the Jewish people, can "defile" the sanctuary and thus drive out God's presence through ritual impurity and, by extension, by their infidelity to the dictates of the covenant through their moral, ethical, and ritual behavior.

If we move beyond the biblical text itself, the picture regarding sacred space that emerges is even clearer. The foundational text of rabbinic Judaism is, of course, the Mishnah. The order Mo·eid, the section devoted to the Sabbath and the holy days of the Jewish calendar, takes up one-sixth of its corpus. In contrast, the orders of Zera·im, Kodashim, and Tohorot, which focus on laws rooted in the holiness of the land of Israel and the mitzvot that are applicable exclusively in that locale—the laws of the Temple, sacrifices, and ritual purity,[15] as well as laws that focus on holiness of place, objects, and human beings and the avoidance of sacrilege of those entities— take up a more than half of the text of the entire Mishnah. And it is not simply a question of relative space accorded to each of these themes. The entire text of the Mishnah, even outside of those orders, is permeated with the concepts of the holiness of the land of Israel and its consequences, as well as the holiness of the Temple and its attendant concerns, especially the sacrificial rite and the laws of ritual purity. These areas of concern make their mark in other areas of the Mishnah, far removed from the tractates that deal directly these issues. To cite one example: consider the *mishnayot* included in tractate Eiduyot, which contains a veritable cross-section of various *halakhot* cited by various sages on one specific day. Roughly two-thirds of the *mishnayot* recorded there focus on areas of ritual purity, laws tied to the land of Israel, and laws of sacrifices—all of which go hand in hand with the idea of sacred space. The next-largest category of halakhic material is laws related to marriage and personal status, with only occasional forays into matters dealing with torts and or with the holidays and Shabbat.

In short, a perusal of the biblical and rabbinic material yields the undeniable conclusion that Heschel's paradigm is extreme in its formulation and does not accord with the evidence of the foundational texts of Judaism. It is no doubt true that with the destruction of the Temple and the exile from the land, the centrality of the laws relating to the land, to the Temple and sacrifices, and to ritual purity waned—both in the practical sphere and in the theoretical consciousness of both the scholarly elite and the average Jew. Indeed, with these of areas of *halakhah* relegated to *hilkh'ta di-m'shiḥa* (that is, laws that would only be operative in some far-off and distant messianic utopian age), the other areas of Jewish law took on greater centrality in Jewish consciousness. Laws relating to rituals for home and synagogue, personal status, and business now received the lion's share of the attention of sages and laypeople alike, and the "temples of time" that were Shabbat and the holidays took on even greater significance. Moreover, as many scholars have noted, it was during the period of the aftermath of the destruction of the Temple that the great enterprise of aggadic ethicization and reinterpretation of the laws of sacrifices and ritual purity took place, in order to give to these laws meaning and resonance in a world where they could not be practiced. It is during this period that great works such as Vayikra Rabbah were written, which reinterpreted and reinvigorated the "dead letter" laws of ritual purity, sacrifices, and agricultural matters with new meaning and religious purpose in a world that had lost the living, breathing reality of the entire diverse and rich reality that had existed in the time of the Temple.

Moreover, one has to raise the question of whether Heschel's extreme formulation is a by-product of his hasidic upbringing. In many of its core texts, Hasidism engages in a spiritualization of the concrete reality of the land of Israel, and shifts that to the "temple of the heart" or to the court of the rebbe. Gershom Scholem, the pioneering scholar of Kabbalah and Hasidism, put it this way in an early essay on this topic:

> The terms [Egypt, Zion, Eretz Yisrael, Galut (exile) and *ge'ullah* (redemption)] were turned into allegorical catchwords denoting no longer only what they actually mean, but standing for a personal state of mind, for a moral condition, or, as we would say in contemporary jargon, for existential situations of man. Notions like these have lost their concrete historical or geographical meaning, they have no longer to do with the fate and future of the nation, but with the individual's struggle for his own salvation. If Egypt, the house of bondage, is a sphere that exists in every man, it is only logical that the same applies to the land of Israel and to the inner redemption.[16]

But to retroject that paradigm shift back onto the central texts of the tradition does violence to the historical truth and to the reality of the original and primary message presented to us as the word of God in those texts.[17]

And Yet, Profound Insight

With all of the justified critique of Heschel's sharp dichotomy between holiness of space and holiness of time, it is important to note that he did highlight an important idea that warrants reiteration.

Holiness of space in the Jewish tradition is not something detached from the God of Israel. Paralleling the extensive work done by noted biblical scholar Yeḥezkel Kaufmann, Heschel is correct to point to the distinction between the nature of sanctity of space that we find in the Bible and that which appears in many other ancient Near Eastern and pagan cultures. The land of Israel, or the Temple, or any synagogue, is not holy because of any independent primordial power that resides in it, in some sort of magical sense. Space is imbued with sanctity by God: it is God's presence and God's desire to fill a space with sanctity that gives it special status. There are no forces independent of or co-equal to the Divine that inhere in any space that can be a source of holiness or that can act as foci of holiness in the absence of God's will. This is expressed clearly in the book of Ezekiel and in many rabbinic comments on the exile of the Divine Presence (the Shekhinah).[18] One of the central messages of these texts is that God removes the Divine Presence from the Temple when humans, both individually and collectively (as part of k'neset yisrael, the Jewish people) fail to live to live up to the covenant. The Temple does not have an independent status, disconnected from God's choice to infuse the locale with holiness. And thus, when God chooses to remove the Divine Presence from the Temple, symbolically expressed by the image of divine chariot coming down to escort the Divine Presence out of the Temple, it then becomes open and vulnerable to destruction and plunder. At that point it is simply a structure of wood and gold and silver, and it can neither withstand the assault of the enemy nor can it protect itself.[19] Indeed, the prophets Jeremiah and Ezekiel often run up against the mistaken ideology of the masses, who believe that Jerusalem and the Temple can never be overrun because of some inherent holiness that will protect them from any harm. In the eyes of these groups, the Temple has some form of inherent power that will ward off all evil and any threat. As David Henshke has written:

> This idea that holiness of space is rooted in God's conscious choice to manifest His glory and presence is a deeply rooted theme throughout the Bible. The Bible speaks of the tent

of meeting, where God "comes down" to interact with and communicate His will to Moses and the Jewish people. The Temple is the place which God chooses to "have His name dwell" and the "house" that He establishes for human beings to come and bring sacrifices and pray and encounter the presence of the Divine.[20]

This theme finds continued expression in the rabbinic language used to describe the synagogue as well. The *aggadot* in the first chapter of tractate Berakhot, for example, consistently uses phrases such as "when God comes to the synagogue"—once again highlighting the notion that there is no inherent primordial sanctity that inheres in these structures and locales. Rather, the core of the holiness of these sacred spaces is solely a function of God's rendezvous, as it were, with human beings in this special venue, which is set aside for prayer and study.

It is, of course, true that there are halakhic aspects of the holiness of the Temple area that remain in place even after the destruction of the Temple. In a famous passage in the Mishneh Torah, Maimonides notes that the sanctity of Jerusalem, with its attendant ramifications for the laws pertaining to sacrifices, ritual purity, and other aspects of *halakhah*, continues even today, although the status of the rest of the land of Israel is dependent on other factors. Here too, however, it is striking to note that Maimonides' formulation once again highlights the point that we have articulated:

> Why do I say that the original consecration sanctified the Temple and Jerusalem for eternity, while in regard to the consecration of the remainder of Eretz Yisrael, in the context of the Sabbatical Year, tithes, and other similar [agricultural] laws, [the original consecration] did not sanctify it for eternity? Because the sanctity of the Temple and Jerusalem stems from the Shekhinah, and the Shekhinah can never be nullified. Therefore, [the Torah] states: "I will lay waste to your sanctuaries" (Leviticus 26:31). The sages declared:

"Even though they have been devastated, their sanctity remains."[21]

The Temple environs, and more broadly Jerusalem itself, are eternally sacred because their sanctity is rooted in God's ongoing presence in those locales. It does not rest on any inherent sanctity of the places, or on any sort of sanctity that is disconnected from the will of God investing that space with ongoing holiness by means of God's presence.

The Theological Conception of the Holy Place

From a multitude of biblical and rabbinic sources, one indeed gets a strong sense of what Louis Jacobs termed an "objective" notion of the presence of God in the holy places deemed sacred by Jewish tradition and law.[22] In the language of the Bible and in many rabbinic texts, God personally—or the Divine Presence, or God's glory—is said to "dwell" in these spaces. There is a palpable sense of a real concrete presence of the Divine that animates these places. This notion is most fully identified with thinkers in the Middle Ages such as Yehudah Halevi[23] and Naḥmanides,[24] and in more contemporary times with the thought of Rabbi Avraham Yitzḥak Kook.[25]

In some *midrashim*, the process by which God "shoehorns" the Divine Presence into this sacred space is called *tzimtzum*, an act of contraction, in which the Divine Presence permeates the area of the sacred. In later kabbalistic literature, this very term will be used to explain the theological conundrum of a finite world emerging from an infinite God who seems to leave no room for any other matter to exist. And indeed there were, and no doubt continue to be, many Jews who adhere to an essentialist notion of the holy as having some inherent manifestation of the Almighty.

This perspective, of course, was—and continues to be—challenged by those who identify with a more rationalist understanding of

Judaism. The questions posed include: What does it mean for God's presence to dwell in a place? How should we understand the concept of a "holy place" in a Jewish monotheistic worldview that rejects the corporeality of God? Echoing these concerns is the rhetorical question that King Solomon expressed at the dedication of the Temple: "But will God, in truth, dwell on the earth? Behold the heavens and the heaven of heaven cannot contain You: how much less so this house that I have built!" (1 Kings 8:27). Medieval Jewish philosophers sharpened this formulation; Saadiah Gaon, for example, expressed this idea as follows:

> A *propos* of place, I say that it is inconceivable for several reasons that He should occupy any place whatsoever. First of all, He is Himself the Creator of all space. Also He originally existed alone, when there was no such thing as place....Furthermore space is only required by a material object which occupies the place of the object that it meets and comes into contact with....This is, however, out of the question as far as the Creator is concerned. As for the assertion of the prophets that God dwells in the heavens, that was merely a way of indicating God's greatness and His elevation, since heaven is for us the highest thing we know of. The same applies to statements that God dwells in the Temple....The purpose of all of this was to confer honor upon the place and upon the people in question. Besides that, it is to be remembered that God had also revealed in that place His specially created light, of which we have spoken previously, that was called *shekhinah* and *kavod*.[26]

And thus, in this more subjectivist interpretation of the notion of holiness of space, the reason that Judaism chooses to maintain that notion of sacred place is to teach us the proper approach that we should have to God and to ensure that we have the proper respect and behavior in our approach to the sacred rituals associated with serving God in those places.

A second approach within this more rationalistic camp is found in the commentary of Don Isaac Abravanel to the biblical narrative of the building of the tabernacle in the wilderness:

> The divine intention behind the construction of the Temple was to combat the idea that God had forsaken the earth and that the divine throne was in heaven, remote from humankind…It is all a parable and allegory representing the immanence of God's presence and providence.[27]

In this reading, once again the subjective note comes to the fore. The sanctity of these spaces and the notion of God dwelling in them are simply code words for the ongoing notion of God's providential care (hashgahah) of humanity—and of the Jewish people in particular. It reflects a philosophical dogma about God's involvement with the world without violating the canons of the pure monotheism that is at the heart of the rationalist conception of God.

In a similar vein, Professor Menachem Kellner has argued at length that Maimonides did not believe in any concept of inherent holiness in objects, persons, or time. In his words:

> According to this view holiness is a status, not a quality of existence. It is a challenge, not a given; normative, not descriptive. It is institutional (in the sense of being part of a system of laws) and hence contingent. This sort of holiness does not reflect objective reality; it helps constitute social reality. Holy places, persons, times, and objects are indubitably holy, and must be treated with all due respect, but they are, in and of themselves, like all other places, persons, times, and objects. What is different about them is the way in which the Torah commands that they be treated.[28]

Another theme that is sometimes highlighted in these discussions is the notion that holiness is derivative of the great number of *mitzvot* that are associated with a specific locale or person. Thus, many who take an anti-essentialist view of holiness often point to the following *mishnah*:

> There are ten levels of holiness. The land of Israel is the holiest of all lands....And what makes it holy? They bring from it the omer [barley offering], the first fruits, and loaves of bread [the elevation offering of the first grains on Shavuot]—things that are not brought from other lands (M. Keilim 1:6).

Moving from medieval times to the modern era, the sharpest expression of this notion is found in a celebrated passage written by Rabbi Meir Simḥah of Dvinsk, a noted talmudic scholar of the late nineteenth/early twentieth century, in his Bible commentary entitled *Meshekh Ḥokhmah*. In addressing the question of why Moses broke the tablets of the law upon seeing the Israelites sinning with the golden calf, rather than simply returning the tablets to God, he posits a calculated educational purpose in Moses' behavior. Moses was trying to convey to the people this profound religious message:

> I am not holy. I am a man just as you. The Torah is not dependent upon me. Even had I not returned, the Torah would have continued in my absence. The sanctuary and its utensils are not intrinsically holy. Their sanctity derives from God's presence in our midst. If you sin, these objects lose their holiness. Even these tablets of testimony—the word of God—are not holy, in and of themselves. Their sanctity derives from your relationship with God and your willingness to observe God's law. Now that you have sinned, these tablets are mere stone, devoid of any sanctity. As proof of my point, I shatter them before you![29]

And in our contemporary age this idea was often highlighted by Dr. Yeshayahu Leibowitz and his sister, Professor Nechama

Leibowitz, in their respective writings. Moreover, this notion also found great expression in the writings of the leading light of modern Orthodox thought, Rabbi Joseph B. Soloveitchik, who wrote:

> Judaism has always maintained that holiness is not something objective, inherent in an object, prevailing independently of the way this particular sacred object is treated. We denied the idea that there is sanctity *per se*, a metaphysical endowment which persists irrespective of man's relationship to the object. Such an approach to the idea of the sacred would border on fetishism and primitive taboos. Sanctity is born out of man's actions and experiences and is determined by the latter. The very instant man adopts a coarse attitude toward the hallowed object—the moment of sacredness is eliminated. Sanctity expresses itself not in the formal quality of the object or institution but in a relationship between the latter and man. It is an experience rather than an endowment...[30]

And so, in addressing this fundamental tension, we are left with conflicting positions in the sources and voices within our tradition, regarding how we are to understand the concept of sacred space in Jewish thought. Do we push forward with a full-throated conception of an objective reality of God's presence in some form that animates those areas and locales? Or do we scale back these ideas and, guided by a rationalist sensibility, translate them into terms that relate more to human feelings and practice? Whatever philosophic conclusion we come to, it is undeniable that in the realm of praxis and halakhic expression, the idea of sanctity of place—of things—remains a central concept in the corpus of Jewish law and Jewish thought. Moreover, it animates our vision of the eschaton, which the committed Jew thrice daily expresses at the conclusion of the Amidah prayer:

> May it be Your will, Eternal One, our God and God of our ancestors, that the Temple be rebuilt speedily in our days... and there we shall serve You with reverence, as in the days of old and as in former years.

A Final Note

One of the unique aspects of the notion of the holiness of place in Jewish law is the role played by the human being in achieving the status of sanctification of the locale. For example, although the land of Israel was endowed by God with sanctity at the time of the patriarchs (if not earlier), there remain large dimensions of holiness, with great halakhic ramifications, that are dependent on human acts of sanctification. For the land of Israel to be fully endowed with sanctity, the Jewish people—through various ritual and symbolic acts—need to imbue the land with its full potential of halakhic *k'dushah*. The Jewish people play a central role in enhancing and expanding the inherent sanctity that exists in the land, and it is they who formally establish its parameters. Rabbi Joseph B. Soloveitchik expressed this notion very directly in one of his printed halakhic discourses:

> We say [in the liturgy]: "God who sanctifies Israel and the holidays," [which is interpreted by the Talmud to mean:] "who sanctifies the people of Israel, who [then] sanctify the holidays—i.e., the people establish the holidays [through the calendar]. So too in the land of Israel and the Temple, the act of sanctification is accomplished by the Jewish people. Entire tracts of *halakhah* exist relating to the sanctification of the city of Jerusalem and various sections of the Temple environs; how and through what objects we sanctify these spaces...the holiness of the human being is rooted in the holiness of the Torah [which has sanctified the individual]... for the Torah is an object that imbues sanctity in other things.[31]

He further expressed this notion in a number of his philosophical discourses, as in the following passage:

> Holiness, *k'dushah*, sanctification is a venturesome undertaking. It is not given a grant but is created by man.

The creative gesture which engenders holiness draws on inner resources contained in the realm of man's naturalness; the holiness of the personality, even though it comes into full bloom in one's spiritual dimension, in his noble, sublime emotions, profound thoughts, great volitions and strivings, is deeply rooted in the physical layers of his existence, in his carnal drives, in his being integrated into the kingdom of nature....Judaism considers the body the wellspring of *k'dushah*. That is why it focused its attention on the body.[32]

These notions were recently reiterated in a published interview with my revered teacher, Rabbi Soloveitchik's preeminent disciple and son-in-law, Rabbi Aharon Lichtenstein, who eloquently expresses these core concepts:

When I was a young man, one summer I heard a lecture from the Rav [Rabbi Soloveitchik] z"l on the topic of the sanctity of place, *k'dushat makom*. However the lecture did not only deal with that topic.

Holiness, the Rav stated at the time, is created by the human being. The blessed Holy One created a neutral world. In that world there is raw material that one can imbue with sanctity. Of course, it is true, the Rav noted that there are things that have sanctity in and of themselves. However, holiness, fundamentally, is created by the human being. The human being receives neutral raw material and gives it a personal imprint, rooted in one's personality and one's personal sanctity, and thus the process begins to snowball. Afterwards I saw something similar to his words in a comment of the *Meshekh Hokhmah* to the verse, "When the call of the *shofar* concludes they may go up on the mountain" (Exodus 19:13). For through the acts of God, nothing is made holy, only when human beings sanctify something...I have presented here a number of examples of the principle that one can add another layer of holiness, through the additional input of the human being, even when we are discussing sanctity that is rooted in the divine sphere, which comes from the blessed Holy One.

Question: From whence does this power of the human being derive, to create holiness or to add a dimension of sanctity? Answer: Clearly, the foundation is to understand that holiness emanates from the blessed Holy One...The verse states: "You shall be holy, for I, the Eternal your God, am holy" (Leviticus 19:2)....I interpret this to mean that there is a heavenly sanctity. God is the apex of holiness, the source of *k'dushah*, and thus the human being who connects to the blessed Holy One, who imbibes that sanctity and sanctifies oneself at that level—that person can also create holiness in other things.[33]

The human being and God become partners in expanding and enhancing the parameters of the holy in the concrete world. As the human being became a partner with God at the time of creation in enhancing and improving the physical world, so too do the individual and the collective play a crucial role in imbuing that created reality with sanctity and spirituality.

NOTES

[1] I would like to thank Dr. Maier Becker, Dr. David Berger, Rabbi Shalom Carmy, Rabbi Yair Kahn, and especially Dr. David Shatz and Rabbi Jacob J. Schacter for their comments and feedback on earlier drafts of this essay.

[2] "Young Adults Thrilled and Inspired by JFSA Birthright Trip," *Arizona Jewish Post* (August 9, 2012), online at http://azjewishpost.com/2012/young-adults-thrilled-and-inspired-by-jfsa-birthright-trip.

[3] Abraham Joshua Heschel, *The Sabbath: Its Meaning for Modern Man* (New York: Farrar, Straus and Giroux, 1951), pp. 8–10.

[4] On the relationship between sacred time and sacred space in religion in general, see the classic work by Mircea Eliade, *The Sacred and the Profane: The Nature of Religion* (New York: Harcourt, Brace & World, 1957).

[5] *The Sabbath*, p. 81.

[6] Nechama Leibowitz, *Studies in Shemot, Exodus* (Jerusalem: World Zionist Organization, 1978), vol. 2, pp. 654ff.

[7] It is true that the term *kadosh* does not appear in Genesis 2 in describing the Garden of Eden; but, as indicated in the next few lines of text and the next footnote, the Bible does intimate that this is a special place where God is manifest.

[8] Cf. Genesis 3:8 and 4:16.

[9] See the opening to the book of Jonah.

[10] Many writers have noted the parallels between the narrative of the Garden of Eden and that of the holy spaces of the tabernacle and the Temple in later biblical narratives. (For one example, see Amnon Bazak's online essay, "A Return to Eden," at http://vbm-torah.org/archive/parsha72/19-72teruma.htm.) It is interesting to note that in Ezekiel 28, the prophet describes the former glory of the king of Tyre by first noting that the king saw himself as living in an idyllic situation, "in Eden, the Garden of God" (verse 13), and then moving on to a second image of the king who fancied himself as being in the "holy mountain of God" (verse 14). The juxtaposition of "Eden" and the "holy mountain of God" in this passage is telling, once again intimating that there is something special about the physical locale of Eden.

[11] Cf., e.g. Rambam's comment at M.T. Hilkhot Ma·aseir Sheini V'neta Reva·i 2:1.

[12] The exact meaning of the root *kof-dalet-shin* in the Bible is in dispute. It clearly has various nuances in different contexts. We use it in this essay in the most common sense of the term, "holy."

[13] For a contrary view that rejects this interpretation of Rashi and the midrashim he builds upon, see the online essay by Yair Kahn, "Build for Me a Sanctuary," at http://vbm-torah.org/archive/parsha71/19-71teruma.htm.

[14] See, for example, his commentary to Exodus 31:28.

[15] The exact relationship between the concept of *k'dushah* (holiness) and that of *tohorah* (purity) requires its own analysis, which is beyond the scope of this essay. Suffice it is to say that the two concepts often go hand in hand in the Bible, with the requirement to maintain ritual purity as an indication of the holy status of the place or person under discussion.

[16] Gershom Scholem, *The Messianic Idea in Judaism* (1971; rpt. New York: Schocken, 1995), p. 200.

[17] In a parallel phenomenon from a wholly other historical and cultural context, scholars have noted that part of certain early Christian replacement and supersessionist theologies tended to downplay the reality of Jewish holy places. Earthly Jerusalem relating to a specific people and covenant was replaced by a spiritual Jerusalem that was to embrace all of humanity. This was of a piece with the move to replace carnal Israel—Israel of the flesh—with Israel of the spirit.

[18] Ezekiel 8 and 10, and cf. the midrashic material at Eikhah Rabbah 1:32 and 1:33.

[19] This is forcefully hinted at in the famous midrashic comment that the Jewish people take comfort in the fact that God poured out divine wrath on "wood and stone" but not on the people of Israel (Eikhah Rabbah 3:14). The Hebrew is *shafakh ḥamato al ha-eitzim v'al ha-avanim.*

[20] This passage is taken from David Henshke's important essay, "Mishkan Ha-eidut U-veit Ha-b'ḥirah," first published in *Megadim* 11 (1990). The essay discusses the exact distinction between the nature of the holiness of the tabernacle and tent of meeting, on the one hand, and that of the Temple in Jerusalem, on the other.

[21] M.T. Hilkhot Beit Ha-b'ḥirah 6:17.

[22] Louis Jacobs, "Holy Places" in *Judaism and Theology* (London: Valentine Mitchell, 2005), pp. 51–65.

[23] See, for example, *Kuzari* II 14–22.

[24] See, for example, his commentary to Leviticus 18:25.

[25] See for example, *Orot Eretz Yisrael, Ha-milḥamah* (Bet El [Israel]: Sifriyat Ḥavah, 2007), or idem, *Orot* (Jerusalem: Mosad Harav Kook, 1973), ch. 1.

[26] *The Book of Beliefs and Opinions* II 11, trans. Samuel Rosenblatt (1948; rpt. New Haven: Yale University Press, 1995), pp. 124–125. For more on the notion of the Shekhinah as God's special light, see Maimonides, *Guide to the Perplexed*, trans. Shlomo Pines (Chicago: Chicago University Press, 1974) I 64, pp. 156–157.

[27] Abravanel to Exodus 25:2.

[28] Menachem Kellner, *Maimonides' Confrontation with Mysticism* (Oxford and Portland, OR: Littman Library of Jewish Civilization, 2006), p. 88.

[29] Commentary to Exodus 32:17. See further the discussion in Marvin Fox, "The Holiness of the Holy Land" in Jonathan Sacks, ed., *Tradition and Transition: Essays Presented to Chief Rabbi Sir Immanuel Jakobovits* (London: Jews' College, 1986).

[30] *Family Redeemed: Essays on Family Relationships* (New York: KTAV, 2000), p. 64.
[31] *Shiurim L'zeikher Abba Mari* (Jerusalem: Mosad Harav Kook, 1984), pp. 175–176.
[32] Family Redeemed, p. 74.
[33] *M'vakshei Panekha: Siḥot Im Ha-rav Aharon Lichtenstein*, ed. Hayyim Sabbato (Tel Aviv: Yediot Ahronot, 2011), pp. 116–124, passim. In part of the passage omitted here, Rav Lichtenstein outlines a number of examples of the notion that in areas of *halakhah* that appear to reflect sanctity that emanates exclusively from above—e.g., the sanctity of Shabbat, for the human being adds a dimension of *k'dushah* through one's personal actions and words to the existing level of holiness.

Sanctity Beyond the Law[1]

Yitzchak Blau

How should a religious Jew go beyond the letter of the law in the pursuit of sanctity? Even after affirming the desirability of such an endeavor, how does he or she then determine an appropriate course of action? *Halakhah* provides concrete guidelines for proper behavior within the realm of what is required according to Jewish law, but gray areas not covered by *halakhah* depend upon more subjective judgments—which may or may not accord with Torah ideals. What can committed Jews do to ensure that their attempts to go above and beyond the strict demands of the law remain faithful to Jewish values?

A close reading of the most famous traditional source on this topic provides insight and guidance. Leviticus 19:2 contains the general mandate to "be holy," *k'doshim tihyu*; and Ramban[2] interprets this as a call to pursue sanctity even when not explicitly mandated by Jewish law, and to thus avoid becoming a "scoundrel with the Torah's permission"—that is, someone who lives a dissolute lifestyle while adhering to every jot and tittle of the law. A person could eat glatt kosher meat and drink rabbinically approved wine, while still speaking coarsely and cohabiting indecorously with one's spouse— and such a person would not be in technical violation of a single halakhic norm. Yet, such a lifestyle lacks sanctity. The Torah's mandate to be holy charges us to strive for more.

How do we go about extending Torah values beyond that which is clearly set forth as our minimum responsibilities? Granting validity to our human reasoning and ethical intuitions makes the path easier. Assuming that Judaism instructs us to rely upon our capacity for ethical reasoning, we have adequate means for making good decisions. Even when not given definitive halakhic direction, we can rely upon our own analysis and intuitions to select ways in which we might strive to exceed the minimum requirements of our religious obligations.

Ramban himself does give such credence to human ethical intuitions. When explaining why the sin of *ḥamas* ("lawlessness"[3]) specifically brought about the deluge in the time of Noah, Ramban writes: "Because it [i.e., the prohibition of *ḥamas*] is a rational commandment that does not need a prophet's command."[4] The generation of the flood was guilty of sins of theft and violence, whether or not prior divine revelation had expressly cautioned them against engaging in such behavior, because human reasoning alone is sufficient to arrive at the conclusion that such behavior is wrong. Having accepted the validity of human reasoning in this case, Ramban could have continued in the same vein and said that we should utilize the same human reasoning to guide our determination of what constitutes appropriate religious striving beyond the minimum requirements of the law. Interestingly, he does not do so; rather, Ramban highlights resources within the tradition that offer guidance in this regard. After outlining his interpretation of *k'doshim tihyu*, Ramban explains how to undertake this crucial enterprise:

> Therefore, after having listed the matters that God prohibited altogether, Scripture followed them up by a general command that we practice moderation even in matters that are permitted. One should minimize sexual intercourse, similar to that which the rabbis have said, "So that the disciples of the sages should not be found together with their wives as often as roosters [with hens]" (B. Berakhot 22a), and one should not engage in it [i.e., intercourse] except as required in fulfillment of the commandment thereof. One should also sanctify oneself [i.e., by exercising self-restraint] by using

wine in small amounts, just as Scripture calls a nazirite[5] "holy" (Numbers 6:8), and one should remember the evils that the Torah mentioned as following from [drinking wine] in the cases of Noah and Lot. Similarly, one should keep oneself away from impurity, even though we have not been admonished against this in the Torah, similar to that which the rabbis have said: "For the *p'rushim*, the clothes of the unlearned are considered as if trodden upon by a *zav or zavah*" (B. Hagigah 18b), and just as nazirites are called "holy" because of guarding themselves from the impurity of the dead. Likewise, one should guard one's mouth and tongue from being defiled by excessive food and by lewd talk, similar to what Scripture states: "And every mouth speaks wantonness" (Isaiah 9:16). Moreover, one should purify oneself in this respect until one reaches the degree known as [complete] self-restraint, as the rabbis said concerning Rabbi Hiyya, that he never engaged in idle chatter.[8]

A close reading of this passage reveals four sources of instruction regarding Torah ideals put forward by Ramban as guides to helping us determine the scope of any supererogatory behavior: (1) the worldview espoused in various rabbinic statements, (2) extrapolation from existing *halakhot*, (3) value judgments set forth in prophetic passages, and (4) helpful instruction gleaned from biblical narratives.

Let us begin with the first category. Ramban cites three different rabbinic sayings in his presentation. Rabbinic praise of Rabbi Hiyya for always avoiding idle chatter conveys an important Jewish value, irrespective of the fact that *halakhah* does not specifically prohibit such discourse. Along similar lines, rabbinic statements instruct us to not overindulge in marital relations and to avoid ritual impurity—neither of which practice is actually required by *halakhah*; these are both examples of going above and beyond the minimal requirements of the law. This method (namely, scrutinizing rabbinic dicta to uncover the values underlying the texts) works, but it raises the question: how did the sages themselves know which ideals to promote? The problem may be solved if we assume they had well-developed traditions regarding these matters. On the other hand, if we think that they relied on their best human ingenuity to independently make religious evaluations, then we must return to our opening quandary: how do religious people, even those of great stature, decide precisely how to approach going beyond the letter of the law?

Ramban also extrapolates from the corpus of existing *halakhah* (i.e., the second category in the enumeration above). Calling a nazirite "holy" (as the Torah does) implies that these practices deserve emulation. Thus, we can infer that it is ideal to minimize wine intake and to avoid defilement by corpses. Clearly, this kind of halakhic inferencing does not fully circumvent the need for human judgment. Is the ideal to avoid alcohol altogether, or simply to minimize its consumption? Should all forms of ritual impurity be avoided, or only those that derive from contact with a corpse? More fundamentally, the analysis depends upon our understanding of the status of the nazirite. If we view this institution as a concession to human weakness more than an ideal, we certainly cannot hold up its details as models for emulation. Ramban here, however, tends to see the nazirite as an ideal: in his opinion, the nazirite brings a sin offering upon completing the term of the vow because of leaving this exalted state and returning to mundane reality (and not because there was anything inherently problematic about having assumed the role of the nazirite in the first place).[9] Though Ramban's analysis is cogent, the fact remains that extrapolating from *halakhot* depends upon our analysis of the teleology of the *mitzvot*—that is, our human reasoning does come into play. Learning from the commandments mandates an approach that abandons religious formalism and makes assumptions about reasons for the commandments.[10]

Prophetic utterances also offer guidance (cf. Ramban's third item), as do passages from biblical wisdom literature. Isaiah declares: "Therefore the Eternal shall have no joy in their young men, neither shall God have compassion on their orphans and widows; for every one is ungodly and an evildoer, and every mouth speaks wantonness. For all this God's anger is not turned away, but the divine hand is stretched out still" (9:16). The prophetic critique of wanton speech emerges clearly, whether or not such discourse violates the formal requirements of Jewish law. Of all biblical books, perhaps Proverbs has the most potential in this regard. The judicious advice contained in numerous proverbs directs the pursuit of sanctity and ethics above and beyond halakhic norms.

Finally, we have biblical narratives (the last item on Ramban's list). No verse specifically forbids drunkenness, but various scriptural stories effectively convey the dangers of inebriation. For example: Noah gets drunk and suffers some form of humiliation at the hands of his son (Genesis 9:20–27); Lot drinks too much and ends up committing incest with his daughters (Genesis 19:30–38). These stories effectively convey a cautionary approach toward alcohol consumption. In analogous fashion, we can utilize this methodology to argue that the Torah is critical of both anger and polygamy. The Torah may not prohibit anger but that trait seems to repeatedly get Moshe into trouble. Similarly, although the Torah does allow polygamy, its stories suggest that marrying multiple wives invariably leads to significant family tension.[11] Thus, reading between the lines of biblical stories provides an effective way to convey Torah principles, as we may infer from those stories underlying values— which we may then choose to emulate in our striving to go beyond the letter of the law in our religious lives.

The four methods discussed by Ramban bear strong resemblance to a similar list found in David Shatz's review of Walter Wurzburger's *Ethics of Responsibility*.[12] According to Shatz's reading of Wurzburger, when we use our ethical intuitions (as informed by Torah values) in order to go beyond halakhic norms, we must rely upon: (1) the study of specific laws, (2) moral conduct in conformity with Torah norms, (3) *aggadah* and biblical narratives, and (4) personal contact with Torah scholars. The second item on this list highlights a point not mentioned in Ramban's presentation. We do not simply analyze *mitzvot* intellectually, in the hope of extracting themes that can apply beyond a given set of laws; crucially, a lifetime of practicing the commandments helps us to cultivate the refined character traits that enable us to then apply those values to additional situations. We shall also examine the last factor in Shatz's list—encountering role models—which is not explicitly articulated in Ramban.

Having explored Ramban's various methods for expanding religious commitment, we may wonder why it is even necessary for us to do so. Instead of leaving it up to us to strike out beyond the limits *halakhah* on our own, God could have given us a more expansive, extensive legal code that codifies all of our responsibilities as formal obligations; why was this not done? In a different passage, Ramban implies that the problem is quantitative. According to Ramban, the verse "And you shall do what is right and good in the eyes of the Eternal" (Deuteronomy 6:18) commands us to suffuse all of our interpersonal interaction with an extra measure of kindness, even when not specifically delineated in specific *halakhot*. He explains:

> Now this is a great principle, for it is impossible to mention in the Torah all aspects of a person's conduct with one's neighbors and friends, and all of one's various transactions, and the ordinances of all societies and countries. But since God mentioned many of them—such as "you shall not go about as a talebearer" (Leviticus 19:16), "you shall not take vengeance, nor bear any grudge" (Leviticus 19:18), "neither shall you stand idly by the blood of a neighbor" (Leviticus 19:16), " you shall not curse the deaf" (Leviticus 19:14), "you shall rise before the elder" (Leviticus 19:32), and the like— God reverted to state in a general way that, in all matters, one should do what is right and good, including even compromise and going beyond the requirements of the law.[13]

Note how Ramban lists several interpersonal commandments explicitly included in the Torah. Apparently, here too we extrapolate from the data offered by explicitly enumerated *mitzvot*, to extend beyond those *mitzvot* and encompass additional behaviors not explicitly commanded. Furthermore, he explains that it would be impossible for the Torah to address every possible scenario demanding ethical behavior. Human social interactions include too much variety; no law code could hope to cover each and every case in a specific fashion. Therefore, God chose to delineate some specifics, from which we can then infer an overarching moral mandate.[14]

Perhaps there are other factors in play that led to the *halakhah* specifically *not* encompassing all principles in concrete and detailed law. We all experience a wide variety of interpersonal encounters in a lifetime; moreover, many issues are not clear-cut and do not allow for a one-size-fits-all response. The list of forbidden foods is the same for every Jew; however, the amount considered appropriate for any individual to consume depends upon time, place, and personal inclination. Accordingly, it would be impossible to craft a comprehensive code to apply to all situations that could possibly arise. Rabbi Isaiah Horowitz (165–1630)[15] offers just such an explanation of Ramban. Different times and circumstances generate different standards; people themselves change over the course of a lifetime; and character and inclination differ from person to person. The Torah could not give universal guidelines determining what constitutes overeating, excessive indulgence in marital relations, or too much idle chatter; instead, it simply commands us to pursue a life of holiness—and this pursuit demands personalized work in all those areas of life.[16]

Rabbi Naftali Zvi Yehudah Berlin (1816–1893)[17] uses a parallel idea to solve a textual problem. The verse commanding holiness begins with the unusual phrase *dabbeir el kol adat b'nei yisrael* ("Speak to the entire nation of the Israelites," Leviticus 19:2). This phrase appears five times in the Torah but only once as the introduction to a specific commandment. Berlin explains that the Torah needs to emphasize the inclusion of all Israel precisely because this commandment includes a "sliding scale." Universal objective commandments obviously apply to every Jew and thus do not need a formal introduction. However, commandments that are dependent upon context and individual constitution do not clearly pertain to all, and the Torah therefore stresses how this subjective command applies to each Jew according to his or her own situation.

Strikingly, Rabbi Yehonatan Eybeschütz (1690–1764) interprets the phrase in a diametrically opposing manner.[18] He expresses concern about people who take on ascetic practices beyond the Torah's obligations, noting that the Pharisees objected to ascetic practices of other Second Temple sects. According to Eybeschütz, the phrase *kol adat b'nei yisrael* in Leviticus 19:2 actually informs us that one should only take on aspects of *p'rishut* (that is, ascetic behavior) that the whole community can follow. In this way, those seeking to expand their religious commitments will not cut themselves off from their community. Whereas Berlin and Horowitz see this *mitzvah* as setting forth a scale with varying applications, Eybeschutz sees here a commandment with a more fixed standard.

Rabbi Eybeschütz's position serves as an important counterbalance to the other view. If we assert both that we need to go beyond the law and that this demand works differently for each person, then we open the danger that select individuals may adopt extreme practices in their striving for supererogatory behavior. For example, someone might adopt a severe form of asceticism as a purported fulfillment of *k'doshim tihyu*. We need to balance the idea of varying and individual obligations, on the one hand, with the good judgment necessary to prevent wild and harmful applications, on the other.[19]

The Mishnah commentary of Rabbi Israel Lipschitz (1782–1860)[20] further develops the approach of Rabbis Horowitz and Berlin. According to the Mishnah, "Anyone not involved with *mikra, mishnah,* or *derekh eretz* is not part of civilization" (Kiddushin 1:10). Those who contribute to society, according to this text, need to be engaged in study of Scripture (*mikra*), study of the Oral Law (*mishnah*), and acts of kindness and decency (*derekh eretz*). Lipschutz explains that these categories represent the three realms of human obligation—belief, action, and character. Beliefs emerge from Scripture: although the Bible never states a list of fundamental beliefs, the idea of a single, benevolent, and just God running the universe is implicit in almost every biblical book. Actions commanded by *halakhah* are found in the Mishnah and Talmud. Character finds expression in *derekh eretz*, the realm of our interactions with others, and does not receive legal treatment in the Bible or in the Talmud: no commandments specifically forbid arrogance, anger, laziness, or gluttony, and no *mitzvot* instruct people to be merciful, sympathetic, patient, and kind.

Why did the Torah not include clear commandments regarding *middot* (that is, the personal character traits that inform our conduct in the realm of *derekh eretz*)? Lipshcutz writes that no law can give precise directives regarding these matters, since they vary based on time, place, generation, and the matter at hand. These matters require a subtlety and complexity that a set of laws cannot fully address. Could we imagine a legal code outlining exactly when it is appropriate to get angry? Would the challenge of appropriate pride play out identically for a king and a tailor? We can learn more about these matters by spending time with people of upstanding character than we can by reading a rule book. For this reason, the rabbis prized the practice of *shimmush talmidei ḥakhamim*, "attending the sages"—which speaks to direct personal interactions, and not merely attending their classes or lectures. Only a live model of refined character can help us navigate the nuance and variety of ethical challenges that we are likely to encounter in our lives.[21]

Thus, it was not merely a penchant for brevity that precluded the Torah from including a rule book for every situation; some things simply do not allow for encapsulation in law. Knowledge and insight of such matters can only be acquired via encountering the rich texture of the human personality in the crucible of life. In addition to flesh-and-blood experience, narratives present us with even more examples of human interaction—and provide us with the opportunity to draw upon their nuances and complexities, as we distill from those narratives the values we will then seek to pursue in our own lives. Rather than telling us exactly how much to eat or precisely how much pride to exhibit, the Torah asks us to reflect deeply about the individuals in its narratives, in order to find there both positive and negative role models. Ultimately, this sets the groundwork that allows us to pursue our own path toward excellence in ethics and sanctity, more powerfully than would be possible from exclusive reliance on a rule book.

While arenas of action that depend on individual temperament and circumstance prove more resistant to legal precision, it would be a mistake to draw a sharp dividing-line between interpersonal commandments (*mitzvot bein adam la-ḥaveiro*) and commandments treating the relationship between ourselves and the Divine (*mitzvot bein adam la-makom*). *Halakhah* certainly includes concrete demands in the realm of the former; it also calls for going beyond the law in our attempt to fulfill the spirit of the latter. Ramban says that the commandments regarding sacred rest are intended to ensure that Shabbat and the festivals are true days of rest. According to biblical law, a Jew could spend all of Shabbat moving heavy items around the house or engaging in business dealings, without technically violating the prohibition against performing work (*m'lakhah*) on the Sabbath; yet, such behavior would hardly constitute a sanctified day of rest. Therefore, the Torah directs us with a general command to create a *shabbaton*.[22] Why did the Torah employ a generality here, rather than a more detailed directive? We could answer this by returning to the quantitative problem of the difficulty of covering every scenario, as described above. Alternatively, it may be that determining the "spirit of Shabbat" also depends upon contextual and individual factors, which make it too complex to be treated comprehensively in an itemized rule book.[23]

Before concluding with the implications of this analysis, I want to add one more possible reason why the Torah does not codify every Jewish ideal into binding law. In an important letter, Rabbi Avraham Yitzḥak Kook (1865–1935)[24] writes that the Torah purposely left certain items to be fulfilled as middat ḥasidut (that is, supererogatory piety) or as behavior specifically characterized as being li-f'nim mishurat ha-din (that is, above and beyond the strict requirements of the law), because there is great value in the voluntary exercise of free will not present in obedience to command.[25] Obviously, Rav Kook does not minimize the value of adhering to divinely given directives. Yet something would be amiss if a religious person never felt inspired to act beyond the strict confines of the law's demands. God left us an incomplete world and asks us to perfect it; in the same way, God did not locate all goodness in the Torah and therefore asks us to complete the picture on our own.

Of course, this still leaves open the question why God chose to codify particular demands while leaving specific others open for human initiative to fill in. The distinction between that which is codified and that which is discretionary points to an advantage of the approach described above. If we can successfully show that certain issues within religious life lend themselves to codification whereas others do not, we may be able to point to a logical basis for understanding when God made specific demands and when God did not. On the other hand, Rav Kook's approach leaves us without a clear method for explaining the distinction between the two realms.

According to Ramban, the directives to "be holy" and to "do the right and the good" both demand that we go beyond the law in our pursuit of sanctity and ethical decency. What provides the necessary guidance that enables us to do so? Careful investigation of Ramban's commentary on k'doshim tihyu reveals four sources of guidance: the insight of our sages, prophetic wisdom, biblical narratives, and the data provided by concrete halakhot. These last two sources each carry particularly interesting implications.

Narrative points to the subtle quality of human experience necessary for accumulating wisdom. While legal works provide enormous guidance, there is no substitute for existential encounter—mostly in real-life situations, but also expanded through the world of imaginative literature. We can gain greater understanding into ambition from Macbeth, and jealousy from Othello, than we would by reading a work entitled "The Code of Character Traits." Thus, it would be a mistake to convert these areas of religious life into subjects fit for their own Shulhan Arukh. Laws are necessary insofar as they lay out a basic rubric for what is expected of us in general terms, but they cannot teach precisely when to get angry or what constitutes overindulgence.

Applying the implicit ideals of the laws also carries philosophical assumptions. As noted, we can only use the data of *halakhah* if we can rely on our analysis of the purpose of specific *mitzvot*. For example, the underlying message of the nazirite depends on whether we view this institution as a religious ideal or as necessary concession to someone struggling with their inclinations. Pure halakhic data will at times prove insufficient, without an accompanying ideology. This point needs to be addressed by those emphasizing the need to develop a Jewish philosophy purely from within the *halakhah*.

Acknowledging our reliance upon an ideology of halakhah, biblical narratives, and aggadic teachings in order to achieve a more robust spiritual life forcefully highlights the need to supplement *halakhah* in the fulfillment of religious aspirations. While Judaism may be most defined by its law, rigorously defined statutes do not constitute a complete, all-encompassing system. "Being holy" and "doing the right and the good" remind us that the pursuit of sanctity and ethical excellence depend upon thinking beyond the *halakhah*. Ramban's classic commentary provides various models for how to accomplish this.

NOTES

[1] The author thanks Dr. David Shatz for his helpful comments in discussing this essay.

[2] Rabbi Moses ben Naḥman, also known as Naḥmanides (Spain, 1194–1270).

[3] NJPS translation.

[4] Ramban, commentary on Genesis 6:13, s.v. *hamas*.

[5] A nazirite is a person who voluntarily decides, for a limited period of time, to abstain from drinking alcoholic beverages and consuming grape products, to not get haircuts, and to avoid all contact with the dead; see Numbers 6:1–8.

[6] The Hebrew *p'rushim*, sometimes anglicized as "Pharisees," denotes a class of Jewish persons in late antiquity given over to a range of supererogatory pietistic practices, some of which went far beyond the simple requirements of the law.

[7] *A zav* (male) and *zavah* (female) are those who have become ritually impure due to ongoing discharge, and they must separate themselves from the community until they undergo a purification ritual; see Leviticus 15.

[8] Ramban, commentary on Leviticus 19:2. The translation, with minor changes, is taken from Charles B. Chavel's translation (New York: Shilo, 1971–1976).

[9] Ramban, commentary on Numbers 6:14.

[10] On the broader question of utilizing *taamei ha-mitzvot* for halakhic analysis, see my "*Taamei Ha-mitzvot*: Halakhic Analysis and Brisker Conceptualization," in Reuven Ziegler, ed., *That Goodly Mountain* (Yeshivat Har Etzion: Alon Shevut, 2012), pp. 97–108.

[11] Two examples: (1) After she encourages Abraham to marry Hagar, Sarah ends up resenting her former maid-turned-rival and drives her out of the house. (2) Due to Laban's deception Jacob ultimately marries four wives, setting up a pattern of competition, jealousy, and enmity that spills over to the next generation and has serious consequences for the well-being of the family.

[12] David Shatz, "Beyond Obedience: Walter Wurzburger's *Ethics of Responsibility*," in Tradition 30:2 (Winter 1996), p. 80; commenting especially on Walter Wurzburger, *Ethics of Responsibility: Pluralistic Approaches to Covenantal Ethics* (Philadelphia: Jewish Publication Society, 1994), pp. 37–38.

[13] Ramban to Deuteronomy 6:18; translation is based on Charles B. Chavel (see note 8 above).

[14] For a parallel analysis, see the famous comments of Rabbi Vidal of Tolosa in his *Maggid Mishneh*, to M.T. Hilkhot Shekheinim 14:5.

[15] Also known as the Shelah or the Shelah Hakadosh (after his best-known work, *Sh'nei Luḥot Ha-b'rit*), Horowitz lived in Prague and later in Jerusalem and was an important influence on the Hasidic movement.

[16] Isaiah Horowitz, *Sh'nei Luḥot Ha-b'rit, Asarah Maamarot, Maamar 7*.

[17] Also known as the Netziv. Rabbi Berlin led the Volozhin yeshiva in Lithuania

from 1854 to 1892. See his *Ha·ameik Davar* to Leviticus 19:2.

[18] See his Torah commentary, *Tiferet Y'honatan*, to Leviticus 19:2.

[19] I thank David Shatz for pointing out the danger of extremism in this context.

[20] Also known as the Tiferet Yisrael, after the title of his well-known commentary to the Mishnah.

[21] Yisrael Lipschitz, *Tiferet Yisrael* commentary to M. Kiddushin 1:10, *Yakhin*, no. 79.

[22] Ramban, commentary to Leviticus 23:24.

[23] David Shatz also uses the Ramban on *shabbaton* to minimize a sharp distinction between ethical law and ritual law regarding going beyond the law; see Shatz, "Beyond Obedience," p. 86.

[24] Rav Kook was the Ashkenazic Chief Rabbi of British Palestine from 1921 through his death in 1935.

[25] See Rav Kook's *Ig'rot Ha-ra·ayah* (Jerusalem: Mosad Harav Kook, 1985) vol. 1, p. 97.

Reflections on What It Means To Be Holy

Reuven P. Bulka

Defining Holiness

Shabbat is obviously the most holy day of the week, and arguably the most holy day in the calendar. At its end, in the Havdalah ("delineation") service, we conclude with the words, "who delineates between the holy (*kodesh*) and the profane (*hol*)." That is the standard translation. But what type of praise is it, for delineating between the sacred and the profane? This should be obvious to anyone. Even the alternate translation of *hol* as meaning "secular" is somewhat lacking. A more accurate translation of *hol* would be "ordinary." We bless God who distinguishes between the holy and the ordinary. The world is full of ordinariness. Average, ordinary, good enough, is better than nothing, but a far cry from holy. It is the difference between acceptable and excellent, between doing alright and doing our best.

Perhaps there is in this simple observation a clue as to the general sense of "holy." Holy is beyond ordinary, and moving toward excellence in all of life's affirmations. To be sanctified, as we express in all blessings prior to fulfilling a divine dictate (*mitzvah*), is to be endowed with the means to attain excellence, or at least to be oriented toward excellence. This works best when the *mitzvah* is fulfilled with full concentration and understanding.

In the Torah, we read: "Speak to the entire congregation of Israel and say to them, 'You shall be holy, for I the Eternal your God, am holy'" (Leviticus 19:2). God is the ultimate model, the focal point in aspiring for holiness. But God is a tough act to follow. Accentuating the difficulty is the midrash, cited by Rashi, in explaining the verse: "My holiness is higher than your holiness" (Vayikra Rabbah 24:9). The midrash in effect states the obvious: that God's holiness is utterly transcendent, and by definition it will always be higher than human holiness. The midrash thereby makes an already difficult task an impossible one. Judaism is difficult enough without venturing into the realm of the impossible.

A better understanding of holiness might offer an insight into this complexity. When God says "My sanctity is higher than yours," the message is clear. No human being will ever, can ever, bridge that gap between the human and the Divine. We are human, and God is God. We will never reach the peak.

But the peak will always be there to reach. This means that there will always be something for which to strive. However good we may be, we can always be better. Any achievement will give birth not to self-satisfaction, but to the desire for even greater achievement.

It is clear that if we define holiness as reaching up to God, we are setting ourselves up for a fall. It will never happen that we reach that height. K'dushah, holiness, is therefore not a defined, or definable, destination. Instead, it is a process of continual striving, absent any self-delusion that we are as good as we can be.

Returning to the problematic verse and its explanation, it now makes more sense. We define holiness as *the continual process of getting better*. To be holy requires that one never think of oneself as merely "good enough." As if to guarantee that this process is never ending, God tells us to be holy because God is holy—God is so transcendently holy that we will never reach such holiness, and because we can never attain such holiness, the process of reaching, aspiring, can never cease.

One of the more immediate implications of this definition is that holiness is not only elusive and unreachable; it is simultaneously beyond self-definition. The moment you think you have attained holiness, you cease to be holy. Holiness is a process, a continuous challenge. Holiness is also enmeshed with humility. Both these attributes are ultimately intangible, and severely compromised through the awareness of them. Those who say "I am holy" and those who say "I am humble" are both living in a false world. One cannot be humble and aware of it, or holy and aware of it.

The Holiness Model

If that is so, how can we strive to be holy? The immediate obligation following the charge to be holy is to be in awe of one's parents (Leviticus 19:3). The ladder to God starts with how we embrace our parents. In the interaction with our parents, we are on the way to apprehending the awe we are to have for God, who is the ultimate Parent.

There are defined parameters for what it means to hold our parents in awe. These include not sitting in their designated places, not contradicting them or condescendingly agreeing with them, and not calling them by their first names.[1] It is possible to adhere to all these regulations yet still not be in awe of one's parents. The rules create the ambience of awe, but the *feeling* of awe comes from the child. The feeling is facilitated by, rather than established by, the rules.

Why are we asked to be in awe of our parents? More precisely, what is achieved by being in awe of our parents, more than by simply honoring our parents? And what justification is there for being in awe of our parents?

The justification derives from the simple fact that our parents gave birth to us. Without that, we would not exist. The act of creation, of giving birth, involves all sorts of sacrifices. Carrying a child for nine months is no picnic. Giving birth is painful. The period after birth is likewise painful. The time, energy, and expense of raising a child are intrusions on the sedentary, uncomplicated, and perhaps even relatively burden-free life. Yet the parents enter into this challenge cognizant of the challenges, but not fully aware of the extent of the complications. This should be elicit awe. Once we have embraced this sense of awe, honoring one's parents flows much more naturally. As beautifully developed by Rabbi Aaron Halevi of Barcelona, the fullness of appreciation of parents is the conduit toward full appreciation of God, and provides for all the needs anyone may have.[2]

Holiness of a People

Until now, we have concentrated on individual holiness. There is, however, another sphere of holiness worthy of attention: the holiness of the group, of Israel as an entity. In this regard, there are two distinct references to the holiness of the group that link holiness with compliance, with fidelity to the Godly covenant. The first is found in the book of Exodus: "And you shall be for Me a kingdom of *kohanim* (priests) and a *holy* nation" (19:6). This is preceded by a condition: "If you will listen attentively to Me and observe My covenant" (19:5). This assurance is echoed later in the Torah: "God will establish you for God as a *holy* people, as God swore to you, if you observe the commandments of the Eternal your God, and walk in God's ways" (Deuteronomy 28:9).

Very clearly, the way to holiness is contingent on our fulfilling the commandments and walking in God's ways. Are these two contingencies? It certainly seems so. One might ask: how does "walking in God's ways" differ from fulfilling the *mitzvot*? It seems that there is indeed quite a distinction.

Rabbi Ḥama the son of Rabbi Ḥanina expounded: "What is the meaning of 'You shall follow after the Eternal your God...' (Deuteronomy 13:5)? Is it possible for any mortal to follow the divine presence? It has already been said that 'the Eternal your God is a consuming fire' (Deuteronomy 4:24).

Rather, it means to follow the attributes of the blessed Holy One. Just as God clothes the naked...you too should clothe the naked. The blessed Holy One visited the sick...you too should visit the sick. The blessed Holy One comforted mourners...you too should comfort mourners. The blessed Holy One buried the dead...you too should bury the dead."[3]

Maimonides, in commenting on the words "and walk in God's ways" (Deuteronomy 28:9), also invokes the rabbinic understanding of these words, underscoring the humanistic thrust of Rabbi Ḥama: "Just as God is called gracious, you too be gracious; just as God is called compassionate, you too be compassionate; just as God is called holy, you too be holy."[4] Maimonides calls these the good and upright ways. These are the ways we follow in God's path; literally, this is the path to holiness. Rabbi Aaron of Barcelona follows along these same lines in explaining that very precept to "walk in God's ways":

We are commanded to perform all our actions in an honest and good manner, with all our strength, and to channel all matters that are between us and others in a kind and compassionate manner, as we know from our Torah that this is the way of God, and this is what God desires from God's creations....The sages of blessed memory said, in explanation of this precept: Just as the blessed Holy One is called compassionate, you too be compassionate; just as the blessed Holy One is called gracious, you too be gracious; just as the blessed Holy One is called righteous, you too be righteous; just as God is called holy, you too be holy.[5]

The language in Maimonides and *Sefer Ha-ḥinnukh* are almost identical, and very definitively link compassion, grace, and holiness.

It is instructive to note that following in God's ways (Deuteronomy 13:5) and walking in God's ways (Deuteronomy 28:9), essentially the path to holiness, are linked to acts of kindness—deeds that we would be inclined to endorse as virtuous, even absent an explicit mention in the Torah. Why is following in God's ways not linked to the ritual obligations that are unique to Jews, such as Shabbat, *t'fillin*, *m'zuzah*, and *kashrut*? What are we missing here?

One possible explication links to the following insightful observation: "For Judaism sheer compliance with the Law as such was never regarded as the ultimate value, it rather represented a means to the fulfillment of the Divine Will."[6] Is it possible that unique *mitzvot* are the contours, the outer boundary within which we are urged to travel, and within which we walk in God's ways by acts of kindness and compassion?

There is nothing intrinsically kind about putting on *t'fillin*, or observing the Shabbat. However, the covenantal reinforcement offered by these precepts creates the ambience for kind expression. This is especially the case in the instance of Shabbat, as setting apart a day free from work creates the time and space for bringing other human beings into our orbit.

The Holiness Track

The blessings we recite prior to the fulfillment of a precept include the words *asher kid'shanu b'mitzvotav*, "who has sanctified us with [God's] commandments." This theme resonates in our prayers, where we often express our gratitude to God for, among other notable acts of grace to us, having sanctified us with the *mitzvot*. This is expressed as thanks for what is; it is not a request. On the other hand, we often do ask God to sanctify us with the commandments (*kad'sheinu b'mitzvotekha*). And sometimes we do both: for example, in the Musaf Amidah on festivals, we first thank for what is, and then ask for the very same thing for which we have just thanked God. What is the sense of this? The answer to this may seem obvious, but bears some elaboration. What do we mean when we thank God for sanctifying us with the divine commands? Are we thereby presuming that we are by definition holy? That would be, at the least, presumptuous, and at worst bordering on arrogance. The fact that we ask God to sanctify us via the precepts suggests that we do not claim presumed holiness.

Another possibility follows in line with our suggestion that holiness is a process rather than a destination. The process begins with our being placed on the holiness track, so to say. That is achieved via being given the tools: namely, the *mitzvot*. How far along the track we go, on a track that is endless, but continually moving forward (should we so choose), depends on us.

We express gratitude to God for being put on the track, and then ask for God's help as we endeavor to continue the process.

Exterior and Interior

The Talmud records a fascinating exchange of views on how to actualize the immortal words of Moshe Rabbeinu, "This is my God, whom I will adorn" (Exodus 15:2). One view is that this is achieved via adorning oneself in the fulfillment of the commandments: by making a beautiful *sukkah*, by acquiring a beautiful *lulav*, a beautiful *shofar*, beautiful *tzitzit* [fringes], etc.[7]

Another opinion about this verse, that of Abba Shaul, goes a bit further. Abba Shaul sees this as the charge to be like God, playing on the complicated word *v'anveihu* (literally, "I will adorn Him") and seeing it as a play on the words *ani va-hu* (literally, "I and He"— with the third-person pronoun referring to God). For Abba Shaul, the verse is an imperative that we should emulate God. Just as God is gracious and compassionate, so too should we be gracious and compassionate.

Abba Shaul seems more concerned about "interior decorating" as the proper way to partner with God. Adorning the precepts is fine, he says, but not enough. We need to also adorn ourselves, by adopting and embracing the ways of God as our own. All signs point to an understanding of holiness as the divine way in which we interact with others. This might sound surprising, as one would presume that the way to holiness is via the ritual commandments that are between us and God, such as *lulav*, *shofar*, and keeping kosher.

Why is it that the conduit to holiness is through person-to-person interaction? Perhaps because there are no holier objects in our world than other human beings. Other objects (such as a *sefer torah*, *t'fillin*, or a *m'zuzah*) have a significant and defined sanctity. Yet nothing compares with God's own creations: other human beings.

In the way that we interact with others, in the Godly way we behave toward them, we affirm their holiness—and, by definition, the holiness of God. It is through this that we achieve the desired holiness that God asks of us. It is through this that we become holy like God—not as holy as God, but holy like God.

Object Holiness

A word about object holiness. At first blush, object holiness does not seem to fit the dynamic "process" of holiness described above. After all, a Torah is a Torah, and its holiness is hardly compromised by anything external to it. On the other hand, we do have a grasp of what it means to not ascribe holiness to the Torah scroll. We are all too familiar with the desecrations of the Torah that have haunted our history.

The fact that a Torah is holy is, in actuality, related to a holiness process: namely, the process of continually ascribing holiness to the Torah, and behaving in a way that affirms this sanctity in increasing measure. The same applies to the sanctity of *t'fillin* or of a *m'zuzah*. Shabbat and the festivals are not exactly objects, but they are inanimate manifestations of holiness. As much as Shabbat and the festivals are holy, we nevertheless sanctify these days at their beginning (by reciting Kiddush) and at their end (by reciting Havdalah). And we can actually add to this sanctity by bringing in Shabbat earlier and concluding it later.

In what way do we sanctify days that are already holy, independent of us? By accepting the holiness of these days as obligations for us, and sanctifying them through the appropriate behaviors that accrue to these days. This too is a process, rather than working on a same old, same old pattern. Ideally, the way we sanctify this week's Shabbat should be an improvement over how we sanctified last week's Shabbat.

Finally, I wish to include a reflection on the sanctity of marriage. It is not for naught that we call the first part of the marriage ceremony kiddushin (literally, "sanctification"). It is actually an obligation to betrothe one's bride: "Whoever marries a woman without first betrothing her has failed to fulfill this obligation."[8] What is the meaning of this? In *kiddushin*, the groom sanctifies and hallows his wife-to-be. It is a process wherein the groom is made aware that this is a sacred relationship, not a narcissistic exercise. Were one to rush straight into marriage without clearly sanctifying one's spouse, effectively sanctifying the union itself before entering into it, one would miss a crucial step in assuring the meaningfulness of the union.[9] Knowing that the union is sacred means that the dynamic process associated with holiness applies to marriage: every day, the sanctity needs to be an improvement over that of the day before.

The Holiness of Israel

We come now to the culminating holiness, the holiness of Israel—which brings together the notions of holiness as a dynamic process, and the holiness of the land and its people. The land of Israel is often referred to as holy. We affectionately refer to it as *artzeinu ha-k'doshah*, "our holy land." The land itself is holy, Jerusalem has an elevated level of holiness, and within Jerusalem, the Temple, the *beit ha-mikdash* (literally, "the holy house"), is the ultimate holy place. These are all places that are holy by designation; but, like other holy objects, they call upon us to revere these places, to ascribe holiness to them, and to further sanctify them through our behavior within them.

Israel provides us, in our time, with a unique opportunity to live out the idea of the holy as a constant commitment to doing better today than yesterday. It is evident in the passionate search for cures of ravaging illnesses. It is evident in the high-tech breakthroughs that Israel has generated, improving so many aspects of life.

Israel is a place where the Torah—its history, its glory, and its agony—comes alive. The glory is in the learning; the agony is in the stark and searing reminders of the times when the Torah was desecrated, and when those who embraced the Torah were brutally murdered. And, in a most inspiring expression of holiness as the kind, gracious, compassionate manner in which we venerate human life, Israel as a country has become the first responder to emergencies all around the world: to earthquakes, tsunamis, and more. The holiness of life is the underlying value that fuels this passion to save. This is actualized not merely by going to these places, but by expending the energy and resources dedicated to building and perfecting the equipment and expertise, which can then be employed in the service of intervening and saving effectively.

Surrounded as it is by enemies bent on its destruction, Israel has repeatedly shown that for those who will allow them in, nothing—not distance, not degree of difficulty, not expense—will deter them.

This, to me—and this observation is certainly consistent with our discussion—seems to be a state-sponsored holiness, a fusion of all the components that comprise holiness. In an age when the entire world can literally explode into nothingness, the most effective antidote and preventive is to affirm the holiness of life and of every human being, and to implement policies and behaviors that reinforce this affirmation.

NOTES

[1] Mishneh Torah, Hilkhot Mamrim 6:3.

[2] See his *Sefer Ha-ḥinnukh*, §33.

[3] B. Sotah 14a.

[4] Mishneh Torah, Hilkhot Dei·ot 1:6.

[5] *Sefer Ha-ḥinnukh*, §611.

[6] Walter S. Wurzburger, "Covenantal Imperatives," in Gershon Appel, ed., *Samuel K. Mirsky Memorial Volume: Studies in Jewish Law, Philosophy, and Literature* (New York: Yeshiva University Press, 1970), p. 8.

[7] B. Shabbat 133b.

[8] *Sefer Ḥareidim*, p. 98, no. 6 (commenting on Deuteronomy 24:5).

[9] See my *Best-Kept Secrets of Judaism* (Southfield, MI: Targum/Feldheim, 2002), pp. 90–98, for a more complete study of this topic.

Sanctity of Time, Sanctity of Place, and Sanctity of the Human Being

Shlomo Riskin

Introduction

One of the most intriguing, absorbing, and significant theological topics is the concept of *k'dushah*, sanctity. All who deal with this fascinating subject agree that sanctity is the encounter between the human and the Divine, for "holy, holy, holy is the Eternal One of Hosts" (Isaiah 6:3)—God is the source of all holiness. And because God is generally conceived as the transcendent, ineffable Master of the Universe, beyond human understanding and beyond the limits of nature, conventional wisdom would identify and equate sanctity with spirituality—and thus the search for spirituality would entail escaping from the material world roundabout and attempting to enter a supernal, ethereal world far away. This is the essence of Soloveitchik's depiction of the typological "religious man" in his important work, *Halakhic Man*.[1]

To a great extent, the major commentaries on the biblical commandment "You shall be holy" (Leviticus 19:2) follow this line of interpretation. Rashi, for example, interprets the words "be holy" to mean "be separate," thus commanding separation from sin and especially from forbidden sexual relationships. Naḥmanides goes even further, advocating general abstention from the excess materialism of this world, suggesting that one ought separate oneself even from materialistic pleasures that are biblically permissible. According to these views, holiness requires separation from the material world in which we live.

My teacher and mentor, Rav Yosef Dov Halevi Soloveitchik of blessed memory, provides a very different perspective in his article "Sacred and Profane, *Kodesh* and Chol in World Perspective."[2] He rejects escaping, abstaining, and withdrawing from the physical world in order to find sanctity and spirituality, and prescribes instead bringing God into every aspect of our physical universe, and increasing the places of God's entry to embrace every aspect of our material world. After all, the entire universe belongs to the blessed Holy One and "there is no place devoid of the potential for actualizing the presence [of God]." In the words of the famed Rebbe Menahem Mendel of Kotzk, "'Where is the place of God's glory?' Wherever you let God in!" And we must do everything in our power to enable God to enter into every moment and into every place in our lives and in our world.

In this essay, I hope to follow in the footsteps of Rav Soloveitchik, and demonstrate how sanctity must be brought into the world (1) through the human encounter with the Divine in the dimension of time, as it is manifested in our festivals, and (2) through the human encounter with the Divine in the dimension of space, as it is manifested in the sanctuary and the world at large. And it is the human being who is responsible to bring this about, the human being created in God's image and thereby endowed with a spark of the Divine, who is empowered to actualize the divine sanctity within every aspect of the universe.

Let us begin with "time" and the festivals. The first biblical reference to sanctity is in conjunction with time, with reference to the Sabbath: "And God blessed the Sabbath day and made it *holy*" (Genesis 2:3).

Reflections of the Biblical Chapter of the Festivals

Let us now turn to the chapter of the festivals in Leviticus 23. This passage, as we will shortly see, raises a number of questions.

The word *mo·eid*, "festival," literally means "meeting," "rendezvous," or "appointed time," as the use of the same root in Amos 3:3 demonstrates: "Do two walk together, unless they have agreed to meet (*no·adu*)?" The annual festivals are "meetings" or "encounters" in two senses. First, they are an encounter between the Jewish people and God, as the Torah says: "Three times a year, all your males shall be seen toward the face of the Master, the Eternal" (Exodus 23:17). Second, they are an encounter between the Jewish people and specific momentous events in its history, moments when the Divine Presence had been especially manifest. Each of the three pilgrimage festivals testifies to a different historical event: Pesah, our freedom from Egyptian enslavement; Shavuot, our receiving of the Torah of ethics, morality, and human responsibility at Sinai; and Sukkot, our survival despite our wanderings through an alien and hostile desert environment. Hence in these moments of time we encounter the God of Freedom, the God of Torah and Morality, and the God of Protection.

The Sabbath Day

The Torah's chapter about the festivals, Leviticus 23, opens with Shabbat, which the Bible apparently sees as a primary festival, a *mo·eid*, an appointed time of human meeting with the Divine:

> And the Eternal spoke to Moses, saying, "Speak to the Israelites and say to them, 'These are My appointed festivals, the appointed festivals of the Eternal, which you are to proclaim as sacred assemblies. For six days work may be done, but the seventh day is a day of Shabbat rest, a day of sacred assembly. You are not to do any work, wherever you live; it is a Shabbat to the Eternal'" (verses 1–3).

Calling Shabbat a sacred, appointed time means that Shabbat is a time in which we meet God, a time of momentous significance, a time that touches eternity.

Time without God is an undifferentiated succession of seconds, minutes, hours, days, weeks, months, years—periods that move on inexorably, automatically, impervious to human beings and their experiences, in which people live out their lives between the tick-tocks of a blind and unfeeling Master Clock. The prophet of futility, Kohelet, says it frighteningly well: "A generation goes and a generation comes, but the earth [i.e., the clock] continues forever. The sun rises and the sun sets, and at the place where it yearned to rest, it only rises again from there. [The sun] goes toward the South, veers round toward the North; round and round it moves with the wind, and on its cyclical journey it returns with the wind" (Kohelet 1:4–6).

Time without God is cyclically sisyphean, repetitive without meaning or endgame, mocking the foolish strivings and sacrifices of the various peoples who move in its wake. As Shakespeare put it, "Tomorrow, and tomorrow, and tomorrow, / Creeps in this petty pace from day to day, / To the last syllable of recorded time."[3] It is a petty pace—not a progressive, meaningful march (halakhah)—because individual life, even the life of humans in the world, is nothing more substantive than the vapor (hevel) we exhale on a cold day. It is "a tale told by an idiot, full of sound and fury, signifying nothing."[4]

But this is not so, if life is a tale told by God—if world and life were created by a God of love and plan, and purpose. This is the message of that primordial seventh day, distinguished from what came before it and after it, a special day on which humans are bidden to share with God a rendezvous in sacred time:

And God saw all that God had made [in creating the world] and behold it was very good; and it was the evening and the morning of the sixth day. And the heavens and the earth were completed, and all their array. And God completed on the seventh day the creative work that God had done; and God rested on the seventh day from all the creative work that God had done. And God blessed the seventh day and made it holy, because on it God rested from all the creative work that God had created to do (Genesis 1:31–2:3).

What occurred on that momentous and significant seventh day? God recognized the "goodness" of creation, seeing that it was not necessary to repetitively do again what had already been accomplished without ever arriving at a finish line. This seventh day grants a glimpse into the eventual possibility of reaching fruition, of arriving at an endgame, of enjoying the light at the end of the tunnel. On that seventh day God created redemption, the possibility of bringing the entire material world into the orbit of the Divine.[5]

At the same time, in placing Shabbat as the first of the mo·adim, the appointed meeting places between people and God, the individual is empowered to enter into close relationship with God in time, during an entire day—thereby making that day with God qualitatively different from any other day of the week. This sacred Shabbat reveals the enormous implication of humanity having been created in God's image, endowed with a portion of God, and commanded to emulate God's characteristics:[6] just as God creates worlds, so too must we create worlds, and just as God rested on the Sabbath, thereby activating world redemption (which Rashi calls the creation of m'nuḥah), so too must we rest on the Sabbath, thereby glimpsing the reality of world redemption.

If indeed the Sabbath day establishes our fellowship with God, even our partnership with God ("Just as God…so must we…")—a meeting in which we actually "shake hands" (as it were) to work together—then we must devote this seventh day to coming closer to our Partner-in-Heaven, to learning better how to make our smaller worlds part of God's greater world, how to prepare ourselves and our world for redemption. Then Shabbat can truly become a time that touches eternity, and can become a truly sacred day. And we must make Shabbat so; we must actively "do" Shabbat. The Torah tells us: "And the Israelites shall observe Shabbat, to make [or "do"] Shabbat for their generations, as an eternal covenant [or: a covenant with the world]" (Exodus 31:16). This is the higher meaning of our "making Kiddush," of our sanctifying the Sabbath day along with the Creator of the universe.

The Festivals

The verse that marks the weekly Shabbat as a special, prototypical appointed time of the human-Divine encounter also opens the biblical discussion of other sacred times, the days of the yearly festivals: "These are the appointed festivals of the Eternal, sacred assemblies, which you shall announce in their due season" (Leviticus 23:4). This general introduction is followed by the festival of *matzot* (unleavened bread), the first of the festivals, on the fourteenth day of the month of Nisan, the first month of the year (Leviticus 23:5–8). The next verses deal with the reaping of the *omer* barley offering and the reaping of the first of the ripened grain (which is the fundamental base of physical sustenance), which express the human encounter with the Universal Sustainer in the land of Israel (Leviticus 23:9–22). The *omer*-count then continues for seven weeks, forty-nine days, culminating in the festival of the first fruits, Shavuot: its offering of two *hallah* loaves, representing the ripening of the last of the grains—wheat, which produces bread, the staff of life—thus symbolizes the completion and perfection of Israel's produce and God's bounty (but note that the initial barley *omer* offering was considered to be the grain eaten by animals). And the Oral Law adds that Shavuot is likewise the day of the divine revelation at Sinai, when Israel encountered God as the Teacher of Torah and morality.

Beginning the Jewish calendar of sacred days with the festival of our freedom, Passover, following the sacred Sabbath day, intensifies the profound message of our having been created in the divine image: just as God is free, so must every human being be free. Our God-encounter on those days must teach us our responsibility as God's partners—to attempt to free every human being who is enslaved by any other human being—as well as the necessity of making ourselves free of negative character traits, of toxic human addictions. And the command for us to begin counting every day "from the morrow of the Sabbath" (rabbinically interpreted to mean the day following the first day of the festival of *matzot*) emphasizes the truth that it is only a free individual who is able to count time, who is empowered to make time count; a master removes such an ability from slaves, and thereby robs them of the very essence of their humanity, the ability to encounter God and fulfill the divinely mandated responsibility to perfect the world in the sovereignty of God.

Marking the agricultural cycle from barley to bread (including the magnificent fruits for which Israel is praised) and leading up to our festival of first fruits likewise expresses our partnership with God in working the land and providing human sustenance; such an occupation is a sacred endeavor and a meaningful divine encounter. The Torah—the constitution we received from God at Sinai—defines our mission as a nation; it emphasizes the ethical and moral responsibilities of freedom and allows us a glimpse into what free individuals can accomplish together with God: ending enslavement and exile, reaching a homeland, and establishing a successful agricultural society providing for a sabbatical year of rest for the land as well as for the farmers, or a respectable avenue of employment for the poor, the widow, and the stranger. The prophetic vision of the Temple was of a place to serve as a guidepost and beacon of light to all the families of the earth, teaching Torah to all humanity (Isaiah 2:2–4, Micah 4:1–3).

Following the cycle of the year, the next festival mentioned in the Torah is Rosh Hashanah: "And the Eternal spoke to Moses, saying: Speak to the Israelites and say to them: 'In the seventh month, on the first of the month, you will have a *shabbaton* of remembrance of the *shofar* blowing, a sacred assembly. You shall not do any work, and you shall present a fire offering to the Eternal'" (Leviticus 23:23–25). In verse 24, Rosh Hashanah is described as a shabbaton, as is the very next festival of Yom Kippur: "But on the tenth [day] of this seventh month is a Day of Atonement, at-one-ment, [i.e., forgiveness].

You will have a sacred assembly, and you shall afflict your souls; you shall offer a fire offering to the Eternal….It is a *shabbat shabbaton* for you….From the evening of the ninth day of the month, until the following evening, you are to observe your Shabbat" (Leviticus 23:27–32). These two festivals empower us to encounter the God of Creation and the God of Forgiveness.

Next comes the festival of Sukkot, which is not described as a *shabbaton*; rather, we read: "On the fifteenth day of this seventh month is the festival of Sukkot, seven days for the Eternal" (Leviticus 23:34). The biblical text then mentions the festival of the Eighth Day (Shemini Atzeret), declaring the special sacredness of the first and last days which forbid work, but it does not in any way explain the ritual of the *sukkot* (booths), nor does it make reference to the taking of the four species, or explain in any way the significance of Shemini Atzeret.

And then comes the conclusion of the entire festival passage: "These are the Eternal's appointed festivals, which you are to proclaim as sacred assemblies for bringing fire offerings to the Eternal—the burnt offerings and grain offerings, sacrifices and drink offerings required for each day, in addition to those for the Eternal's Shabbat-days, and in addition to your gifts and whatever you have vowed and all the voluntary offerings you give to the Eternal" (Leviticus 23:37–38).

However, this apparent conclusion is then followed by a return to and further discussion of the festival of Sukkot, but this time the Bible introduces the commandment of the four species and explains the significance of the *sukkot*:

> But on the fifteenth day of the seventh month, after you have gathered the crops of the land, celebrate the festival to the Eternal for seven days; the first day is a *shabbaton* and the eighth day is also a *shabbaton*. On the first day you are to take the fruit of a special tree, palm branches, a leafy branch, and a willow

sprig—and rejoice before the Eternal your God for seven days. Celebrate this as a festival to the Eternal for seven days each year. This is to be a lasting ordinance for the generations to come; celebrate it in the seventh month. Live in booths (*sukkot*) for seven days: All native-born Israelites are to live in such booths, so that your descendants will know that I had the Israelites live in booths when I brought them out of Egypt. I am the Eternal your God." (Leviticus 23:39–43)

And then comes the final conclusion: "Thus Moses announced the Eternal's appointed times to the Israelites" (Leviticus 23:44). It is unclear why the verses about the festival of Sukkot are divided into two parts by what now seems to have been a pseudo-conclusion. It is important to note that in the second part, Sukkot is classified as a *shabbaton*, whereas in the first part, it is not described thus. And it is noteworthy that the term *shabbaton* is used in conjunction with Rosh Hashanah, Yom Kippur, and the second passage that describe Sukkot, but not in the passages describing Pesah, Shavuot, and the first passage about Sukkot.

In summary, this chapter presents us with three major problems:

1. Why is the term *shabbaton* used for Rosh Hashanah, Yom Kippur, and the second Sukkot passage, but not for the first Sukkot passage and not for the other festivals? And what is the significance of the linguistic linkage between *shabbaton* and Shabbat?
2. Why is the description of Sukkot divided into two parts, with only the second part mentioning the four species?
3. The festivals can be categorized in two ways: one approach pertains to the agricultural cycle of gathering, harvesting, planting, etc., and the other approach relates to the commemoration of historical events such as the Exodus from Egypt, the journey through the desert, and the revelation at Sinai. Rosh

Hashanah and Yom Kippur, however, do not fall into
either approach: they are not related to the agricultural
cycle, nor do they seem to commemorate any
particular historical event. If so, how can we
understand these two festivals and their relation to
the other appointed times of the Jewish year?

Toward the conclusion of this essay, we shall attempt to answer
these questions.

Further Reflections on the Concept of Sanctity

As we attempt to answer our questions and arrive at a more nuanced
understanding of sanctity, it is important to reflect on two works of
secular scholarship that discuss the concept of sanctity. The first is
Rudolph Otto's *The Idea of the Holy*,[7] where the word "numinous" is
used to describe the idea of sanctity; it is a word that evokes awesome
mystery, the different and the unknown, the mysterious bordering on
the occult. In this context, sanctity becomes connected with fear of
God, the sublime and awe-ful *mysterium tremendum*. The numinous
fascinates but also repels, inspiring frightful admiration but also
suggesting distance and human diminution.

The second book, *The Sacred and the Profane*, is by Mircea Eliade,[8]
an anthropologist and historian of religion. As mentioned above, my
mentor and teacher Rabbi Soloveitchik, of blessed memory, also wrote
an article by the same title, which expresses similar ideas to those of
Eliade, and emphasizes the desire of humans to find God in every
aspect of world. Rav Soloveitchik adds that sanctity is a "paradox"
rather than a "paradise": sanctity requires perpetual striving, sacrifice,
commitment, and creativity. This definition contrasts significantly
with the classical Jewish understanding of avoidance and restraint,
a separation from the material which is largely a passive expression;
sanctity according to Rav Soloveitchik is an active enterprise of
seeking God in time and place. It requires perpetual creativity,

ceaseless activity on the part of the human being to reach out and up in order to bring God into the here-and-now, everywhere.

The Sacred as a Link to God and Eternity

This approach to sanctity is an encounter between the human and the Divine, the fleeting and the ephemeral with the Permanent and the Eternal. God is the only real entity in the world, who bestows actual being, true existence. Outside of God we are left only with the vapor (*hevel*) of Kohelet, the appearance of substance but doomed for almost immediate disintegration. An encounter between God and a particular time creates sanctity, sanctity of time. Similarly, an encounter between God and a particular place creates sanctity of place. Because God is the entity who grants eternity to both time and place, the encounter between God and a particular event in history or a particular place in the world necessarily creates sanctity, enabling that time or that event or that place to interact and interface with the Divine, and thereby to participate in eternity.

The Sacred Dance between God and Humans in Time and Space

This is evident in the first appointed time, when the idea of sanctity is first mentioned in the Bible: "And God blessed the seventh day and made it sacred" (Genesis 2:3). And, as we have seen earlier, the first *mo·eid* or "holy convocation" in the book of Leviticus is Shabbat (23:3).

This idea is also echoed in the holiest of places, in the Temple (or sanctuary), the *mikdash*. Since the sanctuary is a meeting-place between God and humans (cf. Exodus 25:8, "They shall make Me a sanctuary so that I may dwell among them"), it may be seen as a Shabbat in space. The Temple is the place that humans make for God, complementing the world that God made for humans. God declares the Sabbath to be a sacred day where humans can meet with the Divine through the medium of the world, which God has made for them as a sanctuary in time; humans declare the Temple a sacred space where God can meet with us through the medium of a place that we have made for God, a Shabbat in space.[9] And in both realms, time and space, eternity is achieved by a sacred dance between God and human. In time, it is God who brings humans close to the Divine; in space, it is humans who must bring God down to them. Ultimately humans must re-create the *entire* world as a sanctuary fit for God, and herein lies the human task of *tikkun olam*.

Tikkun Olam: Bringing God Down

The Kedushah prayer declares, "Holy, holy, holy is the Eternal One of Hosts, the whole world is filled with God's glory" (Isaiah 6:3), and the Zohar explains, "No place is [potentially] devoid of God." Sanctity does not result from withdrawing and abstaining from the world, but rather from our bringing God down into the world and filling it with God's glory. Similarly, Maimonides[10] interprets the notion of "God's glory" (*k'vodo*) as God's presence in the world, the Shekhinah or the immanent Divine Presence. In the morning blessings before the Shema, we follow the praise "Holy, holy, holy is the Eternal One of Hosts, the whole world is filled with God's glory" with a verse from Ezekiel: "Blessed is the glory (*kavod*) of the Eternal One, from God's place" (Ezekiel 3:12). This is usually taken to mean that God's glory emanates from an exalted supernal place in the heavens. However, I would instead interpret this verse to mean, "More blessed is the [immanent] glory of the Eternal [on earth] than [is the transcendent glory from] God's exalted place in the heavens."[11] There is transcendental divinity and immanent divinity; Judaism emphasizes the need to incorporate the transcendental divinity into the world so that it becomes immanent. God is more blessed when present in this world, than when located in isolated splendor beyond this world.

This idea is also expressed in the prayer U-va L'tziyyon Go·eil ("A Redeemer Will Come to Zion"), which cites the Aramaic translation-interpretation of Targum Yonatan to the verse from Isaiah (6:3). In this prayer, the celestial beings receive permission from one another to praise God and they interpret the three domains of God's holiness: "Holy in the highest heavens, home of God's presence; holy on earth, the work of God's power; holy forever and for all time." Here, the three degrees of sanctity of God are presented in ascending order: first, we mention the holiness of the transcendental divinity, "holy in the highest heavens"; then, we mention the holiness of immanent divinity, "holy on earth, the work of God's power"; and finally, we mention the holiness of the divinity throughout history, "holy forever and for all time."[12]

The greatest challenge for humankind, therefore, is to bring God into this world and into our time, to transform the transcendental Eternal One into the immanent Shekhinah. In the book *Halakhic Man*, Rabbi Soloveitchik explains that the way to achieve this immanence is through *halakhah*, which explains the dictum of our talmudic sages, "The blessed Holy One has nothing in this world but the four cubits of the Law" (B. Berakhot 8a). Thus, the laws of *kashrut* bring the sanctity of the Divine into the kitchen, the laws of family purity bring the sanctity of the Divine into the bedroom, and the Jewish legal laws of *Ḥoshen Mishpat* bring the sanctity of the Divine into the workplace.

I once heard a wonderful teaching about this from Rabbi Aharon Soloveitchik, of blessed memory. There are two contradictory verses in the book of Psalms, which need to be harmonized. The first verse reads, "To the Eternal is the earth and all of its fullness" (Psalm 24:1), while another verse states, "The heavens, the heavens belong to the Eternal, while God gave the earth to humankind" (Psalm 115:16). How does one reconcile these two ideas? The Talmud explains: "One verse applies before one offers a blessing, and the other applies after one offers a blessing" (B. Berakhot 35a). The conventional commentaries (including Rashi) explain that before one makes a blessing the food belongs to God, and afterward the food belongs to the person who made the blessing. Indeed, it is the blessing that gives us the right to partake of God's world and requisition a specific aspect of it for our own personal use.

Rabbi Aharon Soloveitchik, however, interprets the tension between the verses in a completely different way. According to him, a person who has not yet recited a blessing (or does not recite a blessing at all) sees two separate worlds or two separate realms: heaven, which belongs to God, and earth, which belongs to people. Never do the two worlds meet. However, a person who is immersed in the world of blessings is able to perceive the sublime within the mundane, the Godly within the earthly, the transcendent nature of God within the immanent universe. The food he or she is about to eat becomes a bridge between this world and God. Through the blessing, a person is able to bring God down into this world. Therefore, *after*—and as a result of—eating the fruit with a blessing, an individual can truly feel that "the entire world belongs to God." Indeed, a person can bring God into the material world even by means of an object as mundane as an apple or a piece of bread.

Through this, one can understand Rabbi Yosef Dov Soloveitchik's teaching that one of God's names is *ha-makom* ("the Place, or "the Omnipresent in the Here-and-Now"): since it is this world in which God yearns to be eternally present, it is up to us—the inhabitants of this world—to make this entire world God's sanctuary. The verse recited by Ashkenazic Jewish visitors to a house of mourning is, "May the Omnipresent (*ha-makom*) comfort you among the mourners of Zion and Jerusalem." It is a prayer for the future, that the time will come when the Shekhinah will be ever-present, and then even this world will be a place of consolation and salvation, as I will discuss below.

Rosh Hashanah: Our Coronation of God as Sovereign as We Repair and Perfect a Broken World

The sanctity of Rosh Hashanah is mainly related to sovereignty, to anointing God as Sovereign of the world: "It is taught that Rabbi Judah said in the name of Rabbi Akiva…On Rosh Hashanah, say before Me *malkhuyyot* (sovereignty), *zikhronot* (remembrances), and *shofarot* (blasts) to crown Me over you. How? Through the shofar." (B. Rosh Hashanah 16a) This sovereignty of God in the world is made explicit on Rosh Hashanah in the fourth blessing of the Amidah, concerning the holiness of the day (*k'dushaht ha-yom*): "Blessed are You…Sovereign over all the earth…" This coronation is a fulfillment of the need to bring God into the world, to induce immediate, immanent divinity. The purpose of blowing the *shofar* is for us to anoint God as sovereign; the *shofar* was traditionally used in ancient Israel for coronation ceremonies (see, e.g., 1 Kings 1:39). Hence, the Bible's reference to Rosh Hashanah as yom *t'ruah*, "a day of sounding the *shofar*" (Numbers 29:1), marks it as the day of God's coronation as Sovereign of the world—over the world from within the world. And the Hebrew word *t'ruah* would then refer to the exultant shouts that accompany and punctuate a coronation ceremony.

In contrast, a later discussion in the Talmud (B. Rosh Hashanah 33b) interprets yom *t'ruah* as a day of groaning or sobbing, based on the derivation of the word *t'ruah* from *ruah*. Indeed, the Talmud queries whether the term is related to *ginnuhei gannah*, the broken groaning sighs known as the sh'varim tones, or to the broken, sobbing, wailing sounds known as the *t'ruah* tone, *y'lilei yalil*—or perhaps to both "sighing" and "wailing" together. If so, how can we reconcile a day of weeping and sighing, as this passage interprets *yom t'ruah*, with the idea of the day of God being crowned as Sovereign of the world?

The answer to this question is that as long as the presence of God is not felt in the world, as long as the world is far from being perfected under the sovereignty of God's name, the world is indeed a "valley of tears." The midrash is tragically succinct: "God's name is not complete and God's throne is not complete…as long as Amalek is in the world" (Rashi to Exodus 17:16). In the words of Rabbi Simha Bunim of Przysucha (1765–1827), "There is nothing more broken than a broken heart."[13] This vision of an incomplete (and even broken) world is documented by a startling verse in Isaiah, which all too honestly depicts the world created by God: "Producer of light and Creator of darkness, the One who makes peace and creates evil—I am the Eternal, who makes all of these" (Isaiah 45:7). God created a world that contains evil as well as good, darkness as well as light, chaos as well as order. Our world is imperfect, incomplete, and broken. And this is the reason Rosh Hashanah is a day of wailing, weeping, and sighing: because of the chasm between our present reality and our anticipated vision, between what we now have and what we still yearn for.

For the bridge to unite vision with reality, we must return to the initial biblical reference to the Sabbath:

> Then the heavens and the earth were completed, and all their array. With the seventh day, God completed creative physical activity that had been performed; God rested on the seventh day from all the creative physical activity that had been performed. And God blessed the seventh day and declared it holy, because on it God rested from all the creative physical activity that God had created to do. (Genesis 2:1–3)

The last few words, "God had created to do," are not clear; they seem somewhat superfluous. If these words are deleted, the passage would still make perfect sense. I would suggest that the phrase should be taken to mean, "God rested from all the activity that God had created, [leaving the rest] for *humankind* to do."[14] It is up to us to fill in the gap; it is up to us to complete the work God expects us to do. We must crown God as Sovereign of the world and we must perfect the world under the sovereignty of God's name, which is love and compassion, graciousness (unconditional love), patience, and lovingkindness (cf.

Exodus 34:5-6).[15] This is the essence of Rosh Hashanah: to translate our vision into reality by crowning God as Sovereign over the world, so that God will come down and be manifest in the world so that it may be perfected, completed. We must make the world a suitable sanctuary within which it will be comfortable for God to dwell; then God will be manifest within the world.

This is the essence of the second paragraph of the Aleinu, recited as part of Malkhuyyot on Rosh Hashanah: we must "remove idolatry from the earth...perfect the world (*l'takkein olam*) under the sovereignty of the Almighty, when all mortals will call upon Your name and all the wicked of the earth will turn to You...Everyone will accept the yoke of Your Sovereignty and You will rule over them speedily forever..." This is what coronating God means; this is the essence of taking a transcendent God from an exalted, supernal place and making God immanent in our present world.

The prophets[16] declare that we will eventually succeed in this task in historic time (*zikhronot*) and by means of the nations accepting our Torah teachings (*shofarot*). Hence Rabbi Shimon ben Elazar teaches that ultimately all the Gentiles will convert to Judaism (B. Berakhot 57b), and Maimonides suggests that in the messianic age everyone will return to the true religion (Mishneh Torah, Hilkhot Melakhim 12:1). The nations will come to the Third Temple to accept our teaching of ethical monotheism, they will beat their swords into plowshares, and the world will be redeemed.

And it is this human empowerment and divine guarantee that caused the talmudic sages to add the triumphant *t'kiah* sound of victory to the mournful *t'ruah* sound of angst on Rosh Hashanah— the *t'kiah* that emanates from the Jubilee Year as a taste of redemption (Leviticus 25:9). Even more, our sages mandate two exultant *t'kiah* sounds to every broken *t'ruah* sound and insist that each individual *t'kiah* be at least as long as each individual *t'ruah*.[17] Our faith in our capacity to turn this vale of tears into a Garden of Eden is what makes Rosh Hashanah a festival of joy and gives us the optimism to turn despair into directive, as we continue to work toward the exultant crescendo-climax of our as-yet unfinished symphony.

Shabbat, Sanctuary, and Sanctifying Human Beings

God created time so that we, in historic time, will become a light unto the nations, will meet God in special moments of time (our festivals), and will eventually bring about that long-awaited and anxiously-expected time that will be the day (or epoch) "that is entirely Shabbat," when all of time will be spent in rendezvous with the Divine. This is the *zikhronot* blessing that follows the *malkhuyyot* blessing on Rosh Hashanah: the sanctity of historic time when, in a redeemed world, every day will be Shabbat.

Likewise, in regard to the dimension of place, we long to fulfill God's command to "make a sanctuary for Me, so that I will dwell among them" (Exodus 25:8)—the world must become an extension of the sanctuary! According to Yehudah Halevi's *Kuzari*, the sanctuary symbolizes the world, which we must make worthy of the Divine Presence dwelling in its midst. We must transform the entire world into a sanctuary and we must elevate every day to the level of Shabbat, thus sanctifying the dimensions of space and time by bringing God into these realms. It was so that we could be God's partners in perfecting the world of space and time that we were created in the image of God and charged with perfecting the world.

There is No Sanctity Without Sacrifice

It is an obligation for us humans to sanctify space and time, and every act of sanctity requires sacrifice and commitment. According to Rabbi Isaac Luria ("the Holy Ari," 1534–1572), the great secret and foundation of the world's creation is *tzimtzum*, the diminution or contraction of God's self, as it were. Reflect: if God is wholly goodness, and if the world and all of humanity are emanations of that divine goodness, then from whence did evil, darkness, emptiness and void, the serpential evil instinct, and hedonistic materialism develop?

The question I am posing is probably the most significant question posed to the religionist: from whence, and why, does an imperfect world—a world that admits an Auschwitz —emanate from a perfect God of love?

In the aftermath of the sin of the golden calf, when Moses is desperately seeking God's forgiveness for the nation, the greatest of all prophets asks to see God's glory (*kavod*), to glimpse (as much as is humanly possible) the definition of God's presence in the world. God responds with a second revelation at Sinai, expressing the Thirteen Attributes—the first of which is the Tetragrammaton, the four-letter ineffable name of God (*yod-hei-vav-hei*), which the talmudic sages interpret to mean the God of unconditional love, both before and after we sin, the God of love who is always open to forgiveness (Exodus 33:18 and 34:6; B. Rosh Hashanah 17b). Indeed, the very name YHVH may well mean "love": hav in Aramaic is the verb "to give," so that *hei-vav-hei*, or "givingness," may well be identified with lovingkindness (since the most obvious expression of love is the desire to give to one's beloved). And although *hav* and *ahavah* are spelled with the letter vet and YHVH is spelled with the letter vav, these two homophonous letters may sometimes be interchanged: note that *ta·avah*, "erotic desire," is written with a vav and *tei·avon*, "hungry appetite," is written with a vet, and yet they are considered cognate words! Hence YHVH is the God of forgiving love.

Rabbi Ḥayyim Vital maintains that the Almighty created the world because "it was necessary for God to be perfect in action and in the fulfillment of the divine names," and since love and compassion require others to whom to express love and compassion—love and compassion cannot exist in a vacuum—God created human beings, "other."[19] And that "other" had to be created with freedom of choice; if humans were totally controlled by God, were in actuality mere extensions of God, then divine love for humans would merely be "self-love" on the part of the Divine—it would be devoid of a true "other." So God created human beings with the possibility of choosing to do even that which God would not have wanted them to do; God had to leave room in the world for humanity to be other, to choose other (see Genesis 1:26, and the commentary of Seforno ad loc.). Hence God practiced self-constriction (*tzimtzum*), as it were, limiting divine omnipotence, in order to leave room in the world where God was not, to leave room for evil in an imperfect world, to enable humanity to choose evil, to create free human beings who were not mere puppets or pawns but who could and must become full partners, "only a little lower than God, crowned with glory and honor" (Psalm 8:5)—who will eventually triumph over evil, and will perfect, complete, and repair a broken world.

God initially emanated a world within historical time which was an inextricable part of the Divine. God is the One who fills all worlds and all times, the All in the all. In an act of love and self-sacrifice, God restricted and contracted the divine Being in order to leave room in time and space for others (i.e., humans); the challenge is for those others to re-unite both time and space with the God who initially created them, by restoring the Ineffable Eternal One with the Shekhinah, Tiferet with Malkhut. We must bring God into world by extending the sanctuary to encompass the world, and we must bring God into time by transforming every day into Shabbat. This requires great human effort and sacrifice. We, too, in imitation of God's ways, will be required to limit and contract our individual materialistic desires and needs in order to leave room both for other people and for God. Sometimes this will entail even the ultimate sacrifice of our lives and the lives of our children—for the sake of the continuity of our nation and our religion, and for our mission as God's witnesses and a light unto the nations of the world. But God guarantees through the divine covenant that we will ultimately overcome the challenges and re-create a perfected world. This is the meaning of the final triumphant *t'kiah g'dolah* sounded on Rosh Hashanah and at the close of Yom Kippur.

This is the amazing connection between Shabbat and sanctuary: Shabbat is to the rest of the days what the sanctuary is to the rest of the world. Shabbat is a sanctuary in time, and the sanctuary is an oasis in world.[20]

God created an imperfect world in worldly time for us to live in and work in and develop in, even as God invites us to turn that world into a sanctuary for the Divine to live in with us—in our midst—once humanity becomes worthy; and God created time and history within the world, inviting us to redeem both time and history by effectuating an era that is wholly and holy Sabbath and redemption. In the messianic era, both time and space will be suffused and saturated with divine sanctity; there will be no suffering, no tragedies, no untimely deaths. At that time, God's great name will be magnified and sanctified in the world created in accordance with the divine will—that is, a will that demands that we, God's human partners, sanctify both time and the world by bringing God into both of these spheres (see Ezekiel 38:23). At that time, God's name will be complete and the divine contraction will be expanded by the immanent Divine Presence. At that time, when God will be omnipresent (ha-makom) and suffuse the world with the Divine Presence, every broken heart will be repaired and every mourning soul will be comforted. This is the significance of the Mourner's Kaddish and the formula with which Ashkenazic Jews comfort the mourners.

There is a fascinating dispute between two of the greatest figures of Hasidism, the Kotzker Rebbe and the Vorker Rebbe. The Vorker Rebbe would say that he preferred the mitzvah of sukkah over the mitzvah of taking the four species, because when we hold the four species we are holding sanctity, but when we put them down, the sanctity is gone. When we sit in the sukkah, however, we are being held by a sanctity we cannot put down; it is all around us. The Kotzker Rebbe responded that that was why he preferred the mitzvah of the Sabbath over the sukkah: one can leave the sukkah and walk out of sanctity, but one can never leave Shabbat!

However, I would argue that the issue is not so clear-cut. The sanctity of Shabbat can be broken: when a person transgresses Shabbat, when the peace of a Shabbat table is destroyed by an angry word or a malicious reference, then the individual *has* effectively walked out of Shabbat. Sanctity is always dependent on the thoughts and deeds of people. "Israel must keep Shabbat, making Shabbat in every generation, as an everlasting covenant" (Exodus 31:16). We must "make Shabbat," declaring the sanctity of the Sabbath in our spoken Kiddush in addition to God's own declaration, and in addition to the natural astronomical advent of the Sabbath at sunset on Friday evening. Shabbat must be felt in our lives and in our deeds. By observing Shabbat, we actually "create" a unique and special twenty-five-hour oasis—a sanctuary—in time, a blessed day different and distinct from every other day, which must be made into a model for every day.

A well-known midrash[21] describes how Noah partnered with Satan in planting the first vineyard. Satan killed a sheep and poured its blood on the earth, killed a lion and poured its blood on that same earth, killed a monkey and spilled its blood over that earth, and killed a pig and let its blood mingle with the bloody earth. From this blood-soaked earth, a grapevine sprouted. When one drinks wine, one first becomes mild and sleepy like a sheep; when one continues drinking, one then becomes as fierce as a lion; when one drinks still more, one frolics ridiculously as a monkey; and eventually, when one drinks to surfeit, one becomes repulsive and disgusting, like a pig.

The Talmud asks why wine is red, and responds that under the influence of red wine one may come to shed red blood; moreover, when one recalls how one has acted when drunk, one is ashamed, and one's face flushes red (B. Sanhedrin 71a).

In spite of all this, or perhaps because of all this, we make Kiddush over wine; we seek to sanctify even the most mundane, to bring God into every aspect of our lives, uplifting the most material into the most spiritual. We make a special blessing on wine, which concludes with the words "who creates the fruit of the vine" rather than the expected "who creates the fruit of the tree," because of the special intensity of human labor that is required to bring forth wine from the fruit of the vine. The wine symbolizes that with hard work, humans are able to improve on nature; with hard work, one can improve on one's own human nature, bringing sanctity into every aspect of life. With sacrifice and commitment, humanity can perfect God's world, and can bring the Divine into every realm, sanctifying every space and every day.

A Talmudic Tale Proves the Sanctity of Immanence

In order to understand the concept of sanctity, it is important to study the talmudic story of Rabbi Shimon bar Yoḥai, one of the giants of the talmudic sages who escaped the Romans by hiding in a cave with his son for thirteen years (B. Shabbat 33b–34a). The mystics maintain that during this period he was gifted with the divine revelation that produced the sacred Zohar.

According to one approach by the sages, "The blessed Holy One looked at the Torah, and created the world" (B'reishit Rabbah 1:1)—that is, Torah (including the Oral Law) is none other than a transcendental literature that emanates from the sublime and supernal realm of the Divine. From this perspective, immersing oneself in Torah is essentially immersing oneself in non-physical, otherworldly engagements. Thus, involvement in Torah study came to be seen as a transcendent involvement, totally separated from this world.[22] From this perspective, the study of Torah is clearly an ethereal and spiritual enterprise, demanding disengagement from world; hence, the ultra-Orthodox yeshiva world, in Israel as well as in the Diaspora, might contrast the study of Torah with any secular study or pursuit, seeing the two as being totally incompatible. And since *talmud* torah *k'neged kullam*, "the study of Torah outweighs all other pursuits" (B. Shabbat 127a), the essence of sanctity must be seen as the antithesis of worldly occupations, studies, or engagements.

Let us examine the approach of Rabbi Shimon bar Yoḥai:

> Rabbi Judah, Rabbi Yossi, and Rabbi Shimon were sitting
> and studying, and Judah, a son of converts, was sitting near
> them. Rabbi Judah commenced [the discussion] by observing,
> "How fine are the works of this people [the Romans]! They
> have made marketplaces, they have built bridges, they have
> erected bath houses." Rabbi Yose was silent. Rabbi Shimon
> bar Yoḥai answered and said, "All that they have made, they
> made for themselves: they built marketplaces to set harlots
> in them, bath houses in which unnecessarily to pamper
> themselves, and bridges on which levy tolls for themselves."
> Then Judah, the son of converts, went and related their
> conversation, which reached the ears of the government. [The
> Roman government] decreed: "Judah, who exalted [us], shall
> be exalted; Yose, who was silent, shall be exiled to Sepphoris;
> Shimon, who reviled [our efforts], must be executed."
> He and his son went and hid themselves in the house of
> study, where his wife brought him bread and a jug of water
> for their meals. [But] when the decree became more severe
> he said to his son, "Women are of unstable temperament; she
> may be tortured and expose us." So they went and hid in a
> cave. A miracle occurred and a carob tree and water well were
> created for them.[23] They would strip their garments and sit
> up to their necks in sand. (B. Shabbat 33b)

It is interesting to note how the cave is depicted as a grave of sorts:
they sat up to their necks, buried in sand.[24] In any case, they were
cut off from the world. It would seem that for the author of this
story, Torah isolated from the world is not a living Torah but is rather
an impaired, estranged Torah; it is a living grave! The talmudic tale
continues:

> The whole day they studied; when it was time for prayers they
> dressed, covered themselves, prayed, and then took off their
> garments again, so that their garments would not wear out.

Thus they dwelt twelve years in the cave. Then Elijah came and stood at the entrance to the cave, exclaiming, "Who will inform the son of Yoḥai that the emperor is dead and his decree annulled?" So they emerged. Seeing a man plowing and sowing, they exclaimed in condemnation, "People such as this one forsake eternal life and engage in temporal life!" Whatever they cast their eyes upon was immediately burnt up. Thereupon a heavenly voice came forth and cried out, "Have you emerged to destroy My world? Return to your cave!" So they returned and dwelt there twelve more months, after which they exclaimed, "The punishment of the wicked in Gehenna is only twelve months long."

Apparently, their cave became harder and harder to bear, despite the great amounts of Torah they learned within it. By this point, even Rabbi Shimon was experiencing their isolation as Gehenna, hell— the abyss that the wicked experience after death.

A heavenly voice then came forth and said, "Go forth from your cave!" Thus, they left the cave. Wherever Rabbi Elazar was wounded, Rabbi Shimon healed. He said him, "My son! You and I are all this world needs [for total involvement in study; let the rest of humanity work]." On the eve of the Sabbath before sunset they saw an old man holding two bundles of myrtle and running at twilight. "What are these for?" they asked him. "They are in honor of the Sabbath," he replied. "But should not one suffice for you?" they asked. [He replied to them]: "One is for 'Remember' and one for 'Observe.'" Said [Rabbi Shimon] to his son, "See how precious the commandments are for Israel!" Thus they were placated.

From here, it is clear that the lesson Rabbi Shimon learns from the old man is significant. But before we attempt to understand how Rabbi Shimon viewed the material world and what he gleaned from the old man's response, we must first recall Rabbi Shimon's worldview prior to this encounter outside of the cave. There is a famous dispute between Rabbi Shimon and Rabbi Ishmael regarding the *mitzvah* of Torah study (B. Berakhot 35a):

> It is taught: "And you shall gather in your grain" (Deuteronomy 11:14). What is to be learned from these words? Since it says, "This book of the Torah shall not leave your mouth, you shall meditate therein by day and by night" (Joshua 1:8), one might think that this injunction is to be taken literally. Therefore it says, "And you shall gather in your grain," which implies that you are to combine the study of Torah with a worldly occupation. This is the view of Rabbi Ishmael. Rabbi Shimon bar Yoḥai says: "Is that possible? If one plows in the plowing season, sows in the sowing season, reaps in the reaping season, threshes in the threshing season, and winnows in the season of wind, what is to become of Torah study? Rather, when Israel performs the will of the Omnipresent, their work is performed by others, as it says: 'And strangers [Gentiles] shall stand and feed your flocks' (Isaiah 61:5). And when Israel does not perform the will of the Omnipresent [to study Torah full-time], they will carry out their work themselves, as it says, 'And you shall gather in your grain' (Deuteronomy 11:14). Nor is this all, but the work of others will also be done [by the Israelites]."

It would seem to be clear according to Rabbi Shimon that the ideal is indeed to literally learn Torah "all day and all night"—all of the time! And our material needs will then be taken care of by others.

It is interesting to note that in the subsequent talmudic passage, where the difference of opinion between Rabbi Shimon and Rabbi Ishmael is adjudicated, no one in the later generation of sages agrees with the opinion of Rabbi Shimon—neither Abaye nor Rava nor Rabbah: "Said Abaye: Many have followed the advice of Rabbi Ishmael, and it has worked well; others have followed Rabbi Shimon bar Yoḥai and it has not worked well. Rabbah said to the sages who studied in his academy: I would ask you not to appear before me [in the house of study] during Nisan and Tishrei, in order that you may be able to do the necessary agricultural work so that you will not be anxious about your food supply during the rest of the year."

It would seem that Rabbi Shimon's approach was deemed to be not realistic. Those who followed his conviction of total immersion in Torah study found themselves waiting in vain; "others" never appeared to do their work for them. Moreover, Rabbi Shimon's maximalist interpretation of meditating in Torah "all day and all night" (*yomam va-lailah*) would seem to contradict the universally accepted maxim, "It is good to combine Torah study with a worldly occupation" (Pirkei Avot 2:2). Even more importantly, Rabbi Shimon's strongly worded opinion in this passage seems to contradict another of Rabbi Shimon's own statements: "Rabbi Yoḥanan said in the name of Rabbi Shimon bar Yohai, 'If one only recites the Shema prayer in the morning and the evening, one has fulfilled the commandment of 'This book of the Torah shall not leave your mouth'—[meaning:] you shall meditate therein for a *portion* of the day and a *portion* of the night'" (B. Menaḥot 99b). And similarly, we read in the Mekhilta, on the verse "Six days you shall labor and do all your work" (Exodus 20:9): Rabbi Shimon says, "Work is so important that even if the high priest were to enter the holy of holies on Yom Kippur not as part of the service, he would receive the death penalty; whereas when the Temple was being built, even unclean workers or people with defects were allowed to enter the holy of holies." Even more startlingly, in another version of the same Mekhilta passage just cited, we read: "Rabbi Shimon teaches that 'Six days you shall labor'—this is a positive commandment. It is incumbent for one to work during the week in order for it be recognizable that one is resting on the Sabbath."[25]

All of these texts show the great value that Rabbi Shimon places on work and worldly occupation. Clearly, he must have changed his mind; but if so, can we find a clue as to when and why?

This contradiction can be resolved by reflecting upon the transformation that Rabbi Shimon had undergone by the second time he left the cave. Earlier in his life, he had seen Torah study and any other non-Torah involvement as being mutually contradictory, since any such endeavor would remove the scholar from his single-minded commitment to study Torah. He believed that "If one plows in the plowing season, sows in the sowing season, reaps in the reaping season, threshes in the threshing season, and winnows in the season of wind, what is to become of Torah study?" However, by the time he reemerged from the cave, he had come to view Torah study in a different light. The Shulḥan Arukh comments that Rabbi Shimon left the cave on the thirty-third day of the counting of the omer,[26] a day which came to be marked as a festival on the Jewish calendar. Note that for twelve years, Rabbi Shimon (together with his son) had been immersed in the secrets of the Kabbalah. According to kabbalistic tradition, he was divinely inspired at that time to write the sacred Zohar. However, because he was completely isolated, in a sense he was dead to the world; having been forced to escape the earthly world, his experience in the cave was otherworldly. As we have discussed, this withdrawal is problematic: humanity's challenge is to sanctify *this* world, the world we live in, and not to seek holiness through complete denial of the material world. We must transform this world into the world to come.

This was understood by Rabbi Akiva's students, who fought in the revolt of Bar Kokhba in order to free the land of Israel and bring redemption to the world. They were not content to learn Torah and pray; rather, they took action! They died at the hands of the Sicarii— not by a form of whooping cough (as Rashi understands the talmudic term *ask'ra*), but rather by the sword, as Rabbi Hai Gaon describes: "The students of Rabbi Akiva died by *sh'mada*, having been murdered as a result of the harsh edicts of the Roman Emperor Hadrian, which were related to the revolt of Bar Kokhba."[27]

This is the moral of the old man running at sunset with two myrtle branches, one branch symbolizing the "remembrance" (preparation for) Shabbat and the other symbolizing the "observance" of Shabbat. We have seen that Shabbat is a testimony to the creation of an incomplete world, a broken world. However, Shabbat is also a taste of the world to come, an encounter between this incomplete world and the world to come, perfect and redeemed. During the week, the six days of creation, we need to elevate the real world, our world, into a foretaste of the world to come, a time that is entirely Shabbat. Therefore, we "remember the Shabbat day" during the week, and prepare for our dream to "observe the Shabbat day" on Shabbat itself. In this way we can live in both worlds at the same time; even in our imperfect world, we can catch a glimpse of the world of the future at least every Sabbath day. We can appreciate the disparity between where we are and where we yearn to be and, at the same time, prepare for a more glorious future. And preparing for the Messiah must be seen in itself as a holy pursuit; the effort that goes into bringing God into the world may well be considered a higher rung of sanctity than the passive realization that the Messiah is here. In halakhic terminology, *hekh·sheir mitzvah* is also a *mitzvah*.

How do we prepare for this during the week? By creating sanctity, by performing *mitzvot* in the material world, by elevating that which is worldly, physical, material. Through plowing and planting—by keeping the laws of tithing (*t'rumot* and *ma·asrot*), by not planting forbidden mixtures, by "not restraining the oxen when they plow," by leaving a corner of the field for the poor. And by observing the laws that are pertinent to every part of life: charity laws, laws within the home, laws between neighbors, laws of family purity, laws of *kashrut*. These are the laws that sanctify every aspect of life: commerce, community, life, eating, intimacy. We can reach toward sanctity through our daily lives, through living in this world, not by escaping it—and by preparing every aspect of our lives in the not-yet-holy world for when we will merit the holy world. And even then we will no doubt still be struggling to rise higher and higher in sanctity.[28]

This is precisely what Rabbi Shimon learned from the old man with the two myrtle twigs. He even said to his son, "See how precious the commandments are for Israel"; the observation that "they were placated" indicates that they then understood the value of agricultural pursuit. The commandments require us to be involved in and to engage with this world, in every aspect of our being. That is how we prepare the way for the re-creation of a more perfect world.

If wine can be sanctified, then there is nothing in the material world that cannot similarly be made holy. As Rabbi Avraham Isaac Kook teaches: in this world there are only two categories, the holy and the not-yet holy. There is no unredeemable material, nothing that is wholly *ḥol*: "And God saw everything that had been made, and it was good"—at least in potential. We are entrusted with the task of sanctifying everything in this world.

The same applies to time. Every day is holy, for the same God who created Shabbat also created the six days leading up to it. As we say in our prayers, "God who, in goodness, renews the act of creation every single day." We must recognize the potential in every moment of every day—after all, for six days we must do our work, which is holy in itself, since the preparation for a *mitzvah* is also a *mitzvah*. A person must sanctify every material object,[29] making every moment holy and every place heavenly. This is the lesson that the old man taught Rabbi Shimon: even a branch of myrtle, and even the act of plowing or planting, can be holy—for they are inseparable parts of remembering the Shabbat day to keep it holy, and observing the Shabbat day to keep it holy. They are all preparations for the period that is wholly Shabbat and for the world-sanctuary that will host God within it and within our midst.

The Myrtle: Blooming Even in a Wasteland, a Symbol of Redemption

This is symbolized by the myrtle. The myrtle is mentioned as one of the seven plants that will cause the wasteland to bloom in the time of redemption: "I will put in the desert cedar and acacia, myrtle and olive; I will place in the wasteland cypress, fir, and the box tree together" (Isaiah 41:19). There is a custom (attributed to Rabbi Ḥayyim Vital)—a custom that I myself maintain in my home—to welcome Shabbat on Friday evening by making a blessing on two myrtle branches right before blessing the children, paralleling the blessings on the spices recited Saturday evening at Havdalah.

Myrtle is one of the four species that we bind together on Sukkot, and we then wave the bundle in every direction when we recite Hallel. In the book of Nehemiah we read that myrtle was even used in the actual construction of the *sukkah*: "Go out to the mountain and bring olive branches, oil tree branches, myrtle branches, date branches, and shade tree branches to build a *sukkah*, as it is written" (Nehemiah 8:15). Queen Esther, who redeems herself and the lives of her people after spending her years of growth and development in the pagan hedonistic environment of Persia, nevertheless, at a critical moment, rejoins her Jewish past and secures a Jewish future for herself and her Jewish people. Her Hebrew name is Hadassah, "myrtle"; her Jewishness bloomed in the pagan desert of Persia.

According to the Talmud, all parts of the myrtle tree—its leaves, its branches, and its fruit—taste the same, as in the beginning of creation in the Garden of Eden. It is written: "They said that Rabbi Judah bar Ilai would take a myrtle wand and dance before the bride, saying that the bride is beautiful and graceful" (B. Ketubot 17a). And it is clear from the wedding blessings that every wedding has an aspect of redemption, of faith in the future of Israel, resonating with the wish that there "may be heard in the cities of Judah and in the streets of Jerusalem the sounds of joy and gladness, the sounds of the bridegroom and bride." In a similar vein, it is written that "whoever learns Torah and teaches it in a place devoid of Torah scholars is like a beloved myrtle in the wilderness" (B. Rosh Hashanah 23a)—that is, the myrtle even blossoms in a wasteland. God must be brought unto wherever the Divine Presence is lacking. Similarly, God commanded Abraham: "Walk before Me and be whole-hearted" (Genesis 17:1); and in the prophet's words, "A voice calls out in the desert:

'Make way for the Eternal, clear a path through the wilderness for our God!'" (Isaiah 40:3). A myrtle in the wilderness symbolizes the introduction of holiness into a not-yet holy place. Myrtle is a symbol of the challenge—and the possibility—of bringing redemption to this world.

This is what Rabbi Shimon saw in the myrtle branches the old man was carrying on Shabbat eve. Sanctity can only radiate in all its glory outside of the cave, for only when it shines *outside* of the cave can it reach and illuminate every corner of the world. We must not despair, but strive to sanctify even the most desolate and most godless of places.

Coins, Baths, and Marketplaces: All Potentially Holy

But to truly understand the full meaning of sanctity, we must continue exploring the wondrous tale of Rabbi Shimon and what happened to him after leaving the cave: "Since a miracle has occurred, he said, 'Let me go and fix [*atakkein*, using a word based on the three-letter root *tav-kof-nun*] something, for it is written, *And Jacob came whole* [*to the city of Shechem*] (Genesis 33:18).'" The parallel is clear. Like Jacob, who struggled with Esau and triumphed, so did Rabbi Shimon struggle with Esau's descendant, Edom/Rome. He too triumphed, and he emerged whole:

> As Rav interpreted: whole in body, whole in finances, and whole in Torah. And [Jacob] gave graciously [*va-yiḥan*] to the city, and thereby perfected [i.e., fixed] it significantly. [How so?] Rav said: He instituted coinage for them. Samuel said: He instituted market for them. Rabbi Yoḥanan said: He instituted bath houses for them. (B. Shabbat 33b)

Rabbi Shimon now understood that out of gratitude for God's salvation, he too must actively sanctify aspects of this world, as he learns from our ancestor Jacob. And is it not amazing that precisely those three aspects of Roman society that Rabbi Shimon had reviled at the beginning of our narrative—those were precisely the three things that Grandfather Jacob/Israel had perfected for God! Apparently coins, bath-houses, and marketplaces may become sources of evil and hedonistic materialism, or they may be seen as means to attain societal economic well-being—allowing for the growth of businesses to provide gainful occupation, as well as institutions of hygienic welfare, which allow citizens to maintain sound minds in sound bodies. The Romans developed these institutions to be hotbeds of corruption and immorality; for Jacob, these very same institutions were used as a boon, serving to help repair and perfect society. Rabbi Shimon had indeed become transformed; he no longer saw Torah in opposition to the world, but rather as the means to sanctifying world. The story concludes:

> Rabbi Shimon asked them [the leaders]: "Is there anything that needs fixing, that is in need of repair?" They replied: "There is a place of questionable purity, which has been marked impure by priests, who avoid going there." He said: "Are there people who can vouch for the fact that at one time it had been considered pure?" One old man answered: "Ben Zakkai used to gather lupines here [which must be kept pure; that is, he testified that at one time the area had been pure]." According to this information, every hard place he declared pure; and every soft place he declared impure. [Apparently, the hardness of the ground was a sign that no one had been buried there] (B. Shabbat 33b–34a).

Rabbi Shimon found a large parcel of land that was avoided—especially by priests—because it was of questionable purity, because at least a portion of it had been used as a cemetery. Unfortunately the entire area was now considered impure and rendered off-limits to priests, the teachers of Torah. Rabbi Shimon effectuated his *tikkun*, or repair, by declaring a goodly portion of the area pure and therefore permissible for priests.

Recall that the initial image of the cave—where Rabbi Shimon had fled to—seemed to be that of a cemetery, with Rabbi Shimon and his son buried up to their necks in the sand while they learned Torah (and later, the cave is compared to Gehenna, hell). The symbolism here is striking: Torah in a cave, isolated from world, is a cemetery, a gravesite. However, our Torah is a Torah of life, a Torah by which we must live and not die, a Torah that urges us to "choose life," a Torah that is a "tree of life for all who grasp it" (Proverbs 3:18). It is a Torah that is meant for this world, the world of the living: a Torah that must perfect and sanctify this world, a Torah that must bring God into this world—the living God who wants us to live and not die, the God who is the Sovereign of all living creatures, the God whose greatest praise is in making the dead live again.

Hence Rabbi Shimon's *tikkun*, of the place as well as of himself, was to bring the Torah of the priest to a place where it had been prevented from being, to a place that had moved outside of the world of the living. Rabbi Shimon thus brought the God of life, through the Torah of life, into an area that he had restored from land-of-the-dead to land-of-the-living. This is the truest function of Torah.

The Annual Festivals: The Sanctity of Time

I now wish to return to our discussion of the festivals and our questions regarding the biblical passage in which they first appear together. The first month of the Jewish calendar is Nisan, in which we celebrate the festival of Pesah, which is followed by the counting of the *omer* until Shavuot, seven weeks later. This is a period of the gestation and birth of a nation: both physically, in our exodus from Egyptian slavery to freedom, and spiritually and morally, in the revelation at Sinai. The Torah thus defines the nation of Israel as a people who believes in freedom and the responsibility of freedom, the necessity of linking the freedom of Passover to the ethical laws of the revelation of the Decalogue at Sinai. Freedom dare not be an excuse for lawlessness, for looting and rioting and raping. Freedom under God is a freedom with responsibility: *heirut* with *ahrayut*. But at this point, during the first three months of the year (Nisan with Passover, Iyar with its *omer*-count, and Sivan with Shavuot), the responsibility is limited to the Jewish nation. Passover is a familial or national celebration, with a lamb for each household and the exclusion of all uncircumcised males (Exodus 12:3, 6, 43–48).

Rosh Hashanah, the next festival in line, occurs during the seventh month (Tishrei), and extends the responsibility for nation to the responsibility for world. Rosh Hashanah is a commemoration of the birthday of the world (albeit a broken, imperfect, and incomplete world), a world symbolized by the *t'ruah* sound of the *shofar*. One of the most prominent pieces of the Rosh Hashanah liturgy is the Aleinu prayer (including the *al kein n'kaveh l'kha* paragraph), which emphasizes God's sovereignty while insisting upon the mission of Israel to "perfect the world under the sovereignty of God's name," to repair and heal the broken world, to transform the *t'ruah* into a *t'kiah*. Hence Aleinu is the first blessing of the Rosh Hashanah Musaf liturgy extolling God's universal sovereignty, *malkhuyyot*. Once our nation has developed and matured from its Pesah and Shavuot origins, it must begin to accept the yoke of universal responsibility.

This is analogous to a baby, who thinks that the entire world revolves around him or her, and that it is the sole object of its parents' love. Rosh Hashanah teaches that from the womb of the Shekhinah come innumerable siblings of various colors and ethnic backgrounds, all born in the image of God, all with the DNA of all members of the Divine Nature Association. It is the image of God that makes us each free and inviolate, all indelibly linked together as children beloved to our universal, even cosmic, Parent.

Hence we have two epicenters of the year. In the first month, Nisan, there is the festival that marks the creation of a nation: Pesah. Through the *omer* it is linked to the third month, Sivan, containing the festival that completes the Passover freedom by bringing us from the desert to our homeland, Israel, with the celebration of the first fruits in the Temple. Counting the *omer* takes us from the offering of barley (animal grains) to the offering of wheat (human grains) seven weeks later, and Shavuot commemorates our spiritual freedom through the Torah we received at Sinai, our Divine National Constitution. These festivals define the Jewish nation: its homeland, its values, and its lifestyle.

The second epicenter occurs in the seventh month (which is parallel to the seventh day, Shabbat): the month of Tishrei, which begins with Rosh Hashanah and continues with Yom Kippur, Sukkot, and Shemini Atzeret. This is the universal epicenter of the year, and Rosh Hashanah, the birthday of the world, defines the purpose and mission of the nation Israel in the world: to perfect the world under the sovereignty of God's name. Rosh Hashanah culminates in Yom Kippur, during which Judaism's mission is repeated over and over in the Seliḥot penitential prayers: "for My house [i.e., sanctuary] shall be called a house of prayer *for all nations.*" On Rosh Hashanah Israel has a rendezvous with God which enables the entire nation to be present at the creation of the world and which commands and empowers them to engage and teach the world: "Through you shall all the families of the earth be blessed."[30] Hence Rosh Hashanah is called *shabbaton* (Leviticus 23:24), linking it to the universal Sabbath with which this entire biblical passage of the festivals opens. Passover and Shavuot, national festivals, are not called *shabbaton.*

On Yom Kippur, the nation of Israel meets God not only in time—commemorating the day when God is defined as a God of love and unconditional forgiveness, recalling the day when God forgave the nation for their idolatrous sin with the golden calf by giving the second set of tablets—but also in space, in the sacred sanctuary, which we pray is to be expanded to encompass all the nations of the world. Indeed, the entire world must become a sanctuary, a house of prayer (enabling communication with the Divine) for all the families of the earth (Isaiah 56:7, repeated again and again in the Yom Kippur liturgy).

Yom Kippur is *shabbat shabbaton* (Leviticus 23:32): first, because it enables human beings to re-create themselves through repentance and God's forgiveness; and second, because it broadens the sanctity of space as well as of time, when the Israelites are bidden by God to enlarge the sanctuary to encompass all of humanity, to host the Divine in their midst.

The Festival of Sukkot: A Festival of National and Universal Significance

The festival of Sukkot contains two aspects, with dual significance. On the one hand, it is part of a trilogy of events that transformed a group of shepherds and slaves into a proud nation. This historicity connects the festival of Sukkot to Pesaḥ and Shavuot and emphasizes, from a national point of view, that we have emerged triumphant despite the endless exiles and persecution we have faced. The impermanence of the *sukkah* itself reflects how, despite the harsh and hostile environments threatening the fragile and fleeting structure, the *sukkah* hut-house of Israel has nevertheless not only survived, but has even survived as a holy people. This national aspect of Sukkot—similar to Passover-Shavuot—is not described with the word *shabbaton*: "And the Eternal spoke to Moses, saying, 'Speak to the Israelites, saying: On the fifteenth day of this seventh month is the festival of Sukkot, seven days for the Eternal'" (Leviticus 23:24).

This aspect of the festival is followed with a general statement that summarizes the end of the annual cycle of festivals, and the three festivals of pilgrimage in particular: "These are the Eternal's appointed festivals, which you are to proclaim as sacred assemblies" (Leviticus 23:37). In each of these three festivals, we have had a special and sacred "meeting" with the Divine. On Passover, God chose us as a special and firstborn child and redeemed us from slavery. On Shavuot, God gave us the Torah, which we freely accepted. And on Sukkot, God confirmed that despite exile from host countries and persecutions from pillar to post, we have survived; God remains our national Protector.

But there is further significance to the festival of Sukkot. Sukkot is not only part of the Pesaḥ-Shavuot-Sukkot triad, the national festivals of pilgrimage, but it is also related to Rosh Hashanah and Yom Kippur, the special days of universal significance. Logically, given the sojourning in the desert that it commemorates, Sukkot would have been more suitably placed in Nisan, between Pesaḥ and Shavuot, right after the Exodus from Egypt. However, Sukkot falls in Tishrei, only days after the High Holy Days. From this perspective, the *sukkah* celebrated is "the fallen tabernacle (*sukkah*) of David," the sanctuary-tabernacle that is built in the wake of Yom Kippur, symbolizing the ultimate dwelling place of God in the midst of the world: a house of prayer to all nations. Such a sanctuary does not require proud, strong walls for protection, because it represents the Temple in the period of world peace. It requires the presence of the Almighty, the sheltering shadow of divine love, and the *ushpizin* (guests) who conveyed Torah teachings throughout the generations.

And then the biblical text moves on to the second aspect of the festival of Sukkot, the commandment to take the four species, the universal bounty that symbolizes God's gifts of heaven, earth and rain, to provide sustenance for all—but not without the human input to work the land agriculturally: "So beginning with the fifteenth day of the seventh month, after you have gathered the crops of the land, celebrate the festival to the Eternal for seven days; the first day is a *shabbaton* and the eighth day is also a *shabbaton*" (Leviticus 23:39).

Here, the ingathering of the crops is featured—for Sukkot occurs during the universal harvest-time—and the word *shabbaton* also reveals the universal, supra-national nature of the festival. Here, sanctity of time and sanctity of place intersect, for all gathering of crops—indeed, all raising of crops—is holy. The entire land is holy, and all time spent in the field—planting, plowing, reaping, and threshing—is holy. This holiness is reflected in the manner in which we work the fields: allowing the land to lie fallow every seventh year, not mixing different kinds of seeds together, not yoking an ox to an ass and forcing them to plow together (despite their very different strengths), leaving for the poor both the forgotten sheaves and a designated corner of the field. And it is also reflected in the manner in which we reap: sharing sustenance with the indigent, with the priests, and with the landless Levites, in a sacred partnership with God in nourishing humanity.

Hence, this second mention of Sukkot also specifies the four species: "On the first day you are to take a beautiful fruit of a tree (*p'ri eitz hadar*), palm branches, a leafy myrtle branch, and a willow sprig" (Leviticus 23:40)—items that symbolize the universal fruits of Mother Earth. And these are also fruits that symbolize the universal need for rain, *geshem*; the universal need for the material world, *gashmiyut*; and the universal relationship between rainfall from heaven, human agricultural ingenuity, and hard labor in tilling the soil most effectively—a universal partnership between God and humanity. We must be grateful for and desperately concerned about the food supply for all of humanity.

Not only is the *land* of Israel connected to the world through the universal act of working the earth, but the *nation* of Israel must also be connected to the world, extending the sanctity of Israel and its holiest city, Jerusalem, to all lands and cities of the world, being a light unto the nations as witnesses of God and divine compassionate righteousness, just morality, and peace. These universal festivals stress the interrelationship between all nations—especially important in a global village as we have today. It is therefore symbolic that over the course of the Sukkot festival, Israel must bring seventy bulls as offerings on behalf of the seventy nations of the world.

Following these verses, the commandment of dwelling in a *sukkah* is also repeated, only this time, with the addition of a rationale: "… so that your descendants will know that I had the Israelites live in booths when I brought them out of Egypt" (Leviticus 23:43). The Exodus from Egypt was a public announcement to the entire world that enslavement, tyranny, and totalitarianism are appalling sins. God alone may rule over the whole world. And we, Israel, must always be ready to raise the banner of freedom as part of our blessing for all the families of the earth; God is Owner of heaven and earth, and under

God every individual created in the divine image must be free and inviolate.

Shemini Atzeret, the "Eighth Day of Assembly," is an added gathering: the gathering of the entire world as one. This is the very symbolism behind the offering of a single bull on this day. The festival is marked by prayers for rain from the Universal Fructifier and, as it has developed through the generations, is also a gala celebration of the Torah. It is on this day that we take the Torah to the streets, singing and dancing with the Torah scrolls, and we even invite Gentile leaders to celebrate with us. On Simhat Torah[31] we conclude our yearly reading of the Torah and begin once again the book of Genesis—and the story of creation. This is a fitting climax to the universalism of Rosh Hashanah and Yom Kippur, to the sanctity of God within the world. On Shemini Atzeret–Simhat Torah, we bring God's Torah to the world!

And therefore, in the second passage, Sukkot is twice called a shabbaton—once for the *sukkah*-sanctuary and then again for the universal Torah, the Torah for the world.

If So, What Is Sanctity?

Israel's mission is to bring God into this world and to cause God to dwell within the dimension of time and history, thus bringing redemption and the messianic era. From the very moment that God elected Abraham, God charged him, saying: "I shall make you a great nation, and through you all the families of the earth will be blessed" (Genesis 12:3). Sanctity requires humanity's constant effort, and God's partnership, in order to perfect the world in the name of God's sovereignty. This is the fundamental essence of the festivals, the fundamental mission of Judaism, and the fundamental definition of sanctity. We must join forces with God in order to create a world that is entirely sanctuary, and to create a time that is entirely Shabbat. In short, the sanctity of time and the sanctity of place ultimately depend on the sanctity of Israel and the sanctity of the rest of humanity: we, to teach our God-given Torah; and they, to accept it. At that time, in the words of the Aleinu, "everyone will accept the yoke of divine sovereignty," and "at that time the Eternal shall be One and God's name shall be One." What is the essence of Torah, and what is its most profound message? If we are to suffuse God throughout the world, what is that spirituality that we are spreading round about? Listen to the prophet Jeremiah, the message the sages of the Talmud taught on Tishah B'Av when we are to think of redeeming the world and re-building the holy Temple; hear the last words of Maimonides at the conclusion of his final work, the *Guide for the Perplexed*: "Thus says the Eternal: Let not the wise glorify themselves with their wisdom, let not the strong glorify themselves with their strength, and let not the rich glorify themselves with their riches. But only with this shall one glorify oneself and be glorified: understanding and knowing Me, for I am the Eternal who does lovingkindness, moral justice, and compassionate righteousness on earth; it is these things which are My desire, says the Eternal" (Jeremiah 9:22–23).

NOTES

[1] Joseph B. Soloveitchik, *Halakhic Man* (Philadelphia: Jewish Publication Society, 1983).

[2] Published in Gesher, Student Organization of Yeshiva (Sivan 5728/June 1966).

[3] *Macbeth*, act V, scene 5.

[4] Ibid.

[5] See Rashi to Genesis 2:3: God created *m'nuḥah* (rest) on the seventh day (and cf. *Musaf Rashi*, ad loc.: God desired completion, *ḥemdah*).

[6] See B. Sotah 14a: "Just as God is compassionate, so must you be compassionate; just as God clothes the naked, so must you clothe the naked…"

[7] Originally published in 1917 in German, it was first translated into English in 1923 and has appeared in many editions since then.

[8] Mircea Eliade, *The Sacred and the Profane: The Nature of Religion* (New York: Harcourt, Brace & World, 1957).

[9] This idea is adapted from Abraham Joshua Heschel's *The Sabbath: Its Meaning for Modern Man* (New York: Farrar, Straus and Giroux, 1951).

[10] *Guide for the Perplexed* I 64.

[11] See Radak (Radak David Kimḥi) to Ezekiel 3:12, whose interpretation is in line with my grammatical construction. Radak maintains that *barukh* means "additional goodness and blessing"; he explains the phrase to mean that the immanent glory of God in the world is greater that it had been when it had been merely located between the two cherubs of the desert sanctuary—i.e., that God's glory when manifested throughout the world is greater that the ethereal glory manifested in the heavens above and beyond (and the angelic cherubs symbolize the supernally and transcendentally sacred).

[12] See Abudraham to this passage for a similar explanation.

[13] *Kol Ha-m'vasseir*, vol. 1, p. 287.

[14] See the midrash cited in Kasher's *Torah Sh'leimah* to this verse.

[15] For more about the divine names and the qualities they embody, see the essay elsewhere in this volume by Saul Berman.

[16] See, e.g., Isaiah 2, Micah 4, and Zechariah 7–9.

[17] M. Rosh Hashanah 4:10; B. Rosh Hashanah 32b, and see Tosafot ad loc.

[18] See Maimonides' explanation of the *kavod* in his Guide I 64.

[19] *Sha·ar Ha-hakdamot, sha·ar* 1, *hakdamah* 3.

[20] Hence the various biblical connections between the Sabbath and the sanctaruy, c.f., e.g., Exodus 31:13 and Leviticus 19:30. See Avishai David, *Soloveitchik* on the *Parashah, Va-yak·heil*, and the linguistic use of *m'lakhah* and *va-y'khulu* found in both of these biblical texts.

[21] *Tanḥuma, No·aḥ* §13.

[22] See the opening phrase of Rav Soloveitchik's *Halakhic Man*: "The Holy One, blessed be He, looked into the Torah and the created the world"; as well as the

adage oft-stated in the book, *halakhah v'lo ma·aseh*, theoretical study definitely not for practical application. See also *Nefesh Ha-ḥayyim* by Rabbi Ḥayyim Volozhin.

[23] A carob tree and a stream of water are the two miracles brought in an earlier talmudic debate (B. Bava Metzia 59b) to prove that the *halakhah* is according to Rabbi Eliezer and not according to Rabbi Joshua in the matter concerning a type of oven; Rabbi Eliezer believed that the Torah is still in heaven, that the halakhic ruling is still determined by God, and that the Torah is therefore transcendent. However, the Talmud concludes that this is not the case, and the miracles Rabbi Eliezer performed with a carob tree and a stream of water do not prove that the *halakhah* is in the hands of God. Rather, as expounded by Rabbi Joshua, the Torah is not in heaven but rather on earth, within our reach.

[24] Recall that the grave of our ancestors is called the Cave of Machpelah.

[25] Amos Hakham, *Daat Mikra* to Exodus 20:8, p. 384. Cf. also Mekhilta D'rabbi Shimon bar Yoḥai, ibid., p.149.

[26] In its discussion of laws pertaining to the festival of Lag Ba-Omer; see S.A. Oraḥ Ḥayim 93:7.

[27] See Y. Taanit 4:6.

[28] See Maimonides, Mishneh Torah, Hilkhot Melakhim 12:5.

[29] Note that the Hebrew word for material, *ḥomer*, is similar to the Aramaic word for wine, *ḥamar*.

[30] Genesis 12:3; these are God's words to Abraham at the time of his election.

[31] In Israel, Simḥat Torah is celebrated together with Shemini Atzeret; outside of Israel, it is celebrated on the following day.

The Dead Sea Scrolls Sect as a Replacement Temple

Lawrence H. Schiffman

In Second Temple times, the Temple in Jerusalem was the paramount location in which God, although transcendent, was also most immanent. Here was the pipeline through which the Divine emanated into the world, to be spread out to the land of Israel and from there to all the nations of the world. Here the sacrifices were offered along with the songs and prayers that accompanied them. Here the priests and Levites ministered to connect the sanctity of God with the holiest place on earth, His House in Jerusalem.

Since the Dead Sea Scrolls sect had willfully withdrawn from Temple worship and repaired to the desert, how did they manage to make this connection with the Divine? After all, they were without temple priests and sacrifices, and their settlement at Qumran was not the "place that God had chosen." We shall see how the sect reconfigured their theology to meet their new situation. They developed a particular relationship with the concept of holiness that allowed them to both establish a replacement for the Temple that they eschewed in the short run and, at the same time, pray for the restoration of the Temple cult at the end of days that would be conducted according to their requirements for all eternity. When that day came, they would joyfully resume their participation in the Temple in Jerusalem that now would be under their control. In order to accomplish their short-term goal, they reconfigured the idea of holiness and were thus able to relocate its center to Qumran.

The Holy Community

A long passage in column 8 of the Rule of the Community (1QS) will be our starting point. The passage begins by setting out the nature of a community council (8:1–4) of twelve representatives, presumably one for each tribe, and three priests, presumably for the clans of Gershon, Kehat, and Merari. The text continues that when this council is formed, the community as a whole (*atzat ha-yahad*) will be "founded on truth, as an eternal plantation, a holy house for Israel, and the foundation of the holy of holies for Israel...the most holy dwelling for Aaron, with all their knowledge of the covenant of justice (1QS 8:5–9 = 4Q259 ii 13–17).[1] The text then tells us that after the council has been organized for two years, "they will be separated as a sanctuary in the midst of the council of the men of the community" (1QS 8:11 = 4Q258 vi 5).[2] Further, once this wider community is established, anyone who purposely violates a commandment "may not touch the pure food of the men of holiness" (1QS 8:17 = 4Q258 vi 9).[3] In 8:20 (= 4Q258 vi 11), a long section, termed the sectarian penal code, then starts off by stating: "These are the regulations by which the men of perfect holiness shall conduct themselves."[4]

These passages afford us a detailed sense of what holiness and sanctity meant to Qumran sectaries, in addition to what ideas about holiness they had inherited from the traditions of the Bible. The sect itself is seen as a holy house—which means, for all intents and purposes, that the sect itself replaces the actual physical holy house, the Jerusalem Temple (which the sectarians have shunned because, in their view, it is in violation of the Torah's laws).[5] Further, for the Aaronide priests who constituted the founders and earliest leaders of the sect, the group (or perhaps its council) constituted the true holy of holies. In fact, it is only the sect that makes possible atonement (lines 6–7; not quoted above).

We can already observe that the sectarians have transferred the sanctity of the Jerusalem Temple, usually understood as spatial and as typifying holiness of place, to their group. Just as priests ministered in the Temple, so they themselves led the sect. Just as the sacrifices were supposed to bring atonement for the people and their land (line 6), so the life of the sect performed the same function. It is in consonance with this ideal that the sect never established a sacrificial cult at Qumran.

Another extremely important aspect of the life of the sect and its holiness is its separation from the rest of Israel, described in 1QS 8:12–13 (= 4Q258 vi 6–7[6] = 4Q259 ii 3–4[7]): "When these have become a community in Israel...they are to separate (*yibbad'lu*) from the midst of the assembly of the men of iniquity to go to the desert...." This second aspect of sectarian holiness picks up on the root meaning of *kof-dalet-shin*, "to separate," here expressed with the Hebrew root *bet-dalet-lamed*. However, whereas in the Bible and rabbinic literature separation is from that which is impure or evil, here it is from the "people of iniquity." This concept is closely linked with the idea of the sect as temple. Spatial sanctity of the temple is transferred to the group. What is inside is holy, as led by priests and the sectarian officials, but what is outside is not holy, and therefore to be separated from. The boundaries of a physical temple with its *temenos* and courtyards are here imitated in the life of the group. Its boundaries are understood to be those of the temple. The pure food of the sect (line 17) was equivalent to the sacrifices, and the sectarians were called "holy men." Those who followed the way of the sect were termed "men of perfect holiness" and the sect is a "council of holiness" (lines 20–21).

The Qumran sect also saw holiness as closely linked with ritual purity. From this point of view, like the members of the *havurah* discussed in rabbinic literature, the sectarians sought to observe the laws of temple purity in their regular daily lives. For the sectarians, the system of ritual purity was intimately connected with membership in the sect[8]—which, as we have seen, was tantamount to entry into the holy Temple itself. Effectively, purity functioned in the life of the sect in a way very similar to its role in the Temple: as a sign of greater sanctity and closeness to the Divine.

However, in addition, purity statutes served as a means of demarcation of levels of sanctity and, hence, sectarian status. This was the function of purity as a boundary marker in the Temple—here transformed to the life of the sect.

The Rule of the Community describes the process of admission to the sect (1QS 6:13–23).[9] The first step toward entry into the sect was examination by the *pakid b'rosh ha-rabbim*, the "official at the head of the community." If this official approved the candidate, the novice took his oath of admission and was then taught the sectarian regulations. Only then did the *moshav ha-rabbim*, the sectarian assembly, render a decision regarding the candidate, presumably based upon performance to date. If this examination was passed, the candidate attained a partial status. The novice was not permitted to touch the pure food of the community for one year until examined by the *moshav ha-rabbim* once again. If this examination too was passed, the novice was elevated to a higher status in which personal property was temporarily admitted into communal use, but the novice still was not permitted to touch the liquid food of the community for another year. Only after the third examination by the *moshav ha-rabbim* could the novice be admitted as a full member of the sect with all attendant privileges, including entry into the sectarian assembly.

All these stages serve to link the instruction in sectarian teachings with the initiation into the sect through the medium of ritual purity. While gaining knowledge of the sect's interpretations of biblical law and passing examinations, the novice was gradually admitted into greater confidence amongst the members, and gradually rose in ritual purity until finally being able to partake of all the pure food and drink of the sect.

Jacob Licht explains that the process of initiation accords well with tannaitic *halakhah*, according to which liquids are more prone to contract and transmit impurity than are solids.[10] Thus, the touching of liquids is the last stage to which the novice was admitted.[11] Also, this theory explains why a member of the Qumran sect who sinned was removed from partaking in pure food, as a punishment. Since ritual purity was, to the sectarians, a symbol of inner, spiritual purity, one who transgressed slid back down the ranks through which he had risen. He is once again forbidden from the food of the sectarians until he repents and regains his pure religious state.

Effectively, what has been created here by means of purity is a set of boundaries of increasing sanctity. Entering the sect is like entering the *temenos*, and proceeding through the levels of initiation is like entering further into the courts of the Temple, then into the Temple itself, and finally into the holy of holies. These purity rules and their connection with the initiation rites were what made the Qumran sect truly a Holy House.

Sacred Space

The Temple, in certain Dead Sea Scrolls, is equivalent to the tabernacle in the desert camp. This desert sanctuary was remembered by all Second Temple Jews as concretized in the First Temple and then in the Second. When the Qumran sectarians contemplated the ideal temple, as we see in the Halakhic Letter (4QMMT), they determined that it was equivalent to the tabernacle that stood in biblical times: "But we hold the view that the Temple is [the (equivalent of the) tabernacle of the Tent of Meeting, and Jerusalem is the camp, and outside the camp [is (equivalent to) outside Jerusalem]; it is the camp of their cities" (4QMMT B29–31).[12] Following the prescriptions of the desert camp as a pattern for the present allows the concept of spatial holiness from the Bible to be transferred to the present. As a foundation document of the sect, 4QMMT also opens the way for the sect to replace the Jerusalem Temple, where it no longer worshipped.

In the four copies of the Halakhic Letter found at Qumran, the text lists matters in which the sectarians did not agree with how the Temple worship was being conducted—and were the reason that they had left the Temple service. They write to some official in the hope that he will change the way the Temple is run and will conduct the rituals according to the sectarian rulings. This text dates to 150 B.C.E. and represents a formation document of the sect, in the aftermath of the Maccabean revolt—by which time Pharisaic rulings (as opposed to the Sadducean view) had become the norm in the Temple. These nascent sectarians were protesting and leaving the Temple as a result of their disagreements.[13] Once they stopped participating in the Temple cult, they began to explain their own life as a substitute Temple.

Finding a replacement for the Temple, the central institution of Jewish life at the time, was not so unusual. When the Temple was physically destroyed in 70 C.E., the rabbis similarly would seek to explain Torah study, prayer, and the Jewish home as symbolic replacements for the Temple. Lighting the Sabbath candles recapitulated the lighting of the *menorah*; putting the challah bread on the table beforehand would stand in for setting the bread on the showbread table. This kind of symbolism already goes back to these early ideas:

> When the time comes that men such as these are in Israel, then the council of the Yaḥad will be truly established, an eternal planting, a temple for Israel, and a council of the holy of holies for Aaron; true witnesses to justice, chosen by [God's] will to atone of the land and to recompense the wicked their due...a dwelling of the holy of holies for Aaron, all of them knowing the covenant of justice and thereby offering a sweet savor. They shall be a blameless and true house in Israel, upholding the covenant of eternal statutes. They shall be an acceptable [sacrifice], to atone for the land and to decide the verdict against evil. When these men have been grounded in the foundation[s] of the Yaḥad for two years—provided they be perfect in their conduct with no iniquity—they shall be set apart as holy in the midst of the council of the men of the Yaḥad. (1QS 8.4–11)

In this passage there is some garden imagery, reflecting the notion of the sect as an eternal planting. This garden is reminiscent of the Garden of Eden, the first home of humanity, where Adam and Eve lived with no iniquity. The "dwelling of the holy of holies for Aaron, all of them knowing the covenant of justice and thereby offering a sweet savor" is the substitution of the Temple sacrifices and priesthood by Aaron and his "sweet savor," which accomplish atonement within the sect that replaces the Temple. However, it is understood that this solution only obtains in the short term. In the long term, the Temple will be purified in the end of days (a time period that the Qumran sectarians saw as not a very long way off), and the sect would be able to go back to worshipping there in the holiness that would be reestablished.

The Temple Scroll

The transferal of the biblical tabernacle into the ideal Temple is accomplished most particularly by the Temple Scroll, a composition found at Qumran the sources of which predate the founding of the sect. The Temple Scroll presents an ideal vision of Israel as it should build its Temple, worship its God, maintain ritual purity to the utmost degree, be governed by its king, and observe the laws of the Torah.[14] This ideal plan, according to the explicit statement of the scroll (11QT 29:2–10), was intended for the present age, not for the eschatological future. It was the intention of the author/redactor to put forward his scroll as an alternative to the "constitution" of Israel, religious and political, which was in place in the Hasmonean period. He called for a new temple building and for new settlement patterns as well.

In the area of temple building, settlement patterns, and his approach to the land of Israel, the author took a distinctly utopian view. Throughout, the author is informed by a notion of concentric spheres of holiness,[15] as well as by distinct concern for the sanctity of the entire land as sacred space.

The Temple City

For the Temple Scroll, the central point of the land of Israel and the source of its sanctity was the temple and the surrounding complex.[16]

This new temple, of very different proportions from those obtained in First or Second Temple times, would be characterized by the enclosure of the temple building itself by three concentric courtyards.[17]

The Inner Court (11QT 36:3–7) was to measure some 280 cubits square, with four gates representing the four groups of the tribe of Levi: the Aaronide priests on the east, the Levites of Kehat on the south, Gershon on the west, and Merari on the north. This arrangement corresponds exactly to that of the desert camp as described in Numbers 3:14–39.

The Middle Court (38:12–15) was to be concentric with the Inner Court, 100 meters further out. The entirety was to be 480 cubits square, with three gates on each side. The gates (39:11–13) were to be distributed among the twelve tribes of Israel, each having its own gate.[18]

The Outer Court (40:5–11) was also concentric, with sides measuring some 1600 cubits. This wall would also have twelve gates (40:13–41:11) which are distributed such that they correspond exactly to those of the Middle Court.[19] The chambers in the outer wall that faced inward (41:17–42:6) were to be apportioned (44:3–45:2) to the various tribes as well as to the priestly and levitical groups mentioned above. Aaron is assigned two groups of chambers: as a member of the tribe of Levi as well as one of the levitical priests, and as a firstborn entitled to a double portion.

This unique temple plan represents the layout of the tabernacle and camp of Israel in the desert combined. The architect of this temple plan sought to place the camp of Israel within the expanded *temenos*. Hence, he called for a temple structure that made access to the tribes and even symbolic dwelling places for them, as a basic principle of design. Each tribe was assumed to enter the *temenos* through its prescribed gate and to proceed initially to its chambers. From there all members of the tribe or levitical clan could circulate in the Outer Court. Those not disqualified by some impurity from entry into the Middle Court[20] could then proceed into that court, again through their respective gates. Only priests and Levites could proceed through their gates to the Inner Court, wherein the temple and its furnishings were located.

Underlying this entire plan is the assumption that the temple is the center of sanctity, which can be reached by entering further and further into the concentric spheres of holiness of the *temenos*. The scroll makes clear repeatedly that it is the indwelling of the Divine Presence in the temple that imparts to it this level of sanctity.[21] The addition of the third court was intended to provide further protection for the sanctity of God's precincts. God is to dwell in the temple, among the Israelites forever, according to many passages throughout the Temple Scroll.[22]

Installations Outside the Temple City

Beyond the *temenos* just described were a few installations designed to ensure the sanctity of the holy place. Among them was the place for the latrines (*m'kom yad*), to be located northwest of "the city" (i.e., the temple city), at a distance of three thousand cubits (46:13–16),[23] probably derived from Numbers 35:4–5.

Further, the scroll requires (46:16–47:1) that outside the temple city, specific locations be assigned to the east for three groups that are impure: those with the skin disease *tzara·at* (usually mistranslated as "leprosy"), those with abnormal genital discharges, and those who had had a seminal emission. Actually, the intention of the scroll is to locate the entire residence area outside of the temple city, and to expand the *temenos* to include the entirety of what was Jerusalem in the author's time.[24] In this view, there would be no residents of the temple city, but those who came to the temple for their seven-day purification rites would stay in these areas during the rituals and then enter the temple to offer their sacrifices when their rites were completed and they had attained a state of purity. Clearly, the exclusion of these various groups was intended to guarantee the holiness of the temple precincts.

Beyond the temple city dwelled the tribes, each of whose territory was located directly opposite its respective gate. Indeed, it was through these gates that the tribal territory was to be tied to the sanctity of the central shrine and the Divine Presence, which dwelled there. Each tribe was apportioned territory such that it would have direct access to the temple, from which holiness emanated to the entire land.

The Cities of Israel

Beginning with the discovery of the Zadokite Fragments in the late nineteenth century, and again after the publication of the Temple Scroll in 1977, there has been much discussion generated about the meaning of the term *ir ha-mikdash*, literally "city of the sanctuary."[25] While some have taken this phrase as a reference to the city of Jerusalem as a whole, including the residential areas,[26] we take it as referring only to the temple precincts.[27] Accordingly, the restrictions on entry into the temple city of those with various disqualifications and impurities refer essentially to the *temenos*, the temple precincts.[28] It was the intention of the author of the scroll to expand the size of this *temenos* to cover almost the entirety of what was Jerusalem in his day.

Opposite the temple city were "their cities" (47:8) or "your cities" (47:14, 17) in which, if located more than three days' journey from the temple, non-sacral slaughter was permitted. These cities are to be distinguished from God's city, referred to as "My city" or the temple city. Yet even these cities had to observe certain purity regulations. Areas were also set aside for those with impurities outside these cities: for those with various skin diseases (cf. 49:4) or genital discharges, as well as menstruants and parturients. These locations were to be designated for each city (48:14–17). Likewise, burial in the cities was forbidden (48:11); cemeteries were to be set aside, one for each four cities (48:11–13) and equidistant from all of them.

The cities of Israel were apportioned by tribes. That is, each tribal area was expected to have cities in which the people (presumably of that tribe) dwelled. Not a single passage in the scroll describes anyone as living anywhere but in these cities. Within the cities the residents were all expected to live in stone houses. This is clear from the detailed discussion of the purification of the house in which a dead body had rested (49:5–50:16). The parts of the house and the equipment found in it are also listed in connection with the impurity of the dead.[29]

What was the purpose of this complex geographic master plan? The Temple Scroll called for a total reconstruction of the temple and redistribution of the land around it, so as to grant to all the tribes of Israel direct access to the presence of God and an outflow of holiness to the entire land. Only in this way, the author believed, would the future of Israel upon its land be guaranteed. Holiness and sanctity were the keys to living in the land.

The scroll's plan, as we have examined it here, bears little relationship to the teachings of the Qumran sect as they are known from the sectarian texts.[30] Further, there is no attempt in the architecture of the Qumran structures to follow any ideal blueprint. In this respect, this material supports our general conclusion that some of the sources of the Temple Scroll predate the Qumran sect and that the author/redactor, regardless of his own affiliation, cannot be blamed for having failed to anticipate the ideas of the Qumran sect in his scroll. Neither did our author follow the vision of Ezekiel closely. Yet both he and the prophet shared the desire to see the Jewish people, all twelve tribes, restored to their ancient glory in the sacred land of Israel. One component of this vision was to see the temple and its service conducted at an even greater level of sanctity than was required by the Torah.

Holiness of Heaven on Earth

While we may call the spatial transferring of holiness from the Temple Mount in Jerusalem to the sect and its life a horizontal transference, we may also speak of a vertical transference (or union), in which the holiness of the sect is the result of an angelic presence.[31] This concept is central to the War Scroll and its portrayal of the eschatological war to be conducted both in heaven and on earth. The Rule of the Congregation (1QSa 2:3–11) specifies that eschatological purity requires the absence of those with specific deformities, the impure, and the aged, since the angels are regarded as being present in the assembly.[32] In 1QM 7:6, we find the very same reason for the excluding those impure from a seminal emission from participation in the eschatological battle: "For holy angels are together with their armies."[33] Baruch Bokser suggested that this is actually a reworking of Deuteronomy 23:15, which explains the requirement of ritual purity in the military camp as resulting from the presence of God. Bokser maintains that the Divine Presence is represented here by the angels.[34]

A parallel to this very concept occurs in 1QM 12:7–8, where it is stated that the angels are fighting among the members of the sect: "A host of angels is mustered with us."[35] It was a cardinal belief of the sect that just as the world below is divided into the domain of the two spirits,[36] those of good and evil, so was the world of the angels. Just as the Teacher of Righteousness and the Wicked Priest represented the forces of good and evil to the sect in the present age,[37] so the Prince of Light (the angel Michael) and his enemy, Belial, represent the very same forces on high.[38] These forces would be arrayed against each other in the end of days, just as they are in the present, pre-messianic age.

The great eschatological battle would be fought, therefore, simultaneously both in heaven and on earth. In the actual battle, angels and men would fight side by side. After the long series of engagements described in the War Scroll, the forces of good would ultimately be victorious. For this reason, the sect believed that in the end of days the angels would be present in the military camp described in the War Scroll. At the very same time, the eschatological council would also involve both the earthly and heavenly Sons of Light.[39]

This angelic presence effectively merged the realms of heaven and earth for the sectarians. Living in the present in expectation of the messianic era meant living as though divine representatives were among them. The eschatological dream meant that somehow heaven and earth would meet, and that heavenly sanctity would now be manifest on earth below.

A principle of the Qumran sect was its view that holiness would be perfected only in the end of days. In fact, the perfection of the end of days would involve both the ultimate victory over and elimination of the forces of evil, and also the perfect observance of Jewish law as interpreted by the sectarians. It was believed that when the messianic war would begin, the sect would be mustered to fight the battles against the evildoers and those who do not know the correct interpretation of the Torah, as expounded by the sect. As the sect would finally overcome its enemies and emerge victorious, the righteous of Israel who turn to God and adopt the sectarian way of life would also be included in the sect. Together with the original sectarians, they would constitute the eschatological community. This new community would gather together for the messianic banquet under the leadership of the Zadokite priestly messiah and the messiah of Israel.[40]

The messianic era was understood to constitute the ultimate utopia, a world in which perfection in purity and worship would surpass all of history. The sect of the future age—now really the only Jewish way—would fulfill all the aspirations of "the men of perfect holiness" (1QS 8:10). The end of days was to usher in unparalleled holiness and sanctity as the angels dwelled among the eschatological community.

The sect tried to actuate in the present, pre-messianic age the perfect holiness that they expected in the coming age.[41] For this reason, many of the prescriptions of the War Scroll and the Rule of the Congregation describing the eschatological congregation also parallel regulations found in other texts intended to legislate for the present age. In order to actualize its dreams for the future age, the sect referred to itself as the Sons of Zadok and held this group of priests in special esteem.[42] They expected that these priests would constitute their leadership in the end of days. Likewise, the levitical age limits of the Bible applied in the Dead Sea Scrolls to the present officials of the sect, the officers of the military units who would participate in the eschatological battle, and the leadership structure of the messianic community.[43]

Disqualifications from the eschatological assembly, as described in the Rule of the Congregation (1QSa), also followed levitical legislation regarding those priests who were unfit for temple service. These were the impure and those who suffered from physical deformities or old age (1QSa 2:3–11; cf. 1:19–22). After all, the sect saw itself as constituting a sanctuary, through its dedication to a life of holiness and purity. At the brink of the dawn of the eschaton, during which they were living, the sect had to maintain the highest standard of purity. They pre-enacted the future messianic banquets in their communal meals by eating with a quorum of ten males, requiring ritual purity of the participants, and performing the blessing of wine and bread presided over by the priest who then apportioned the food according to the status of the members of the community (1QS 6:2–5).[44]

The messianic era is portrayed as a second redemption, the Exodus from Egypt being the prototype. To this end, the sect used biblical terminology to describe the messianic era. The Dead Sea Scrolls speak of the encampments of Israel's wandering in the desert,[45] as well as of the restoration of the ancient monarchy, the high priesthood, and the ancient tribal organization. The first redemption from Egypt represented the ultimate closeness to God and direct divine intervention in history. At this stage, Israel was the most receptive to God's revelation and the most obedient to divine law. The sectarians expected the renewal of this perfect condition in the soon-to-dawn eschaton. In addition, the world would attain a level of purity, sanctity, and observance of the law even more perfect than that experienced in the first redemption. The sectarians strove to live in perfect holiness so that they would experience the eschatological battles and tribulations of the dawning of the messianic era and the promised glory of the end of days.

Conclusion

The Qumran corpus as a whole seems to present two basic schemes of holiness and sanctity. According to the sectarian view, the locus of holiness and, therefore, the mode of access to it, is the sect itself, a group of people devoted to representing in their individual lives the commitment to higher levels of purity and, accordingly, to the quest for higher levels of sanctity. This group aspired to the perfection of its holiness and to the fulfillment of its present-day quest in the soon-to-dawn eschaton. Only then would perfect holiness be achieved—not in the temple sancta, but in the life of the group and its victorious members.

The Temple Scroll, however, deriving from sources close to the Sadducean priesthood, hews more closely to the spatial aspect of holiness as known from the concepts of holy land, holy city, and holy temple in the Bible. As a result, it maps out holiness and sanctity in geographical terms, rather than in human or group terms.

Both conceptual frameworks of sanctity do exist in the Bible, and all Jews would have espoused them. What is significant here is the clearly differing emphases in the Temple Scroll and sectarian organizational texts.

This same distinction exists regarding the relationship of sanctity to the human being. Cultic, spatial sanctity maps out an area that a person enters in order to access an already-existing, prepared, perhaps waiting, presence of God. Purity is required of those who seek to enter, as they must qualify to enter the sanctified realm.

Individual or group sanctity required that the individual or the aggregate group of individuals create in themselves a holiness and sanctity that is not externally defined. It comes about only through striving for spiritual and religious growth. Hence, purity—or, more precisely, purification—is a step toward that greater closeness to God. Together, the members of the group seek to raise themselves to approach a deity whom they effectively must bring down into their own daily, mundane lives. For them, the group and its religious life replace the temple and its *temenos*.

These two approaches to holiness existed in Qumran texts as in Judaism as a whole. God and the Divine Presence might occupy a holy place, but the ultimate shrine is constituted of the hearts and souls of those individuals who committed themselves to seeking God's presence, both in this era and in the end of days.

NOTES

[1] Philip Alexander and Geza Vermes, *Qumran Cave 4. XIX: Serekh Ha-yaḥad and Two Related Texts* (DJD 26; Oxford: Clarendon Press, 1998), pp. 139–44; cf. 4Q258 vi 1–3 (DJD 26, pp. 105–109) and 4Q265 (Miscellaneous Rules) in Joseph M. Baumgarten, et al., *Qumran Cave 4.XXV: Halakhic Texts* (DJD 35; Oxford: Clarendon Press, 1999), pp. 69–72. DJD references the scholarly series *Discoveries in the Judaean Desert* published by Oxford University Press over the last sixty-odd years.

[2] DJD 26, pp. 105–109.

[3] Ibid.

[4] Ibid., and cf. Lawrence H. Schiffman, *Sectarian Law in the Dead Sea Scrolls: Courts, Testimony, and the Penal Code* (Chico, CA: Scholars Press, 1983), pp. 155–159.

[5] Bertil Gärtner, *The Temple and the Community in Qumran and the New Testament* (Cambridge: Cambridge University Press, 1965).

[6] See especially DJD 26, p. 107, on the variant readings of the manuscripts.

[7] DJD 26, pp. 144–148.

[8] Schiffman, *Sectarian Law*, pp. 161–165.

[9] Partially paralleled in 4Q256 xi 11–13 (DJD 26, pp. 55–57); 4Q261 3 1 (DJD 26, pp. 177–178).

[10] Jacob Licht, *M'gillat Ha-s'rakhim Mi-m'gillot Midbar Y'hudah* (Jerusalem: Bialik Institute, 1965), pp. 294–303.

[11] Cf. Chaim Rabin, *Qumran Studies* (London: Oxford University Press, 1957); Saul Lieberman, "The Discipline in the So-Called Dead Sea Manual of Discipline," in *Journal of Biblical Literature* 71 (1951), pp. 199–206; rpt. in idem, *Texts and Studies* (New York: Ktav, 1974), pp. 200–207.

[12] Translated by Lawrence H. Schiffman in *Reclaiming the Dead Sea Scrolls: The History of Judaism, the Background of Christianity, the Lost Library of Qumran* (Philadelphia: Jewish Publication Society, 1994), p. 389.

[13] Schiffman, *Reclaiming*, pp. 83–95.

[14] Yigael Yadin, *The Temple Scroll* (3 vols.; Jerusalem: Israel Exploration Society and the Shrine of the Book, 1983).

[15] Wayne O. McCready, "Temple and Temple Scroll: A Sectarian Alternative," *Proceedings of the Tenth World Congress of Jewish Studies, Division A: The Bible and its World* (Jerusalem: World Union of Jewish Studies, 1990), p. 203.

[16] See Yadin, *Temple Scroll*, vol. 1, pp. 177–276; Lawrence. H. Schiffman, "Architecture and Law: The Temple and its Courtyards in the Temple Scroll," in *From Ancient Israel to Modern Judaism: Intellect in Quest of Understanding: Essays in Honor of Marvin Fox*, eds. Jacob Neusner, Ernst S. Frerichs, and Nahum M. Sarna (Atlanta: Scholars Press, 1989), vol. 1, pp. 267–284; Johann Maier, "The Architectural History of the Temple in Jerusalem in the Light of

the Temple Scroll," in G. J. Brooke, ed., *Temple Scroll Studies* (Sheffield: JSOT Press, 1989), pp. 23–62; Johann Maier, "The *Temple Scroll* and Tendencies in the Cultic Architecture of the Second Commonwealth," in Lawrence H. Schiffman, ed., *Archaeology and History in the Dead Sea Scrolls: The New York University Conference in Memory of Yigael Yadin* (Sheffield: JSOT Press, 1990), pp. 53–82; Johann Maier, *The Temple Scroll: An Introduction, Translation & Commentary* (Sheffield: JSOT Press, 1985); Hartmut Stegemann, "The Institutions of Israel in the Temple Scroll," in Devorah Dimant and Uriel Rappaport, eds., *The Dead Sea Scrolls: Forty Years of Research* (Leiden: E. J. Brill; Jerusalem: Magnes Press and Yad Ben-Zvi, 1992), pp. 146–185.

[17] Cf. Johann Maier, "Die Hofanlagen im Tempel-Entwurf des Ezechiel im Licht der 'Tempelrolle' von Qumran," in John Adney Emerton, ed., *Prophecy: Essays Presented to Georg Fohrer on His Sixty-Fifth Birthday* (Berlin: Walter de Gruyter, 1980), pp. 55–67.

[18] The apportionment of gates to the twelve tribes is found in regard to the city of Jerusalem in Ezekiel 48:31–34 and Revelations 21:12–14. Fragments of virtually the same text are found in 4Q365a, published under the title "4QTemple?" by Sidnie White (Crawford), in Harold Attridge, et al., *Qumran Cave 4.VIII, Parabiblical Texts Part I* (DJD 13; Oxford: Clarendon Press, 1994), pp. 323–333. These are probably from the same manuscript as 4Q365 (Reworked Pentateuch). The relation of this manuscript to the Temple Scroll was already noted by Jean Starcky, "Jerusalem et les manuscrits de la Mer Morte," *Le Monde de la Bible* 1 (1977), pp. 38–40. On the relation of these texts to the Temple Scroll, see White, DJD 13, pp. 319–320.

[19] I am unconvinced by Margaret Barker, "The Temple Measurements and the Solar Calendar," in Brooke, *Temple Scroll Studies*, pp. 63–66, who sees the gates of the Outer Court as symbolizing the calendar and serving as a device for its calculation.

[20] See Lawrence H. Schiffman, "Exclusion from the Sanctuary and the City of the Sanctuary in the Temple Scroll," in *Hebrew Annual Review* 9 (1985), pp. 303–306.

[21] Lawrence H. Schiffman, "The Theology of the Temple Scroll," in *Jewish Quarterly Review* 85 (1994), pp. 118–121.

[22] This theme appears in the conclusion of the festival calendar of the scroll (29:3–4, 7–8), the purity laws (45:12, 13–14, 46:11–12, 47:10–11), the commands for the construction of the temple (46:4 [partly restored]), the laws of forbidden food (51:7–8), the prohibition of non-sacral slaughter (52:19–20, 53:1 [restored]), the ban on the skins of such animals in the temple city (47:18), the laws of oaths and vows (53:9–10), and the authority of priests, Levites, and judges (56:5).

[23] See Yadin, *Temple Scroll*, vol. 1, pp. 294–304, and his earlier article, "The Gate of the Essenes and the Temple Scroll," in his *Jerusalem Revealed: Archaeology in the Holy City 1968–1974* (Jerusalem: Israel Exploration Society, 1975), pp. 90–

91. Cf. Schiffman, *Halakhah at Qumran* (Leiden: E.J. Brill, 1975), pp. 93–94, where 2000 (in relation to the 11QT) must be corrected to 3000.

[24] Schiffman, "Exclusion," p. 317; cf. Magen Broshi, "The Gigantic Dimensions of the Visionary Temple in the Temple Scroll," in *Biblical Archeology Review* 13:6 (November/December 1987), pp. 36–37. McCready, "Temple and Temple Scroll," p. 203 suggests that this was essentially a protest against the nature of Second Temple period Jerusalem as a commercial and governmental center.

[25] Cf. Lawrence H. Schiffman, "*Ir Ha-Miqdash* and Its Meaning in the Temple Scroll and Other Qumran Texts," in Alberdina Houtman, Marcel Poorthuis, and Joshua Schwartz, eds., *Sanctity of Time and Space in Tradition and Modernity* (Leiden: Brill, 1998), pp. 95–109.

[26] Yadin, *Temple Scroll*, vol. 1, pp. 277–285.

[27] Baruch A. Levine, "The Temple Scroll: Aspects of its Historical Provenance and Literary Character," in *Bulletin of the American Schools of Oriental Research* 232 (1978), pp. 14–15; Schiffman, "Exclusion," pp. 301–320.

[28] See the complete list in Schiffman, "Exclusion," pp. 314–515.

[29] Lawrence H. Schiffman, "The Impurity of the Dead in the *Temple Scroll*," in *Archaeology and History in the Dead Sea Scrolls*, pp. 135–156.

[30] Stegemann, "Institutions of Israel," pp. 162–166.

[31] For a somewhat different perspective on the priestly aspects of this notion, see Rachel Elior, *Mikdash U-merkavah, Kohanim U-malakhim, Heikhal V'heikhalot Ba-mistikah Ha-y'hudit Ha-k'dumah* (Jerusalem: Magnes Press, 2002), pp. 174–202.

[32] Cf. Lawrence H. Schiffman, *The Eschatological Community of the Dead Sea Scrolls* (Atlanta: Scholars Press, 1989), pp. 37–52.

[33] Yigael Yadin, *The Scroll of the War of the Sons of Light against the Sons of Darkness* [hereafter War Scroll], trans. Batya and Chaim Rabin (Oxford: Oxford University Press, 1962), pp. 290–291. Cf. 4Q491 1, 2+3 line 10 (M. Baillet, *Qumrân Grotte* 4.III (4Q482-4Q520) (DJD 7; Oxford: Clarendon Press, 1982), pp. 13–18. On angels in the War Scroll, see Yadin, War Scroll, pp. 229–242.

[34] Baruch M. Bokser, "Approaching Sacred Space," in *Harvard Theological Review* 78 (1985), pp. 279–299.

[35] Yadin, *War Scroll*, 316317; cf. 4Q491 1, 2+3 line 10.

[36] 1QS 3:13-4:26. Cf. Schiffman, Reclaiming, pp. 149–150; Jean Duhaime, "Dualism," in Lawrence Schiffman and James VanderKam, eds., *Encyclopedia of the Dead Sea Scrolls* (New York: Oxford University Press, 2000), vol. 1, pp. 215–220.

[37] Schiffman, *Reclaiming*, pp. 117–121, 231–235.

[38] Yadin, *War Scroll*, pp. 232–236.

[39] In addition to those with deformities, the impure, and the aged, 1QM 7:3–4 states that women and children are also to be excluded from the military camp. It is most likely that the very same regulation was in force regarding the eschatological council. Although women and children would be part of the sect,

as is evident from 1QSa 1:6–11, their presence among the angels in the council of the community would not be allowed, nor were they permitted in the military camp during the battle at the end of days.

[40] Cf. Lawrence H. Schiffman, "Messianic Figures and Ideas in the Qumran Scrolls," in *The Messiah, Developments in Earliest Judaism and Christianity*, ed. J. H. Charlesworth (Minneapolis: Fortress Press, 1992), pp. 116–129.

[41] Schiffman, *Eschatological Community*, pp. 68–71.

[42] Schiffman, *The Halakhah at Qumran*, pp. 70–75; Elior, *Mikdash U-merkavah*, pp. 202–211.

[43] Schiffman, *Sectarian Law*, pp. 32–35.

[44] Cf. 1QSa 2:11–22 for the eschatological banquet; Schiffman, *Eschatological Community*, pp. 53–67.

[45] Cf. Shemaryahu Talmon, "The 'Desert Motif' in the Bible and in Qumran Literature," in Alexander Altmann, ed., *Biblical Motifs: Origins and Transformations* (Cambridge: Harvard University Press, 1966), pp. 216–254; rpt. in idem, *Literary Studies in the Hebrew Bible: Form and Content: Collected Studies* (Leiden: E. J. Brill, 1993), pp. 55–63.

K'dushah in the Age of Technology: The Challenge

Alfred Cohen

America is a blessed land, and for the Jewish people in particular, it has been a blessing. Here, for practically the first time in all the years of the Diaspora, we have been free to practice our religion as we see fit. The modern age has also brought with it many blessings: modern innovations make our lives so much easier, as we are able to avoid so much of the tedium and hard labor that were once essential t7o provide for the necessities of life.

Thus, it is ironic and sad that precisely at the juncture of so much freedom and so much ease, many Jews have lost sight of a major aspect in our religion: holiness, *k'dushah*. Numerous times, the Torah underscores the importance of striving for holiness, in its discussion of observing the commandments. For example, the third paragraph of the Shema, recited twice daily, instructs us to don *tzitzit*, with the reason given as follows: *l'ma·an tizk'ru va-asitem et kol mitzvotai vi-h'yitem k'doshim*, "so that you will remember to observe all My commandments, and thereby become holy" (Numbers 15:40). Similarly, certain *mitzvot* are introduced with the phrase *v'anshei kodesh tihyun li*, "you shall be holy people for Me" (Exodus 22:30).

As far as Maimonides is concerned, the verse *k'doshim tihyu*, "you shall be holy" (Leviticus 19:2), does not embody a specific *mitzvah* in and of itself; rather, the Torah is telling us that if we are careful to observe the commandments, the end result will be that we will become holy. Whenever the Torah makes general statements such as "be careful to follow My commandments," Rambam does not count these as one of the 613 *mitzvot*, but rather as a general principle affecting all our actions:

> This directive [to be holy] is not a commandment that stands by itself; rather, it applies to any commandment [that the Torah has ordained], and whoever fulfills the commandment is called "holy." And there is no difference whether it says "be holy" or "observe My *mitzvot*."[1]

Others, however, disagree and do see Leviticus 19:2 as a distinct *mitzvah*, one that should inform our every action and thought. (More on these approaches will be found in the next section of this essay.)

Whatever interpretation we follow—whether there is a separate, distinct *mitzvah* to be holy, or whether there is an overarching requirement to live life in such a way that holiness ensues—it is obvious that our lifestyles in America fall far short of this ideal, to the point that striving for *k'dushah* is no longer on the radar screen even for many observant Jews. Walk the streets of any city in America during the summer, and it becomes immediately obvious that the current style of dress, clearly at odds with traditional notions of modesty, is not conducive to holiness. Moreover, the presence of large numbers of women in the workplace has eroded social barriers in daily life, and the increased opportunities for interaction between the sexes in both professional and personal arenas make it difficult to adhere to what used to be common standards of proper behavior, let alone holiness. Sadly, it is an old truism that Jewish mores follow societal mores, and so it is that the values and styles of secular American society are reflected more and more in the modes of behavior prevalent among American Jews.

Perhaps most important for the present inquiry, the ubiquity of "social media" networking and other new technologies have all but obliterated traditional ways of social interaction and societal discipline. There are so many new ways to stray from the ideal of holiness that the very concept may appear, to many, as a relic of the past, an anachronism no longer appropriate for the modern world.

The turmoil this reality introduces into the life of observant Jews was part of the motivation for a huge rally organized by ultra-Orthodox Jewish leaders in New York in 2012, called the "*asifa,*" which urged Jews to avoid or limit use of the Internet and other new technologies.[2] It is a sad comment on our alienation from authentic Jewish values that many people—including many observant Jews—ridiculed the gathering as an attempt to hold back the tides of progress, rather than seeing it as sounding an alarm concerning the danger to our spiritual welfare posed by contemporary lifestyles.

This essay will examine this situation. We shall first seek a definition of holiness, and then examine the pervasiveness of technology in our everyday lives, considering both its deleterious and its beneficial effects. Finally, we shall suggest ways to overcome impediments to achieving *k'dushah* in our own lives, and we shall consider to what extent that goal is compatible with a technologically advanced lifestyle.

K'dushah/Holiness

What is *k'dushah*? As we have already noted, the classic biblical commentators interpret the biblical mandate to "be holy" in a variety of ways, affording us different insights into this elusive desideratum. Maimonides, as noted, does not count it as a separate *mitzvah*, but rather as an overarching goal that should animate all our thoughts and endeavors. There are numerous instances where the Torah specifically notes that performing a certain *mitzvah* (such as wearing *tzitzit*) will lead to an end result of being holy.

Unlike Maimonides, however, there are those who do consider the verse *k'doshim tihyu*, "be holy" (Leviticus 19:2), as a distinct and specific *mitzvah*, and so they seek to define what one should do to be holy, or what holiness entails. Rashi interprets holiness as being removed from forbidden actions or thoughts, such that one should be ever mindful to take precautions not to be attracted to forbidden pleasures or to sin, "for every place that you find a barrier against *ervah* [loosely translated as "immorality," especially referring to sexual immorality], there you find *k'dushah*, holiness."[3] In other words, Rashi sees holiness resulting from conscious separation from ervah and whatever else is proscribed by the Torah. Holiness can ensue only when people are removed from negative thoughts, environments, or actions.

In his own biblical commentary, Naḥmanides cites the views of Rashi but disagrees with his understanding. For Naḥmanides, it is not enough to simply refrain from proscribed behaviors, such as eating forbidden foods or consorting with forbidden partners. He notes that were this the extent of the commandment, then "one with strong appetites for pleasure could constantly indulge one's desires while eating only kosher foods and having sexual relations only with permitted partners, with the result that such a person would be a *naval bi-r'shut ha-torah*"—that is, such an individual could be guilty of degenerate behavior even while technically adhering to the limitations set by the Torah. One could eat kosher meat to excess, gorge on delicacies, drink wine to the point of inebriation—and still be considered to be following the dictates of the Torah! Certainly, exclaims Naḥmanides, simply avoiding forbidden behaviors (such as consuming forbidden wines or meats, or refraining from adultery) cannot by itself qualify one's lifestyle as one of holiness. Instead, he offers an alternate understanding of what we must do to seek *k'dushah*: we are to *be p'rushim min ha-motarot*, refraining from excessive indulgence—even in those things permitted by the Torah. He writes: *kaddeish atzm'kha b'mutar lakh*, "sanctify yourself with that which is permitted to you." Sanctity can only occur when one consciously limits one's indulgence in physical pleasure, including permissible pleasures. For Naḥmanides, sanctity is a step above ordinary behavior, and it cannot occur when a person is steeped in self-gratification. Holiness is to be found in the realm of the spiritual; excessive involvement in material existence will drag one away from that higher realm. We will return to this idea later in this study, as we contemplate the effects of technology on our ability to focus on the Divine.

In the modern era, Rabbi Shimon Yehudah Shkop (1860–1939) offers a positive rather than a negative approach to the search for holiness in our lives. In the introduction to his *Sha·arei Yosher*, he notes that we are urged "to follow the paths of the Almighty" (citing Deuteronomy 28:9, *v'halakhta bi-d'rakhav*). According to classic rabbinic discussion of this verse, one should "imitate" the Creator: just as God clothed the naked (Adam and Eve in the Garden of Eden), visited the sick (Abraham after his circumcision), and buried the dead (Moshe Rabbeinu), so too are we bidden to follow in God's footsteps. And therein lies holiness. Rav Shkop continues:

> The *mitzvah* of *k'doshim tihyu* is a fundamental desideratum of the Torah…that all our services [of God] and our efforts should always be dedicated to the welfare of the whole, that we never use any deed, movement, pleasure, or rejoicing unless there is in it some good for others…and therefore, when one straightens one's paths and strives always that all the parts of one's life be consecrated to the *k'lal* [the community], then whatever one does—even for oneself or for the health of one's mind or one's body— is also turning all [these efforts] to the *mitzvah* of being holy, inasmuch as through one's efforts one is benefitting [not only oneself but] also the many.

Our brief overview indicates just how much diversity there is in the rabbinic delineation of *k'dushah* and how elusive a precise definition of that concept is. For Maimonides, someone who follows all the dictates of the Torah will naturally become an ethical, God-fearing, and God-loving person—that is, a holy individual. Rashi finds that *k'dushah* ensues when one distances oneself from sin and ervah. Nahmanides finds holiness in an individual's rejection of a surfeit of physical pleasures, thus minimizing one's focus on bodily needs and the secular world, and instead directing one's thoughts to spiritual pursuits. And the author of *Sha·arei Yosher* sees holiness as emerging from one's conscious efforts to pattern one's behavior after God's example: following the example of the Holy One will perforce lead to becoming holy.

What all of these opinions have in common is the conviction that holiness is not reserved only for an elite few, but is rather an obligation incumbent upon (and attainable by) every Jewish individual.[4] For Maimonides, it is an outgrowth of careful adherence to the Torah's commands; for Naḥmanides, it is attained through self-discipline and avoidance of excess; for *Sha·arei Yosher*, it is the product of directing one's efforts to the benefit of others rather than toward oneself. Furthermore, all of these understandings clearly bespeak the conviction that in order to achieve holiness, that desire must be the focus and the impetus of all one's actions and thoughts. Holiness is not an incidental benefit of observing the commandments; it must be a conscious goal. These different opinions do not negate one another; it might be more useful to see them as complementary perspectives, emphasizing diverse aspects of the same concept—a constant striving that draws us ever closer to the Divine.

Achieving holiness has never been easy, but seems to be even more elusive in the modern age. We turn our attention now to factors that may either impede or advance our religious dedication in the present day.

Modern Technology

How do technological advances threaten or challenge our commitment to Torah ideals, and specifically the ideal of *k'dushah*?

First of all, we need to define "technology" as we will be discussing it in this essay. "Technology" may be considered as a wide range of inventions and improvements that humans have created over the millennia, which have changed the way people live and work, often making life easier. By that definition, the invention of the bow and arrow is an example of "technology," enabling early people to hunt more effectively; the invention of guns and rifles did the same, on a more advanced level. The invention of the printing press and the typewriter were certainly tremendous boons to spreading ideas and furthering education. And nowadays, instant communication between people all over the world has advanced to an unprecedented level, due to the presence of social media and the Internet, and devices such as smart phones, iPads, and iPods. But obviously, technological innovations have never been an unmixed blessing. Bows and arrows—and guns and rifles—can kill not only animals or predators, but human beings as well. Atomic energy can provide cheap fuel—or destroy the world. And so we must carefully consider not only the benefits, but also the potential downfalls, that computer-related technology may bring to our lives.

It is necessary to recognize a basic truth: technology in and of itself is neither good nor bad; rather, how we use it and what we do with it determines whether it is ultimately an asset or a detriment to our lives. Indeed, the rabbis understood the Torah to be alluding to an argument between Lemech and his wives on just this point.[5] It seems that Lemech (the seventh generation after Adam) was a very talented man, who taught his oldest son the art of animal husbandry and his second son the art of music. The third son was taught by Lemech how to sharpen weapons and fashion all kinds of instruments for waging war. His wives wanted to abandon him because of this, claiming that he had introduced killing and murder to the world. Lemech replied, "*I* have slain a man…" (Genesis 4:23, emphasis added)—thus adumbrating the modern slogan, "Guns don't kill, people kill." Lemech argued with his wives that he was not guilty of any wrongdoing for having taught his third son what he did: the instruments he had fashioned could be used for hunting and helping people survive, and if some chose to use them to kill, that was not his responsibility.[6]

Technological innovation has been part of human development since the dawn of civilization—and so has the controversy surrounding it. When we examine technological advances throughout the centuries, we must conclude that there are both positive and negative aspects to most of them. It is true, for example, that the printing press and the photocopy machine have made the written word available cheaply and easily to millions of people, and we can certainly consider that a positive outcome. Yet, these "advances" have also had an adverse effect on people's ability to memorize or remember poetry or written documents, since the need for memorization no longer exists in the same way that it used to. The printing press, or the Internet, or any kind of telecommunication, are all powerful instruments that can spread all sorts of knowledge (such as Torah, or medical and scientific advances) quickly to all parts of the world. But at the same time that the Internet can make rare libraries and arcane books available to scholars, it also makes it possible to disseminate heretical, immoral, or evil ideas to millions of people, far more rapidly than has ever before been possible in human history.

What should be the "proper Jewish" appraisal of technology? In particular, since we have seen that holiness represents a core Jewish value, we will need to evaluate how use of the Internet (and television, smart phones, and various social media) may impact our ability to strive toward attaining *k'dushah* in a meaningful way.

It is easy to recognize the great benefits that television, the Internet, and other forms of modern technology have had on the sense of unity of the Jewish people. Being able to see events taking place in Jerusalem, on-screen in our homes halfway around the world, virtually as they happen (no pun intended), binds us to fellow Jews living in Israel far more powerfully than was previously possible. The sense of immediacy and closeness has had the effect of galvanizing and connecting all parts of the Jewish people. Decades ago, the Chabad Movement was one of the first segments of the Orthodox community to capitalize on the possibilities of the modern era, transmitting the Rebbe's speeches to a worldwide audience in real time. Nowadays, Jews all over the world have become accustomed to hearing and viewing outstanding rabbinic leaders addressing virtually the entire Jewish people. Families on different continents can be in conversation via Skype, maintaining closeness far more easily than in previous generations. These wondrous developments have given a new meaning to the age-old prophecy that all the Jews "will become bound together" (*agudah ahat*),[7] as for example, hundreds of thousands celebrate the completion of a *daf yomi* cycle together.

But there is no question that these modern technologies at the same time represent a formidable challenge and threat to wholesome Jewish living, and particularly to a holy lifestyle. Television brings the daily news into our homes, but it also brings to us graphic depictions of violence and immorality—and those images are not readily erased from our minds. Even against our conscious desires, our minds become suffused with images, ideas, and language that are antithetical to Jewish values.

The Internet is a marvelous tool for accessing all manner of information that would have been highly difficult to retrieve or access in the past, but it also offers access to areas of thought or action that should never enter a Jewish mind. We are not even taking into account the reality that pornography and *l'shon ha-ra* are readily available in cyberspace; these are, and have always been, outright forbidden for any Jew. But the ubiquity and anonymity afforded to these age-old forbidden behaviors by the new technologies, together with their easy accessibility, do magnify the problem. Everyone is familiar nowadays with the reality that sexual predators lurk in anonymous chat rooms, and that one can easily become inveigled in all manner of dangerous and sinful behavior—yet every day, incautious youngsters (and adults too) find themselves lured into this realm. On the Internet, one can find thousands of *shiurim* on Torah and *musar*, but also thousands of speeches and websites about heretical concepts. And often, the consumer may not be able to discern the authenticity or validity of the ideas disseminated. The Internet also opens the door to blogs or postings on Facebook and the like, which are often little more than rants of *l'shon ha-ra* and denigration of others, made so easy by the anonymity of cyberspace. Lives and reputations have been destroyed by the total invasion of privacy that is possible when someone posts pernicious comments or videos online, which are then forward to and viewed by millions—with complete disregard of whether or not they are true.

There is yet another aspect of modern technology that impacts negatively on lives, especially our Jewish lifestyle, and that is its seductive nature. People often waste away hours daily, idly surfing the Internet. Social media such as Facebook and Twitter, as well as electronic communications such as texting and emailing, seem to have an addictive effect on many, especially on young people, for whom social standing is overwhelmingly important.[8] More than one person has been killed due to texting while driving, as the addictive lure of instant communication monopolizes our attention and makes it impossible to focus elsewhere—sometimes with tragic results.

Also inconsonant with Torah values are the demands that modern technology make on the individual to stay constantly in touch, always connected, and up-to-date with the newest and latest gadget or app. The ancient rabbis note that part of Pharoah's nefarious plan to enslave the Jewish people was to keep them so busy, so involved in physical survival, that they would not have the time to ponder their situation or even complain about it. Pharaoh charged the taskmasters: *tikhbad ha-avodah al ha-anashim v'ya·asu vah, v'al yishu b'divrei sheker*, "Let heavier work be set upon them, so that they may do it and not [spend their time] contemplating nonsense" (Exodus 5:9). This is strikingly parallel to what is happening to myriads of people nowadays, caught up in the technology revolution. By sucking in the mind of users—by keeping people almost frantic to stay in touch, with their finger on the pulse of all that is happening with their acquaintances and in the world, fearful of falling behind the latest and newest innovation—modern technology totally distracts us from our loftier goals, making it difficult to focus on what God wants of us and instead filling every available minute with efforts to keep up with the technology.[9] And the more one is involved in the secular, material world, the further removed one is from a life of contemplating the glory of God, the wisdom of the Torah, and the awesome responsibility we each have to perfect our souls.

Confronting Modern Innovations

Since the dawn of the modern age, the Jewish community has been divided into two basic camps: those who have wanted to isolate themselves from the reaches and effects of the modern world, and those who have wanted to partake of the innovations and opportunities offered to us by the modern world. There are strong arguments to be made for both positions.

Especially in the Hasidic world, one finds entire towns established on the premise that the intrusion of the modern world into the Jewish community is a threat to our dedication to Torah ideals. Consequently, enclaves are created where no TV, computers, or even secular newspapers are countenanced, thereby affording the residents a haven from the corruption, violence, and immorality that is so rampant in the surrounding society. There is much to be said for protecting young minds—and mature ones as well—from the corrosive effects of secular society, thus fostering an environment in which is it possible to live serenely according to the dictates of Torah values and ideals. A problem could arise, however, when individuals from such a protected community come into contact with modern society, which is inevitable in the course of making a living, or travelling, or seeking medical treatment. Unaccustomed to modern innovations, such people could become completely overwhelmed by them, and might totally surrender to the lure of the "outside" world.

The other side of the coin consists of Jewish groups that seek to participate in all aspects of the modern world while still remaining completely loyal to the requirements of Jewish living. They seek out not only Jewish education but also secular knowledge, and they actively engage with modernity and technology, believing that these are compatible with Torah values and can enhance them. In their view, the correct approach for the committed Jew is to participate in the world, meet its challenges, and thereby rise to greater heights of belief and dedication.[10] The downside of this approach is readily apparent not only in the high rate of intermarriage, which has only increased after a few generations of this lifestyle, but even in the weakening of observance of *mitzvot* and diminution of Torah values among those who profess to be strictly Orthodox in the present. In a recent article, for example, Jonathan Rosenbloom laments the frightening number of young people who study in Orthodox yeshivas and Bais Yaakov schools, and who admit to texting one another on

Shabbat. Nor is this a fleeting phenomenon: it even has a name, "half Shabbos."[11] Yet, as many contend, it is also modern technology that makes possible access to information that is beneficial, including Torah lectures, closeness with the land and people of Israel, medical knowledge, and the like.

Therefore, we need to have a discussion about how to approach the modern world with its mixed blessings. Should we try to negate it by holding back the tides of time? Or should we "take the fruit and discard the peel"? And is that even possible? This is not a new conflict, between those who want to block any influence from the non-Jewish world and those who want to engage the modern world and use its innovations to enhance a Torah lifestyle. In truth, this tension is part of a larger debate, seeking to clarify the role of the Torah in our lives and what God expects from each of us.

The Torah contains a *mitzvah* concerning the nazirite, a person who voluntarily takes a vow to live a life of exemplary holiness, eschewing drinking any wine, even avoiding grapes, and not becoming ritually impure through contact with a dead body.[12] At the end of his period of abstinence, the nazirite must offer an atonement sacrifice. The Talmud records a debate about why the nazirite must seek atonement:[13]

> Rabbi Elazar the Kappar…says [he must atone for the fact that] he distressed himself by [abstaining] from wine. And a priori, if this person is considered a sinner when only abstaining from wine, how much more so the person who abstains from any and all pleasures [should be considered a sinner]! But Rabbi Eliezer says, [on the contrary, the nazirite] is considered holy [and must bring an atonement for the fact that he is now abandoning his higher calling and returning to life as an ordinary Jew].[14] And if this is so, and someone who abstains from only one thing [i.e., wine] is considered holy, how much the more so should a person who abstains from other pleasures [be considered holy]!

Thus we see that the two approaches about partaking of all that the world has to offer is not a new debate, nor is it one for which there is a clear-cut "right" answer. Since the reality is that most people will find it almost impossible to cut themselves off from contact with modern secular society, it is important to consider the advice of rabbinic leaders who have sought to address this challenge.

Human beings are not perfect; we all make mistakes. As King Solomon, the wisest of all men, noted: "There is no one who is perfectly righteous and never sins" (Kohelet 7:20). What is important is what a person does after erring.

In a famous letter to one of his disciples, Rabbi Yitzḥak Hutner (1906–1980) quotes the verse, "For a righteous person falls seven times, and rises" (Psalm 88:6). He rejects a common interpretation that the verse teaches that, despite making repeated errors, a righteous person has the resilience to pick oneself up, repent, and continue to grow. Rather, he emphasizes that "wise people know well that the intent [of the verse] is to teach that what *precipitates* a person's becoming a *tzaddik*, is that first one had to fall down seven times…"[15] Rav Hutner is taking a definite position here, reiterating his belief that the true fulfillment of human potential results from confronting the multiple challenges faced by each person. And while it is true that no person will be able to overcome all hardships, one will nevertheless emerge a greater and better person for trying—and maybe failing—and then trying again.

Others point to the sad reality that not everyone (and maybe not even most people) will be able to cope positively with their mistakes, learn from them, and go on to become stronger and better. After all, Jewish law mandates that when a nazirite approaches a vineyard, we are supposed to warn him: "Go away, go away!" Clearly, Jewish thinking recognizes that it is more prudent and practical to *avoid* sin, rather than to be exposed to it and hope for the best. And while it may indeed be an admission of a general weakness of character in our generation, there is no question that if people do not allow

the Internet into their homes, there will be many fewer people
viewing inappropriate material or twittering away their free time over
nonsense.[17]

In his *Nefesh Ha-ḥayyim*[18] Rabbi Ḥayyim Volozhin (1749–1821)
refers to a disagreement between Saadiah Gaon and Abraham ibn
Ezra about who is greater, humans or angels.[19] Rav Ḥayyim Volozhin
writes that in truth they are both right: "Undoubtedly, angels are
superior to humans, in both their very essence and the greatness of
their holiness and their wondrous intellectual grasp; however, in one
aspect humans have a great superiority over the angels, and that is
their ability to overcome adversity and strive to improve themselves,
which no angel is able to do. That is why angels are described as
'standing' [i.e., they cannot move to a higher plane]."

His conclusion harks back to a famous talmudic text describing
the encounter between the angels and Moses, when the latter went
up to heaven to receive the Torah:

> The angels confronted Moses, demanding to know what a
> human being was doing in their midst, and he responded
> that he had come to receive the Torah. Thereupon the
> angels, aghast, turned to God and asked, "Can it be that this
> treasure, which You have kept hidden for 974 generations…
> You intend to give to a flesh and blood [person]!?" The
> Almighty then said to Moses, "You answer them."…Moses
> asked, "God, what is written in Your Torah?"…"I am the
> Eternal…who took you out of the land of Egypt." Then he
> challenged the angels: "And did *you* go down to Egypt, and
> were you enslaved by Pharaoh? And what about 'Remember
> the Sabbath day to sanctify it'—do you angels do any work,
> that you need to sanctify Shabbat [by desisting from work]?
> And what about 'Honor your father and your mother'—you
> angels don't have fathers or mothers!" Straightaway, each of
> the angels became a loving friend to Moses and gave him a
> gift…[20]

This celestial encounter seems to adumbrate the debate between ibn Ezra and Saadiah, alluded to by Rav Hayyim Volozhin: the angels, so to speak, claim superiority in the realm of knowledge and in their ability to contemplate the Divine.[21] On those grounds, they consider themselves to have a stronger claim to the Torah, for humans are subject to shortcomings and physical and mental frailties, and are therefore not to be trusted with God's special treasure. But Moses' claim trumped theirs: it is humans who need Torah, not the angels. Humans can grow; their understanding can develop; their spirit can soar. Yes, humans can also stumble and fall—but they can rise up again, becoming even better and stronger. And on that basis, even the angels agreed that it is more appropriate for humans to possess and learn from the Torah than it is for the angels to adore it.

In the context of our present inquiry, this passage from *Nefesh Ha-hayyim* is most instructive. One way of living life as a Jew is to try and insulate ourselves in our communities, cut ourselves off from the rest of the world, and focus only on our religious obligations.[22] On the other hand, God created us to live in this world: to meet its challenges and to get involved in its problems. Let us remember that after God created humanity, with our quixotic ability to stumble or to grow, God put us into this world to be a part of it—and it was at that point that God concluded that "it was very good" (Genesis 1:31).

There is a fascinating episode recorded in the Talmud: for more than two years, the students of Hillel (Beit Hillel) and the students of Shammai (Beit Shammai) were engaged in a fundamental debate about whether it was better for humanity to have been created or not. Beit Hillel argued that a life of physical existence and endeavor and the opportunity to fulfill God's wishes affords the soul the opportunity to grow, to rise, and to attain great spiritual heights. Beit Shammai, on the other hand, was not so sanguine, and pointed to the countless opportunities for humanity to fall, to stumble, and to sin grievously against God. After years of debate, they finally put the issue to a vote and concluded, "It would have been better for humanity not to have been created" (*mutav lo la-adam she-lo nivra*), seeing how the majority of people cannot overcome the challenges and temptations of physical existence. Despite this conclusion, since the reality is that humanity indeed has been created, the question is effectively moot. Therefore, the sages advised: "Let one examine one's deeds" carefully and avoid sin.[23]

Perhaps the Jewish community would indeed be better off if all the delicious temptations of the modern world had not been made available to them. But that train has long since left the station. For many, the reality is that we have had no choice but to confront the modern world, rather than escaping from it. Nevertheless, this reality does not mean "throwing in the towel" on maintaining or achieving our status as God's holy people. Modifications in our Jewish educational system might fortify young people and help them prepare for the onslaught of technology and modernity they will encounter in the world, and remind them of the imperative to live a life of holiness. The problems need to be addressed, rather than avoided or denied.

All is not bleak. Through our struggles with both the temptations and opportunities afforded by life in the modern world, we can hope to emerge even stronger in our commitment to our Jewish values. But that is only a hope, not a guarantee. As we have noted, our sages considered that "it would have been better for humanity not to have been created." Consequently, we must be cognizant of the depressing reality that many people are not successful in meeting the challenges presented by this world to their spiritual journey.

For many, the pleasures and distractions of the world—presented with all their lure via the Internet or the like—are more than they can overcome. It is quite relevant in this context to note that the temptation (*yetzer ha-ra*) to worship idols was unbelievably strong in ancient times. Despite the numerous warnings in the Torah, and despite centuries of exhortations from the prophets to reject totally any form of idol worship, the Jewish people were not successful in withstanding this temptation. Idolatry was the underlying reason for the loss of the Northern Kingdom and, according to the Talmud, idolatry was at least partially responsible for the destruction of the First Temple.[24] When the Jews returned from the Babylonian exile and built the Second Temple, the sages saw that once again the temptation of idolatry was seducing many people. At that time, the Talmud relates, they prayed mightily that God would allow them to excise this *yetzer ha-ra* (temptation) permanently, because too many people just did not have the strength to overcome it. And then they received a sign from heaven that their request had been granted. At a certain point, if a yetzer ha-ra is just too much for most people to handle, it may be time to eradicate that temptation, to prevent the havoc it will inevitably wreak.[25]

The burgeoning technology of the modern world and its ubiquitous intrusion into our thoughts and habits represent a problem that is ignored by most people, including many Jews committed to a Torah lifestyle. We need to recognize that our increasing participation in the general lifestyle of the secular world introduces obstacles to our ability to maintain appropriate spiritual direction, and may even threaten religious observance. The obstacles presented by the modern world are often beyond the ability of many (if not most) people to overcome. It is not sufficient to bemoan the inroads made by television, the Internet, social media, and instant communications (such as emailing and texting) in whittling away our consciousness of our Jewish mission; it is also necessary to take action against this pervasive erosion of our values and lifestyle.

No matter how diligently Torah values are taught in Jewish schools, children are inherently most powerfully influenced and shaped by the values they absorb from their families and from their homes. Thus, it is the responsibility of Jewish parents to carefully monitor, control, or even remove untoward influences from their children's environment. This would include not only installing filters on computers but also disabling certain functions of their cell phones, iPods, and iPads—or even interdicting them entirely—and making sure to place the computer in the middle of the living room to discourage family members from clandestinely viewing inappropriate material. Many adults cannot overcome the urge to "take a peek" (or worse) at forbidden images on the web. One attempt to deal with these challenges is presented by Web Chaver software, a "buddy system" that shares information about all sites accessed by a user with a designated individual, who accepts the responsibility to monitor the Internet use of his or her friend.

These are attempts to limit the damage that could ensue from improper use of modern technology. But they might not be enough. Although it will go against the grain for some people who are accustomed to living in a thoroughly modern and open environment, it may be necessary to draw back from the customary total involvement in order to preserve one's Jewish commitments. Thus, there is much to be said for those who disdain having all sorts of modern technology in their homes and who shun television, the Internet, and various technological gadgets and devices altogether. Since many people find themselves unable to effectively limit their use of technology or social media, it may be most prudent to interdict them totally.

The problem when it comes to setting guidelines and taking precautions is that it is difficult, if not impossible, to gauge in advance any particular individual's susceptibility to the temptations of technology. Consequently, wise parents will restrict their children and only cautiously and gradually permit them access to this environment, which can be so dangerous. Some parents may find it prudent to restrict access absolutely, while others may decide that their children or teenagers are able to withstand the temptations and use the technology in a responsible manner.

What we have said about the vulnerability of youngsters applies as well to adults. Many individuals feel that they can successfully maintain the delicate balance between using technology for the good of the world and the individual, on the one hand, and the pitfalls of becoming slavishly devoted to the demands of social media and the Internet to keep us constantly in touch and in the know, on the other hand. However, even well-intentioned adults are not always successful in gauging how far they may be sliding down a slippery slope.

An additional factor to be taken into account is that this is not only an individual struggle, but one that has communal aspects as well. We must always be cognizant of the needs of the entire Jewish community and not only of our own personal perspectives. Thus, it is desirable to set community standards to protect those most vulnerable. Some people may be more susceptible to the attractions of modern technology, with its myriad opportunities to stray from the guidelines of Judaism; others may be fairly impervious. Whatever one's particular position on the issue, responsible people in the Jewish community need to engage in conversation within the community about how to increase our dedication to becoming a holy nation.

The Torah's commandments enjoin us to perform certain acts and expect that these actions will transform us into a holy nation, God's people. And it is this goal that should set the guidelines for whether, or to what extent, we allow ourselves to become part of the new technological world. In this essay, we have focused on the dangers that this new world represents for our ancient and enduring commitment to a Torah lifestyle. But technology is only the latest permutation of the threat to Jewish values that arises anew in each generation, and it is not the only one.

Becoming part of secular society has really only been an option for Jews for a few hundred years, and this participation carries with it a continuing threat to the mandate of the Jewish people to seek holiness. *K'dushah*, holiness, is not one of the values of the world around us. To the extent that a Jew engages in a modern lifestyle, the threat becomes stronger; and so, the efforts to overcome the negative drag need to become stronger, too. As Nahmanides pointed out, holiness ensues when one consciously decides to forego an action or an option that is intrinsically permissible, but that may be just too materialistic or physically gratifying—that partakes just a little too much in *olam ha-zeh*.

Writing to a correspondent who had endured a difficult moral test and yet emerged successfully, Rav Eliyahu Eliezer Dessler (1892–1953) commends him and makes the following observation:

You should know that there is blessing (*b'rakhah*) and there is grace (*haninah*). A blessing is bestowed from [God's] lovingkindness and mercy, but grace comes also from the aspect of justice, which means that it is obligatory from the force of justice...Because when one suffers for the sake of heaven, withstanding a temptation [or trial], and accepts one's suffering with love, because one considers oneself fortunate to have been able to make this sacrifice for the Creator—with this, by the quality of divine justice, one is entitled [for God to] bestow grace and grant many good things, in this world and in the next.[26]

Conclusion

It is not the purpose of the present study to chart a definitive path that sincerely committed Jews should follow with regard to rejecting or employing modern technologies, but rather to point out the pitfalls and benefits of both alternatives. It is readily evident, moreover, that whatever one's decisions with respect to technology, it is more and more important in the modern age to remember always that we are bidden to be a holy people.

Reviewing the variety of understandings for the concept of *k'dushah* adduced by our rabbis, it may be valid to surmise that there are differing degrees or modes of holiness. While each of us must strive for holiness, just as each of us must strive to learn Torah, we will surely not all accomplish our goals in the same way or to the same degree.

Holiness is not a one-size-fits-all attribute; that was a basic mistake made by Korah when he challenged Moses and Aaron, arguing that "the entire congregation [of the Jewish people] are all holy (*kullam k'doshim*)...and therefore why do you set yourselves above God's people?" The ensuing debacle, wherein Korah and his cohorts were swallowed alive by the earth, definitively proved the superiority of

Moses.[27] A similar failure to comprehend that there are differing levels of *k'dushah*, closeness to God, was what provoked Miriam to speak against Moses, when she protested that he had separated himself from his wife due to the demands of his prophetic responsibilities: "Was it only with Moses that the Eternal spoke—didn't God speak with us as well?" (Numbers 12:2). She assumed that since she (and many others) had also experienced the transcendent phenomenon of prophecy, and none of them had been instructed to separate from their spouses, it was pretentious for Moses to assume a different mode of behavior. But God clarified that there are, in fact, different modes of prophecy, each denoting a distinct level of holiness. It was only with Moses that God spoke peh el peh, "mouth to mouth" (Numbers 12:8); communication with others was on a more "mundane" level.

Although the directive to be holy applies to the entire Jewish people, that does not mean that all people can, or do, achieve the same level of holiness. What is clear is that all of us are bidden to rise as high as we can, and no one is entitled to opt out with the claim that such a goal is not appropriate for him or her. Nor need all people follow the same path for achieving holiness. Some may find their path to holiness impeded by their constant interaction with social media, while others can access technology in moderation, deriving maximum benefit without impediment to their focus on the sublime. Not all people are the same, and one size does not fit all when it comes to lifestyles either. What is essential, however, is that we embark upon a serious discussion about how to infuse our homes, our families, our workplaces, and the entire Jewish community with a greater sense of *k'dushah*. A prerequisite to engaging in such a conversation is the acceptance of the goal of becoming a holy nation.

NOTES

1 *Sefer Ha-mitzvot, k'lal* 4 (Jerusalem: Mosad Harav Kook, 1990), p. 17.

2 Ironically, the overflow crowd was able to gather "virtually" and view the rally by means of modern technology. For a report of the *asifa* in the mainstream Jewish press, see Ari L. Goldman's article in the *The New York Jewish Week* of May 22, 2012, also available on the newspaper's website at http://www.thejewishweek.com/news/new_york/will_asifa_net_results.

3 Rashi to Leviticus 19:2.

4 It must be pointed out, however, that there is a broad spectrum of holiness. Not every individual will attain the same degree of *k'dushah*, yet everyone must strive to reach the highest possible level for him or herself.

5 Genesis 4:23; see comments of Naḥmanides there.

6 Rashi to Genesis 4:23.

7 The Hebrew phrase is found at 2 Samuel 2:25.

8 This is without even considering the invidious effect that pernicious posts and cyberbullying can have on individuals. There is more than one instance on record of teenagers committing suicide because of hurtful or hateful postings about them online.

9 Part of the fascination with technology may arise, for some people, from lack of involvement in ideas or thoughts that they find meaningful. Nature abhors a vacuum, and that may in part explain why young people get so caught up in playing with their technological toys. If their minds and hearts were filled with Torah, or *ḥesed*, or community involvement, they might find that they have considerably less interest in technological distractions.

10 There are some people who maintain that since most of us do not have (or will not choose) the option of isolating ourselves and our children from the outside world, it is important to increase our Torah knowledge and study, so that we are fortified against letting the secular world overwhelm our values. People well-grounded in Torah wisdom are less susceptible to being overly impressed by modern science and technology. So for example, when students learn that our rabbis two thousand years ago knew that hemophilia is a disease that presents in males but is genetically transmitted by females—a fact that modern science did not appreciate until about a century ago—it can only strengthen their faith that the Torah is divinely inspired. Such faith will then be better able to withstand the lure of the outside world. Another example would be discovering that many of Freud's brilliant insights into the human psyche and the symbolism of dreams are also found in the Talmud, written more than a thousand years earlier. Modern medicine has concluded that a fetus's gender is determined by the sixth week of gestation—which the ancient rabbis knew almost two thousand years ago. If people want to take on the intellectual challenges of the modern world, some will say that we should adjust their education to help them withstand its

attraction, as seeing the wisdom of the ancient rabbis can only bolster one's *emunah* (faith).

[11] Jonathan Rosenblum, "Half Shabbos Is No Shabbos," *Jewish Action* (Spring 5722), p. 12.

[12] Numbers 6:1–20.

[13] B. Taanit 11a.

[14] This is also the view of Naḥmanides in his commentary to Numbers 6:1-20.

[15] *Paḥad Yitzḥak* §128. The same idea is expressed also in *P'ri Tzaddik, parshat Va-yeilekh 1*; *Tzidkat Ha-tzaddik* §234.

[16] B. Bava Metzia 92a and Shabbat 13a.

[17] It has been suggested that Jewish schools should refuse to enroll any student whose parents have the Internet in the house without a filter, and only provided that the parents need it for work.

[18] *Sha·ar* 1:6.

[19] Cited in the commentary of ibn Ezra to Genesis 1:1.

[20] B. Shabbat 88b.

[21] See the introduction of of Rabbi Shlomo Avraham Razachta to his collection of responsa, *Bikkurei Sh'lomo* (ed. Pietrikow, 1894), p. 12.

[22] The *S'fat Emet*, commenting on Numbers 14, analyzes the motivation of the spies in the wilderness along these same lines. He explains that they deliberately painted a frightening picture of what awaited the Jews in the promised land because they feared that the confrontation with the mundane requirements of having to earn a living and being involved with the myriad needs of fashioning a society would pull the Jews down from the pinnacle of holiness that exemplified their existence in the wilderness. There, they saw daily that their sustenance came directly from God and that they were totally dependent on divine bounty. This closeness to God, this high level of holiness, would be lost when they entered the land. Therefore, suggests the *S'fat Emet*, the spies deliberately chose an alternative that would keep the Jews in the wilderness.

[23] B. Eiruvin 13b. See also Rashi, ad loc., s.v. *y'fashfeish*: "One should review one's deeds, clarify what one did wrong, and repent." The Talmud notes that some versions of the rabbinic debate have a slightly different conclusion: *y'mashmeish b'ma·asav*, "let one examine the quality of each of one's actions"; see Rashi, ibid.

[24] B. Yoma 71a.

[25] We should point out in this context that when the sages prayed that the temptation for idolatry be eradicated because it was too powerful a lure for the majority, the outcome was not entirely positive—because the removal of the great pitfall, idolatry, had to be balanced by the removal of its great opposite attraction, prophecy. With the end of idolatry, the Jewish people also experienced the end of prophecy. Removing the impediment meant also removing the opportunity to attain high spiritual summits. Furthermore, the Talmud notes that the sages initially also sought to abolish other forms of temptation, but that

abolition had a negative effect on the world's dynamic growth and productivity. No one wanted to strive for achievement anymore. Recognizing that they had gone too far, the sages later changed course in order to permit humanity to function according to the divine plan.

26 *Mikhtav Mei-Eliyahu* (Jerusalem, 1997), vol. 5, p. 532.

27 Numbers, chapter 16; quoted verse is 16:3.

Sanctification

Hillel Goldberg

I

Sanctification.
> It's objective.
> Laid out.
> With boundaries.
> Defined spaces.
> Places you enter.
> Or don't.
> If you define the spaces and places your own way,
>> you do not enter. Do not get to the sanctification.
> On its face, sanctification is restrictive.
> Limiting.
> Dismissive of human struggle, human initiative, human
>> achievement.
> On its face, sanctification is narrow.
> Insular.
> Forbidding.
> Actually, the opposite is true.
> Within the boundary is the expansiveness.
> And the individuality.
> Within the boundary is the liberation.
> The closeness to God.
> God?
> Yes, the process and the purpose of sanctification is
>> to come close to God.

To stretch beyond the human boundaries.
To see, to sense, to reach beyond the limitations of
    cells and organ systems, of species and ratiocination.
God is limitless. But the way to God—the
    sanctification—is delimited.
Bound.
Given.
Revealed.
God is infinite, but God's presence "fits" into the
    defined, limited, and quite small dimensions of Exodus'
    tabernacle.
A paradox?
Actually, the ultimate paradox.
The limitless God becomes available in the limited
    space.
And the limited time.
In place, exactly defined.
In time, exactly defined.
In these defined, objective spaces and times:
    sanctification.
Step in, if you want it.
Move from where you are to the defined space, to
    the boundaries of the land of Israel; or to the defined times,
    such as the Sabbath day—and there you find sanctification.
There you find God.
There, you struggle.

II

Sanctification is a given, as a *potential*.
    Sanctification is available, but it needs to be grasped,
        appropriated.
    Sanctification is a presence—if, within the boundaries,
        you seek it.
    If you inquire.

And study.
With your mind, your soul, and your character.
God, up to a point, may be understood.
And God's will, in its revelation, may be understood.
Then the mind, in its understanding, must impinge on
    the heart.
The soul.
Must shape the soul.
Build it.
Open it.
Expand it.
Then both the mind and the soul must impinge on
    character.
On acts.
Deeds.
To be sanctified, you enter the defined space and time—then
you begin.
Struggle within the boundaries yields the highest
    human stature.
Struggle outside the boundaries may take the earnest,
    searching human being to a certain height, at a certain angle.
But the funnel, the direct link to God, is through God's
    objective, revealed channels.
Divine instructions.
Divine commandments.
Divine vessels, divine funnel, divine defined spaces
    and times.
Divine will.
Divine gifts.

III

For example: God's commandment to observe the Sabbath day.
    The Sabbath has a beginning.
    And an end.

A very specific, closely defined beginning.

And end.

It is not "Saturday."

Its beginning is not when one feels the time ripe.

And it itself is not simply a "special time."

A "time for prayer."

Or "rest."

Or "reflection."

Or "spirituality."

Rather, it is a frame.

A structure of acts to do, and not to do.

Objective, these thirty-nine acts, if refrained from,
  constitute the boundaries. By refraining from these thirty-
  nine acts, there is the Sabbath day.

Refraining from them, one steps into something preexistent.

One steps inside.

One crosses the boundary.

Then, from within that spiritual space, is the potential
  for struggle, for upward movement.

For expansiveness.

For building the mind, the soul, the character.

For reaching, touching, God, the Creator of the frame.

The Revealer of the Sabbath.

Of what it is, and how it is: the observance of these thirty-nine
acts.

They frame the frame.

God's gift.

Perhaps, after creation itself, God's greatest gift.

The most spiritually potent channel for accessing God.

But, once within the frame, once observant of the
  thirty-nine acts, the struggle begins.

The opportunity.

To open the soul to God.

To use the mind to access God's will.

The opportunity—for sanctification.

The struggle—also, the tranquility.

Seeking God—and having God.

Human initiative—and human submission to the defined space, to the Sabbath day.

The ultimate paradox: one may reach the highest
  heights when, by refraining from the thirty-nine acts, one
  does nothing.

Nothing physical.

Through the objective command.

The Sabbath day.

IV

The human being eats.

  Anything?

  Or is eating, too, an opportunity?

  A God-given frame?

  If this I eat, and this I don't: does it make any spiritual
  difference?

  Here, too, is the opportunity for sanctification.

  In Leviticus' dietary (kosher) frame.

  This I may eat; this I may not.

  The human being is intimate.

  Any way? With any person?

  Or, are intimacy and procreation also an opportunity?

  A God-given frame?

  Here, too, is an opportunity for sanctification.

  In Leviticus' *mikveh* frame.

  This person I may be intimate with; these others, not. At this time, yes; at other times, no.

  The human being wears clothing, the human being
  earns money, the human being speaks: here, too, are
  opportunities for sanctification.

  This I may wear; this I may not.

  This money I may take; this, not.

  This I may say; this I may not.

A cascade of frames.
A concentric circle of overlapping and expanding—
    objective—acts.
Places to enter.
More gifts.
Across the expanse of life.

V

Only within the frames?
    Sanctification is nowhere else?
    What about on the mountaintop or at the seashore?
    What about in the garden or under the rushing rain?
    What about in the snow or at the sunset?
    These are not frames?
    Not opportunities for sanctification?
    They are not.
    They are preparations for sanctification.
    They can sensitize.
    Can enrich the human spirit.
    Can inspire.
    Amaze.
    Take one to the realization, or the consciousness, of God, of
    God's presence.
    Yet, they are fluid.
    They come.
    And go.
    They need the frame to last.
    Yes, they can build and nurture the human being, who
        is then able to want a lasting sanctification.
    Yes, they can confirm the closeness to God disclosed by
    sanctification.
    Yes, they can enhance the beauty, the artistic sense,
        encouraged by sanctification.
    They can take us to the revelation.

Then, within the objective, revealed frame, the given,
the defined space and time, sanctification awaits.

VI

Back up.
To the mind.
To its capacity.
To the revealed will.
To the Torah.
To its study.
The Torah is not just words, not just instructions,
not just the divine disclosure of the frames for sanctification.
Not just an instrument.
A guidebook.
Not just narratives of the paragons and paradigms of
sanctification.
Not just a spiritual "need to know."
Not even, primarily, a window on the history of
sanctification, whether in instances of its success or instances
of its failure.
Study of the Torah is not just the acquisition of
knowledge.
Not just a great challenge to the mind.
Or a great reward for, or a tool of, the sharpening of
the mind.
The study of Torah is sanctification itself.
To engage with the divine will is to engage with the
Divine.
To study Torah is the specific frame, itself commanded
by the Torah, with the greatest potential for sanctification.
To study Torah is the opportunity to come close to
God.
In Torah study, not only does the will of God speak:
God's very Self speaks.
The wrong analogy: what the person of Jesus is to

Christianity, the Messiah is to Judaism.

The right analogy: what the "Incarnation" is to
   Christianity, the Torah is to Judaism.

Actually, God never takes the form of a human being;
   God is disclosed via the Torah. There is no other "Incarnation."

When the words of Torah are studied, not only is the
   divine will accessed, but the Divine Self is accessed. For
   Christians, God lived through Jesus. For Jews today, God
   lives through the Torah.

VII

Back up. Again.

   To speech.

   To the commandments of speech.

   Specifically, to what the divine will says people may
      not say.

   We many not say denigrating words.

   Or incendiary words.

   Or false words.

   Within this threefold frame of what is not to be said—
      insults, provocations, falsehoods—is sanctification.

   Which, simultaneously, is character building.

   Through the frame of prohibited speech, one comes
      close to God.

   And to people.

   The struggle for closeness to God and the struggle for
      harmony among people are coextensive.

   Sanctification is not only a divine gesture.

   It is a human gesture.

   The human being is created "the human face Divine," as Rabbi
   Aaron Lichtenstein translated *b'tzelem*
      elohim (Genesis 1:27).

   The objective definition of sanctification, and the
      opportunities for it, include the material.

Sanctification, yes; stretches beyond human boundaries.
Within human boundaries.
Sanctification reaches beyond body and mind.
Within body and mind.
Sanctification is vertical.
Also, horizontal—within human society.
Sanctification aspires upwards.
And sidewards.

VIII

Back up, still again.
　"Sanctification."
　It is general.
　You shall be sanctified (Leviticus 19:2).
　This pertains to every move, every gesture, within
　　　　every frame, every *mitzvah*.
　"Sanctification" is also specific.
　A single *mitzvah*.
　A single frame: that of marriage, called "sanctification"
　　　　(*kiddushin*).
　In its specificity, sanctification is the most restrictive;
　　　　and, on that account, the most liberating frame in the Torah.
　If I wish to marry a non-Jewish person and call it
　　　　"sanctification" (*kiddushin*), I cannot.
　It is akin to division by zero.
　Division by zero is indefinable in our number system.
　Kiddushin, applied to the marriage of a Jew and a
　　　　non-Jew, is indefinable in the Torah.
　It is not there.
　If I am a *kohen*, a priest, a descendant of Aaron the high priest,
　the brother of Moses, and I wish to marry a divorcee, I cannot.
　It is not there.
　"*Kohen* marries divorcee": it is indefinable under the
　　　　Torah.

It is not *kiddushin*.
If I am a male and wish to marry a male.
If I am a female and wish to marry a female.
It is not there.
Not *kiddushin*.
It is indefinable under the Torah.
If I wish to divorce my spouse, then marry others,
    "taking a sample of spouses," then come back to remarry my
    original spouse.
Not there.
Not *kiddushin*.
Indefinable under the Torah.
"Sanctification," *kiddushin*—the most searing of objectivities, the
most restrictive of boundaries, the most elevating of opportunities,
disclosed by God via the Torah.
Kiddushin: God's holiest vessel.

IX

Sanctification: What is its opposite?
    The thinnest line, as wide as the Grand Canyon,
        separates sanctification from its opposite.
    So thin, this line:
    If I take water, and guide it to ground, using no vessel,
        nor certain other handmade or natural materials, voilà! I
        have a pool of water, a *mikveh*, that purifies. Immersion in it
        elevates a person from one spiritual status to another.
    If I take the very same water—exchanging not so
        much as a single molecule—yet guide it to ground via a
        vessel, the water is flat. Lifeless. Empty of spiritual vitality.
        It elevates nothing.
    Same water: This time, within the objective frame, laid
        down in the Torah.
    This time, not.
    This time, sanctification.

This time, not.
If I slaughter an animal with a knife that has the
    slightest nick, I may not eat of the animal.
If I slaughter it with a perfect, flawless blade, I may eat
    thereof.
Same animal.
Same moment of death.
Virtually, the same instrument of slaughter.
This, I may eat.
This, I may not.
If I lend money and take no interest, I may use this
    money.
If I lend on 0.1% interest, I may not.
Virtually, the same amount.
This, I may take.
This, I may not.
The thinnest line marks the largest chasm: between
    that which elevates, and that which does not; between that
    which I may do, and that which I may not.
Sanctification and sin: So similar. So different.

X

Is sanctification only for those who live and study the
    Torah?
Are non-Jews excluded?
In an obvious sense, yes.
In other senses, no.
Yes, those who do not live and study the Torah do not
    access its frames.
God's act of choosing is via the divine revealed frames.
Via God's gift of the potential for sanctification.
Yet.
No one is excluded. Anyone may adopt the Torah.
It is not a closed system.

Not the property of a race.
Or an ethnicity.
Or a nationality.
Any human being may convert to the life of Torah.
There is no guard at the Gate of the Torah.
Still more: even without conversion to Judaism, seven
    of the frames of the Torah are universal.
Not just for adherents of the Torah.
The "seven commandments of the sons of Noah"—of
    humanity—are incumbent upon and accessible to all people.
The commandments of justice.
Of morality.
Of faith.
Of kindness to animals.
To cite four of the seven universal frames of the Torah.
They unite all of humanity.
They *define* humanity.
They constitute God's ways of choosing every human
    being.
They constitute God's gifts to humanity.
God's objective frames.
God's sanctification.
For everyone.

XI

Sanctification is a spiritual and experiential certainty.
    And a philosophical conundrum.
    Sanctification is Godlike, and humanlike.
    Beyond.
    And here.
    Above.
    And below.
    Out of this world.
    Through this world.

Prayer.
And society.
Sabbath.
And weekday.
Torah study.
And marriage.
Transcending cells and organ systems—and infusing them.
Sanctification is hidden, in prayer. In speech for God.
Sanctification is visible. In speech for people.
Sanctification is a conundrum, the most hidden, and the most visible.
The late Rabbi Aryeh Levine observed that when a
> new baby is born, the friends and relatives rejoice, while the baby cries. But when a person dies, the friends and relatives cry, while the soul rejoices, exulting in eternal closeness to God.

Sanctification is both: the objective, revealed, divine
> frames that elevate the human being in this world.

And guide him or her to the next world.
Both.
You shall be *sanctified*.

The Holiness of God:
Its Meaning, Actualization, and Symbolic Embodiment

Saul J. Berman

Seven separate times in the Torah, God is identified by saying "I, the Eternal your God, am holy (*kadosh*)." Religious thinkers and scholars have expended much effort and ink in attempting to explain the meaning of the word *kadosh* in this context, as well as in the multitude of other passages in which the word is used in the Torah. This essay is an attempt at a modest additional contribution to the prior literature on this matter.[1] The central focus of this article will be on the usage of term *kadosh*/holy in the text of the Torah, in order to elicit the patterns of its use as a way of arriving at a systematic understanding of its meaning. But throughout the article I will integrate rabbinic teachings, to explicate biblical usages and to demonstrate application of those usages within Jewish thought and law.

The urgency of understanding the meaning of the term *kadosh* derives first from the fact that God is cited as using that quality more frequently than any other characteristic to describe the divine self. Since imitating God is itself a command that necessitates an understanding of the nature and qualities of the Divine, it would be a forfeiture of significant dimension for us to lack understanding of the term. Second, the Torah also uses the word *kadosh* to describe a broad series of other entities in the divergent realms of time, persons, objects, and places. Those latter references are not random, but appear in coherent parallel sets. It is to these sets that we will then turn our attention, as a way of evaluating the ways in which *k'dushah* (holiness) is embodied in these symbolic vessels.

The Meaning of the Holiness of God

While the Torah contains many self-proclamations of God's own holiness and a broad range of entities are seen to embody the notion of holiness, the text of the Torah contains only intimations of the essential meaning of the term. Let us trace a line of reasoning in verses of the Torah that might lead us to one possible meaning of the term "holiness."

In Leviticus 19:2, God demands of the Jewish nation: "You shall be holy, for I, the Eternal your God, am holy." This verse implies that the very holiness of God can be discovered in its echo in the holiness of the Jewish people. In what, then, does their holiness reside?

Deuteronomy 28:9–10 sheds more light on the idea of the holiness of the Jewish people: "The Eternal will establish you as a holy people, as God has sworn unto you, if you will keep the commandments of the Eternal your God and walk in God's ways. And all the peoples of the earth shall see that the name of the Eternal is called upon you, and they shall be in awe of you" (Deuteronomy 28:9–10). The meaning of *k'dushah* here is unequivocal. The holiness of the Jewish people is actualized through two realms of conduct: observance of the divine commandments and walking in God's ways.

These two components, which constitute the essential character of the holiness of the Jewish people, is indicated as well in a prior passage in Deuteronomy, where Moses confirms the people's entry into an eternal, mutual covenant with God: "You have acknowledged this day the Eternal to be your God, in that you would walk in God's ways and keep God's statutes and commandments and ordinances, and hearken unto God's voice. And the Eternal has acknowledged you this day to be God's own treasure…that you may be a holy people unto the Eternal your God, as God has spoken" (Deuteronomy 26:17–19). Here, as in the preceding passage, the holiness of the Jewish people appears to be actualized in the same two components: obedience to the law and walking in God's ways. The former component is quite clear, but what exactly is meant by "walking in God's ways"?

Let us return now to Deuteronomy 28:10, where Moses describes the extraordinary consequences, the impact, of the perception that the Jewish people is holy: "And all the peoples of the earth shall see that the name of the Eternal is called upon you, and they shall be in awe of you." The simple meaning of this verse is that when the nations of the world perceive the holiness of the Jewish people, they will sense that the very name of God is actualized within the Jews, and therefore they—those other nations—will experience awe. What, then, is the connection between holiness and the name of God?

The verses above have taught us that one of the central components of achieving holiness is "walking in the ways of God." Writing about this commandment, Maimonides says:

> The eighth *mitzvah* is that we are commanded to emulate blessed God to the best of our ability. The source of this commandment is God's statement…"And you shall walk in God's ways" (Deuteronomy 28:9). This commandment is repeated in the verse, "to walk in all of God's ways" (Deuteronomy 11:22). This is explained in the words of the Sifrei (Eikev): "Just as God is called merciful, so too you must be merciful. Just as God is called kind, so too you must be kind. Just as God is called righteous, so too you must be righteous. Just as God is called pious, so too you must be pious." This commandment is also repeated in the verse, "Walk after the Eternal your God" (Deuteronomy 13:5). This too is explained as emulating the good deeds and fine attributes that are used to allegorically describe our exalted God, who is immeasurably exalted over everything.[2]

The basis of the passage in the *midrash halakhah* quoted by Maimonides is Exodus 34:5–8, which informs us that the "ways of God" are manifest in God's names. In that passage, when Moses requests to be shown God's presence, God responds by indicating that while Moses cannot directly see God, the divine relational qualities can be revealed to Moses—which God then does by reciting the divine attributes, which embody those relational virtues. Maimonides further elaborates on this matter:

> We are commanded to walk in these intermediate paths—and they are good and straight paths—as it says, "And you shall walk in God's ways" (Deuteronomy 28:9). [Our sages] taught [the following] explanation of this *mitzvah*: Just as God is called gracious, you shall be gracious; just as God is called merciful, you shall be merciful; just as God is called holy, you shall be holy. In a similar manner, the prophets called God by other names: "slow to anger," "abundant in kindness," "righteous," "just," "perfect," "almighty," "powerful," and the like. [They did so] to inform us that these are good and just paths. A person is obligated to accustom oneself to these paths and [to try to] resemble God to the extent of one's ability. Since the Creator is called by these terms and they make up the middle path, which we are obligated to follow, this path is called "the path of God." This is [the heritage] that our ancestor Abraham taught his descendants, as it says: "For I have known him, that he will command his descendants...to keep the path of God" (Genesis 18:19).[3]

What all of this suggests is that the divine mandate of holiness to the Jewish people requires two dimensions of human response. It requires obedience to God's commandments, and it also requires the acquisition of noble personal virtues in imitation of the divine qualities revealed in the Torah itself, through their being embedded in the divine attributes (*middot*). Then, to understand the meaning of the holiness of God, we need to understand the divine attributes, and the virtuous qualities that they reflect. Those virtues are the underlying foundation and purpose of the commandments of the Torah—so that through their performance the virtues themselves will be actualized in the real world. Those virtuous qualities are in turn embodied and reflected in the dimensions of symbolic times, persons, objects, and places, as vessels or instruments through which the consciousness of those virtues is maintained and transmitted.

We need then to comprehend three layers of holiness. First, we need to understand the relational qualities that constitute the meaning of the holiness of God. Second, we need to understand how doing *mitzvot* constitutes the actualization of those same virtues in daily life, for the individual and for the society of which he or she is a part. And third, we need to examine the process by which the Jewish religious symbols in which those virtues are embodied may alert us to, and instill within us, the aspiration to partner with God in spreading those virtues and enabling us to transmit them to future generations.

The Names of God as Virtues and Their Actualization in Law

We will begin with an analysis of the *middot* of God declared in Exodus 34:6–7. There is much debate as to precisely which of the words of these verses constitute the traditional count of thirteen divine attributes. There is also much debate concerning how to accurately translate and interpret the varied divine qualities suggested in these names. The following is an attempt at one possible understanding of the individual qualities and of the set as a whole:

> And the Eternal passed by before him, and proclaimed: "Adonai, Adonai, God, merciful and gracious, long-suffering and abundant in goodness, and truth; keeping mercy unto the thousandth generation, forgiving iniquity and transgression and sin, and acquitting…"[4]

Now, the same passage with the names and attributes numbered:

> And the Eternal passed by before him, and proclaimed:
> 1. Adonai,
> 2. Adonai,
> 3. God,
> 4. merciful and
> 5. gracious,
> 6. long-suffering and

7. abundant in goodness and
8. truth;
9. keeping mercy unto the thousandth generation,
10. forgiving iniquity
11. and transgression
12. and sin, and
13. acquitting...

Name #1: _Adonai_ The first divine name is the Tetragrammaton, YHVH (_yod-hei-vav-hei_), pronounced as _Adonai_ and often translated as "Lord" (although generally rendered as "Eternal" in this volume). It represents the value of productivity—of being productive in the material world. In Genesis 1:1–2:3, the story of creation in seven days, the deity is identified by the generic name _elohim_, meaning "God." The Tetragrammaton, the four-letter name of God (YHVH), appears for the first time in the Torah in Genesis 2:4, in the compound form _YHVH elohim_, "Adonai God," meaning "the elohim (i.e., deity, God) whose name is Adonai (i.e., the Eternal)." That identification of God by the name "Eternal" then appears again in verses 7, 8, 9, and 15. In each of those five appearances, the name is specifically joined with a verb describing the divine actions in producing the material world. Thus, "the Eternal made," "the Eternal formed," "the Eternal planted," "the Eternal made grow," and finally "the Eternal took the man and put him into the Garden of Eden, to work it and to protect it."

Imitation of this divine value would demand that a person be productive in the material world. It is then not accidental that the human is placed in the Garden of Eden "to work it and to protect it," and that he is granted a mate with whom to procreate—since the productive transformation of the earth, and the re-production of further generations of humans, are the paradigmatic realms of human productivity in imitation of the Divine.

Name # 2: _Adonai_ The second divine name is a repetition of the Tetragrammaton, YHVH, which here represents the value of interdependence. This meaning of the divine name is manifest in the second use of the word YHVH as the name of God, as it appears in Genesis 2:5: "No shrub of the field was yet in the earth, and no herb of the field had yet sprung up; for the Eternal, God, had not caused it to rain upon the earth, and there was not a human to till the ground." This verse indicates that God's productive purpose in the material world was not to be achieved solely through the actualization of the divine will and word, but was dependent upon the establishment of interdependence, of partnership with humans. Thus the next two verses indicate that God watered the earth and then created the human as a living being, thus creating the conditions under which this interdependence could be actualized.

The imitation of this divine value of interdependence by humanity is immediately made manifest in the Torah in both its affirmative presence and then in its negation. The start of Genesis chapter 4 is the account of the intimate partnership between Adam and Eve, which results in reproduction (the birth of Cain and Abel); this is followed by the farmer Cain's rejection of an interdependent productive relationship with his shepherd brother Abel, in which he not only kills Abel but then goes on to deny that he bears any responsibility for him (for which he is then punished by God).

Name # 3: *El*   The divine name *El* represents the value of responsiveness to danger or distress. This name first appears in Genesis 14 where in rapid succession God is referred to as *El Elyon*, "Supreme God," four times—first in describing Melchizedek, king of Shalem, as "the priest of *El Elyon*" (Genesis 14:18), then twice by Melchizedek himself (Genesis 14:19-20), and finally once by Abraham in his response to the king (Genesis 14:22). The term *El* is opaque in its particular meaning. However, it is significant that not only does Abraham refer to God with this term, but moreover that God self-identifies with this term when first entering into formal covenant with Abraham, a few chapters hence: "When Abram was ninety-nine years old, the Eternal (YHVH) appeared to Abram and said to him: 'I am God Almighty (*El Shaddai*); walk before Me and be whole-hearted. And I will make my covenant between Me and you, and I will multiply you exceedingly" (Genesis 17:1-2).

What divine quality is manifest in the name *El*? Beginning with its earliest use in the blessings of Melchizedek and continuing to its later uses by Jacob, the term *El* seems always to reflect God's responsive use of divine power to rescue from danger. In the passage referred to above, Melchizedek recognizes that it was God as *El* whose power was manifest in the victory of Abraham, and Abraham recognizes that it was the power of God that made for his victory and therefore does not want to allow the King of Sodom to share in the glory. Later, Jacob refers to his desire to move his family to Beth-El where he "...will make an altar unto God (*El*), who answered me in the day of my distress and was with me in the way which I went" (Genesis 35:3).

The imitation of this divine value by people would be reflected in using human power to rescue others from danger and distress. The broad pattern of the various duties regarding rescue, which the Torah imposes upon Jews in their relationship to fellow Jews (and sometimes even in relation to those outside the covenantal community), is reflective of precisely this divine quality being actualized by persons in their relationship to others. It is not accidental then that the name El is used in the context of covenantal responsibilities (Deuteronomy 7:9), or that Moses particularly uses that name of God when he pleads with God to rescue his sister Miriam from the disease that afflicted her (Numbers 12:13).

Name # 4: *Rahum* The divine name *Rahum*, translated as "merciful," is obviously related to the word *rehem* (meaning "womb"), and it represents God's quality of extending unearned love. Strikingly, the words *rahum* and *rahamim* are used in the Torah only once in regard to human feelings. Otherwise, these words refer exclusively to God's own feelings of loving forgiveness, extended to the Jewish people—despite the fact that they have not acted in a manner that earned such feelings.[6] The one instance in which human *rahamim* is referenced occurs in Jacob's prayer upon sending Benjamin to Egypt with his brothers, when he prays that "God Almighty (*El Shaddai*) give you mercy (*rahamim*) before the man, that he may release unto you your other brother and Benjamin" (Genesis 43:14). Clearly the prayer for an experience of unearned love is a petition that God imbue a person with this divine quality. Indeed, the fulfillment of Jacob's prayer is directly indicated in a subsequent verse when Joseph, upon seeing his brother Benjamin, is overcome by fiery feelings of love (*nihm'ru rahamav*), a love that Benjamin has not earned through any prior interaction with Joseph; Joseph then flees the room to cry privately (Genesis 43:30).

The human imitation of this divine quality is self-evident: it is the cultivation of the capacity to feel loving care even for persons who have not earned it, who do not deserve such a loving response. To respond lovingly to one who deserves such a response by virtue of their prior conduct, or by virtue of the history of the prior relationship, would be an act of justice. The quality of *rahum* is distinctively applicable when justice would not require such conduct—that is, when it is fully a reflection of mercy.

Name #5: *Hannun* The divine name *Hannun*, meaning "gracious" or "compassionate," is an expression of God's virtue of empathy, the ability to share the feelings of joy and pain of another. The Torah provides a vivid example of God's embodiment of this virtue in Exodus 22:24–26: "If you lend money to My people, to the poor among you, do not act toward them as a creditor: exact no interest from them. If you take your neighbor's garment in pledge, you must return it to them before the sun sets. It is their only clothing, the sole covering for their skin; in what else shall they sleep? Therefore if they cry out to Me, I will hear, for I am compassionate (*hannun*)." A further expression of divine empathy is found in the divine declaration to Moses that God is aware of the suffering of the Jewish people in Egypt and intends to redeem them from their enslavement: "And the Eternal said: 'I have surely seen the affliction of My people...and have heard their cry...for I know their pains" (Exodus 3:7).

In both of these passages, God's "hearing" (just like God's "seeing" and "knowing") is an expression of God's own perception of the feelings of pain being experienced by the victims of oppression, which then leads God to act on their behalf. A most powerful indication of this empathy by God is expressed in Exodus 22:21–23: "You shall not oppress any widow or orphan. If you do afflict them, I will hear their outcry as soon as they cry out to Me. And My anger shall blaze forth and I will put you to the sword, and your own wives shall become widows and your children orphans."

The human imitation of this divine virtue of empathy is also demanded by the Torah. While God's empathy for suffering and oppression is not based on God's own experience of those states, there is divine awareness that for humans, empathy is significantly based on having themselves experienced suffering, or being deeply aware of the feelings associated with the oppression and affliction that they now observe others experiencing. Therefore, God's demands for empathy from the Jewish people often makes reference to their experience of enslavement. Thus, for example: "You shall not wrong a stranger or oppress him, for you were strangers in the land of Egypt" (Exodus 22:20). In six separate instances in the Torah, God's demand of empathy for the oppressed and the disadvantaged is justified by the assertion that the Jewish people need to have special feelings for such situations due to their own experience of oppression and enslavement in Egypt. No wonder then that the celebration of Passover requires that every individual Jew in every generation not only retell, but actually re-experience the enslavement of Egypt. It is only based on that virtual experience of oppression that the feeling of Jewish empathy for the oppressed can continue to be strong in every subsequent generation.

Name #6: _Erekh Apayim_ The divine name _Erekh Apayim_ describes the divine virtue of patience (forbearance), the capacity to postpone acting even in the face of strong emotions such as anger. The single instance in the Torah where God is described as actualizing this quality, described by this very phrase _erekh apayim_, is in the interaction between God and Moses in response to the sin of the spies as told in Numbers 14. God, furious over the refusal of the Jewish people to move directly to the conquest of the land of Canaan due to the frightening report of ten of the twelve spies, desires to destroy the entire people and to start over again by forming a new elect people out of Moses and his descendants (Numbers 14:11–12). Moses responds with a plea to God to forbear from doing so—not because the people do not deserve such punishment, but based on God's own best interests. Moses essentially makes three arguments in favor of God's forbearance (Numbers 14:13–19).

First, he argues that if God were to destroy the Jewish people immediately, the other nations of the world would conclude that God was powerless to actualize the divine will—that is, knowing that it would be impossible to achieve victory against the Canaanite nations and not wanting to suffer an ignominious defeat at their hands, God simply chose to destroy the Jews in the wilderness. Second, Moses suggests that such divine action would be an act of disloyalty toward God's covenantal partners, who had been publicly intimate with God and had been protected and shielded with such evident divine love. Third, Moses contends that if God were to forgive the Jews, it would demonstrate to the nations of the world that God's true power lies not in destructive punishment of wrongdoing (as in Egypt), but rather in merciful forbearance. It would show that true power is evident in control over anger, God's ability to be *erekh apayim*— that is, having the necessary patience to allow the Jewish people to evolve into a nation truly worthy of their covenantal relationship with God. God accedes to Moses petition and forgives the people, but will punish them in a manner that will avoid the negative and highlight the positive outcomes of divine forbearance by having the generation of weak-willed, rebellious adults who emerged from Egypt die out before attempting to bring the next generation into the land of Canaan (Numbers 14:20–24).

Human imitation of this divine virtue of patience or forbearance is demanded by many laws of the Torah, and it is often couched in terms resonant with the motives that Moses suggested as its basis. Thus, Leviticus 19:17–18 forbids acting vengefully in response to hatred, instead requiring loving chastisement. Acting thus is a manifestation that one is not powerless to achieve the desired end, and that hope for a restored relationship is not lost. It is imperative to partner control over the desire for instant gratification of negative feelings together with the demand for gaining control over the desire for instant gratification of positive feelings, because such action can easily undermine the covenantal commitments that one has with an intimate partner. Thus, for example, no leeway is allowed in the Torah for adulterous relationships. In similar manner, the Torah unequivocally deprives parents of the authority to take the lives of rebellious children—a power fully recognized in virtually every ancient legal system (and still preserved in some modern societies in the guise of "honor killings"). According to the Torah, parents can do no more than bring their children to a court for trial (Deuteronomy 21:18–20). Thus parental authority is manifest not in the power to punish, but rather in the power to control anger, to manifest patience in the hope that the child will be able to be properly redirected through the intervention of the legal system.

<u>Name #7: *Rav Hesed*</u> The divine name *Rav Hesed* is a compound phrase that presents God as acting to satisfy human needs (*hesed*) in a manner that exceeds reasonable expectations (*rav*). The act of *hesed*, as it appears in various relationships in the book of Genesis, bespeaks not only being with a person in his or her time of need, but also taking action in a manner that serves some fundamental human need: saving life (Genesis 19:19), finding a wife (24:12, 14, 27), enabling economic success (32:11), and causing a person in power to look favorably upon one in a disadvantaged state (39:21). In every one of these instances, the beneficiary of the action could not meet his own need without the affirmative act of *hesed* performed by the divine benefactor.

The addition of the adjective rav, reflecting the great magnitude of the kindness manifested by God, appears in the Torah only in the two instances where the phrase is used to characterize the great magnitude of divine kindness (Exodus 34:6 and Numbers 14:18). In all other instances, where the act of beneficence is performed by a person, or a divine messenger, the term *hesed* is used alone without the indication of its special magnitude.[7]

In regard to the duty of human imitation of this divine quality, it is not accidental that every manifestation of kindness described in Genesis as an act of *hesed* is identified by the Torah itself (or by rabbinic teaching) as a personal obligation resting upon every Jew. Thus the obligations to save life, enhance commercial success, facilitate marriages, enable the poor to achieve financial independence, bring peace between persons, and liberate slaves are each either considered as independent *mitzvot,* or are encompassed within the biblical command of "Love your neighbor as yourself" (Leviticus 19:18). The prophet Micah captures the centrality of the human imitation of this divine quality when he encapsulates the essence of God's expectations of the Jewish people as including (in part) the duty "... to love *hesed*" (Micah 6:8).

Name #8: *Emet* The divine name *Emet* represents God's virtue of trustworthiness. The word *emet* appears in the Torah with two different meanings. One usage is to describe the accuracy of some information pertaining to an event, confirming that the information is "true." Thus, when the Torah records the law of destruction of an idolatrous city, it requires that there be evidentiary certainty of the fact that idols had been worshipped: "Then you shall inquire and make search and ask diligently; and behold if it be truth (*emet*) and the thing certain, that such abomination was wrought in your midst..." (Deuteronomy 13:15; the same phrase appears in Deuteronomy 17:4). Similarly, in regard to an accusation of a bride's lack of chastity, the Torah says, "If this thing [i.e., the accusation] be true (*emet*)..." (Deuteronomy 22:20). The second usage of the word *emet* is to describe a personal virtue, that one is "trustworthy." Thus, Jethro advises Moses that judges need to be *anshei emet* (Exodus 18:21)—that is, trustworthy men, "truthful" in the sense of having the virtue of personal integrity, who can be trusted to be honest in administering justice. Rather than focusing on the accuracy ("truthfulness") of a past event, this sense of emet is focused on the inner quality of a person. When the Torah identifies one of the names of God as *Emet* (Exodus 34:6), the word is intended not to suggest the objective "truth" of God, but rather that an essential divine virtue is God's trustworthiness—that is, God's honesty and integrity.

That humans are obligated to imitate this divine quality is evident in the multitude of biblical laws that regulate the requirements of honesty and integrity in both commercial and interpersonal relationships. It is not accidental that the consummate divine command to the Jewish people, "You shall be holy, for I, the Eternal your God, am holy" (Leviticus 19:2), is soon followed by:

> You shall not steal; neither shall you deal falsely, nor lie to one another. You shall not swear by My name falsely so as to profane the name of your God; I am the Eternal. You shall not oppress your neighbor, nor rob them; the wages of a hired servant shall not remain with you all night until the morning. You shall not curse the deaf, nor put a stumbling-block before the blind, but you shall fear your God; I am the Eternal. (Leviticus 19:11–14)

These verses (and many others) attempt not only to command honest behavior, but also to cultivate the inner quality of *emet*, integrity and trustworthiness. It is precisely this point that the sages emphasized when they asked why this particular passage concludes with the phrase "but you shall fear your God." They responded by noting that with so many forbidden activities, the underlying motive of the actor is unknown and therefore human prosecution is often impossible. People need, therefore, to be reminded that God knows what our motives are, and so we need to exercise control over our behavior based on our cultivation of proper inner virtues even when they will not be enforced by human agents.[8] The importance of human imitation of this divine virtue of trustworthiness is perhaps nowhere more forcefully expressed than in the command: "That which goes out of your lips, you shall observe and do" (Deuteronomy 23:24).

Name #9: *Notzeir Hesed La-alafim*   This divine name, "keeping mercy unto the thousandth generation," is an expression of the virtue of gratitude. The nature of this gratitude can best be understood through the only two other instances in the Torah in which a form of the Hebrew root *nun-tzadi-reish* is used. When Moses, toward the end of his life, describes the intensity of the covenant between God and the Jewish people, he reminds the people that God, as it were, "… found him [Jacob—that is, the Jewish people] in a desert region, in an empty howling waste. God encircled him, watched over him, and guarded him (*yitzrenhu*) as the pupil of God's eye" (Deuteronomy 32:10). It is striking that the Jewish people's willingness to remain in the desert for forty years with God is described by the prophet Jeremiah as *hesed ne'urayikh*, "the kindness of your youth," which God gratefully remembers to their merit (Jeremiah 2:2). It is thus the ancient *hesed* of the Jewish people that continues to elicit God's gratitude (which is manifest in specific behaviors) for "a thousand years." The divine virtue of gratitude, recognizing the loyalty of the Jewish people, is reflected in a slightly different form in the next chapter of Deuteronomy. In blessing the tribes, Moses refers to Levi as *ish hasidekha* (Deuteronomy 33:8), and he then goes on to relate that the tribe of Levi was able to disregard the natural love of their fellows in order to execute God's justice against those who had worshipped the golden calf. They thus placed their loyalty to God over their loyalty to their fellows, says Moses: *et b'rit'kha yin'tzoru*, "they guarded Your covenant" (Deuteronomy 33:10). Here, loyalty to God is considered an act of *hesed*, which in turn elicits divine gratitude as manifest in the eternal appointment of the tribe of Levi as the teachers, leaders, and priests of the Jewish nation (Deuteronomy 33:10–11). These two examples show that when humans act with *hesed* toward God, divine gratitude in remembrance of that *hesed* will be manifest for many generations.

The mandate for humans to imitate this divine quality of gratitude is deeply embedded in the Torah. After years of Egyptian enslavement and oppression of the Jews, it must have come as an extraordinary shock to the people to hear Moses declare in the name of God, "you shall not abhor an Egyptian, for you were strangers in their land" (Deuteronomy 23:8). That same verse also forbade enmity toward the Edomites, despite the history of antagonism between them and the Israelites, "for he is your kinsman." Loyalty toward kinsmen, and gratitude for ancient kindnesses, are essential expressions of the imitation of this divine quality.

To these texts one must certainly add the central nature of the peace offering (sh'lamim) in the sacrificial practice. Repeatedly in the Torah we are commanded to bring offerings to God in expression of gratitude for the goodness that we experience in life—for both personal occasions (such as the birth of a child, rescue from great danger, or a successful harvest) as well as for the expression of national celebration of historic moments.[9] Certainly the later rabbinic transformation of these offerings into liturgical expressions, as blessings of gratitude toward God at the culmination of every prayer service, was an embodiment of the essential nature of our duty to integrate the divine virtue of gratitude into our own personalities.

Name #10: _Nosei Avon_ The divine name _Nosei Avon_, "forgiving iniquity," is a compound name in which both Hebrew words are of great significance. The word _nosei_ appears frequently in the Torah with the related meanings of "to bear," "to tolerate," or "to forgive." Its first appearance is, in fact, in conjunction with the word _avon_. When God confronts Cain about having killed his brother Abel and then metes out punishment for that crime, Cain responds by asking a rhetorical question: "_Gadol avoni mi-n'so?_ Is my sin too great for You to bear/forgive?" (Genesis 4:13, as per Rashi's comment to the verse). God does forgive Cain and mitigates the punishment (although it is not cancelled altogether): Cain is provided with protection so that the prescribed penalty of exile—that is, permanent wandering— will not become a death penalty (Genesis 4:15). Cain apparently had expected that divine forgiveness would result in God simply disregarding the crime, but he was mistaken. Divine forgiveness still required accountability of Cain for his action, but it also ensured that Cain would have another opportunity (albeit as a wanderer) to make a new life for himself, armed with the wisdom that he had now acquired. What, then, is the meaning of the word *nosei*? In five other instances in the Torah, it is clear that this word means that one will bear responsibility for one's conduct. The phrase *tissa alav heit* means "he will bear responsibility for the action as a sin" (Leviticus 19:17, 22:9; Numbers 18:22, 32; Deuteronomy 15:9). Thus the word *nosei* bears the dual meanings of both "forgiving" and "holding accountable."

We will now explore the word *avon*, in order to establish its meaning with greater clarity. As discussed above, this noun is used by Cain to describe his sin, which is homicide. Strikingly, elsewhere in the Torah, the word *avon* is only used to describe other crimes of a particularly grave nature. It is the word used in conjunction with adultery (Numbers 5:15) as well as various incestuous relationships (Leviticus 20:19), as well as with idolatry (Exodus 20:5) and other forms of inappropriate conduct toward the sanctuary and its material accouterments (Exodus 28:38, 43). Moreover, Judah describes the theft of Joseph's enchanted cup as an avon (Genesis 44:16). The word avon is used to describe the sin of acting dismissively (*b'keri*) toward God (Leviticus 26:27, 40). And, in an unclear passage, the unspecified sins of the Amorites, which will eventually justify God's subjecting them to destruction at the hands of the Israelites, are also referred to as *avon* (Genesis 15:16).

The particularly grave set of sins referred to as *avon* appears to be almost perfectly consonant with the set of fundamental laws that the sages termed the Seven Noachide Laws, which they understood to represent the will of God for all of humanity. These include prohibitions against murder, idolatry, theft, and sexual immorality (including adultery and incest)—all of which, as we have seen above, are described with the word *avon*. The Noachide Laws also require the establishment of a court system, to ensure basic standards of justice, and we may reasonably propose that the crime of the Amorites (referenced above) was precisely their failure to create such a just society. Moreover, the further Noachide Law prohibiting blasphemy, which is the despicable action of cursing God, may be precisely what is abrogated by the inappropriate behavior toward God and the divine precincts, as referenced above. The only Noachide Law that we have not seen described by the Torah as *avon* is the prohibition of eating the limb torn from a living animal—an act of exceptional cruelty that was almost universal in antiquity. Thus, the word *avon* might be the Torah's term to describe the breach of fundamental, universal human standards of moral conduct (which are, in turn, laid out by the sages in the Noachide Laws).

What does it mean, then, to say that God is *nosei avon*? Building on the insights above, we may suggest that while God will exact punishment for degraded behavior and will hold individuals (and nations) accountable for their actions, the promise of divine forgiveness will always be held out as well, with the assurance that a second chance will be offered so that the sinner can pursue a better, more noble path. This is, in fact, exactly what the Torah tells us happened, every time that Israel sinned and God forgave them. After they made the golden calf, God forgave the people, just as Moses asked—but insisted that those individuals who actually worshipped the calf be punished, while the nation as a whole would have a renewed opportunity to make a new future for themselves in the land that God had promised to their ancestors (Exodus 32:31–33:2). When the people were swayed by the report of the ten spies and refused to enter the promised land, God did in fact forgive them (as Moses pleaded)—yet still exacted punishment of the entire nation by requiring them to wander in the desert for forty years, and only thereafter allowing the new generation to enter the land (Numbers 14:20–31). And this is also the basic pattern of the *toheikhah*, the national chastisement that spells out the consequences that will ensue if the people forsakes the covenant: God warns that there will be destruction and exile, but God will also forgive and provide a future opportunity to choose a better path, by ultimately restoring the people to the land (Leviticus 26:14–45).

Thus the core meaning of this tenth name of God, *Nosei Avon*, is that God demands accountability for human behavior, but divine forgiveness will also provide people with a second chance to redirect the course of their lives toward the fulfillment of the divine will. That is: even after despicable human conduct (*avon*), God will hold accountable but also forgive (*nosei*). God demands that we too act in this manner, and so this intersection of the twin ideas of accountability and forgiveness is built into the very structure of the Jewish judicial process. For example: a thief who is unable to repay a loss caused to a victim may be sold into indentured servitude, but the term of service is limited to six years and, in order to ensure that the individual will be able to make a transition to a new and honest life after the period of servitude, the owner is obligated to provide him with a grubstake upon manumission (Deuteronomy 15:13–14, in light of Exodus 21:37–22:2).

Name #11: *Nosei Pesha* The divine name *Nosei Pesha*, "forgives transgression," carries forward the central elements of the preceding name by incorporating the word nosei, which (as we have seen) means that God both forgives and holds accountable. The distinctiveness of this particular name, then, must be embedded in the distinct meaning of the word pesha. This term is used only twice in the book of Genesis: once spoken by Jacob and once alleged to have been spoken by Jacob. The first instance occurs when Jacob indignantly defends his own integrity, after Laban accuses him of having stolen the latter's household idols: "And Jacob was angry...and he said to Laban, 'What is my transgression (*pishi*)? What is my sin, that you have pursued me?'" (Genesis 31:36). Jacob continues with a lengthy speech, avowing that he had always honored his work-responsibilities toward Laban, even going beyond what he was duty-bound to do. In the second instance, Joseph's brothers address him after the death of their father, fearful that he will now take revenge for the fact they had sold him into slavery. They allege that Jacob had instructed them to deliver the following message: "Thus you shall say to Joseph, 'Please forgive, I beg you, the transgression (*pesha*) of your brothers and their sin, for they did you wrong'; and now, please forgive the transgression (*pesha*) of the servants of the God of your father. And Joseph wept when they spoke to him" (Genesis 50:17).

The distinctive element in the use of the word *pesha*, as illustrated by these two examples, is not primarily the gravity of the crime (as in the case of *avon*). Rather, it is the betrayal of a relationship that demands trust. In the first instance, Jacob understands Laban's accusation to intimate a breach of trust, both as a member of the family and as an employee. In the second instance, the brothers understand that they have betrayed the trust due to a brother. It is not surprising, then, that the few subsequent usages of the word *pesha* in the Torah that are related to specific wrongdoing also have to do with betrayal of trust. In Exodus 22:8, the term *pesha* is used to describe loss or damage to a person's property that has been entrusted to someone else's care. In Exodus 23:20–21, Israel is warned not to betray the messenger appointed by God to lead them into the promised land.

But, in the face of betrayal of trust, how can forgiveness still be possible? The passage about the brothers' speech to Joseph provides us with insight as to how people—or God, for that matter—might grant forgiveness even in the face of betrayal. The verse quoted above (Genesis 50:17) actually contains two separate pleas for forgiveness: the first by Jacob and the second by the brothers themselves. Jacob's plea is based simply on the fact they are all brothers, part of the same family. The plea for forgiveness by the brothers, however, is based instead on the assertion that they are all common servants of the God of their father. In Jacob's plea, it is the sheer power of the relationship between family members—the breach of which would generate fury at having been betrayed—that can serve to impel forgiveness, and the consequent opportunity to restore the familial relationship to its proper covenantal commitment. In the plea of the brothers, the fact that they all share a covenant with the common ancestral God is determinative; this serves as both the source of intense anger at betrayal, and also as the source of reconciliation and a second chance, made possible through forgiveness.

Why, then, does God forgive sins of *pesha*, sins of betrayal of trust? No doubt, it is due to a combination of the above reasons—which we have seen above operating in the realm of human relationships, but is just as incisive in the realm of the divine. Foremost, God is party to a covenant with us; and that covenant is designed to achieve a common mission, a common vision for the world, and achieving that reality depends on the divine-human partnership. This is already intimated in the first and second names of God, *Adonai Adonai*. As indicated earlier, the first of those names describes God's purposefulness in creation, and the second name indicates the further quality of interdependence between God and humanity in achieving the purposes of creation. Thus the divine-human covenant (later: the divine-Jewish covenant) is motivated by God's own vision for the world.

But what quality would lead God to forgive and try again, not only after serious misconduct but even after behavior that betrays the covenantal relationship itself? The Talmud asserts: "In every place where you find manifestation of the mightiness of God, there you find also manifestation of divine humility" (B. Megillah 31a). It is the divine quality of humility that overcomes God's pride and allows God to forgive us and to allow us another chance at achieving our joint covenantal mission in the world (even while still holding us accountable for our misdeeds). Thus, the divine name *Nosei Pesha* carries further the quality of *nosei avon* insofar as God not only forgives grave sins, but does so even for sins that manifest betrayal of the covenantal relationship with God—and this is due to God's additional quality of humility.

The human imitation of this divine quality of humility—generating forgiveness despite betrayal—is frequently implied in laws of the Torah. For example, when the Israelites sought to pass peacefully through the land of Edom (and even offered to pay for whatever goods they would need while there), the Edomites refused to allow them to do so (Numbers 20:14–21). Despite this hostile conduct, the Torah commands: "You shall not loathe an Edomite, for he is your brother" (Deuteronomy 23:8). The very fact that Edom is Israel's "brother" made their refusal such a disappointing betrayal of the trust that should have existed between two related nations. Yet,

God demands that we act with humility and not harbor a grudge against the Edomites, but rather forgive them and allow for the possibility of an improved relationship in the future. In like manner, when an individual is personally offended by the conduct of another, the Torah expects an amicable resolution of the injured feelings: rather than exacting vengeful retribution, one should chastise the wrongdoer and attempt to secure an apology (or at least have the opportunity to clear the air)—so that following forgiveness, it will be possible to restore a caring relationship (Leviticus 19:17–18). Here too, the critical quality to be demonstrated by the hurt party is humility: one cannot be so personally offended by the betrayal that one would be willing to simply terminate the relationship. Rather, humility must lead to forgiveness, providing a second chance, while also holding the wrongdoer accountable for his or her conduct.

It is not accidental that the Torah informs us that "the man Moses was most humble of all persons living on earth" (Numbers 12:3) precisely at the moment when he had been betrayed by his own sister and brother. As God reprimanded them for their behavior and punished Miriam with a skin disease, Moses pleaded with God to heal her. It was precisely Moses' humility that enabled him to forgive immediately. God reminds Moses, however, that that even in the face of forgiveness, accountability is essential; therefore, God imposed upon Miriam the punishment of seven days' exclusion from the camp. The biblical narrative thus lays out both God's own virtue, and the way in which humans are expected to imitate that virtue.

Name #12: _Nosei Hatta·ah_ The divine name _Nosei Ḥatta·ah_, "forgives sin," is the third time that we see divine forgiveness juxtaposed with holding individuals accountable for their behavior. In this instance, the forgiveness is for action characterized as _ḥeit_ or _ḥatta·ah_. What do these terms mean? How does _ḥata·ah_ differ from avon and pesha, and what divine characteristic is necessary in order for this quality to be manifest?

First, what is _ḥeit_ or _ḥatta·ah_? The word _ḥeit_, both as a noun and in its related verbal forms, is actually the most common word used in the Torah to describe sinful or wrongful action. It is used to describe the most serious of crimes, such as adultery (Genesis 20:6), homicide (Genesis 42:22), and idolatry (Exodus 32:30), as well as unspecified crimes of sufficient magnitude to warrant the total destruction of Sodom (Genesis 18:20). And it is also used as a generic term to describe any crime at all (Leviticus 4:3), as well as both serious and less serious acts of rebellion (Numbers 21:7; 22:34). The term ḥeit is used to describe both intentional and unintentional wrongdoing (Exodus 9:34 and Leviticus 5:15, respectively). It encompasses both wrongdoing against God (Exodus 10:16) and against fellow humans (Leviticus 5:21). The term can point to wrongdoing performed by a common person (Leviticus 5:1), a gentile king (Genesis 20:6), an anointed priest (Leviticus 4:4), a prince of the Israelites (Leviticus 4:22), or even the legislature (Leviticus 4:13). Compounding the complexity of the word ḥeit, it should be noted that sometimes the word appears to be used not for the sin itself, but rather for the punishment due for the sins (Genesis 20:9 and Exodus 32:34). And as happens (albeit rarely) with other words in the Torah, the same Hebrew root can, in some instances, be used to connote precisely the opposite—that is, the process of being cleansed from the stain of the sin (Leviticus 14:52 and Numbers 19:19).

Given the broad range of meaning associated with this word, it should come as no surprise to discover that the very first time that the Torah speaks of human wrongdoing, it is with a word derived from this root. There is no general word for "sin" used in the biblical passage recounting the misdeeds of Adam and Eve that results in their expulsion from the Garden of Eden. However, God's warning to Cain—containing a personification of sin—reads as follows: "… sin (ḥattat) lies at the door; and to you shall be its desire, and yet you may rule over it" (Genesis 4:7). This generic usage of the word ḥattat (from the same root as ḥeit) stands in stark contrast to the term avon, by which Cain refers to his own crime of fratricide a few verses hence (Genesis 4:13). As we have seen, the Torah continues to use avon for particularly grave sins that are universal; similarly, the Torah reserves the use of the term pesha for a particular set of crimes, which involve betrayal of trust in a relationship. This leaves the term *heit* (and its related forms) available for use in the broadest generic sense to encompass all forms of wrongdoing.

If we have already learned, from the prior divine attributes, that God forgives (albeit with accountability) sins of the magnitude of *avon* and *pesha*, then why is it necessary to add this third name to the series? Is it not self-evident that if God forgives both grave universal sins (*avon*) and sins of betrayal (*pesha*), then potentially milder sins (*heit*, *hattat*, *hatta·ah*) would certainly be forgiven? Understanding the former two names helps us realize that God does forgive wrongdoing, and that the quality of humility even allows God also to forgive crimes involving personal betrayal; but what does this third name add to our understanding of divine qualities? Is there some other divine quality that is being suggested, which would only be manifest in God's forgiveness of *heit*?

On two separate occasions early in the book of Genesis, it appears as if God despairs of the capacity of humans to achieve and sustain goodness. The first instance is in the passage just cited, when God acknowledges to Cain that the temptation to do evil is ever-present (Genesis 4:7). The second instance is after the flood, when Noah emerges from the ark and offers sacrifices, and God responds by saying: "I will not again curse the ground any more due to humankind, for the imagination of the human heart is evil from youth; nor will I again destroy every living thing, as I have done" (Genesis 8:21). In this latter instance, God may be despairing specifically because of Noah's violence against animals (a plausible suggestion, since it was violence—albeit violence by humans against other humans—that had prompted God to destroy the world in the first place). Alternatively, God may be recognizing that while human evil cannot be eliminated, it might at least be balanced by expressions of gratitude in recognition of divine power and goodness. In either case, God is determined to go forward with the experiment of seeing whether humans with free will can be brought into partnership with the Divine, in moving toward a more perfected world. God remains filled with hope.

It is this divine quality of hope that makes it both necessary and possible for God to forgive the broad range of wrongful conduct that is, as it were, the norm of human existence—which needs to be governed and moderated, but which can never be fully extirpated. It is this same quality of hope that needs to be imitated by every parent—ever hopeful of inculcating in one's children basic norms of moral conduct, but at the same time fully aware that one's own moral commitments are not automatically passed on to one's offspring. It is precisely for this reason that the Torah needed to mandate the teaching of Torah as a parental responsibility (Deuteronomy 6:7), and needed to create a national obligation to assure the exposure of all citizens to the values and the laws embodied in the Torah (Deuteronomy 31:12). Neither individuals nor society as a whole can lose hope in the potential for goodness that is contained within every human being, despite the understanding that temptation and failure will always be present. Thus, the distinctive characteristic of this twelfth name of God, *nosei hata·ah*, inheres in the quality of hope—which yields the divine capacity for forgiveness, even of the routine sins and wrongdoing reflected by the terms *heit* and *hata·ah*.

Name # 13: *Nakeih*   The thirteenth of the divine names is a matter of substantial dispute among commentators. Maimonides considers the entire latter part of this verse to be a single divine attribute, which is the only one of the thirteen that is not a characteristic of mercy. He reads Exodus 34:7 as: "[God] will by no means clear the guilty, but will visit the iniquity of the ancestors upon the descendants, upon the children's children to the third and fourth generations."[10] Nahmanides agrees with that understanding, but sees it as denoting a quality of mercy: God will not forgive the sinner, but will instead spread out the punishment over many generations as an act of mercy toward the wrongdoer.[11] In yet a third approach, Samson Raphael Hirsch reads the first part of the statement ("yet remitting nothing") as a separate divine quality of mercy, because it refers to a sinner who fails to repent—thereby implying that with complete repentance, God forgives fully.[12] This understanding is also implied in the writings of Recanati,[13] and is in conformity with the traditional mode of public reading of this passage in the synagogue on fast days during the Torah service, when the reader pauses after the word *v'nakeih*—indicating that God does indeed pardon when repentance has taken place. This allows the latter part of the verse to be read in reference to a sinner who does not repent, in regard to whom "[God] does not forgive, but will visit the iniquity of the parents upon the children..." While these readings differ from each other, they all share an understanding that the thirteenth divine name is a quality of mercy related to forgiveness. But what precisely does this name mean?

The divine name *Nakeih* moves us beyond the qualities of forgiveness and accountability, implicit in the preceding three names, to that of pardon in the framework of justice. The most frequent meaning of the word *naki* (and its associated root, *nun-kof-hei*) in the Torah is "innocent." If the suspected adulteress emerges healthy from the ordeal of the bitter waters, she is thereby deemed to have been innocent (*v'nik'tah*, Numbers 5:28). The court is adjured not to put to death a *naki*, an innocent person (Exodus 23:7), but to be sure to avenge the shedding of the blood of a *naki*, an innocent victim.[14]

However, the very earliest use of this term in the Torah is in the story of Abraham's servant finding a wife for Isaac, and in that context it has a slightly different meaning. The servant asks Abraham what to do if he finds a woman who refuses to return to Canaan with him: should he bring Isaac to Ḥaran? Abraham responds vehemently in the negative, but then takes account of the servant's concern, reassuring him: "If the woman does not consent to come back with you, then you will be relieved (*v'nikkita*) of this oath to me" (Genesis 24:8). The servant repeats this usage twice more, in his subsequent report to Rebecca's family concerning the oath that Abraham imposed upon him: "Then you will be relieved (*tinnakeh*) of my oath; if you come to my family and they do not allow you [to take her]; you shall be relieved (*naki*) of my oath" (Genesis 24:41). In two additional instances, the word naki also seems to mean to be relieved of responsibilities. A man newly married is to be *naki*, relieved of all communal responsibilities (including military service in discretionary wars), for the entire first year of his marriage (Deuteronomy 24:5). Also, the two and a half tribes who desired to remain on the eastern side of the Jordan were told that they must share in the national responsibility of the conquest of the land of Canaan: if they would enter the land and battle with their kinsmen, they could later return to the eastern side of the Jordan and be reunited with their families there. If they fulfill this condition, Moses tells them that they would then be *n'kiyyim*, relieved of their responsibilities both to God and to the rest of the Jewish people (Numbers 32:22).

Of these two related meanings—"innocent" and "relieved"— how are we to understand the use of *nakeih* as a quality of mercy? It would seem that it cannot refer to innocence, since that is a quality of justice, not of mercy. On the other hand, to grant pardon to one who has committed a crime and then repented, thus mitigating the full extent of the punishment that would have otherwise been meted out, is a quality of mercy within the framework of seeing justice done. And this is exactly the meaning of the talmudic teaching of Rabbi Elazar that most commentators rely upon, and which is reflected in our discordant reading of the verse on fast days. But if the preceding three divine attributes spoke to accountability as well as forgiveness, then what element of punishment could still be pardoned? And how is this quality of mercy to be enacted by humans? In the divine admonition (*tokheihah*) of Leviticus 26, and again in that of Deuteronomy 29–30, it is clear that the national rebellion of the Jewish people against God's covenant with them warrants the most dire and severe punishment. But in each case, there is divine reassurance that God will not completely and totally withdraw from the covenant. Instead, God will await the people's repentance. When that occurs, God will accept their return and will restore the divine presence among them (Leviticus 26:40–45; Deuteronomy 30:1–10). Divine pardon thus effects restoration of God's presence within the Jewish nation, bringing to an end the period of divine hiddenness (*hesteir panim*).

The human analogue to this divine quality is treated at length in the Tamud (B. Yoma 87a–b), and then codified in detail by

Maimonides (M.T. Hilkhot Teshuvah 2:9–11). It is reported there that for any wrongdoing committed against a person, repentance is not complete until the sinner both compensates the victim for the loss suffered and also appeases the person wronged—and gains forgiveness from the wronged party. Rambam adds: "It is forbidden for a person to be cruel and not to be appeased. Rather, one should be easy to appease but difficult to anger; and at the moment that a sinner pleads to be forgiven, one ought to forgive wholeheartedly and with a willing spirit. Even if one suffered from much anguish and wrongdoing, one should not take revenge in actions nor revenge in words" (Hilkhot Teshuvah 2:10). Rambam does not quote the end of the biblical verse that prohibits the varied forms of revenge, but those words are of critical importance to us: "... and you shall love your neighbor as yourself" (Leviticus 19:18). The role of a human pardon, like the role of divine pardon, is to overcome the alienation between the wrongdoer and the wronged party—to restore the covenantal love that needs to exist between God and the Jewish people, as well as among individual members of the Jewish people. That alienation is the consequence of (or: the punishment for) crime or sin, but it can be overcome by proper repentance, and the subsequent pardon that results from appeasement of the wronged party after just compensation has been made.

<u>In summary</u>: divine holiness is the set of thirteen qualities of mercy made manifest in God's relationship with the world. Human holiness emerges when people make those qualities part of their own personalities, and actualize those qualities through their behavior. The thirteen divine attributes, which reflect those qualities, are as follows:

1. The Tetragrammaton (YHVH), *Adonai* (often translated as "Lord" or "the Eternal"), is the value of productivity—of being purposefully productive in the material world.

2. Again, the Tetragrammaton (YHVH), *Adonai* (often translated as "Lord" or "the Eternal"), which here represents the value of interdependence.

3. *El*, "God," represents the value of responsiveness to the danger or distress of others.

4. *Raḥum*, "merciful," obviously related to the word *reḥem* (meaning "womb"), represents the quality of extending unearned love.

5. *Ḥannun*, "gracious" or "compassionate," is an expression of the virtue of empathy, the ability to share the feelings of joy and pain of another.

6. *Erekh Apayim*, "long-suffering," describes the virtue of patience (forbearance), the capacity to postpone acting even in the face of strong emotions such as anger.

7. *Rav Ḥesed*, "abundant in goodness," is a compound phrase that presents God as acting to satisfy human needs (*ḥesed*), in a manner that exceeds reasonable expectations (*rav*).

8. *Emet*, "truth," represents the virtue of trustworthiness—that is, having the qualities of honesty and integrity.

9. *Notzeir Ḥesed La-alafim*, "keeping mercy unto the thousandth generation," is an expression of the virtue of gratitude.

10. *Nosei Avon*, "forgiving iniquity," means that while God will exact punishment for degraded conduct (*avon*), God will also forgive—granting a second chance, in order to pursue a more noble path.

11. *Nosei Pesha*, "forgiving transgression," indicates that God bears that same quality of forgiving while still demanding accountability, but even in relation to sins that are rooted in and manifest personal betrayal of the covenantal relationship—and this is due to the additional divine quality of humility.

12. *Nosei Ḥata·ah*, "forgiving sin," represents the quality of hope, which makes it both necessary and possible for God to forgive (again, with accountability) the broad base of wrongful conduct that is, as it were, the norm of human existence—which needs to be governed and moderated but which can never be fully extirpated.

13. *Nakeih* moves beyond the qualities of forgiveness and accountability included in the preceding three names, to that of pardon in the framework of justice. God will await repentance and, when that occurs, the divine presence will be restored.

The Symbolic Embodiment of Holiness

I noted at the outset of this essay that aside from using the term *kadosh* to describe the virtues and values of God, the Torah also uses the term *kadosh* to denominate a broad series of entities in divergent realms within which normal human existence is experienced: the realms of time, persons, objects, and places. These latter references to holiness are not random, but appear in coherent parallel sets. It is to these sets that we will now turn our attention as a way of evaluating the way in which holiness is embodied in these symbolic vessels. We will examine the process by which the Torah embedded the divine virtues and values within Jewish religious symbols in order to alert us to, and instill within us, the aspiration to partner with God in actualizing those virtues, and enabling us to transmit them to future generations.

Layers of Holiness: Maimonides on the Meaning of *Mitzvot*

The manifestation of holiness in these realms suggests that the instances of holiness are actually educational instruments through which God transmits truths, virtues, and values that are to be integrated into the lives of God's human covenantal partners. This notion conforms to the approach taken by Maimonides in *The Guide to the Perplexed*, where he argues that:

The Torah as a whole aims at two things: the welfare of the soul and the welfare of the body. As to the welfare of the soul, it consists in people acquiring correct opinions according to their capacity. Some of these truths are set forth explicitly and some are set forth allegorically....As to the welfare of the body, it comes about through the proper management of the relations in which we live one to another. This we can attain in two ways: First, by removing all violence from our midst—that is to say, that every person does not do as they please, desire, and have the power to do; but every one of us does that which contributes toward the common welfare. Second, in the acquisition by every human being of moral qualities that are essential for life in society, so that the affairs of the society may be well ordered. (*Guide* III 27)

According to Maimonides, each commandment of the Torah serves one or more of three purposes. First, it may teach a fundamental truth about God or the world, or instruct as to what is false so that we do not lead our lives in the darkness of falsehood. For example, the Torah mandates that we believe in the absolute unity of God and in God's creation of the universe, because those are essential truths; and it explicitly forbids engaging in communication with the dead, because that is humanly impossible and is simply a fraud perpetrated to exploit naive people. A second purpose would be to regulate social conduct in consonance with fundamental social values designed to constrain people from injuring each other, and mandating their beneficial actions within society. Thus, for example, the Torah explicitly forbids murder, theft, and tale-bearing, while it mandates the rescue of endangered persons, the return of lost property, and the support of the poor and the stranger. A third purpose that underlies the laws of the Torah is the cultivation of noble personal qualities, which serve as the constant underpinnings of both of the previous purposes—since personal moral virtues are necessary to sustain and enhance moral social conduct, and they are essential as well to sustain the commitment to truth and to eradicate falsehood and exploitation.

But Maimonides has alerted us to the fact that these truths, virtues, and values are not only conveyed in the Torah explicitly;

they are often conveyed as well allegorically, in parables, or through rituals in which the truths, virtues, and values are embedded and expressed through symbolic actions. This proposition is essential for Maimonides' contention that no *mitzvah* is without purpose, that every law of the Torah is intended to have some human benefit (contrary to the position of some of his philosopher antecedents). He is then able, in the later chapters of Book III of *The Guide*, to spell out in substantial detail how both the practical laws of the Torah for human governance, as well as the ritual laws (which some others see as purely expressive of divine will—that is, they are absent any purpose other than to demonstrate human compliance and submission to the divine will), are in fact all expressions of divine wisdom about human nature. All of the laws thus serve the common set of purposes leading to the perfection of both body and soul.

It is in the spirit of this teaching that we need to understand that the careful layering of different expressions of holiness in time, persons, objects, and places are not just random phenomena, but are in fact part of the broader design through which the Torah's rituals related to holiness can reinforce for us the fundamental virtues and social values that inhere in the divine attributes.

Holiness of Time

The earliest appearance of the notion of holiness in the Torah is found at the very end of the story of creation, where we read: "God blessed the seventh day and made it holy" (Genesis 2:3). It is striking that despite the fact that this investment of holiness in the seventh day comes after the creation of man and woman, the humans themselves play no role whatsoever in this investment of holiness in time; nor is there any indication that this change in the nature of the seventh day is communicated to them. In fact, neither the Sabbath nor its holiness is mentioned again in the book of Genesis. It is only in the book of Exodus, when the Israelites are in the desert and God provides them with the manna, that Moses instructs them to collect a double portion of the manna on the sixth day instead of searching for it on the seventh day, for "…tomorrow is a solemn rest, a holy Sabbath unto the Eternal" (Exodus 16:23).

The implications then are clear. The holiness of the Sabbath is invested by God, without human participation, and is therefore absolute and inalienable. The Jewish people, according to the sages, are only commanded to verbally declare the fact of the holiness of the Sabbath, but they need not engage in any action that would imply that they are actually effecting its sanctification. Thus for the rabbis, the fourth commandment of the Decalogue, "Remember the Sabbath day to keep it holy" (Exodus 20:8), creates a legal duty only to make the appropriate verbal declarations of the holiness of the Sabbath at its inception (Kiddush) and at its exit (Havdalah). Neither that verse nor any other presumes to grant people the capacity to alter the innate holiness of the seventh day, which was invested in it by the declaration of God at the time of creation.

When the Torah later commands, "You shall observe the Sabbath, for it is holy unto you" (Exodus 31:14), it is clear that the Sabbath is time made holy by God, which humans need to observe—only, as it were, to bask in the glow of the divinely invested holiness. Even the rabbinically mandated action of lighting candles just prior to the inception of the Sabbath is clearly intended as a preparatory act in which the individual ritually marks the onset of the Sabbath, after which time no other materially productive labor (including the kindling of lights) will be permitted. But neither the action of kindling the lights, nor the blessing recited over the act that acknowledges its mandated character, are actions that actually invest the time itself with holiness. That investment of holiness was done once, by God, at the outset of creation. Humans have only the capacity to observe and rejoice in the gift of the Sabbath, but not to see themselves as the masters, the creators, of that holy time.

What divine name, what divine quality, is manifest in the performance of the commandments associated with the Sabbath?

The central element of the observance of the Sabbath resides in ritual inaction, in refraining from performing *m'lakhah*, labor (Exodus 20:10)—that is, not engaging in the material transformation of objects in a manner that reflects human power and control. As in all other instances of temporary withdrawal from normally permissible activities, the purpose of the withdrawal is definitely not to negate the significance of the abstained-from activity, nor is it a suggestion that the activity is in any way wrongful. Rather, such temporary withdrawals—such as not eating on Yom Kippur, or refraining from sexual intercourse during a women's menstrual period—are designed to confirm the essential human nature of the activity, and to provide a periodic withdrawal for the sake of evaluating the activity. Thus, refraining from productive labor on Shabbat involves the recognition that such purposeful work is in fact essential for every human being. But it is also critical to recognize that human productivity is itself a manifestation of imitating God, whose purposive productivity was (and remains) the very foundation of all material existence. Therefore, human productivity must be tested by determining whether it conforms to the divine purposes of integrity and human benefit that characterize God's own productive force in the world, thereby reflecting the influence of the first divine name—that is, God's own attribute of being purposely productive in the material world.

How different is the language of the Torah in regard to the holiness of the festivals. The Torah never refers to a divine act or speech through which the holiness of the festivals is invested, such as, "And God blessed the festival days and made them holy." Rather, the Torah repeatedly emphasizes that "these are the festivals of the Eternal, holy occasions, which you shall proclaim in their appointed season" (Leviticus 23:4; cf. also verse 2; emphasis added). God invested these dates with the potential for holiness, but the actualization of their holiness is contingent upon the festivals being proclaimed by humans at the appropriate time. In this manner, the rabbis understood that the actual investment of holiness in the festivals was dependent upon the Sanhedrin declaring the correct day to start the Hebrew month in which the festival would fall. Thus, the fifteenth of Nisan *could* be the holy day of Passover by divine determination, but no holiness would be invested in any actual day until the Sanhedrin declared which day would be the first of the month of Nisan. In consequence of that human declaration of Rosh Hodesh, the potential holiness of the fifteenth of that month came to be actualized in a specific day.

In contrast to the holiness of the Sabbath, which is absolute and inalienable, vested by God in every seventh day, the holiness of the festivals is the product of partnership between God and humans. The actualization of the divinely ordained potential for holiness of the dates of the festivals is contingent, and can occur only in consequence of the action of humans partnering with God to "proclaim" those holy days. The necessary proclamation was not an optional act on the part of the people; the central legislature (known most commonly as the Sanhedrin) was mandated to establish the calendar and proclaim the new moon, which would indicate the start of each new month. Thus, in this second layer of holiness of time, God invested a specific date with the potential for holiness, but then commanded human beings to act as partners with the Divine in actualizing that potential, by proclaiming the new month—thus effectuating the divine investment of holiness in a specific day.

This distinction between the two forms of holiness is further recognized by the sages, who saw significance in the fact that the mandate to rejoice (v'samaḥta, Deuteronomy 16:14) applies exclusively to the festivals, but not to the Sabbath. They further distinguish between the term simḥah, meaning rejoicing, and the term oneg, used by Isaiah (58:13) in reference to the Sabbath. They understood oneg to be of rabbinic authority, generating a less intense duty of happiness in the celebration of the Sabbath, as compared to the duty of simḥah created by the biblical mandate concerning the festivals. Despite the fact that the holiness of the Sabbath is derived exclusively from God, the joy generated by the festivals is indeed more intense, precisely because its holiness is derived from the partnership between God and people. The term simḥah seems to have been reserved in rabbinic usage for those contexts in which the character of the joy is shaped by partnership, rather than by the effort of a sole individual. It is not surprising, therefore, that the most prevalent term used to describe the joy of a wedding is not oneg, but rather *simḥah*—as it is a joy born of communal, rather than individual, effort. The term *simḥah* refers to the intense joy taken in the product of the joint effort of partners; the term oneg reflects the lesser joy experienced by an individual basking in the pleasurable benefits of the distinct and separate action of another. Thus, the Sabbath—despite its higher level of holiness—produces a lesser experience of joy, because it results from taking pleasure in what God has created for us, in which process we humans have played no essential productive role.

What divine name, what divine quality, is manifest in the observance of the festivals? Obviously, the overriding quality that inheres in this second layer of holiness in time is that of the second divine name, which represents God's value of interdependence. In contrast to the Sabbath, which commemorates God's own exclusive action, each one of the festivals commemorates either a historical event or a potential performance in which the partnership between persons and God is of the essence. This is an element that is common to the entire cycle of festivals; in addition, each of the festivals contains some additional reflection on a particular divine attribute that we symbolically enact on that distinctive festival.

In Passover, the interdependence between God and the Jewish people is clear from the outset. When Moses is sent to lead the people out of Egypt, God emphasizes repeatedly that he needs to bring the people along, and Moses repeatedly insists that the people will not follow him (Exodus 3:13–4:9). In fact, the midrash to Exodus 13:18 suggests that only one-fifth of the Jews chose to leave Egypt with Moses, as the rest lacked the faith to join in the Exodus.[15] That small fraction of the enslaved Israelites became the Jewish people: they entered into an enduring, eternal covenantal partnership with God, thus making manifest the second divine name. Moreover, Moses reminds the people that God did not elect them as a holy nation due to their own exceptional qualities, but rather because of God's love for their ancestors, who had been promised that their descendants would inherit the land of Canaan after their liberation from Egypt (Deuteronomy 7:6–9). This festival thus reflects another essential divine attribute: the lovingkindness that God showed in taking Israel out of Egypt was unearned love, a manifestation of the fourth divine name, *rahum*. In the observance of the ritual holiness of this festival, there is thus an opportunity to experience and to transmit the qualities of both interdependence and of unearned love.

The festival of Shavuot is also the product of the interdependent relationship between God and the Jewish people. The revelation at Sinai is preceded by God's offer of covenant to the nation, and is clearly contingent upon their acceptance. The vital importance of the people's acceptance is underscored by their declaration, "all that the Eternal will speak to us, we will do" (Exodus 19:8). Beyond this reflection of the second divine attribute, the starting point of the revelation at Sinai is the truth of the unity of God, who is both Creator and Redeemer. This serves as the foundation for the conviction of the truth of revelation, and the trustworthiness of God to maintain the covenantal promises to the Jewish people (Numbers 23:19), thus reflecting the eighth divine attribute: *emet*, God's trustworthiness.

The festival of Sukkot commemorates God's protection of the Jewish people as they wandered in the desert for forty years. The prophet Jeremiah describes God's appreciation of the Israelites' loyalty during those difficult years: "I remember the kindness of your youth, the love of your marriage, that you followed Me in the wilderness, in a desolate land" (Jeremiah 2:2). God's need, as it were, of Israel, is commemorated in the festival of Sukkot as manifestation of the second divine attribute, that of interdependence. But again, a further divine quality is manifest in this festival, and that is the sixth attribute: *erekh apayim*, God's forbearance and patience. The forty years of wandering in the desert is the result of the people's refusal to enter the land of Israel due to the report of the spies, God's threat to destroy the people, Moses' plea on their behalf, and God's consent to forgive them—but also condemning the entire generation to death in the desert, due to their unfaithfulness (Numbers 14:1–25). Our observance of Sukkot thus embodies the intense awareness of the divine quality of patience and forbearance.

The holy day of Rosh Hashanah, with its use of the shofar as a call to repentance, provides a critical element in the understanding of God's desire for partnership with the Jewish people. God does not presume that humans are perfect, as the early narratives of the Torah make clear. But God does presume that humans have the capacity to change, to repent for their errors, and to redirect their futures. The essence of our experience of Rosh Hashanah is that if we engage in honest repentance, God will forgive our sins and allow us a second chance to pursue a more noble path in life—thus on Rosh Hashanah, we experience the tenth divine name: *nosei avon*, forgiving iniquity. On Yom Kippur our essential ritual practice is that of the *innuyim*, the varied forms of withdrawal from bodily pleasures (such as fasting), while in antiquity the high priest performed the Temple service in order to purify the sanctuary and achieve atonement for the entire Jewish people (Leviticus 16). The ultimate purpose of this entire process is to restore the fullness of the relationship between God and the Jewish people. This is precisely the experience of the thirteenth divine quality, *nakeih*, in which divine pardon yields the restoration of the full presence of God. There is thus in these two specific layers of holiness of time a rich awareness, achieved through symbolic behaviors related to seven different divine qualities.

A third layer of holiness in time places even greater responsibility on human beings for the actualization of holiness. The singular example of this layer is the law of the Jubilee Year. Here, the Torah neither declares that God invested the time with holiness, nor does it refer to the time of the Jubilee Year as a festival of God. The essential biblical verse enjoins the Jewish people to sanctify the Jubilee Year, which will then be holy unto them: "And you shall make holy the fiftieth year, and proclaim liberty throughout the land unto all the inhabitants thereof; it shall be a Jubilee (*yoveil*) unto you" (Leviticus 25:10). Likewise in the one other Torah passage that discusses the Jubilee, the year is referred to as the "Jubilee of the Israelites" (Numbers 36:4), not as a time holy unto God. In this layer of holiness, then, God neither invests the time with holiness nor partners with humans by initiating the potential for holiness. Instead, there is simply a confirmation that human effort will produce a form of holiness that God personally recognizes and accepts. God commands people to act, and confirms that such autonomous human action will be efficacious in creating holiness.

We will now move on to examine the other three dimensions of holiness found in the Torah, with an eye toward discerning this three-layered pattern of holiness in those realms, as well.

Holiness of Persons

The primary form of holiness of persons present in the Torah is that of Aaron and his sons as priests. The dedication of Aaron and his sons to the service of God in the sanctuary is described in great detail in Exodus 28–29. One essential element in that process of dedication was the sanctification of Aaron and his sons—that is, making them holy. That process appears to be described in stages. First, Moses is commanded to "speak to all who are wise-hearted, whom I have filled with the spirit of wisdom, that they may make Aaron's garments to sanctify him, that he may serve as a priest unto Me" (Exodus 28:3). Making the holy garments was obviously a precondition to the process that would lead to the investment of holiness in Aaron and his sons. Next, God says to Moses, "This is what you shall do unto them to make them holy…" (Exodus 29:1), and this is followed by instructions to bathe them (Exodus 29:4), to dress them in the holy garments (Exodus 29:5), and to anoint them with anointing oil (Exodus 29:7). The instructions for the sacrifices which follow (Exodus 29:10–43) are interrupted by a further instruction to sprinkle a mixture of blood and anointing oil on Aaron and his sons, as a result of which "he and his garments shall be holy, and his sons and his sons' garments with him" (Exodus 29: 21).

However, all of these actions by Moses apparently do not actually complete the process of the hallowing of Aaron and his sons. That comes in a later verse, when God declares, "Aaron and his sons also will I sanctify, to minister to Me as priests" (Exodus 29:44). While all of the human preparation is necessary, it is not sufficient: the ultimate investment of holiness in Aaron and his descendants is by the direct declaration of God. This clear statement of the inception of priestly holiness by divine declaration led the sages to understand that such holiness cannot be abandoned. A *kohen* cannot alter his personal status as a kohen by renunciation, or even by violating the laws regulating priestly conduct. A *kohen* can be denied the privileges of his status (for example, if he commits homicide), but even then he remains constrained by the laws that restrict his conduct, such as the restrictions on whom he can marry. And even if a *kohen* violates these laws, his personal status is not changed—even though his male offspring will then be disqualified from the priesthood. As was the case in regard to the holiness of the Sabbath, this first layer of holiness of persons is absolute and inalienable, because it was directly invested by God.

In regard to the realm of holiness of time, we saw that the second of the thirteen divine qualities—that of interdependence with humans—first appeared in the second layer, regarding the holiness of the festivals. In contrast, in the realm of holiness of persons, the quality of interdependence appears in the very first layer. God uses the priests as the medium through which divine blessing is extended to the Jewish people, at the close of every service in the sanctuary (Numbers 6:23–26). God concludes that instruction to the *kohanim* by saying, "And you shall place My name upon Israel, and I will bless them" (Numbers 6:27). But at the same time, the priests are the ultimate enablers of the Jewish people's worship of God. They conduct the sacrificial rite, through which the nation engages in its regular, ongoing service of God. Thus, this second divine name or quality of interdependence is doubly expressed in the holiness of the priests, and thereby modeled for the entire Jewish people, as the *kohanim* partner both with God and with the people in intimate interdependence.

After the holiness of the priests, the second layer of holiness of persons is the holiness of the entire Jewish people. The language of the Torah in regard to this holiness is quite distinctive: "You shall be holy, for I, the Eternal your God, am holy" (Leviticus 19:2); similarly: "you shall be unto Me a kingdom of priests and a holy nation" (Exodus 19:6). The clear implication of these verses is that the holiness of the Jewish people was to be achieved by the conduct of the people themselves; it was not fully invested in them by God. Thus, in contrast to the holiness of the *kohanim*, the rest of the Jewish people were invested with potential for holiness—perhaps even some rudimentary level of holiness that might be inalienable—but which requires their own further action in order for their holiness to become fully evolved. This balance between a fragmentary divine investment, on the one hand, and the actualization of its fullness through the necessity of human action, on the other, is reflected in yet another verse: "Verily, you shall keep My Sabbaths, for it is a sign between Me and you throughout your generations—that you may know that I am the Eternal, who sanctifies you" (Leviticus 31:12). This verse acknowledges that God invests the Jewish people with holiness, yet that declaration is linked explicitly with the mandate to observe the divine commandment of the Sabbath.

This is precisely the balance we saw above in the second layer of holiness in time—the holiness of the festivals—in which God had invested a potential for sanctity, which then required human partnership in order to become fully actualized. Here too, then, in regard to the holiness of the Jewish people, there is a similar necessity for partnership between God and people, in order for the fullness of the holiness of these persons to be actualized (although we might also see here, unlike in the realm of holiness in time, that there is the presence of a spark of holiness that can be seen as absolute and inalienable). Beyond the inherent interdependence embedded in the holiness of the Jewish people, there is yet another aspect to the holiness of persons, which finds expression in legislation governing the relationships among fellow Jews: the existence of a duty of rescue. This means that Jews must not only refrain from doing harm to others (particularly, but not exclusively, to other Jews), but must also rescue others from harm—and this obtains in multiple arenas of interpersonal responsibility, including responsibility for property as well as for physical, emotional, and spiritual health and well-being. For example, the command of "You shall not stand idly by the blood of your neighbor" (Leviticus 19:16) imposes the duty to intervene to attempt to rescue the lives of others—even if one did not do anything personally to bring about the situation that is endangering another person's well-being. The breadth and scope of this duty is reflective of yet another divine quality, embedded in the third divine name, *El*: namely, the value of responsiveness to the danger or distress of others. The legal imposition of such duties (primarily toward fellow Jews, although often toward non-Jews as well) is what the sages describe as duties of *areivut*, which derives from the shared holiness invested by God in the Jewish people.

As with holiness of time, there is likewise a third layer in regard to holiness of persons, wherein God mandates human action to create holiness. In this layer, God neither invests the holiness personally, nor partners with humans in its investment, but simply confirms that holiness has, indeed, been created through human action. Such is the case in the divine command to Moses to prepare Israel for the revelation at Mount Sinai. God says: "Go to the people and sanctify them today and tomorrow, and let them wash their garments" (Exodus 19:10). The Torah then confirms that Moses has fulfilled the divine command, as he "went down from the mountain to the people, and he sanctified the people, and they washed their clothes" (Exodus 19:14). In contrast to the two prior layers of holiness of persons, this layer refers to the creation of a form of holiness that is distinctively temporary—in this instance lasting only three days, until the completion of the revelation at Sinai. A further instance of this third layer of holiness of persons is the holiness of the nazirite. Here, too, God neither invests the holiness personally, nor partners with the person in producing the holiness; but again, God does confirm that a form of temporary holiness has been created through human action: "All the days of his naziriteship he is holy unto the Eternal" (Numbers 6:8, and cf. 6:5). The investment of holiness is the product of the nazirite's own righteous actions in dedicating himself as a *quasi-kohen*—identifiable by his abstention from wine, his hair growth, and his observance of the priestly purity laws (even though he was not mandated by God to act in such a manner).

One other instance of the temporary holiness of persons is distinct from the two we have discussed, and this is the holiness of the firstborns, which was indeed invested by God personally: "For all the firstborns among the Israelites are Mine, both human and beast; on the day that I smote all the firstborns of the land of Egypt, I sanctified them for Myself" (Numbers 8:17). However, in the very next verse God tells us that the status of the firstborns was revoked, and they were replaced with the tribe of Levi: "I have taken the Levites, instead of all the firstborns among the Israelites" (Numbers 8:18). In contrast to the time-limited holiness of the Israelites at Mount Sinai, and the time-limited holiness of the nazirite, the holiness of the firstborns was invested by God personally and would have been permanently absolute and inalienable, except for God's own power to terminate that status—which, in fact, was exercised. Strikingly, although the Torah emphasizes the holiness of the firstborns and also reports their replacement by the Levites, there is no indication of investment of holiness in the Levites when they replace the firstborns. God declares that "they are wholly given unto Me, from among the Israelites; instead of all that open the womb, even the firstborns of the Israelites, have I taken them unto Me" (Numbers 8:16). The closing phrase of this verse almost echoes what God had said to Moses earlier concerning the dedication of the firstborns: "Sanctify unto Me all the firstborns; whatever opens the womb among the Israelites, both humans and beast, it is Mine" (Exodus 13:1–2). But in the case of the firstborns, their sanctification was explicitly invested; no such mention of holiness is recorded regarding the Levites.

Holiness of Objects

There are very few objects that the Torah deems to be holy, all of which have to do with the portable sanctuary (the *mishkan*) built by the Jews in the desert and transported with them into the land of Israel. Here, too, there appear to be three layers of holiness, analogous to the layers we have seen elsewhere.

The primary form of holiness of objects is seen in the divine declaration, "And I will sanctify the tent of meeting and the altar" (Exodus 29:44). As with the sanctity of the priests, here too preliminary actions need to be undertaken by Moses and the people, to construct the objects in response to the God's command. Thus, Moses had been previously instructed, "Seven days you shall make atonement for the altar and sanctify it, thus shall the altar become most holy" (Exodus 29:37). The objects are constructed by humans in order to be invested with holiness, but the actual investment of sanctity in the objects is done by God personally.

There is a second layer to the holiness of objects, which encompasses all of the objects made for and used in the service of God in the sanctuary. God commands that all of them, including the tent of meeting and the altar of burnt offerings, should be made by Bezalel and his assistants:

> ...and in the hearts of all that are wise-hearted I have placed wisdom, that they may make all that I have commanded you: the tent of meeting and the ark of the testimony, the ark-cover that is upon it and all the furniture of the tent; the table and its vessels, the pure candelabrum and all its vessels, and the altar of incense; the altar of burnt offering with all its vessels, and the laver and its base; the plaited garments and the holy garments for Aaron the priest, and the garments of his sons, to minister in the priest's office; the anointing oil and the incense of sweet spices for the holy place. According to all that I have commanded you, so shall they do. (Exodus 31:6–11)

But in contrast to the tent of meeting and the altar, in which God personally invested sanctity, for all other objects the investment of holiness takes place through the human partnership with God. God indicates the potential for holiness of these utensils, used in the sanctuary service, which is then actualized through the human effort of actually shaping the objects, in accordance with the divine instructions indicating their sacred intent. Thus God declares, regarding all of these utensils: "And you shall sanctify them [the utensils], that they may be most holy" (Exodus 30:29); and, at the culmination of this process, we read: "On the day that Moses had made an end of setting up the tabernacle, and had anointed it and sanctified it, and all the furniture thereof, and the altar and all the vessels thereof, and had anointed them and sanctified them..." (Numbers 7:1). The potential for holiness had then been fully actualized in this partnership between God and persons.

A further instance of this layer of holiness of objects is seen in regard to tithes of agricultural produce and animals, which require actualization by persons designating the particular produce or the particular animal as a tithe. Thus: "All the tithes of the land, whether of the seed of the land or the fruit of the tree, are the Eternal's, they are holy unto the Eternal. And all tithes of the herd or the flock, whatsoever passes under the rod, the tenth shall be holy unto the Eternal" (Leviticus 27:30, 32). The separation of the tithe is mandated by God, but the investment of holiness is not actualized until the owner of the produce or the animal performs the action of designating the particular produce or animals.

All of these holy objects—including the sanctuary itself, the altar, and all of the implements—were devoted to the sacrificial practice described in Leviticus 1–7. Within those chapters the order of sacrifices is twice presented: once as instructions to the Jewish people, in the ordering of their worship of God (chapters 1–5), and then as instructions to the priests, in their implementation of the divine worship (chapters 6–7). In both instances, there are three sets of offerings that form the essential core of the sacrificial service: the olah (whole burnt offering), the *hattat* and the *asham* (sin offerings), and the *sh'lamim* (peace offerings). Each of these captures a distinctive aspect of human striving to imitate the divine virtues.

The first kind of sacrifice, the *olah*, embodies an affirmation of the covenantal relationship between the Jewish people and God. The essence of that covenant is rooted in two critical biblical narratives. The first describes the formation of the family of Abraham: God feels the pain of Sarah in her infertility, whereupon Abraham and Sarah learn that a child will be born to them within the next year (Genesis 18:1–15). This divine empathy, the quality of *hannun* (the fifth divine name), is echoed on the national level in the second narrative, as God prepares to take the fledgling nation of Israel out of Egypt. God explains the reason behind the divine liberation as follows: "I have surely seen the affliction of My people that are in Egypt, and have heard their cry by reason of their taskmasters, for I know their pains" (Exodus 3:7). When Jews, either as a nation or as individuals, offer an *olah* sacrifice, they affirm that the covenantal relationship between themselves and God is founded in that quality of empathy, in the virtue of *hannun* that Israel is duty-bound to emulate. The second kind of sacrifice, the *hattat* and the *asham*, are both offerings designed to restore the relationship with God after some particular sinful conduct on the part of an individual, a community, or the leadership of the nation. The underlying premise of these sacrifices is that a combination of confession of sin and a sacrificial offering will elicit divine forgiveness. As we have noted in discussion of the twelfth divine name, *Nosei Hatta·ah*, God's forgiveness holds individuals accountable for their conduct while still allowing for the restoration of the relationship that had been ruptured by the wrongdoing. Forgiveness is founded in the hope that a person can truly change in the future, and it is that quality that is modeled for us in the experience of offering these sacrifices. The third kind of sacrifice, the *sh'lamim* or peace offering, is an expression of gratitude by an individual toward God—a woman who has given birth, a person who has survived a dangerous situation, or a person who has appeared before God at the sanctuary on a festival. In all of these instances, the sacrifice elicits imitation of God's own virtue of gratitude, as reflected in the tenth divine name, *Notzeir Ḥesed La-alafim*, "keeping mercy unto the thousandth generation." These three forms of offering are the core of sacrificial worship in the sanctuary. The holiness embodied in this worship enables the Jewish people to both experience God's virtues and to emulate those same virtues in their own lives. Thus, the holiness of objects models for us the divine qualities of empathy, forgiveness (founded in hope), and gratitude.

The third layer of holiness of objects is also related to the sanctuary, and is founded on the principle that any gift to the sanctuary (consisting of either property or a pure animal) becomes holy simply by virtue of being a gift—despite the fact that the gift itself was purely voluntary, and not mandated by God. It is striking that when one makes a vow of money as a gift to the sanctuary, the Torah does not claim that the money itself becomes holy; it notes only that the money has to be in the form of *shekel ha-kodesh*, "the shekel of the sanctuary" (Leviticus 27:3). However, if one vows to give an actual object (such as a pure animal, a house, or land), then the act of giving the gift itself is described with the words *v'ish ki yakdish*, "when a person shall sanctify" (Leviticus 27:14ff.). That is, God did not pre-ordain that any particular animal or property should become sanctified, but human actions have the capacity to invest an animal or piece of property with holiness—analogous to the capacity of a person to invest holiness in oneself as a nazirite.

It seems clear that the Torah exercised extreme caution in regard to the investment of sanctity in objects. Direct divine investment of holiness in objects pertains exclusively to the structure of the singular sanctuary and its major altar. Even the second layer, the partnership between God and persons to produce holiness in objects, pertains exclusively to the remaining objects that were commanded to be constructed as the instruments of service in that sanctuary. And in the third layer, wherein persons have the capacity to initiate holiness in objects, they could do so only in the form of gifts to the sanctuary, which then came under the exclusive control of the priests and Levites. It is reasonable to assume that this constrained investment of holiness in objects was part of the Torah's design to reduce the likelihood of idolatrous conduct, which might result from widespread use of sanctified objects by the population as a whole. It is not hard to see the possibility of popular veneration of household sancta leading to worship of those same objects as either deities or as representations of deities.

Holiness of Place

The concluding verses of the Song at the Sea, the poem that the Jewish people sang after they were saved at the Sea of Reeds, speak prophetically of the direction in which God is leading the people. God directs them toward the place where the divine home, God's own (sacred) sanctuary, will be established: "You will bring them in and will plant them in the mountain of Your inheritance: the place, Eternal, that You have made for Yourself to dwell in, the sanctuary of the Eternal (*mikdash Adonai*), which Your hands have established" (Exodus 15:17). This verse points to the merger of the holiness of the sanctuary-as-object with the holiness of the place where that sanctuary will be permanently located. Thus the sages immediately link the phrase *mikdash Adonai* of this verse with the occurrence of the same word in the divine command of Exodus 25:8, "You shall make for Me a sanctuary (*mikdash*), and I will reside among them" (cf. B. Ketubot 62b).

Indeed, after the construction of the portable sanctuary in the book of Exodus, which was to travel with the people in the desert, the book of Deuteronomy indicates nearly two dozen separate times that God intends to locate that sanctuary at a particular place, to be chosen by God. Thus, for example, after the command for Israel to destroy, upon their entry into the land of Canaan, the multiple local places of idolatrous worship that existed there, God mandates that proper divine worship through sacrifices and offerings be done exclusively at the place to be designated as the location of the sanctuary:

> Only the place that the Eternal your God shall choose out of all your tribes to place the divine name there—that habitation shall you seek, and there you shall come. There you shall bring your burnt offerings, and your sacrifices, your tithes and the offerings of your hand, your vows and your freewill offerings, the firstlings of your herd and of your flock. And there you shall eat before the Eternal your God, and you shall rejoice in all that you put your hand to—you and your households, with which the Eternal your God has blessed you. (Deuteronomy 12:5–7)

In numerous additional verses in Deuteronomy,[16] the Torah emphasizes that God will select a permanent place as the location of the sanctuary. And, in nine of those instances, that will be the place where God's name "will be placed," or "will rest."[17]

It is no wonder, then, that the rabbinic tradition was unequivocal about the nature of the holiness of the place where the Temple eventually stood. As the Mishnah testifies, the divine sanctification of this place "made it [i.e., the Temple Mount] holy for its time [i.e., while the Temple stood], as well as for all future time" (M. Eiduyot 8:6). As we have seen with the other three domains of holiness, here too do we see something similar regarding holiness of place: in the first layer, the sanctity of the Temple Mount was purely the result of divine investment of holiness in that place and is therefore absolute and inalienable. To this day—despite the fact that the Temple in Jerusalem was destroyed more than nineteen centuries ago, and despite dispute as to exactly where the Temple stood—there is no debate in Jewish law about the continued holiness of that specific place, with the result that ritually impure people are forbidden from walking there.

The identification of the *makom kadosh*, the holy place, with the location of the portable sanctuary, the Tent of Meeting, is made explicit in three instances in the Torah. For example, in regard to the priests eating the remainder of the meal offering accompanying the daily sacrifice, we read: "And that which is left of it, Aaron and his sons shall eat; it shall be eaten as unleavened bread in a holy place (*makom kadosh*); in the court of the tent of meeting they shall eat it" (Leviticus 6:9).[18] In six subsequent places the Torah simply refers to activities taking place "in the holy place,"[19] relying on our understanding that this refers to the location of the portable sanctuary (until its permanent location will be divinely selected—at which point in time there will be only that single, absolutely holy place).

A second layer of holiness of place is reflected in the verse, "You in Your love lead the people whom You have redeemed; You guide them in Your strength to Your holy habitation (*el n'veih kodshekha*)" (Exodus 15:13, cf. commentary of Rashbam ad loc.). While this verse is the sole explicit assertion in the Torah of the holiness of the land of Israel, the sages seem to have arrived at far-reaching implications based on the nuances of the verse itself. Firstly, the Mishnah asserts that the entire land of Israel is holy[20]—albeit granting that the holiness of the entire country is the lowest of the ten degrees of holiness that are manifest within the land. That is to say: the entire land is the base upon which ever-higher degrees of holiness can become manifest, ultimately leading to the highest degree of holiness possible, as we would expect, within the sanctuary at the place of the holy of holies.

The way the Mishnah expresses the holiness of the land of Israel is itself of great significance. It says:

> There are ten degrees of holiness. The land of Israel is holier than all [other] lands. And what [constitutes] its holiness? [That] they bring the omer from it, and the first fruits and the two loaves, which they may not bring from [any of] the [other] lands (M. Keilim 1:6.).

The Mishnah teaches that the holiness of the land depends on the actions of the Jewish people, in bringing national offerings to the sanctuary. This understanding may already be implied in the language of the biblical verse cited above, which may be read to imply that the holiness of the divine "habitation" depends on the prior arrival of the people, whom God has redeemed, so that they may be settled there. In fact, this seems to be the central assumption of the talmudic assertion that the holiness of the land of Israel was actualized not by divine decree, but rather by the arrival of the Jewish people and their conquest of the land under Joshua, and their resultant settlement in the land (B. Arakhin 32b). While an alternative understanding is considered, it is precisely this assumption that led the sages to conclude that, upon the destruction of the Temple and the exile of the Jewish people from their land, the very holiness of land itself was nullified. Furthermore, the restoration of the holiness of the land was only achieved when the Jews returned to the land and rebuilt the Temple under the leadership of Ezra.

This rabbinic teaching is strikingly different from that of the Mishnah, dealing with the holiness of the place of the Temple itself. There, the law was clear that even the destruction of the Temple would leave God's chosen place invested with holiness—precisely because God personally had invested that location with holiness in choosing it as the permanent location of the sanctuary. By contrast, the holiness of the rest of the land was invested by God only with potential for holiness, which needed to be actualized by the Jewish people through their own efforts: initially their conquest and settlement of the land, and later their conduct in bringing the produce of the land to the Temple according to the divine command.

It is in this manner that the rabbis must have understood the passage in Leviticus in which, after warning the people not to engage in any forms of sexual immorality or child sacrifice, God issues a powerful threat that such conduct will result in the land becoming impure and vomiting them out:

> You shall not defile yourselves by any of things—for the nations, whom I am sending away from before you, have defiled themselves with all these things. And the land became defiled, and I visited its sin upon it, and the land

vomited out its inhabitants. But as for you, you shall observe
My statutes and My ordinances, and you shall not do
anything like these abominations—neither the citizen nor
the stranger who sojourns among you. For the people of the
land who preceded you committed all of these abominations,
and the land became defiled. And let the land not vomit you
out for having defiled it, as it vomited out the nation that
preceded you. (Leviticus 18: 24–28)

The sages must have understood that it is the very holiness of the land
that could not tolerate the impurity of grossly immoral behavior—
that is, the actualization and maintenance of the holiness of the land
is contingent upon the continued obedience of the Jewish people to
the commandments.

The holiness of the Land of Israel, first actualized through the
conquest under Joshua, ended with the destruction of the Temple and
the exile of the people from the land. This was not the case with the
second actualization of the holiness of the land at the time of Ezra.
That investment of holiness in the land was, according to the sages,
never completely terminated, but remained "eternally sanctified."[21]
However, as we have noted in regard to the second layer of holiness
of persons (that is, the holiness of the Jewish people), this element of
continuous or ongoing sanctity is only partial. In regard to the Jewish
people as a whole, the partial sanctity needs to be fully actualized by
the ongoing conduct of the people. And here, in regard to the sanctity
of the land, it too can only be fully actualized by the conduct of the
people: specifically, by the actual settlement of the land—that is, by
the arrival of the majority of the Jews of the world in the land of
Israel. Maimonides speaks almost prophetically about this matter:

In the present era, even in the areas settled by the Jews who
came from Babylonia, even those [settled] in the era of Ezra,
[the obligation to separate] t'rumah does not have the status
of a scriptural commandment, but merely that of a rabbinic
decree. [The rationale is that] the scriptural [commandment
to separate] t'rumah applies only in eretz yisrael and only

when the entire Jewish people are located there. [This is derived from the phrase] "When you enter…" [Implied is that] the entire [Jewish people] must enter [the land], as they did when they took possession of the land originally and as will happen in the future when they take possession of the land a third time. In contrast, the second time [the people] took possession of the land, in the time of Ezra, only a portion entered. Hence, they were not obligated according to scriptural law. Similarly, it appears to me that the same concept applies with regard to the tithes. In the present era, this obligation [as well] has the status of a rabbinic decree like *t'rumah*."[22]

The holiness of place, for both the *mikdash* and the entire land, carries symbolic significance regarding two fundamental divine virtues. First, the very fact that God fulfilled the promise to give the land of Canaan to the descendants of Abraham was an act of rav *ḥesed*, kindness exceeding reasonable expectations (the seventh divine name). That is exactly why the Jewish people insisted that they could not succeed in entering the land, that such an attempt was doomed from the outset and would be impossible to achieve (Numbers 14:1–3). And that is why Moses' response to the people was, "If God desires [that for] us, then God will bring us into this land and give it to us" (Numbers 14:7). And, in turn, that is why God's response was, "How long will this people despise Me? How long will they not believe in Me, despite all the signs that I have wrought among them?!" (Numbers 14:11). This exchange is reminiscent of the moment of God's informing Abraham, and Sarah overhearing, that they would have a child together, and Sarah's apparently disbelieving laughter in response (Genesis 18:9–12). God's response to her was, "Is anything too wondrous for the Eternal [to do]?" (Genesis 18:14). In both of these instances, humans respond to the magnitude of a promised divine kindness with disbelief. In both instances—but particularly in the situation of the promise to give the holy land of Israel to the holy people whom God had chosen—God insists that the divine capacity for kindness exceeds human imagination. That is precisely the divine quality of rav *ḥesed*: the fact that God's ability to meet those needs far exceeds what humans would consider to be reasonable expectations. To imitate this divine quality, which is embedded in the symbolic holiness of the land of Israel, we are asked to transcend the perception of our own limitations in performing acts of kindness for our fellow humans.

Later in the narrative of the spies, we find Moses' plea to God to forgive the people. Moses offers a number of different reasons why God should forgive them, rather than destroy them and start over again with Moses himself. His concluding plea is that God should forgive the people because God should act in consonance with the divine virtues, the eleventh of which is *nosei pesha* (Numbers 14:13–19). We had noted previously that the term pesha connotes actions that manifest betrayal of personal relationships (including betrayal of the covenant with God). In fact, Moses describes the refusal of the Jews to follow the instruction to enter the land as an act of pesha, but he pleads with God to forgive them nevertheless. God does consent to forgive the people, manifesting divine humility, but still holds them accountable for their conduct and condemns all Jewish adults to death in the desert over the next thirty-eight years. This pattern of divine conduct—forgiving with humility, while still holding the wrongdoers accountable for sinful behavior and administering punishment for such conduct—becomes the central function of the service in the Temple in Jerusalem, the sanctuary at the holy place chosen by God. That very place came to embody this divine quality: the awareness that humility demands that forgiveness be granted (even for sins of betrayal), but that justice nevertheless demands that wrongdoers be punished for the sinful behavior. Thus two fundamental divine attributes, *rav ḥesed* and *nosei pesha*, are symbolically embodied in the Jewish experience of the holiness of the Temple Mount, as well as the holiness of the land of Israel.

The third layer of holiness of place is exemplified by the temporary holiness of Mount Sinai. God instructed Moses to warn the Jewish people against actually ascending the mountain during God's appearance on it, and Moses responded that no such additional warning was needed, since God had already instructed Moses to "set bounds around the mount and sanctify it" (Exodus 19:23). But God instructs Moses nevertheless to command the people not to ascend, and Moses does so. Moses clearly assumes that the people would understand that designating the mountain as holy would preclude them from intruding upon it. God apparently does not share this assumption and therefore demands that Moses explicitly instruct the people not to enter the area during God's revelation. Moses then complies: "So Moses went down to the people and told them" (Exodus 19:25). The holiness of Mount Sinai is never referred to as an investment of holiness by God personally, nor does the Torah ever indicate that Mount Sinai is holy unto God. Rather, God commands Moses to sanctify the mountain by engaging in actions and speech that demonstrate the distinctively holy character of that place for a limited period of time—namely, the time that God's presence will be manifest there as the people enter into covenant with the Divine. Moses had assumed that it would be self-evident that a holy place should be entered only by the spiritual elite (himself and Aaron), but that belief seems to be repudiated by God, who declares that it is only in this instance that the masses must keep their distance. Indeed, when the sanctuary is later constructed, God specifically desires that the entire people to be able to experience the divine presence among them: "And you shall make for Me a sanctuary so that I may dwell among them" (Exodus 25:8).

Conclusion

In each of the four dimensions of holiness—time, persons, objects, and place—there are three distinct layers of holiness. The first layer is holiness that is absolute and inalienable, because it has been fully invested by God personally. The second layer is holiness in which the potential is invested by God, but actualizing that potential fully depends on people entering into partnership with God. The third layer of holiness may be authorized or even commanded by God, but its full investment—the words and actions that are then necessitated by, and reflective of, that holiness—is executed by persons. The following chart summarizes the three layers of each of the four dimensions of symbolic holiness found in the Torah:

Holiness God Leviticus 19:2				
	Time	Persons	Objects	Place
potential and actualization by God: *inalienable*	Shabbat (Genesis 2:3)	Priests (Exodus 29:44)	Tabernacle and Altar (Exodus 29:44)	Location of Temple (Exodus 15:17, Deuteronomy 12:5-7)
potential by God, actualization by humans: *alienable by human conduct*	Festivals (Leviticus 23:2, 4)	Jewish People (Leviticus 19:12)	Sanctuary Implements (Exodus 30:29, Numbers 7:1)	Land of Israel (Exodus 15:13, Leviticus 18:24-28)
potential by God, declaration and actualization by humans: *rare or temporary*	Jubilee Year (Leviticus 25:10)	Nazirite (Numbers 6:5, 8)	Tithes (Leviticus 27:30, 32)	Mount Sinai (Exodus 19:23)

What, then, is the meaning of the holiness that is embodied in these symbolic times, persons, objects, and places? Each of these manifestations of holiness is a symbolic expression through which one or more of the virtues expressed in the thirteen divine attributes is brought to our attention, so that we may become aware of our duty to imitate those qualities and transmit them to the following generations.

The divine virtues embedded in the symbolic expressions of holiness are as follows:[23]

Holiness of Time:

<u>The Sabbath</u>. Virtue #1, the Tetragrammaton ("Adonai"), represents the value of productivity—of being purposefully productive in the material world.

<u>The Festivals</u>.

> Passover. Virtue #4, the divine name *Rahum* ("merciful"), obviously related to the word *rehem*, meaning womb) represents the quality of extending unearned love.

> Shavuot. Virtue #8, the divine name *Emet* ("truth"), represents the virtue of trustworthiness.

> Sukkot. Virtue #6, the divine name *Erekh Apayim* ("long-suffering") represents the virtue of patience (forbearance), the capacity to postpone acting even in the face of strong emotions such as anger.

> Rosh Hashanah. Virtue #10, the divine name *Nosei Avon* ("forgiving iniquity"), means that God will both exact punishment for degraded conduct (*avon*) but also forgive, granting a second chance to pursue a more noble path.

> Yom Kippur. Virtue #13, the divine name *Nakeih* ("acquitting"), represents the idea of pardon in the framework of justice: God will await repentance and, when that occurs, will restore the divine presence.

Holiness of Persons:

<u>The Priests</u>. Virtue #2, the second divine name, is a repetition of the Tetragrammaton ("Adonai"), which here represents the value of interdependence.

<u>The Jewish People</u>. Virtue #3, the divine name *El* ("God"), represents the value of responsiveness to the danger or distress of others.

Holiness of Objects:

The *Mishkan*, Altar, and the Sanctuary Implements.

> The olah. Virtue #5, the divine name *Hannun* ("gracious"), is an expression of the virtue of empathy, the ability to share the feelings of joy and pain of another.

> The *hattat* and the *asham*. Virtue #12, the divine name *Nosei Hatta·ah* ("forgiving sin"), represents the quality of hope, which makes it both necessary and possible for God to forgive (albeit again with accountability) the broad base of wrongful conduct that is, as it were, the norm of human existence, which needs to be governed and moderated but which can never be fully extirpated.

> The *sh'lamim*. Virtue #9, the divine name *notzeir hesed la-alafim* ("keeping mercy unto the thousandth generation") is an expression of the virtue of gratitude.

Holiness of Places:

The Temple. Virtue #11, the divine name *Nosei Pesha* ("forgiving transgression"), indicates that God bears that same quality of holding accountable but forgiving, even in relation to sins that are rooted in and manifest personal betrayal of the covenantal relationship—due to the presence in God of the additional quality of humility.

The Land of Israel. Virtue #7, the divine name *Rav Hesed* ("abundant in goodness"), is a compound phrase that presents God as acting to satisfy human needs (*hesed*), in a manner that exceeds reasonable expectations (*rav*).

****

The challenges that confront us in the modern era are the same as those that have confronted Jews throughout our history. How can we be constantly conscious of the divine virtues in which the holiness of God personally is expressed? How can we use the symbolic models of holiness with which the Torah provides us? How can we sustain an awareness of the ways in which every law of the Torah moves us to integrate those same qualities in our personalities, to actualize them in our conduct in the real world, and to transmit them passionately to the next generation of Jews?

These are the questions that matter. And it is only through a recognition of God's *k'dushah*, and our own commitment to strive to emulate these divine qualities in our own lives, that we can begin to answer these questions.

NOTES

[1] See, e.g., the sources listed by Theodore Friedman, Baruch A. Levine, and Eliezer Schweid in their essay on holiness in the 2nd edition of the *Encyclopaedia Judaica*, eds. Michael Berenbaum and Fred Skolnik (Detroit: Macmillan Reference USA, 2007), vol. 12, pp. 50–56. The essay is entitled "Kedushah."

[2] *Sefer Ha-mitzvot*, positive commandment #8. The talmudic passage referenced is B. Sotah 14a.

[3] M.T. Hilkhot Dei·ot 1:5–7 (emphasis added).

[4] This rendering is based on the 1917 JPS translation of the biblical passage, with a slight modification in the thirteenth name to conform with rabbinic understanding.

[5] Note that his name is still "Abram," at this point in the biblical narrative.

[6] See, for example, Exodus 33:19 and Deuteronomy 13:18.

[7] Some examples of this kind of (non-divine) *ḥesed* include the kindness done by the angels to Lot (Genesis 19:19), requested by Abraham from Sarah (Genesis 20:13), done by Avimelekh to Abraham (Genesis 21:23), requested by Abraham's servant from Laban (Genesis 24:49), requested by Joseph from the butler by Joseph (Genesis 40:14), and requested of Joseph by Jacob (Genesis 47:29.)

[8] B. Kiddushin 32b.

[9] With respect to the latter category, cf., e.g., Deuteronomy 27:7.

[10] See Rambam's *Guide to the Perplexed* I 54.

[11] See commentary of Naḥmanides to Exodus 34:7, ed. Chavel (Jerusalem: Mosad Harav Kook, 1959), vol. 1, p. 523.

[12] Hirsch, *Commentary to the Pentateuch* (trans. Isaac Levy; 3rd edition [London: Isaac Levy, 1967], pp. 650–651) is here following a suggestion of Rabbi Eleazar in the Talmud (B. Yoma 87a).

[13] Menahem ben Benjamin Recanati (1250–1310), one of the great rabbinic authors of medieval Italy, is cited in Chavel's footnotes to Naḥmanides' commentary (see note 10 above).

[14] Cf., e.g., Deuteronomy 19:10, 21:8, and 27:25.

[15] Cf., e.g., the Mekhilta, Bo 12, or the introduction to *B'shallah*, s.v. *va-ḥamushim*.

[16] See Deuteronomy 12:5–7, 11–12, 14, 18, 21, 26; 14:23–24, 25; 15:20; 16:2, 6–7, 11, 15, 16; 17:8, 10, 15; 18:6, 23:17, 26:2; and 31:11.

[17] Deuteronomy 12:5, 11, 21; 14:23–24; 15:20; 16:2, 6, 11; and 26:2.

[18] The other two instances of this explicit identification are Leviticus 6:19 and Exodus 29:30–31.

[19] Leviticus 6:20, 7:6, 10:13 and 17, 16:24, and 24:9.

[20] M. Keilim 1:6–9.

[21] M.T. Hilkhot Terumot 1:5.

[22] M.T. Hilkhot Terumot 1:26, trans. Eliyahu Touger (Jerusalem and New York:

Moznaim Publishing, 2005), p. 214. The Hebrew *t'rumah* denotes the special produce tax owed by farmers to the landless priestly caste. The phrase "when you enter" is not obviously used in Scripture with reference to *t'rumah*, but Rambam seems to be citing Numbers 15:18 in light of the discussion in the Talmud at B. Ketubot 25a.

[23] The virtues themselves are, as noted above: (1) Adonai, (2) Adonai, (3) God, (4) merciful and (5) gracious, (6) long-suffering and (7) abundant in goodness and (8) truth; (9) keeping mercy unto the thousandth generation, (10) forgiving iniquity (11) and transgression (12) and sin, and (13) acquitting.

Translation
Grant peace everywhere goodness and blessing,
Grace, lovingkindness and mercy to us and unto all Israel

Transliteration
Sim shalom tovah u-v'rakhah
ḥein va-ḥesed v'raḥamim aleinu ve-al kol Yisrael amekha

שִׂים שָׁלוֹם*

שִׂים שָׁלוֹם טוֹבָה וּבְרָכָה
חֵן וָחֶסֶד וְרַחֲמִים עָלֵינוּ וְעַל כָּל יִשְׂרָאֵל עַמֶּךָ

---

* **Sim Shalom** (Hebrew: שִׂים שָׁלוֹם; "Grant Peace") is a blessing that is recited near the end of formal Jewish prayer services. The precise form of the blessing varies depending on the service and the precise denomination along the Jewish spectrum.

Author Biographies

Jonathan Sacks

A global religious leader, philosopher, author of over twenty-five books, renowned speaker and moral voice for our time, Rabbi Lord Jonathan Sacks is currently the Ingeborg and Ira Rennert Global Distinguished Professor of Judaic Thought at New York University, the Kressel and Ephrat Family University Professor of Jewish Thought at Yeshiva University and Professor of Law, Ethics and the Bible at King's College London. Previously, Rabbi Sacks served as Chief Rabbi of the United Hebrew Congregations of the Commonwealth between September 1991 and September 2013. A frequent contributor to radio, television and the press both in Britain and around the world, Rabbi Sacks holds sixteen honorary degrees and has been presented with several international awards in recognition of his work, including the Jerusalem Prize in 1995 for his contribution to diaspora Jewish life and The Ladislaus Laszt Ecumenical and Social Concern Award from Ben Gurion University in Israel in 2011. He was knighted by Her Majesty The Queen in 2005 and made a Life Peer, taking his seat in the House of Lords in October 2009.

Benjamin Blech

A Professor of Talmud at Yeshiva University since 1966. Rabbi Benjamin Blech is the author of fifteen highly acclaimed books, the last one of which – *The Sistine Secrets: Michelangelo's Forbidden Messages in the Heart of the Vatican* – is now available in twenty-six countries and has been translated into sixteen languages, in addition to hundreds of articles in both scholarly and popular publications.

Saul J. Berman

A leading Orthodox teacher and thinker. Rabbi Saul Berman is a scholar and an educator. He has made extensive contributions to the intensification of women's Jewish education, to the role of social ethics in Synagogue life, and to the understanding of the applicability of Jewish Law to contemporary society. Rabbi Berman was ordained at Yeshiva University, from which he also received his B.A. and his M.H.L. He completed a degree in law, a J.D., at New York University, and an M.A. in Political Science at the University of California at Berkeley. He now serves as an associate professor at Yeshiva University and teaches at Columbia University Law School.

Yitzchak Blau

A teacher at the Yeshivah of Flatbush and Yeshivat Hamivtar, and a writer for the Yeshivat Har Etzion Virtual Beit Midrash, Rabbi Yitzchak Blau currently serves as the Rosh Kollel at Yeshivat Shvilei Hatorah in Jerusalem. Rabbi Blau is on the editorial board of *Tradition* and publishes widely in journals of Jewish thought. He lives in Alon Shevut with his wife and four children.

Reuven P. Bulka

The spiritual leader of Congregation Machzikei Hadas in Ottawa since 1967, Rabbi Dr. Reuven Bulka received rabbinic ordination from the Rabbi Jacob Joseph Rabbinical Seminary in 1966 and a Ph.D. in Logotherapy from the University of Ottawa in 1971. He is married to Leah (Kalish-Rosenbloom) and is blessed with many children and grandchildren, and one great-grandchild.

Shalom Carmy

Rabbi Shalom Carmy teaches Jewish Studies and Philosophy at Yeshiva University and serves as editor of *Tradition*. A student of the late Rabbi Joseph B. Soloveitchik, he has published many essays on a wide variety of subjects.

Alfred Cohen

The rabbi of Congregation Ohaiv Yisroel in Monsey, NY, Rabbi Alfred Cohen is a rebbe in the Yeshiva University High School for Boys (YUHSB) of Yeshiva University and is editor of the *Journal of Halacha and Contemporary Society*.

Rachel Friedman

A noted teacher, author and lecturer in the areas of Bible and Jewish liturgy, Rachel Friedman is Founding Dean of Lamdeinu, a center for Jewish learning in northern New Jersey and served for many years as Associate Dean and Chair of Tanakh Studies at Drisha Institute for Jewish Education in New York City. She has an M.A. in Bible from the Bernard Revel Graduate School at Yeshiva University and a J.D. from the Columbia University School of Law.

Hillel Goldberg

Rabbi Hillel Goldberg earned his rabbinic ordination in Jerusalem and a doctorate in Jewish intellectual history at

Brandeis University, and has taught at The Hebrew University and at Emory University. He has written for the Intermountain Jewish News (IJN) for forty-seven years, twelve years as its Israel correspondent, and now as executive editor. He has won first-place journalism awards in news, features, profiles, arts, editorials, commentary, reportage from Israel and graphic design.

Nathaniel Helfgot

Rabbi Rabbi Helfgot is Chair of the Department Talmud and Rabbinics at the SAR High School in New York City. He serves as spiritual leader of Congregation Netivot Shalom in Teaneck, NJ. He is on the faculty of the YCT Rabbinical School, the Drisha Institute for Jewish Education and the Wexner Foundation. He is the author of *Community, Covenant, and Commitment: Selected Letters and Communications of Rabbi Joseph B. Soloveichik* (Ktav, 2005) and most recently of *Mikra and Meaning: Essays on Bible and Its Interpretation* (Maggid Publishers, 2012).

James Kugel

Born in New York, Dr. James Kugel was Starr Professor of Hebrew Literature at Harvard University from 1982 to 2003. He retired from Harvard to become Director of the Institute for the History of the Jewish Bible at Bar Ilan University in Israel, where he has also served as chairman of the Department of Bible.

David Mescheloff

Rabbi Dr. David Mescheloff has served as community rabbi, university lecturer, and author in Israel for over four decades and writes on Jewish law and thought. A recent publication is "The Marital Agreement to Mediate," published in Tradition 43:3, the fall 2010 issue.

Shlomo Riskin

Born and raised in New York City, Rabbi Shlomo Riskin graduated from Yeshiva University, having majored in the classics, and received his Master's degree, in Jewish History. In 1982, Rabbi Riskin was awarded his Ph.D. in Near Eastern Studies by New York University and received rabbinical ordination from Rabbi Joseph B. Soloveitchik at the Rabbi Isaac Elchanan Rabbinical Seminary.

David Shatz

University Professor of Philosophy, Ethics, and Religious Thought at Yeshiva University and editor of the *Torah u-Madda Journal*. Professor David Shatz was a winner in the John Templeton Foundation Course Competition in Science and Religion and was awarded the Presidential Medallion at Yeshiva University. His recent publications deal with interfaith relations, theodicy, artistic creativity, religious fanaticism, and the ethics of persuasion.

Lawrence H. Schiffman

Professor Lawrence Schiffman is Judge Abraham Lieberman Professor of Hebrew and Judaic Studies at New York University's Skirball Department of Hebrew and Judaic Studies. He is also a Director of the Global Network for Advanced Research in Jewish Studies. Lawrence Schiffman is a specialist in the Dead Sea Scrolls, Judaism in Late Antiquity, the history of Jewish law, and talmudic literature. His recent books include *The Courtyards of the House of the Lord: Studies on the Temple Scroll* (Brill, 2008) and *Qumran and Jerusalem: Studies in the Dead Sea Scrolls and the History of Judaism* (Eerdmans Publishing, 2010). He is past chair of the International Jewish Committee on Interreligious Consultation (IJCIC), the Jewish Liaison Committee to the Vatican, and other Jewish academic groups.

Avivah Zornberg

Dr. Avivah Zornberg lectures on Bible and Midrash at a number of Jerusalem institutions for advanced Torah study, as well as in Jewish and psychoanalytic settings in the U.S., England and other English-speaking countries. She is the author of *The Beginning of Desire: Reflections on Genesis, The Particulars of Rapture: Reflections on Exodus*, and *The Murmuring Deep: Reflections on the Biblical Unconscious*, all published by Schocken. *Bewilderments: Reflections on the Book of Numbers* will be published by Schocken later this year.

MESORAH MATRIX

10-BOOK SERIES
150 - 180 Essayists

dimensions of

Spirituality & Kedushah

THE SPARK OF THE INFINITE DIVINE

David Birnbaum / Mesorah Matrix Series

LIGHTS OF CREATION & TRANSCENDENCE

Mesorah Matrix Series

David Birnbaum

Editor-in-Chief

10-theme 10-volume series in-progress

MESORAH MATRIX

2015 2015 2016

2016 2017 2017

2018 2018 2019 2019

200+ original essays 150 - 180 global thought leaders

jewish thought & spirituality a decade-long unified endeavor

MESORAH MATRIX

10-BOOK SERIES
150 - 180 Essayists

Sanctification

Tikkun Olam

Birkat Kohanim

The Kaddish

Modeh Ani

Havdalah

Search for Meaning

U-VACHARTA BA-CHAYIM

Eheyeh asher Eheyeh

V'Shamru

THE SPARK OF THE INFINITE DIVINE

Mesorah Matrix Series

Sanctification ("Kedushah")

Tikkun Olam ("Repair the World")

Birkat Kohanim (The Priestly Blessings: a contemporary take)

The Kaddish (specifically, The Mourner's Praise of God)

Modeh Ani (The solo daily morning prayer of Gratitude)

Havdalah (separating Holy from Secular: Sabbath > secular)

Search for Meaning (pegging-off of Viktor Frankl's classic)

U-VACHARTA BA-CHAYIM (The 613th precept-Choose Life)

Eheyeh asher Eheyeh ("I Will Be That Which I Will Be" – at the Burning Bush)

V'Shamru (The Sabbath)

21st CENTURY PUBLISHING

NPM1000@yahoo.com

www.NewParadigmMatrix.com

MESORAH MATRIX

LIGHTS OF CREATION & TRANSCENDENCE

David Birnbaum / Mesorah Matrix Series

Sanctification

David
Birnbaum & Benjamin
Blech

Editors

New Paradigm Matrix™

EXPLORING HIGHER DIMENSIONS

TIKKUN OLAM

JUDAISM, HUMANISM & TRANSCENDENCE

LIGHTS OF CREATION & TRANSCENDENCE | David Birnbaum | Mesorah Matrix Series

Editors

David
Birnbaum &
Martin S.
Cohen

Associate Editor: **Saul J. Berman**

New Paradigm Matrix™

EXPLORING HIGHER DIMENSIONS

MESORAH
MATRIX

BIRKAT
KOHANIM

Editors

David
Birnbaum & Cohen

Martin S.

Associate Editor: **Saul J. Berman**

New Paradigm Matrix™

LIGHTS OF CREATION & TRANSCENDENCE

David Birnbaum / Mesorah Matrix Series

EXPLORING HIGHER DIMENSIONS

KADDISH

David Birnbaum / Mesorah Matrix Series
LIGHTS OF CREATION & TRANSCENDENCE

Editors

David
Birnbaum & Cohen
Martin S.

Associate Editor: **Saul J. Berman**

New Paradigm Matrix™

EXPLORING HIGHER DIMENSIONS

LIGHTS OF CREATION & TRANSCENDENCE

David Birnbaum / Mesorah Matrix Series

Modeh Ani

THE TRANSCENDENT PRAYER OF GRATITUDE

Editors

David
Birnbaum & **Cohen**
Martin S.

Associate Editor: **Saul J. Berman**

New Paradigm Matrix™

EXPLORING HIGHER DIMENSIONS

MESORAH MATRIX

LIGHTS OF CREATION & TRANSCENDENCE
David Birnbaum
Mesorah Matrix Series

HAVDALAH

Editors

David
Birnbaum & Martin S.
Cohen

Associate Editor: **Saul J. Berman**

New Paradigm Matrix™

EXPLORING HIGHER DIMENSIONS

MESORAH
MATRIX

David Birnbaum / Mesorah Matrix Series

LIGHTS OF CREATION & TRANSCENDENCE

SEARCH FOR

MEANING

Editors

David
Birnbaum &
Martin S.
Cohen

Associate Editor: **Saul J. Berman**

New Paradigm Matrix™

EXPLORING HIGHER DIMENSIONS

LIGHTS OF CREATION & TRANSCENDENCE / Mesorah Matrix Series

David Birnbaum

U-VACHARTA
BA-CHAYIM

Editors

David
Birnbaum & **Cohen**
Martin S.

New Paradigm Matrix™

EXPLORING HIGHER DIMENSIONS

MESORAH
MATRIX

Eheyeh asher Eheyeh

Editors

David
Birnbaum & Martin S.
Cohen

New Paradigm Matrix™

EXPLORING HIGHER DIMENSIONS

LIGHTS OF CREATION & TRANSCENDENCE
David Birnbaum / Mesorah Matrix Series

D'shamru

Editors

David
Birnbaum & Cohen
Martin S.

EXPLORING HIGHER DIMENSIONS

New Paradigm Matrix™

ESSAYISTS

Avivah Zornberg
Author

London, UK

David Ellenson
HUC-JIR

New York, NY

Saul Berman
Y.U. / Stern

New York, NY

Jonathan Sacks
United Hebrew
Congregations
London, UK

James Kugel
Bar Ilan University

Ramat Gan, Israel

Shalom Carmy
Yeshiva University,
Tradition Magazine
New York, NY

Or Rose
Hebrew College

Newton Centre, MA

Rachel Friedman
Lamdeinu

New York, NY

W. Zeev Harvey
The Hebrew University of Jerusalem
Jerusalem

Rachel Adelman
Hebrew College

Newton Centre, MA

Shlomo Riskin
Ohr Torah Stone Colleges,
Efrat, Israel

Shai Held
Mechon Hadar

New York, NY

Hillel Goldberg
Intermountain Jewish News
Denver, CO

Lawrence Schiffman
Yeshiva University
New York, NY

Alan Cooper
Jewish Theological Seminary
New York, NY

Yonatan Feintuch
Bar Ilan University

Tel Aviv, Israel

Jacob Schacter
Yeshiva University

New York, NY

Aryeh Cohen
American Jewish
University
Los Angeles, CA

Avrăm Reisner
Chevrei Tzedek
Congregation
Baltimore, MD

Elliot Dorff
American Jewish
University
Los Angeles, CA

Michael Graetz
Congregation Eshel
Avraham
Omer, Israel

Steven Kepnes
Colgate University

Hamilton, NY

Reuven Bulka
Congregation
Machzikei Hadas
Ottawa, Canada

Adena Berkowitz
Kol Ha-neshamah

New York, NY

Alan Mittleman
Jewish Theological
Seminary
New York, NY

Tzvi Sinensky
Rosh Beit Midrash

Lower Merion, PA

Bradley Artson
American Jewish
University
Los Angeles, CA

Jill Jacobs
T'ruah: The Rabbinic
Call for Human Rights
New York, NY

Michael Broyde
Emory University

Atlanta, GA

Noam Zion
Hartman Institute

Jerusalem

Sid Schwarz
CLAL

New York, NY

Raḥel Berkovits
Pardes Institute

Jerusalem

Howard Addison
Temple University .

Philadelphia, PA

Robert Harris
Jewish Theological
Seminary
New York, NY

Samuel Lebens
Rutgers University

New Brunswick, NJ

Richard Hidary
Congregation
Shearith Israel
New York, NY

Michael Chighel

Jerusalem

Eliezer Shore
Hebrew University
of Jerusalem
Jerusalem

Roberta Kwall
DePaul University
Law School
Chicago, IL

Alon Ferency
Heska Amuna
Synagogue
Knoxville, TN

Aubrey Glazer
Congregation Beth
Shalom
San Francisco, CA

Rebecca W. Sirbu
Rabbis Without
Borders, CLAL
New York, NY

Geoffrey Claussen
Elon University

Elon, NC

Jeremy Gordon
New London
Synagogue
London, U.K.

**Shoshana Klein
Poupko**
Ahavath Torah
Englewood, NJ

**Michael
Wasserman**
The New Shul
Scottsdale, AZ

Daniel Greyber
Beth El Synagogue

Durham, NC

Gail Labovitz
American Jewish
University
Los Angeles, CA

James Jacobson-Maisels
Or HaLev, Center for Jew-
ish Spirituality & Meditation
New York, NY

Yeshaya Dalsace
Dor Vador Com-
munaute Massorti
Paris, France

Shaiya Rothberg
Conservative
Yeshiva
Jerusalem

Karyn Kedar
B'nai Jehoshua
Beth Elohim
Deerfield, IL

Nina Cardin

New York, NY

Aryeh Klapper
Center for Modern
Torah Leadership
Sharon, MA

Jonathan
Wittenberg

London, UK

Michael Knopf
Temple Beth-El

Richmond, VA

Rivon Krygier
Congregation
Adath Shalom
Paris

Elie Spitz
Congregation
B'nai Israel
Tustin, CA

Ira Bedzow
Aspen Center for
Social Values
Aspen, CO

Yitzchak Blau
RCA

Jerusalem

Alfred Cohen
YU High School

New York, NY

Elliot Cosgrove
Park Avenue
Synagogue
New York, NY

Yehonatan
Chipman
Hitzei Yehonatan
Israel

David Flatto
Penn State Law

University Park, PA

Shohama H. Wiener
ALEPH: Alliance for
Jewish Renewal
Philadelphia, PA

David Evan Markus
Temple Beth-El

City Island, NY

Nathaniel Helfgot
Yeshivat Chovevei
Torah
New York, NY

Cass Fisher
University of South
Florida
Tampa, FL

Admiel Kosman
Postdam University

Germany

Simcha Krauss
Eretz Hatzvi

Jerusalem

Melanie Landau
Monash University

Australia

Vernon Kurtz
North Suburban
Synagogue Beth-El
Highland Park, IL

Rolando Matalon
B'nai Jeshurun

New York, NY

Daniel Nevins
JTS

New York, NY

Peter Knobel
Beth Emet

Evanston, IL

Jan Urbach
The Conservative
Synagogue
Hamptons, NY

Aryeh Frimer
Bar-Ilan University

Ramat Gan

Martin Lockshin
York University

Ontario, Canada

Shai Cherry
Shaar Hamayim

Del Mar, CA

David Shatz
Yeshiva University

New York, NY

Jeremy Rosen
Persian Jewish
Center
New York, NY

David Greenstein
Congregation
Shomrei Emunah
Montclair, NJ

Avraham Walfish
Herzog College and
Michala Jerusalem
Tekoa, Israel

David Mescheloff
RCA

Israel

Alan Brill
Seton Hall University

South Orange, NJ

Lawrence Troster
GreenFaith

Highland Park, NJ

Ron Margolin
Tel Aviv University

Israel

Lenn Goodman
Vanderbilt
University
Nashville, TN

Dan Ornstein
Ohav Shalom

Albany, NY

Dena Freundlich
Ma'ayanot AMIT

Jerusalem

Yael Leibowitz
Stern College

New York, NY

Pinchas Allouche
Beth Tefillah

Scottsdale, AZ

Orna Triguboff
Neshama Life
Organisation
Sydney, Australia

Nehemia Polen
Hebrew College

Newton Centre, MA

Sandy Sasso
Congregation
Beth-El Zedeck
Indianapolis, IN

David Singer
Congregation
Shearith Israel
Dallas, TX

Avi Olitzky
Beth El Synagogue

St. Louis Park, MN

David Ingber
Romemu

New York, NY

Shmuel Trigano
Paris X University

Nanterre, France

Herbert Bronstein
Lake Forest
College,
Lake Forest, IL

Avraham Feder
Beit Knesset
Moreshet Yisrael
Jerusalem

Elyse Goldstein
City Shul

Ontario, Canada

Kerry M. Olitzky
Big Tent Judaism

New York, NY

Sheila Weinberg
Institute for Jewish
Spirituality
New York, NY

Jason Rubenstein
Mechon Hadar

New York, NY

Herbert Yoskowitz
Adat Shalom
Synagogue
Farmington Hills, MI

Mark Sameth
Pleasantville Com-
munity Synagogue
Westchester, NY

Catharine Clark
Congregation
Or Shalom
London, Ontario

Jacob Adler
Temple Shalom of
Northwest Arkansas
Fayetteville, AR

Jonathan Jacobs
John Jay College,
CUNY
New York, NY

Ysoscher Katz
Yeshivat Chovevei
Torah
Brooklyn, NY

Michael Marmur
Hebrew Union
College
Jerusalem

Mordechai Luria
Institute for Jewish
Ideas & Ideals
New York, NY

Noah Farkas
Valley Beth Shalom

Encino, CA

Marc Angel
Institute for Jewish
Ideas & Ideals
New York, NY

Benjamin Sommer
JTS

New York, NY

Elie Kaunfer
Mechon Hadar

New York, NY

Alex Sztuden
The Herzl Institute

Jerusalem

David Golinkin
Schechter Institute
of Jewish Studies
Jerusalem

Efrayim Unterman
Congregation
Torat Emet
Columbus, OH

Avital Hochstein
Mechon Hadar

New York, NY

Baruch Frydman-Kohl
Beth Tzedec
Congregation
Toronto, Canada

Bradd Boxman
Congregation Kol
Tikvah
Parkland, FL

Chaim Seidler-Feller
Hillel at UCLA

Los Angeles, CA

DovBer Pinson
IYYUN Center for
Jewish Spirituality
Brooklyn, NY

Erica Brown
The Jewish
Federation
Rockville, MD

Ethan Tucker
Mechon Hadar

New York, NY

Everett Gendler
Shomer Shalom
Institute
Stonypoint, NY

James Diamond
University of
Waterloo
Ontario, Canada

Jane Kanarek
Hebrew College

Newton Centre, MA

Jeffrey Fox
Rosh Yeshiva of
Yeshivat Maharat
Bronx, NY

Ariel Mayse
Hebrew College
Newtown Centre,
MA

Ruth Walfish
Herzog College and
Michala Jerusalem
Tekoa, Israel

Berel Dov Lerner
Western Galilee
College; Herzl Inst.
Northern Israel

Mark Greenspan
Oceanside Jewish
Center
Oceanside, NY

Alfredo Borodowski
Skirball Center for
Adult Jewish Learning
New York, NY

Yehuda Gellman
Ben-Gurion
University
Negev, Israel

David Kunin
Beth Shalom
Synagogue
Edmonton, AB

Michelle Levine
Yeshiva University

New York, NY

Mishael Zion
The Bronfman Youth
Fellowships
Delmar, NY

Edwin C. Goldberg
Temple Sholom of
Chicago
Chicago, IL

Ilana B. Grinblat
The Board of Rab-
bis of S. California
Los Angeles, CA

Howard Wettstein
University of
California
Riverside, CA

Zvi Grumet
Yeshivat Eretz
Hatzvi
Jerusalem

Senior Editors

Benjamin Blech
Yeshiva University,

New York, NY

Martin S. Cohen
Shelter Rock,
Jewish Center

Roslyn, NY

Sanctification

'Sanctification'
from Essay by Chief Rabbi Lord Jonathan Sacks

... And there is the priestly task of kedushah, sanctifying life by honouring the sacred ontology, the deep moral structure of the universe, through the life of the 613 commands, a life of discipline and self-restraint, honesty and integrity, respect and love, the code set out in the chapter of the Torah that opens with the momentous words, "Be holy for I, the Lord your God, am holy." Other cultures and faiths drew inspiration from its wisdom and prophetic traditions, but kedushah remained a specific Jewish imperative that made us different. Even so, it contains a message for the world, which Jews bear witness to whenever and wherever they remain faithful to it.

Our vocation remains, to be mamlechet cohanim vegoi kadosh, "a kingdom of priests and a holy nation."

                                                    - The Ethic of Holiness, August 2012

to view series updated authors list,

see www.MesorahMatrix.com

Mesorah Matrix Series

Editors

David Birnbaum

Benjamin Blech

Benjamin Blech
Editor

Benjamin Blech, bórn in Zurich in 1933, is an Orthodox rabbi who now lives in New York City.

Rabbi Blech has been a Professor of Talmud at Yeshiva University since 1966, and was the Rabbi of Young Israel of Oceanside for 37 years. In addition to his work in the rabbinate, Rabbi Blech has written many books on Judaism and the Jewish people and speaks on Jewish topics to communities around the world.

Benjamin Blech
Yeshiva University,
"Understanding
Judaism"

Education

Rabbi Blech received a Bachelor of Arts degree from Yeshiva University, a Master of Arts degree in psychology from Columbia University, and rabbinic ordination from the Rabbi Isaac Elchanan Theological Seminary.

Milestones

Rabbi Blech is the author of twelve highly acclaimed and best selling books, with combined sales of close to half a million copies, including three as part of the highly popular Idiot's Guide series. His book, *Understanding Judaism*: The Basics of Deed and Creed, was chosen by the Union of Orthodox Jewish Congregations as "the single best book on Judaism in our generation".

Martin S. Cohen

Martin S. Cohen

Martin S. Cohen has been a Senior Editor of the inter-denominational Mesorah Matrix series since 2012.

From 2000-2014, he served as Chairman of the Editorial Board of the quarterly journal *Conservative Judaism*, which was published under the joint auspices of the Jewish Theological Seminary and the Rabbinical Assembly.

Rabbi Cohen also served as the senior editor of *The Observant Life*, a landmark compendium of Jewish law and custom published by the Rabbinical Assembly in 2012.

His weekly blog can be viewed at www.TheRuminativeRabbi. blogspot.com. He has served as rabbi of the Shelter Rock Jewish Center in Roslyn, New York, since 2002.

Rabbi Cohen was educated at the City University of New York and at the Jewish Theological Seminary, where he was ordained a rabbi and received his Ph.D. in Ancient Judaism. He is the recipient of fellowships at the Hebrew University in Jerusalem in 1983 and Harvard University in 1993.

Martin Cohen has taught at Hunter College, the Jewish Theological Seminary, the Institute for Jewish Studies of the University of Heidelberg, as well as at the University of British Columbia and the Vancouver School of Theology.

His published works include *The Boy on the Door on the Ox* (2008) and *Our Haven and Our Strength: A Translation and Commentary on the Book of Psalms* (2004), as well as four novels and four books of essays.

Rabbi Cohen is currently writing a translation and commentary on the Torah and the Five Megillot.

Saul Berman
Mesorah Editor

Saul J. Berman is one of the world's leading Jewish intellects.

He is an American Jewish scholar and Modern Orthodox rabbinic.

Rabbi Berman was ordained at Yeshiva University, from which
he also received his B.A. and his M.H.L. He completed a degree
in law, a J.D., at New York University, and an M.A. in Political
Sciesnce at the University of California, Berkeley, where he studied
with David Daube. He spent two years studying mishpat ivri in
Israel at Hebrew University of Jerusalem and at Tel Aviv University.
He did advanced studies in Jewish Law at Hebrew University
and Tel Aviv University Law Schools. Since 1971 Rabbi Berman
serves as Associate Professor of Jewish Studies at Stern College
for Women of Yeshiva University. Rabbi Berman was Rabbi of
Congregation Beth Israel of Berkeley CA (1963-1969), Young Israel
of Brookline, MA (1969-1971) and of Lincoln Square Synagogue in
Manhattan (1984-1990.) Since 1990 he has served as an Adjunct
Professor at Columbia University School of Law, where he teaches
a seminar in Jewish Law. Aside his academic appointments, from
1997 until 2006.

Rabbi Berman is a contributor to the *Encyclopedia Judaica* and
is the author of numerous articles which have been published in
journals such as *Tradition, Judaism, Journal of Jewish Studies,
Dinei Yisrael*, and others.

Rabbi Berman was the founder and director of the Edah
organization for the promotion of Modern Orthodoxy. Edah was
ultimately absorbed into Yeshivat Chovevei Torah.

He is married to Shellee Berman; they have four children and seven
grandchildren.

Saul Berman
Yeshiva University,
Stern College

Shalom Carmy
Contributing Editor

Shalom Carmy is an Orthodox rabbi teaching Jewish Studies and philosophy atYeshiva University, where he is Chair of Bible and Jewish Philosophy at Yeshiva College. He is an affiliated scholar at Cardozo Law School of Yeshiva University. He is also Editor of Tradition, an Orthodox theological journal.

Shalom Carmy
Yeshiva University,
Tradition Magazine

A Brooklyn native, he is a prominent Modern Orthodox theologian, historian, and philosopher. He received his B.A. in 1969 and M.S. from Yeshiva University, and received his rabbinic ordination from its affiliated Rabbi Isaac Elchanan Theological Seminary, studying under Rabbis Aharon Lichtenstein and Joseph Soloveitchik. He has edited some of R. Soloveitchik's work for publication. Carmy has written many articles on Biblical theology, Jewish thought, Orthodoxy in the 20th century, and the role of liberal arts in Torah education. He edited *"Modern Scholarship in the Study of Torah*: Contributions and Limitations" (ISBN 1-56821-450-2), *"Jewish Perspectives on the Experience of Suffering"*, as well as several other works. He writes a regular personal column in *Tradition*, and contributes regularly on Jewish and general subjects to *First Things* and other journals. In addition to his exegetical and analytic work, Carmy's theological contribution is distinguished by preoccupation with the way religious doctrine and practice express themselves in the life of the individual.

http://en.wikipedia.org/wiki/Shalom_Carmy (accessed May 7, 2014)

Sanctification

TIKKUN OLAM

BIRKAT KOHANIM

KADDISH

Modeh Ani

SEARCH FOR MEANING

U-VACHARTA BA-CHAYIM

Eheyeh asher Eheyeh

U'shamru

Birnbaum & Blech

Birnbaum & Cohen

Birnbaum & Cohen

Birnbaum & Cohen

Birnbaum & Cohen

Birnbaum & Cohen

Birnbaum & Cohen

Birnbaum & Cohen

Birnbaum & Cohen

Birnbaum & Cohen

New Paradigm Matrix

New Paradigm Matrix

New Paradigm Matrix

New Paradigm Matrix

New Paradigm Matrix

New Paradigm Matrix

New Paradigm Matrix

New Paradigm Matrix

New Paradigm Matrix

New Paradigm Matrix

2015

2015

2016

2016

2017

2017

2018

2018

2019

2019

March 2017

Blau

Zornberg

Bulka

Carmy

Friedman

Blech

Cohen Helfgot

Goldberg

Kugel

Mescheloff

Berman

Shatz

Schiffman

Sacks

Riskin

For the mountains shall erode

and the hills indeed collapse,

but My grace towards you shall never waver.

- Isaiah 54:10

כִּי הֶהָרִים יָמוּשׁוּ

וְהַגְּבָעוֹת תְּמוּטֶינָה

וְחַסְדִּי מֵאִתֵּךְ לֹא יָמוּשׁ

- יְשַׁעְיָהוּ 54:10 -

21st CENTURY PUBLISHING

David Birnbaum
Editor-in-Chief

New Paradigm Matrix
589 Fifth Avenue
Suite 710
New York, NY 10017

DBprivate@aol.com

$36.00 / book

Sanctification / Kedushah

ISBN: 978-0-9843619-9-1